Office Skills

The Finishing Touch

SECOND EDITION

JOIN US ON THE INTERNET

WWW: http://www.thomson.com
EMAIL: findit@kiosk.thomson.com   A service of I(T)P®

South-Western Educational Publishing

an International Thomson Publishing company I(T)P®

Pacific Grove • Albany • Belmont • Bonn • Boston • Cincinnati • Detroit • Johannesburg • London • Los Angeles • Madrid
Melbourne • Mexico City • New York • Paris • San Francisco • Singapore • St. Paul/Minneapolis • Tokyo • Toronto • Washington

Office Skills

The Finishing Touch

SECOND EDITION

Charles Barrett

Automated Office Occupations Instructor
Regional Occupational Program (ROP)
San Mateo County Schools

Grady Kimbrell

Educational Consultant
Santa Barbara, California

Pattie Odgers

Computer and Business Instructor
Coconino Community College
Flagstaff, Arizona

Vice President of Publishing: Peter McBride
Team Leader: Bob Cassel
Project Manager: Lynda Kessler
Senior Production Editor: John Orr
Editor: Bette Darwin
Design Coordinator: Vickie Grandchamp
Production Artists: Vickie Grandchamp and Matt Thiessen
Copyeditor: Suzanne Franklin DeFazio
Indexer: Bob Marsh
Prepress Services: Parkwood Composition, Inc. New Richmond, Wisconsin
Cover Design: Mario M. Rodriguez and Vickie Grandchamp

Cover Photography Credits: Westlight, Los Angeles, CA and Index Stock Photography, Inc., New York, NY.

ISBN: 0-314-20550-0 (SE)
ISBN: 0-314-12986-3 (TAE)

05 04 03 02 01 00 99 98   8 7 6 5 4 3 2 1 0
Printed in the United States of America

International Thomson Publishing

South-Western Educational Publishing is an ITP Company. The ITP logo is a registered trademark used herein under license by South-Western Educational Publishing.

I(T)P

Contents in Brief

PART IV COMMUNICATION AND PROBLEM-SOLVING SKILLS 325

PART V EMPLOYMENT SKILLS 425

REFERENCE MANUAL   R-1

GLOSSARY   G-1

INDEX   I-1

PHOTO CREDITS   PC-1

Contents

PART II   TECHNICAL SKILLS AND KNOWLEDGE   93

PART III   OFFICE SUPPORT SKILLS   159

PART IV COMMUNICATION AND PROBLEM-SOLVING SKILLS 325

PART V   EMPLOYMENT SKILLS   425

Preface

The inspiration for **Office Skills: The Finishing Touch** resulted from the experiences of one of the authors, who spent several summers as a contract employee in a wide variety of offices. These experiences, combined with consultations with many of the most knowledgeable people in office employment, showed clearly that changes in the business office curriculum were needed to prepare students for the office of the twenty-first century.

Office Skills provides practical, up-to-date information that will prepare students for working in offices. Students will study information processing, telephone procedures and recordkeeping, basic communication and math skills, and decision making and problem solving. The emphasis is on practical applications—everyday skills and knowledge needed to be successful—rather than on theoretical office concepts and methodology. This includes extensive information on effective use of computers and software programs, new telephone equipment, and other new office technology.

Office Skills also focuses on attitudes and human relationships, emphasizing the fact that office success depends on "people skills" as much as on functional skills. This includes understanding the importance of teamwork and the value of self-confidence. Because many office workers will work for more than one boss, students are also provided information on how to prioritize their work and satisfy their bosses. Finally, career information and employability skills introduce students to the vast array of job opportunities and the most effective methods for pursuing those opportunities.

In response to comments that many office skills texts are dull and lifeless, the authors have attempted to make **Office Skills** interesting, as well as informative. In addition to using an easy to understand, lively, conversational writing style, they have developed an abundance of high-interest features to capture and hold the students' attention.

◆ Each chapter of **Office Skills** opens with "Before You Begin" questions to help spark student interest. These questions are repeated as "In Conclusion" questions at the end of the chapter so that students can see how their knowledge and opinions have changed as a result of studying the chapter.

◆ Special features within each chapter, such as "Making Office Decisions," "What's Your Attitude?", and "Human Relations," emphasize the importance of these topics through the use of real-life scenarios.

◆ Perspectives of managers from major corporations are provided in the feature "Industry Focus."

◆ Practical suggestions are provided in the marginal "Office Tips."

◆ "Large Office/Small Office" compares the tasks and environments in large and small offices, thus giving students help in evaluating their personal career interests and objectives.

◆ A comprehensive section of end-of-chapter study aids concludes each chapter.

◆ You will find an ongoing "Career Portfolio" project at the end of each of the five parts of the text to provide an interesting approach to word processing practice and reinforcement.

◆ A "Reference Manual" is included in the appendix.

The Authors have also developed an extensive package of supplementary materials to help you teach with **Office Skills.**

Supplements to the text include the following:

◆ *Teacher's Annotated Edition*
◆ *Teacher Resource Book*
◆ *Computer Applications Supplement with Template Disk*
◆ *Student Activity Workbook*
◆ *Computer-Test Generator*

Office Skills contains an abundance of practical information, high-interest features, and study material in both the text and in the supplements. The authors believe that this approach will ensure content comprehension and thoroughly prepare students to enter the job market and move successfully toward their ultimate career goals.

The authors would like to thank the following teachers / consultants for their valuable comments and suggestions throughout the development of this textbook:

Joan Adamski
De Soto High School
De Soto, Texas

Gloria Ballard
La Porte High School
La Porte, Indiana

Diane Best
North Gaston High School
Dallas, North Carolina

Judy Bush
North Dallas High School
Dallas, Texas

Debbe Dubey
Wylie Grove High School
Beverly Hills, Michigan

Kathryn Glisson
Harris County High School
Hamilton, Georgia

Dawn Grooms
Harris County High School
Hamilton, Georgia

Cecelia Luksa Hartney
Miami Palmetto High School
Miami, Florida

Doris Horton
Sterling Heights High School
Sterling Heights, Michigan

Ronald Katzer
Alexander Hamilton High School
Milwaukee, Wisconsin

Joe Komaromy
Dundee Crown High School
Carpenterville, Illinois

Trudie A. Marks-Dooley
Kalamazoo Central High School
Kalamazoo, Michigan

Dolores Martin
Lakewood High School
Lakewood, Ohio

Wendy McKeever
Chambersburg High School
Chambersburg, Pennsylvania

Jim McMahon
James Madison High School
Milwaukee, Wisconsin

Toni Ellen Norton
Lake Mary High School
Lake Mary, Florida

Glenna J. Pyzik
Morton East High School
Cicero, Illinois

Kathryn Scott
Nacogdoches High School
Nacogdoches, Texas

About the Authors

Charles Francis Barrett received his Bachelor of Science degree from Stonehill College and his Master of Arts degree from San Francisco State University. For over 20 years he has been an office careers instructor for the San Mateo County Office of Education's Regional Occupational Program. In addition he has taught at the community college and university level and has done teacher-training classes for the California State Department of Education. He also has conducted business writing skills workshops for industry personnel. For many years Mr. Barrett has been an active member of the California Business Education Association of which he has been a section officer and held statewide committee chairs. He has kept current in his teaching by working as a contract employee in the private sector.

Grady Kimbrell has been involved in business and career education for more than twenty-five years. He began as a business education teacher in Kansas and California, supervising his students on the job who were part of a school-sponsored work-experience program. Later he served as District Coordinator for Work-Experience Education in Santa Barbara, California.

An interest in research and computers led to Mr. Kimbrell's serving as Director of Research in Santa Barbara Schools. This experience, in turn, led to a variety of consultancy opportunities both in schools and private businesses.

Kimbrell's first business and career publications were motivated by the apparent lack of realistic goals voiced by students in California schools. Those early efforts were well received and provided encouragement for developing new programs and more than a dozen books dealing with business and career education.

Mr. Kimbrell holds degrees in business administration, educational psychology, and business education.

Dr. Pattie Odgers is a product of the worlds of both business and education. She is recent Past President of Arizona Business Education Association (ABEA), currently serves as Associate Editor for the *ABEA Journal*, and is a long-standing member of NBEA and WBEA. Dr. Odgers has taught a variety of courses in computer systems and applications, office and personnel management, and office skills to high school, community college, and university students in Arizona and overseas in West Berlin and Stuttgart, Germany.

Having served as Associate Dean of Instruction at Coconino Community College in Flagstaff for its first two years of operation, Dr. Odgers returned to the classroom and is currently teaching computers to nearly 150 students each semester. Her business experience has progressed through a wide range of positions, from student secretary while in college to educational services representative and manager for IBM, to sales representative for both IBM and Papermate/Gillette Corporations, and now to operating a successful computer consulting and training business that serves Northern Arizona.

As a result of research she has completed on the *InfoTech* worker and the *America 2000* initiative, Dr. Odgers has become a recognized speaker at state, regional, national, and international business conferences. She has published numerous articles in business education journals over the years, in addition to authoring three textbooks.

Dr. Odgers received her Bachelor's and Master's degrees from Arizona State University and her Doctorate from Northern Arizona University. She lives in Flagstaff, Arizona with her husband, two teenage children, and numerous kitty cats.

PART
I

Your Place in the Modern Office

OBJECTIVES

After completing this chapter, you will be able to do the following:

1. Describe an office environment.
2. Describe how partitions divide work areas in an office.
3. Describe an office employee's workstation.
4. List adjustments that can be made to a workstation to make it more comfortable for an employee's size.
5. List adjustments that can be made to eliminate glare on a computer screen.
6. List suggestions for relieving the stress of sitting too long at a computer.
7. Explain the flow of work in an office environment.
8. List two examples of the organizational makeup of an office environment.
9. List hazards to office safety and preventive measures for each.
10. List examples of reasonable accommodations employers have made to comply with the Americans with Disabilities Act.

NEW OFFICE TERMS

ergonomics
modular design
office work flow
organizational makeup

partitions
safety hazard
workstations

BEFORE YOU BEGIN . . .

Answer the following questions to the best of your ability:

1. How does an office environment, including an employee's workstation, look?

2. What are four office safety hazards? Give examples of ways to prevent them.

Anne is a student in an office careers program in the Midwest. Someday she wants to work as an office support employee for a large company. Anne understands the clerical tasks that are done in an office, but she has no knowledge of what an office looks like. Does it look like her classroom? Does it look like the school office? Does it look like the local copy center?

Anne's teacher gave her the names and phone numbers of three former students who are currently office workers. Anne made appointments to visit each person at his or her office.

Anne visited Ivan, who works for a food processing company. Ivan gathers sales figures for the marketing department. Anne also visited Sylvia, who works in the office of a bank. Sylvia processes time sheets for the payroll department. Finally, Anne visited Darrell, who works part-time for a computer parts manufacturer. Darrell uses a PC to merge and save letters for the office services department.

◆ *Large areas can be divided into many workstations with partitions of varying heights, depending on the need for employee interaction.*

At each company, Anne was able to tour the entire office facilities. She realized that although the companies handled different products, the offices were similar.

Office Design

The three offices Anne visited were all cheerfully decorated with brightly painted walls and matching carpeted floors. Soft colors and texture (wood and fabric) enhanced their tasteful quality. The office spaces appeared to be comfortable, yet efficiently planned to promote productivity.

Many executives had their own private office rooms. However, the office support employees' work areas were divided by carpeted partitions that averaged approximately five to six feet tall.

Partitions are panels used to separate or divide a large area into smaller work areas. Research by the National Office Products Association has shown that in some offices, how tall the partitions stand depends on the work done. For example, a marketing department may have three-foot-high partitions, a recreation area may have four-foot-high partitions, work areas of lower-level managers may have five- to six-foot-high partitions, and work areas of executives may have floor-to-ceiling partitions (walls).

In some work areas, employees share space so that they may perform as part of a team and share job functions. In these situations, partitions are low and serve merely as connections for furniture additions, not as walls separating employees. This type of design provides a more open environment for employee interaction. It also accommodates the computer systems that have become an important part of an office environment. The employees in this type of work area frequently share records, equipment, and information.

Workstations

Years ago, office employees worked at desks. Today, most office employees work at workstations. **Workstations** are areas that are similar to desks except that they are larger and contain more electronic equipment. In many offices, partitions separate the workstations, providing for more privacy.

Many of the workstations in the offices Anne visited contained a personal computer and a multifunction telephone. They also contained shelves and storage space for paper, binders, manuals, pens, pencils, books, printouts, and computer disks. Near the workstations were computer printers that were shared by two or more employees. Anne was told that in some offices, employees also shared electronic typewriters for preparing office forms.

The workstation in Figure 1.1 on page 7 is a **modular design.** This means that it is made of pieces that can easily be taken apart, rearranged, and put back together. The design is simple yet functional. It allows equipment to be moved anywhere on the desk with easy

OFFICE TIP

Automation is important in office life these days. However, the basic human skills still are critical. Politeness, enthusiasm, a desire to do one's best—these are the skills that we need most in business.

Ramon is a support staff person in the corporate office of a large bank. He works for Mr. Martin, a senior vice president.

Mr. Martin came out of his office one afternoon and gave Ramon back some letters he had typed. Mr. Martin said, "Please redo these letters. You should not have indented the paragraphs."

Ramon looked at the letters and said, "You told me to do it that way."

Mr. Martin simply returned to his office without saying a word, and Ramon corrected the letters.

About an hour later Mr. Martin called Ramon into his office and said, "Never again talk to me the way you did when I gave you the letters to correct. If any boss in this company asks you to redo some work, you will do it without comment. That is your job."

1. *Was Ramon right in what he said when he got the letters back? Why or why not?*

2. *Did Mr. Martin handle the situation the correct way? Why or why not?*

3. *If you were Ramon, what would you do now?*

access to power sources. It provides storage to keep frequently used reference manuals within arm's reach, but not on the desk itself.

ERGONOMICS

Have you read or heard the word *ergonomics?* **Ergonomics** is the study of the relationship between people and their work environments. It includes the study of ways to change conditions to make tasks easier and more natural. Studying ergonomics can also lead to increased productivity.

◆ *Workstations made from modular units can be taken apart, rearranged, and reassembled as office needs change.*

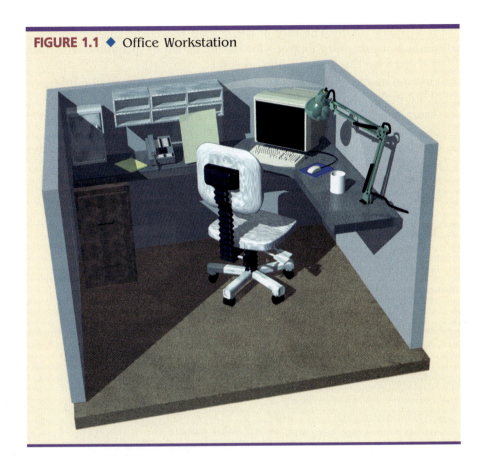

FIGURE 1.1 ◆ Office Workstation

Ergonomics includes the design of the workstation because the design is critical to the physical well-being of the worker. A workstation that is proportioned for the employee's size helps the employee to be more productive and to feel less fatigue.

Figure 1.2 is an example of a well-designed workstation containing a personal computer. This workstation was designed by the National Safety Council to comply with the following guidelines: (Reprinted with permission from the National Safety Council booklet, "Video Display Terminals . . . The Human Factor," Chicago; National Safety Council.)

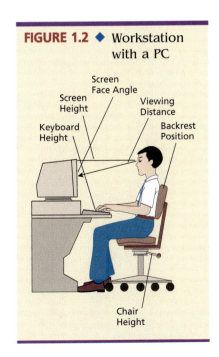

FIGURE 1.2 ◆ Workstation with a PC

◆ *Keyboard height.* The keyboard height should be comfortable—about 2½ inches from the top of the table to the top surface of the space bar and bottom row of keys. At that height, the desk top can give the needed support to the operator's wrists. If the desk top is the right height, approximately twenty-four to twenty-eight inches, the worker's upper arms will form a comfortable angle of approximately ninety degrees. The upper arms will then hang naturally at the sides, taking the strain off the upper back and shoulders.

◆ *Screen height.* The top of the screen should be no higher than eye level to minimize eye movement.

◆ *Screen face angle.* The face of the screen should be tilted back about ten to twenty degrees for easier viewing—provided this does not increase the glare on the screen.

◆ *Viewing distance.* For comfortable viewing, the screen should be about eighteen inches from the eyes.

◆ *Chair height.* The chair is at a comfortable working height when the worker does not feel excessive pressure on the legs from the edge of the seat. Pressure from the seat front could make the legs go to sleep.

◆ *Backrest position.* The backrest of the chair should fit comfortably at the small of the worker's back to give the back good support.

ADJUSTMENTS

Some employees may find their workstations are not ideal and do not meet the above guidelines. If so, the National Safety Council recommends making the adjustments listed in Table 1.1.

TABLE 1.1 ◆ Workstation Adjustments

PROBLEM	SOLUTION
Keyboard Height The keyboard is too high and not adjustable.	Place pads under the wrists to elevate them to a more comfortable position.
The keyboard is too low and not adjustable.	Set a pad of paper or a flat piece of wood under the keyboard.
Screen Face Angle The screen is too vertical and not adjustable.	Place a small wedge under the front of the monitor to tilt it back.
Chair Height You do not know what the proper height of the chair should be.	Complete the following steps: 1. Sit with the soles of the shoes flat on the floor. Keep the shins perpendicular to the floor and relax the thigh muscles. 2. Measure the distance from the hollow of the knees to the floor. 3. Subtract one to three inches. The resulting measurement is the correct height for the top of the chair seat.
Desk Height The desk top is too high.	Raise the chair seat beyond the recommended height. Now the legs are dangling, so use a footrest to minimize pressure from the seat front on the legs.

Recall Time

Answer the following questions:

1. According to research done by the National Office Products Association, would marketing departments or lower-level managers use higher panels to divide their work areas? What height panels do executives prefer?

2. What five items may you find in the storage area of an office workstation?

3. If the workstation desk top is the right height, describe the positioning of the worker's arms while she or he types on the keyboard of a computer.

4. How far should a computer screen be from the operator's eyes?

5. How does the National Safety Council recommend correcting the following problems?

   a. A keyboard is too high and not adjustable.

   b. A keyboard is too low and not adjustable.

OTHER ERGONOMIC CONCERNS

Employees encounter other ergonomic concerns in the office work environment. Being aware of these problems can also lead to a more productive workplace.

Lighting and Glare   Sometimes glare and poor lighting make it difficult to read a computer screen or copy from which an employee is working. To help solve these problems, the National Safety Council suggests the following:

◆ Adjust the screen's brightness and contrast controls to compensate for reflections on the screen.
◆ Close blinds or pull shades to block daylight coming through a window from behind the terminal.
◆ Try to eliminate or adjust any intense light source shining directly into the eyes.
◆ Adjust the angle of the screen to minimize the glare.
◆ Place a glare filter over the monitor to cut down on the glare.

Sitting Too Long   No matter how comfortable the workstation, sitting still for long periods of time can be tiring and stressful. The following strategies are recommended:

◆ Stretch occasionally and look away from your work.
◆ If possible, get up from your terminal and do other tasks.
◆ If possible, alternate different tasks throughout the workday to vary the work rhythms. Take time out to collate papers or deliver completed work.

OFFICE TIP

Have you been sitting at that computer too long? Do some stretching exercises. Raise your arms and stretch as high as you can. Wrap your arms around your chest—give yourself a hug. Hold your hands out straight, palms down, and spread your fingers as far apart as you can. Repeat all these actions.

INDUSTRY FOCUS

Susan Schenck
*Internship Coordinator, Business Careers
National Aeronautics and Space
 Administration / Ames*

Q. Ms. Schenck, what is a real office environment like for a secretary?

A. Some secretaries have private offices and the newest in computer hardware and software. Others plead for second-hand furniture and equipment. Some secretaries can decorate their own space, putting up posters and choosing paint colors. Others work in conservative areas where the company or manager designs identical anonymous spaces.

Q. What are some of the excitements or pleasures gained from being an office worker?

A. Satisfactions include:

◆ Tangible completion of projects such as reports and correspondence.
◆ Seeing that one's work makes a difference in the function of an office.
◆ Learning new software and implementing new techniques.
◆ Ability to get a job in any industry or any geographic location.
◆ Seeing how a company works from the inside, and being able to take advantage of promotion opportunities.

Q. Have you seen any examples of workers who have been terminated because of poor attitude?

A. Yes, mainly due to poor attitude. Poor attitude may be demonstrated through sloppy dress, poor attendance, poor interpersonal relations, and sullen facial expressions. A good attitude is the vital ingredient for success.

Posture   Shoulder or neck pain may be caused by poor posture while working at a computer terminal. The following solutions are recommended:

◆ If a person must lean backward to read the screen, new eye-glasses may be necessary.
◆ If a person cannot read source copy that is lying flat on the table, an upright copy stand may be the solution.

◆ If a worker leans back too far on the chair or leans away from the chair, the chair may need adjustment.

Federal Legislation Affects the Office Environment

The Americans with Disabilities Act (ADA) has also had an effect on the work environment. This Federal Act states, "if an individual has a disability and is qualified to perform the essential functions or duties of a job, with reasonable accommodation if necessary, that individual is protected from job discrimination by the ADA."

Since this legislation passed, employers have provided reasonable accommodations by making their workplaces readily accessible to and usable by people with disabilities. An example of reasonable accommodations would be placing grab bars in rest room stalls for individuals in wheelchairs. Other examples would be (1) devices in telephone handsets for hearing-impaired individuals, (2) page-turning devices for individuals with hand problems, (3) braille training materials for sight-impaired individuals, and (4) modified furniture for individuals with various disabilities.

◆ *Workers with disabilities who are otherwise qualified for a job are finding more acceptance in the workplace today than in previous times.*

Work Flow

All the office workers with whom Anne spoke talked with excitement about the jobs performed in the office section of their companies. The workers explained that their jobs were part of the **office work flow,** which is the activity that revolves around the processing of information. In the business world, information is input (gathered), processed, stored, and output (distributed) in a cycle, referred to as the information processing cycle (see Figure 1.3).

Here are examples of the information processing cycle from the companies Anne visited:

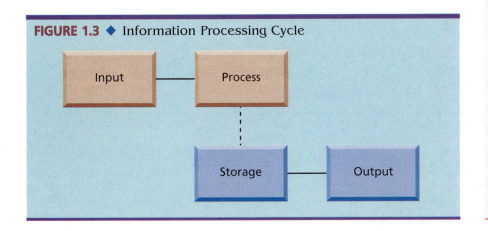

FIGURE 1.3 ◆ Information Processing Cycle

Input — Process

Storage — Output

◆ Ivan receives input of sales figures from the marketing representatives in different states. He puts these figures into his computer, where they are processed into percentages for each district. Then they are stored on disk. Finally they are sent by electronic mail to the regional manager. (Electronic mail means the information was sent from Ivan's computer to the regional manager's computer via telephone lines.)

◆ Sylvia receives time sheets from all the employees in the bank. She verifies the time sheets and then enters the total hours into the computer. The computer processes the hours and prints paychecks. The information remains stored in the computer. The checks are given to the personnel department to be distributed to the employees.

◆ Darrell receives an inventory of parts from the warehouses every three months. This information is entered into his computer. The computer processes the information and prints a report that shows which parts must be reordered. The information is stored on CD-ROM. The printed report is sent to the accounting department.

The information processing cycle performed by office workers makes you realize the importance of the office operations to the entire business. Without office operations, companies would not survive. Manufacturing companies depend on office workers to keep inventory and budget figures. Law firms depend on office workers to process and store accurate legal documents. Retail stores depend on office workers to provide sales figures on a daily basis. All companies need office workers to edit and distribute correspondence, and depend on office workers to process their payroll and keep accounting records for tax purposes.

Chapter 5 explains more about the information processing cycle and the electronic equipment that does the processing.

Ethics on the Job

Erlinda is the only office employee in a small graphics company. Her boss leaves every day at 3 p.m. to make sales calls. The boss never returns until the following morning.

Erlinda would like to take a night class at a local community college, but she would have to leave early in order to get to the class on time. The boss will not know she leaves early.

Should Erlinda ask her boss's permission to leave early, or should she just do it? The boss will probably never know.

Recall Time

Answer the following questions:

1. What are two ways to eliminate lighting glare on a computer screen?

2. What may cause shoulder pain while working at a computer?

3. Was the ADA enacted by city, county, state, or federal legislation?

4. What are the four parts of the information processing cycle?

Organizational Makeup

When you become an employee of a company, you will be responsible for producing accurate work within an allotted time. Someone will assign you the work and see that it is completed. Depending on the

MAKING OFFICE DECISIONS

Your boss has a client's meeting scheduled in a conference room that is located on the same floor as your office. The meeting is scheduled for 3 p.m.

Another supervisor began a meeting in the same conference room at 1 p.m. At 2:45 p.m., that meeting is still going on.

It is your responsibility to set up the meeting room. What will you do?

company and the department, the title of this person can vary. Organizational charts illustrate companies' **organizational makeup,** or the way in which employees in positions of authority are determined.

If you were an office services assistant in Company 1, to whom would you report? (See Figure 1.4.) The answer is the office services coordinator. This person would report to the office services supervisor.

Company 2 is a small company (see Figure 1.5). The administrative assistant is responsible to the office manager, who is directly responsible to the owner.

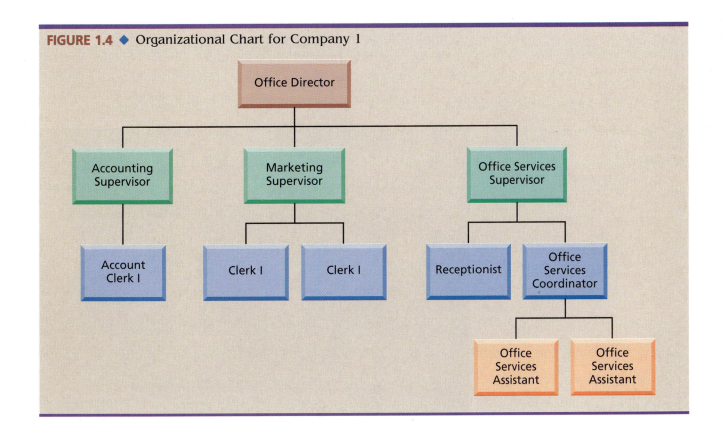

FIGURE 1.4 ◆ Organizational Chart for Company 1

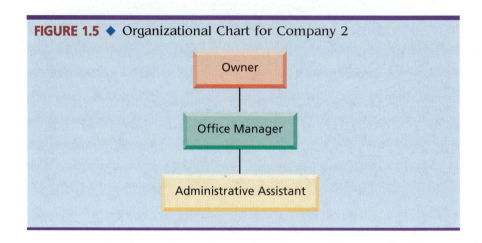

FIGURE 1.5 ◆ Organizational Chart for Company 2

Office Safety

Have you ever tripped over an electrical cord at home? Have you ever had the power go off because too much equipment was plugged into one outlet? Have you ever banged your leg on a drawer that was left open? If not, you are extremely cautious or have been very lucky.

Many people think of work accidents as happening only in factories or at construction sites. However, some accidents also happen in an office environment. These occur when workers are careless or are impatient and try to take shortcuts. Start now to build good safety habits and carry these habits over to your office job.

Office workers have listed the items in Table 1.2 as safety hazards on the job. A **safety hazard** is a danger or a chance of being injured.

◆ *Files or other items left sticking out into an aisle can pose a hazard to workers.*

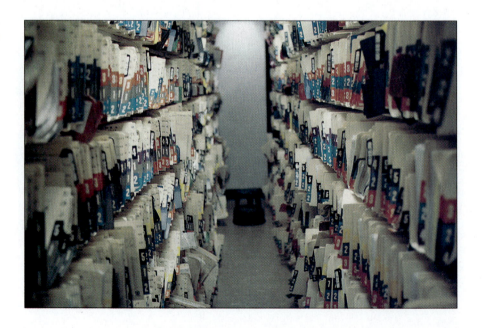

TABLE 1.2 ◆ Office Safety Hazards

HAZARD	PREVENTION
Opening more than one file drawer at a time may cause the cabinet to fall over.	Before you open a file drawer, check to see that all other file drawers are closed.
Leaving a file drawer open may cause someone to trip over it.	Keep file drawers closed when not in use or when you leave for even a short time.
Leaving a handbag or briefcase on the floor in a walkway may cause someone to trip.	Put purses and briefcases into a desk drawer, completely under the desk, or in a cabinet.
Not having enough voltage in the electrical outlet for all the equipment may cause a power shortage or a fire.	Before plugging in new equipment, check with your supervisor to be certain enough voltage is available. Have the company upgrade the electrical system when necessary.
Standing on a chair that is unstable may cause you to fall.	Use a step stool or a ladder to reach high places.
Stooping and lifting improperly may cause back injuries.	Learn the proper lifting procedures.
Leaving electrical cords in a walkway may cause someone to trip.	Keep electrical cords out of walkways or use rubber covers to keep people from tripping.

Recycling in the Business World

Anne noticed that all three companies she visited were concerned with conserving natural resources. They all had recycling programs in operation. However, it was Darrel's company that was the most impressive—it had recently won the Environment Achievement Award.

His company uses different programs to capture office paper, newsprint, magazines, bottles and cans, cardboard, and phone books. Employees in the company even participate in Christmas tree and office equipment recycling. In addition, they use less paper by increasing electronic communications, making two-sided photocopies, and using less preprinted letterhead.

Darrel helps promote the program by doing the graphics for a newsletter on the benefits of recycling. This newsletter is distributed to all employees. The company encourages the public to learn more about these programs by visiting the company's World Wide Web site, which features an extensive environmental section.

Recall Time

Answer the following questions:

1. Refer to Figure 1.4.
   a. To whom is the Account Clerk I responsible?
   b. To whom is the marketing supervisor responsible?
   c. To whom is the office services coordinator responsible?
2. What safety hazard can cause a file cabinet to fall over? How can it be prevented?
3. What safety hazard could cause an employee to trip in an office and how can it be avoided?
4. What may cause a back injury on the job and how can it be avoided?

Summary

We have manufacturing firms, agricultural firms, service firms, government firms, and a variety of others. Although their products and services differ, their office environments are often similar. Many companies use the same type of workstations, and their employees perform the same type of office functions.

All companies should have similar interests in ergonomics and similar concerns about the safety of their employees. The type of work may differ, but the work flow and the organizational setup are similar in most companies.

The following questions may help you decide in what office environment you want to work:

◆ Is the office environment cheerfully decorated?
◆ Are the employee work areas divided to provide privacy and to allow employees to concentrate on work?
◆ Are areas provided for employees to work as a team and to share job functions?
◆ Do the workstations allow for storing materials and manuals as well as for holding the necessary office equipment?
◆ Are the workstations adjustable for the variations in size of the employees?
◆ Does the lighting appear to be adequate for the total work environment?
◆ Does the company comply with the Americans with Disabilities Act?
◆ Is there an organizational setup defining the duties of the employees?
◆ Is office safety a constant concern of the company administrators?
◆ Is the company concerned with conserving natural resources?

IN CONCLUSION . . .

When you have completed this chapter, answer the following questions:

1. How does an office environment, including an employee's workstation, look?

2. What are four office safety hazards? Give examples of ways to prevent them.

REVIEW AND APPLICATION

 ## CHECK YOUR KNOWLEDGE

1. Are all partitions in offices the same height?
2. Which workers usually have their own private offices?
3. Why might workers want to share the same work area?
4. Are workstations used only by executives?
5. Are typewriters still used in offices? If so, what kind?
6. Are all workstations made permanent so they cannot be moved?
7. Why is it important to be concerned with the design of a workstation?
8. Describe how a person's arms should be if he or she is in proper typing position.
9. What is the recommended maximum height at which to place a computer screen?
10. If a person is in proper typing position, where does the backrest of the chair fit?
11. How can a computer screen be tilted if it is too vertical and not adjustable?
12. What does the National Safety Council recommend doing if you do not know the proper height for your computer chair?
13. What is a glare filter used for?
14. List three ways to avoid stress from sitting too long.
15. What do the letters ADA represent?
16. Marcus gathered, processed, and distributed information for his office. What step did he omit from the information processing cycle?
17. Is each of the following an example of input or output?
    a. a movie ticket given to a customer
    b. traffic violations entered into a computer
    c. figures transferred from a CD-ROM into a computer
    d. a paycheck given to an employee
    e. a letter typed into a personal computer
    f. a letter printed from a personal computer
18. What is an organizational chart?
19. Do accidents happen in offices?
20. What safety hazard may cause a power outage in an office?

21. What should an office worker stand on to reach high places?

 ## REVIEW YOUR VOCABULARY

On a separate paper, supply the missing words by choosing from the new Office Terms listed below.

_____ 1. The study of the relationship between people and their work environments is called _____.
_____ 2. Workstations that are made of parts that can easily be taken apart, rearranged, and put back together are made by _____.
_____ 3. Some workstations are divided by _____ for privacy.
_____ 4. The _____ is the area where an employee works that holds equipment and other work-related materials.
_____ 5. The _____ in an office revolves around the processing of information.
_____ 6. Employees in positions of authority are noted by the _____ of an office.
_____ 7. A chance of being injured on the job is a _____.

a. ergonomics
b. modular design
c. organizational makeup
d. partitions
e. safety hazard
f. office work flow
g. workstation

DISCUSS AND ANALYZE AN OFFICE SITUATION

Denise is an office worker for a law firm. One of her duties is directing clients to attorneys' offices.

Denise is going to a party directly after work tomorrow. This is an important party for her, and she plans to wear nice evening clothes. She is thinking of saving time by wearing her evening clothes to work and then going directly to the party.

Should Denise dress this way at her job? Does it make a difference? Why or why not?

PRACTICE BASIC SKILLS

MATH

1. For each item in the following purchase orders, multiply the number purchased by the price listed in the computer supply catalog below. Then add the prices for all the items in the purchase order.

    a. Purchase order 1
        8 printer stands   ———
        6 storage trays   ———
        3 computer dust covers   ———
        4 glare filters   ———
                Total   ———

    b. Purchase order 2
        4 printer mufflers   ———
        12 antistatic sprays   ———
        4 deluxe computer printers   ———
        4 modular tables   ———
                Total   ———

    c. Purchase order 3
        14 storage trays   ———
        3 printer stands   ———
        1 deluxe computer printer   ———
        1 modular table   ———
        5 computer dust covers   ———
                Total   ———

Computer Supply Catalog		
PRICE PER ITEM		
ITEM	If you buy 1–5:	If you buy more than 5:
Printer stand	$ 32.50	$ 30.00
Printer muffler	74.00	70.00
Storage trays	17.75	14.00
Antistatic spray	8.25	7.00
Computer dust cover	28.50	25.00
Deluxe computer printer	390.00	370.00
Glare filter	95.50	90.00
Modular table	580.00	540.00

2. Garrison Contractors does not have the time to do its payroll this month. It hires a computer service company to do the payroll. The computer service company charges $95 per hour. The work will take twelve hours. What is the total cost?

3. Doss Brothers Dairy needs to purchase new draperies for its office because the sun is causing problems with the computer monitors. The draperies cost $62.75 per yard. The company needs eighteen yards. What is the total cost?

4. The supervisor of office services suggests to management that the company pay for eye exams for all the computer operators. The eye exams cost $65 each and the company has eight operators. What will be the total cost to the company?

ENGLISH

1. *Rule:* Most nouns form their plurals by adding s.
    Example: One pencil, two pencils
    Practice Exercise: Form the plurals for the following:

    accountant   desk
    calculator   manager
    computer   typewriter

2. *Rule:* Nouns that end in y with a vowel before the y form plurals by adding s.
    Example: One key, two keys
    Practice Exercise: Form the plurals for the following:

    attorney   day
    boy   delay
    buy   valley

3. *Rule:* Nouns that end in y with a consonant before the y form plurals by changing the y to i and adding es.
    Example: One deputy, two deputies
    Practice Exercise: Form the plurals for the following:

    agency   lady
    baby   laundry
    city   party

4. *Rule:* Nouns that end in o with a vowel before the o form the plural by adding s.

Example: One trio, two trios
Practice Exercise: Form the plurals for the following:

cameo   radio
igloo   stereo
patio   tattoo

5. *Rule:* Nouns that end in *o* with a consonant before the *o* form the plural by adding *es*.
Example: One cargo, four cargoes
Practice Exercise: Form the plurals for the following:

echo   potato
hero   tomato

6. *Rule:* Some nouns form their plurals in different ways.
Example: Foot, feet; man, men; child, children; mouse, mice; deer, deer
Practice Exercise: Form the plurals for the following:

goose   sheep
moose   tooth
ox   trout

PROOFREADING

1. Retype the following report, correcting all errors:

CREATING LOW-STRESS RELATIONSHIPS

Krames Communications suggests the following for creating low-stress relationships on the job.

<u>Listen Actively</u> When you listen with sencitivity toward the speakers feelings, you are better able to understnad the speaker and can then respond by honestly expressing your own thoughs and feelings.
<u>Give Compliments</u> Complimenting people lets them know you have noticed them. Give out at least one complement a day for a job well done, a suggestion at a meeting, or even a neu suit or hairstyle.
<u>Smile at People</u> Smiles and courtecy keep communication open, even when you bring critisism or bad news. But while you are courteous, do not gloss over what needs to be said—express your feelings honestly.

<u>Admit if You are Wrong</u> If you honestly admit when you are wrong, coworkers will trust you more. They will know you are being honest and fare, be more willing to share information with you, and admit when they are wrong.

2. After printing out the report in proofreading exercise 1, make the following changes and print a new copy:

◆ Use uppercase for the underlined words.
◆ Delete all the underlines.
◆ In the paragraph titled "Listen Actively," change the word *honestly* to *truly*.
◆ In the paragraph titled "Give Compliments," delete "a suggestion at a meeting."
◆ Add this paragraph to the bottom:

SHOW APPRECIATION Whether you give a coworker a gift for a job well done, write a letter of commendation, or just say thank you, showing appreciation lets others know you recognize their contributions.

 ## APPLY YOUR KNOWLEDGE

1. Arrange the following words into alphabetical order. Using a personal computer or an electronic typewriter, tabulate the words into three columns.

time sheets   design
panel   workspace
privacy   functional
environment   keyboard
glare   guideline
elevate   height
stressful   posture
process   cycle
responsible   chart
safety   outlet
hazard   electrical
compliment   communication

2. Look around your classroom. Make a list of safety hazards.
3. Using the graphics or tables feature of a word processing program, prepare an organizational

chart for a small company with titles (highest to lowest) of

Owner
Administrative Assistant
Secretary
Receptionist

USING THE REFERENCE MANUAL

Retrieve the file CHIREF on the data disk. Use the punctuation section of the Reference Manual at the back of the book to help you correct comma errors. Save and print.

1. Since the project is not totally correct you will have to spend more time making it acceptable.
2. Shelves and storage space should be available for paper, binders manuals and computer disks.
3. Ergonomics the study of the relationship between people and their work environment is a topic offices today cannot ignore.
4. Consequently the issue is unresolved at the moment.
5. In today's office employees frequently share records, equipment and information.
6. In the business world information is input, processed stored, and output in a cycle.
7. As a result of poor communication there was no one in the office who attended the seminar.
8. Organizational makeup or the way in which employees in positions of authority are determined is illustrated on organizational charts.
9. Today most office employees work at workstations.
10. As soon as Rainey finishes the report make three copies.

CHAPTER
2

Career Opportunities in the Office

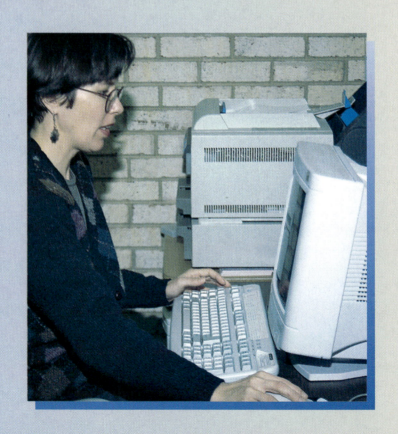

OBJECTIVES

After completing this chapter, you will be able to do the following:

1. List the clerical job classifications that have employment opportunities through the year 2005.
2. List the types of companies that have clerical employment opportunities through the year 2005.
3. List the job duties and qualifications of an adjustment clerk.
4. List the job duties and qualifications of an order clerk.
5. List the job duties and qualifications of a general office clerk.
6. List the job duties and qualifications of a receptionist.
7. List the job duties and qualifications of a secretary.
8. List the job duties and qualifications of a medical assistant.
9. List the job duties and qualifications of a customer service representative.
10. List the soft skills.

NEW OFFICE TERMS

back-office jobs
civil service jobs
Employment Development
   Department
full-time work schedule

Occupational Outlook Handbook
replacement needs
service-producing industries
temporary office workers

BEFORE YOU BEGIN

Answer the following questions to the best of your ability:

1. What is the employment outlook for clerical jobs through the year 2005?

2. What are the job duties and qualifications of a medical assistant?

3. What are the job duties and qualifications of a secretary?

Garrett recently completed business classes that included training in information processing, spreadsheets, and data bases using a PC. He was a good student and is excited now to look for full-time work in an office. The only problem is that he does not know what jobs are available to someone with his training.

Garrett remembers that his neighbor Rochelle works for the **Employment Development Department** (EDD), a state department that handles unemployment and job placement. He makes an appointment to meet with Rochelle at her office. Garrett wants information concerning the projected employment growth of clerical jobs. He also wants information on skills required for clerical jobs, since he is not certain for which jobs he is qualified.

At the meeting, Rochelle first explains to Garrett that much of the information he wants is contained in a publication titled *Occupational Outlook Handbook.* This handbook is published once every two years by the U.S. Department of Labor, Bureau of Labor Statistics. Using it as a reference, Rochelle shares with Garrett some information on job prospects for the future.

Occupational Outlook

Job openings in administrative and support clerical occupations are expected to increase by 6 million jobs between the years 1994 and 2005. The Department of Labor predicts that because of their high number of jobs and substantial replacement needs, clerical occupations will offer abundant opportunities for qualified job seekers in the years ahead.

Garrett asks Rochelle what the handbook means by **replacement needs.** Rochelle explains that these are needs to fill job openings because people leave occupations. Some people transfer to other occupations because they wish to change careers. Others stop working to return to school, assume household responsibilities, or retire.

Most job openings that arise are the result of replacement needs. Therefore, even occupations with little or no employment growth may still offer many job openings. *Employment growth* is an increase in the number of job openings that occurs because new jobs are created in a certain occupation.

Garrett is told that advances in office technology will affect the statistics and classifications for future clerical jobs. Technological advances in mail sorting equipment, for example, will slow demand for postal service clerks. Increased use of personal computers will lead to a decline in the number of typists and an increase in the need for workers with word processing skills.

Jobs that involve interaction with others (see Table 2.1) will generally grow faster than **back-office jobs,** in which employees have little or no contact with the public. The reasons for this growth are varied, but include the following: (1) The tasks performed in the occupation require personal contact; (2) Customer service must be improved; (3) The work is not subject to significant reduction because of technological change.

Rochelle also shares information with Garrett on the types of companies that have the best outlook for employment. She states that the

TABLE 2.1 ◆ Projected Increase in Employment for Selected Administrative Support Occupations, 1994–2005

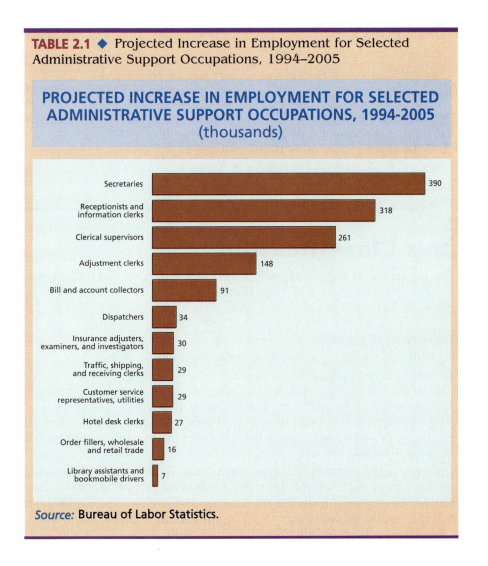

PROJECTED INCREASE IN EMPLOYMENT FOR SELECTED ADMINISTRATIVE SUPPORT OCCUPATIONS, 1994-2005
(thousands)

Secretaries	390
Receptionists and information clerks	318
Clerical supervisors	261
Adjustment clerks	148
Bill and account collectors	91
Dispatchers	34
Insurance adjusters, examiners, and investigators	30
Traffic, shipping, and receiving clerks	29
Customer service representatives, utilities	29
Hotel desk clerks	27
Order fillers, wholesale and retail trade	16
Library assistants and bookmobile drivers	7

Source: **Bureau of Labor Statistics.**

service-producing industries will be hiring the most workers through the year 2005. **Service-producing industries** are businesses that exist to provide service to the public. Business, health, and education services will account for 70 percent of the growth within services.

Health care services will show the most gain with almost one-fifth of all job growth from 1994–2005. Factors contributing to continued growth in this industry include the aging population, which will continue to require more services, and the increased use of innovative medical technology.

All this information concerning the outlook for clerical occupations seems to satisfy Garrett, but now he needs some information on the types of jobs for which he is qualified to apply. Rochelle encourages him to attend a job classification workshop that is being sponsored by the Employment Development Department. She says this may answer his final questions about job classification.

Recall Time

Answer the following questions.

1. Who publishes the *Occupational Outlook Handbook?*
2. Will the number of clerical jobs increase or decrease between the years 1994 and 2005?
3. Are most new jobs in the clerical area due to more work or to the replacement of workers who leave?
4. List three service-producing industries.
5. Which services industry will show the most gain?

Job Classification

The presenter at the job classification workshop that Garrett attends divides office clerical jobs into three categories. The different categories include:

1. entry-level positions
2. positions requiring more than entry-level skills
3. positions requiring advanced skills

The presenter spends time discussing each category. The discussion includes job titles, typical duties, and qualifications required for the positions. The presenter refers frequently to the *Occupational Outlook Handbook* during the workshop.

Real job descriptions that have been collected from private employers and from government agencies are passed out at the workshop. The job descriptions from the government agencies were collected from federal, state, county, and city organizations. These government agency jobs are often called **civil service jobs.**

INDUSTRY FOCUS

Rick Stroud
Communications Director
Professional Secretaries
International (PSI)

Q. Mr. Stroud, what is the job outlook for secretaries? What career paths are available to them?

A. According to the U.S. Department of Labor, the number of secretaries in the United States increased to 3,349,000 in the mid-1990s and 390,000 new secretarial jobs will be added through the year 2005.

This is a very exciting time for secretaries as more and more businesses are operating in a global economy. Companies are creating a multitude of career paths for persons in office professions. Secretaries have moved into training, supervision, desktop publishing, information management, and research.

Q. What are some of the day-to-day tasks of a secretary?

A. ◆ Information flow: Maintaining paper and electronic files and databases, as well as developing methods for organizing and retrieving information.
   ◆ Communications: Editing correspondence and overseeing office communications tools, including voice mail, fax machines, and e-mail.
   ◆ Logistics: Scheduling business travel and meetings, along with planning and developing agendas.
   ◆ Finances: Preparing vouchers and financial data.
   ◆ Customer Relations: Interacting with visitors, salespeople, customers, and members of the community.

The presenter explained that most positions require a **full-time work schedule,** which usually means a forty-hour workweek. In addition, a significant number of jobs are available for individuals who wish to work as temporaries. **Temporary office workers** are employees who work for a few days or a few weeks at one company until a job is completed. They also work at various companies to replace employees on vacation or sick leave. Temporary office workers usually work through private companies known as temporary employment services.

Garrett was pleased that the presenter also spoke about employment for the disabled. The presenter stated that the Americans with Disabilities Act (ADA) has helped increase the number of individuals with disabilities in the workforce. Employers take a variety of measures to insure that disabled persons are not inhibited from applying for openings and that hiring decisions are made on grounds consistent with the ADA. Employment advertisements often include a nondiscrimination statement. Have you noticed these in want ads in your local newspaper?

In addition to advertising, employment application forms often state that disabled applicants will be given equal opportunity and reasonable accommodations. Testing of applicants should be administered in a way that allows disabled candidates to compete fairly; for example, in braille for blind applicants.

Entry-Level Positions

Here is the information from the first category—entry-level positions. It includes two job classifications with a job outlook that is expected to grow faster than the average for all occupations through the year 2005.

ADJUSTMENT CLERKS

Duties   Adjustment clerks investigate and resolve customers' complaints about merchandise, service, billing, or credit ratings. They may work for banks, department stores, utility companies, and other large organizations selling products and services to the public.

Adjustment clerks examine all pertinent information to determine the validity of a customer's complaint. After investigating and evaluating the facts, they report their findings, adjustments, and recommendations. Adjustment clerks also respond to inquiries from customers. They can frequently answer these inquiries with form letters, but other times must compose letters themselves.

Qualifications   Many employers do not require any formal education for adjustment clerk positions. Instead, they look for people who can read and write and who possess good communication and interpersonal skills. They also prefer workers who are skilled at typing.

ORDER CLERKS

Duties   Order clerks receive and process incoming orders for such items as spare parts for machines, consumer appliances, gas and electric power connections, film rentals, and articles of clothing. Most order clerks sit at computers and receive orders directly by telephone, entering the required information as the customer places the order.

The computer provides the order clerk with ready access to information such as stock numbers, prices, and inventory. After the clerk has verified and entered the order, he or she calculates the customer's final cost and routes the order to the proper department to send out or deliver the item.

Qualifications   Most order clerk jobs are entry-level positions. Most employers require applicants to have at least a high school diploma or its equivalent and to be computer literate with good typing ability.

Order clerks must be careful, orderly, and detail oriented in order to avoid making errors and to be able to recognize errors made by others. Once hired, order clerks generally receive on-the-job training to learn company procedures.

Positions Requiring More Than Entry-Level Skills

Here is the information from the second category—positions requiring more than entry-level skills. It includes two job classifications. The job outlook for receptionist is that opportunities are expected to grow faster than the average for all occupations through the year 2005, and the outlook for general office clerks is that good job opportunities will continue to exist.

RECEPTIONISTS

Duties   All organizations want to make a good first impression, and this is the job of the receptionist, who is often the first representative of the organization that a visitor encounters. In addition to traditional duties, such as answering telephones, routing calls to the appropriate individuals, and greeting visitors, a receptionist may serve a security

Ethics on the Job

Rosa is a part-time receptionist for a six-person, privately owned land development company. The office manager, Jennifer, is on vacation, leaving Rosa at the office with the two owners, the accountant, and the sales representative.

Since Rosa's work hours are 1 p.m. to 5 p.m., she never uses the kitchen; but she has seen Jennifer clean up frequently during the workweek. One afternoon the owner, José, left the office at 3 p.m., then popped his head back through the door and said, "Rosa, could you do the dishes before you leave?" Rosa replied, "Why should I clean up when I don't even use the kitchen?"

What do you think of Rosa's response to José? Is cleaning the kitchen a reasonable request for José to make? How would you handle this request if you were in Rosa's position?

◆ *When you visit most business, the first person you are likely to see is the receptionist.*

function—monitoring the access of visitors and determining who belongs and who does not.

Increasingly, receptionists use multiline telephone systems, personal computers, and facsimile (fax) machines. Many receptionists take messages and may inform other employees of a visitor's arrival or cancellation of an appointment. When they are not busy with callers, they may be expected to perform a variety of secretarial duties including opening and sorting mail, collecting and distributing parcels, updating appointment calendars, preparing travel vouchers, and doing simple bookkeeping, typing, and filing.

Qualifications   Skills required of receptionists include typing (45 wpm), general office skills, and knowledge of word processing software. On the job, they learn how to operate the telephone system and how to greet visitors properly. However, some employers also may prefer formal office education or training.

A neat appearance, a pleasant voice, and an even disposition are important. Receptionists do not work under close supervision. Therefore, common sense and a thorough understanding of how the business is organized helps them handle various situations that arise.

GENERAL OFFICE CLERKS

Duties   The duties of the general office clerk are varied and diverse rather than being a single specialized task. The responsibilities of a general office clerk change with the needs of his or her employer. Clerks may spend some days filing or typing, others entering data at a computer terminal. They may also operate photocopiers, fax machines, or other office equipment; prepare mailings; proofread copy; and answer telephones and deliver messages.

MAKING OFFICE DECISIONS

Michelle has been working for six months as a general office clerk for a large company. Her supervisor has been nice and even let Michelle leave early one day because Michelle had some personal business to attend to.

A clerk/typist job opening has become available in the accounting department. Michelle is qualified and would like to apply for the trans-fer. It would mean more money and more interesting work.

Michelle feels guilty because her supervisor has been so nice. She is afraid to tell her supervisor she wants the transfer. Michelle is thinking of forgetting about the opportunity.

What advice would you give Michelle?

Duties also vary by level of experience. Inexperienced employees may operate calculators and record inquiries. More experienced workers may maintain financial records, verify statistical reports for accuracy and completeness, and take inventory of equipment and supplies.

Qualifications Employers usually require a high school diploma, typing skills (40 wpm), general office skills, and computer skills. They also favor workers who are familiar with computer word processing software and applications.

Because general office clerks usually work with other office staff, they should be cooperative and willing to work as part of a team. They should be able to communicate well with people, have good organizational skills, and be detail oriented.

Positions Requiring Advanced Skills

Here is the information from the third category—positions requiring advanced skills. In this category, employment opportunities should be quite plentiful, especially for well-qualified secretaries, through the year 2005.

SECRETARIES

Duties Secretaries, sometimes referred to as administrative assistants, will continue to assume new responsibilities and learn to operate different types of office equipment. In addition, secretaries will continue to perform and coordinate office activities and to ensure that information is given to staff and clients.

Secretaries are responsible for a variety of administrative and clerical duties that are necessary to run and maintain organizations efficiently. They schedule appointments, give information to callers, organize and maintain files, and complete forms. They may also type letters, make travel arrangements, contact clients, and operate office

OFFICE TIP
Ask for extra work in slow times.

◆ *A secretary's job is not only one of the most varied in the work world, but is also constantly evolving in today's changing business environment.*

Large Office / Small Office: What's Your Preference?

WORK PERFORMANCE

It is common for administrative assistants in large offices to work for more than one boss. In a large law office, for example, an administrative assistant may work for two attorneys. This is also true in many other businesses. Therefore, an administrative assistant must be able to schedule the work to meet the needs of all the bosses. An administrative assistant must be able to set priorities. He or she must also have the temperament to be able to take directions from more than one boss and interact with them all regularly.

In a small office, an administrative assistant usually works for and reports to only one boss. Therefore, the daily work is scheduled around only one person. Any priorities can be set with that one boss. Once a work routine is established, an administrative assistant will find it easier to work for only one boss than for several.

Both situations described above have advantages and disadvantages. Would you prefer to work as an administrative assistant in a large office or a small one? Why?

equipment. Secretaries increasingly use personal computers to run spreadsheet, word processing, database management, desktop publishing, and graphics programs—tasks previously performed by managers and professionals.

Qualifications   High school graduates may qualify for secretarial positions if they have basic office skills. Secretaries should be proficient in keyboarding (55 wpm) and good at spelling, punctuation, grammar, and oral communication. Knowledge of word processing, spreadsheet, and database management has become increasingly important to most employers. Because secretaries must be tactful in their dealings with many different people, employers also look for good interpersonal skills. Discretion, good judgment, organizational ability, and initiative are especially valuable.

Testing and certification for entry-level office skills is available through the Office Proficiency Assessment and Certification (OPAC) program offered by Professional Secretaries International (PSI). As secretaries gain experience, they can earn the designation Certified Professional Secretary (CPS) by passing a series of exams given by the Institute for Certifying Secretaries, a department of PSI. The designation is recognized by many employers as the mark of excellence for office professionals.

MAKING OFFICE DECISIONS

You are the receptionist for a large law firm. Your duties include greeting new people, checking a daily sheet to see that each person is expected (approved to enter) by someone in the firm, issuing the person a badge, and directing the visitor to the proper location.

A visitor arrives at your desk and says she has an appointment on the third floor with Kim Singh, the firm's computer analyst. You check your list, but the person's name is not on the list—yet she knew the name, title, and location of Kim.

Should the person be allowed to enter? How do you handle this situation?

Recall Time

Answer the following questions.

1. Employees of what category work only a few days or a few weeks at one company?
2. Does an order clerk have as much responsibility as a secretary?
3. What is the job title of an employee who may serve a security function?
4. What is the job title of an employee who works on a variety of tasks without concentrating in one particular area?
5. What does PSI represent?

Other Areas of Employment

Garrett decided to attend a final workshop sponsored by the Employment Development Department. This workshop covers clerical jobs within specialized areas. These classifications also have a job outlook that is expected to grow faster than the average for all occupations through the year 2005.

MEDICAL ASSISTANTS

Duties Medical assistants perform routine clinical and clerical tasks to keep the offices of physicians, podiatrists, chiropractors, and optometrists running smoothly. Medical assistants perform many clerical duties. They answer telephones, greet patients, update and file patient medical records, fill out insurance forms, handle correspondence, schedule appointments, arrange for hospital admission and laboratory services, and handle billing and bookkeeping.

Medical assistants may also arrange examining room instruments and equipment, purchase and maintain supplies and equipment, and keep waiting and examining rooms neat and clean.

OFFICE TIP

Take notes on everything. Don't trust anything to memory for the first few weeks on the job.

◆   *Medical assistants spend a lot of their time dealing with people.*

Qualifications   Medical assisting is one of the few health occupations open to individuals with no formal training. Some medical assistants are trained on the job. Applicants usually need a high school diploma or the equivalent. Recommended high school courses include mathematics, health, biology, typing (30 wpm), bookkeeping, computers, and office skills. Volunteer experience in the health care field is also helpful.

Because medical assistants deal with the public, they must be neat and well groomed and have a courteous, pleasant manner. Medical assistants must be able to put patients at ease and explain physicians' instructions. They must respect the confidential nature of medical information.

CUSTOMER SERVICE REPRESENTATIVES

Duties   Customer service representatives obtain information that organizations need to enable individuals to open bank accounts, gain admission to medical facilities, participate in consumer surveys, and apply for many other services. They solicit and verify information from people by mail, by telephone, or in person; create and update files; and perform various processing tasks. These clerks are also known as interviewing and new accounts clerks.

Customer service representatives interview people and record the data directly into a computer. They must be familiar with the products and services of the company for which they work. They also may answer telephone inquiries about policies and procedures of the company.

Qualifications   A high school diploma or its equivalent is the most common educational requirement for a job as a customer service representative. However, more important to employers are good inter-

WHAT'S YOUR ATTITUDE?

Roberto has been working for five years as a general office clerk for the same family-owned company. The company has always been successful and has always hired enough office workers for the busy times.

For the last year, the company has not been doing well financially and has had to lay off employees, including office workers. At the same time, those who remain have had to take on more and more work. Roberto occasionally has to do some of the work previously done by office services assistants.

A new executive has been hired who promises to turn the company around and again make it financially successful. In the meantime, all the employees must continue to take on extra work and maintain a positive attitude that things will improve.

Roberto does continue to take on extra work and even does a little overtime without any extra pay. He believes the company has been good to him for the past five years, so he now owes it extra effort during this difficult time.

Do you agree with Roberto's attitude? Why or why not?

personal skills and familiarity with computers, including good typing skills.

Because many customer service representatives work with the public, a neat appearance and a pleasant personality are imperative, as are good problem-solving and communication skills. A clear speaking voice and fluency in the English language are essential because these employees frequently use the telephone.

◆ *A customer service representative might work directly with the public, or by mail, telephone and computer.*

Ethics on the Job

Rita has begun a new job as a file clerk in a large software company. Her first week on the job is spent in the training department learning about the company and the details of her new job.

One of the training sessions includes a segment on "office etiquette." During this session, Rita is told it is best to call her bosses by their last names for the first few months on the job.

Rita is offended by this because she believes she is told to do this because she is a file clerk. She thinks that not all new employees are told to use this procedure, only those in lower-paying positions.

Do you think Rita is correct? What do you think is best when first beginning a job, to call your bosses by first names or by last names?

The Soft Skills

After the workshop, Garrett read through the job descriptions that were distributed by the presenter. He noticed that most of the job descriptions contained what employers refer to as "soft skills." Soft skills are non-technical, interpersonal skills. Garrett compiled a list of the skills and discovered that most companies' job descriptions included the following abilities:

◆ Interpersonal skills
   Workers who can handle difficult people
   Workers who can work with people from different cultures
◆ Organizational skills
   Workers who can keep track of documents
   Workers who can prioritize
◆ Listening skills
   Workers with the ability to grasp the key points of customers' and co-workers' concerns
   Workers with the ability to take notes when necessary
◆ Critical thinking skills
   Workers who are able to analyze and make decisions
   Workers who are able to meet clients' needs
◆ Team players
   Workers who are able to work with others to achieve a goal
   Workers who are able to share ideas
◆ Responsibility
   Workers who can see a task through to its completion
   Workers who can deal with problems and not avoid them

Recall Time

Answer the following questions.

1. Which high school courses are recommended for medical assistants?
2. Why should medical assistants be neat and well groomed?
3. What is another job title for a customer service representative?
4. Give one example of an organizational skill.
5. Give one example of a person who accepts responsibility.

Summary

Many job openings will continue to exist in office occupations through the year 2005. Although some jobs will be available for individuals with entry-level clerical skills, most opportunities will require more than entry-level skills.

In addition to the technical knowledge and skills of personal computer operation and typing, written and verbal communication skills are required for most clerical occupations. Employers prefer hiring individuals who are high school graduates. Jobs including the greatest responsibilities require the greatest abilities.

Do you qualify for any of the clerical positions discussed in this chapter? Use the following checklist to determine for which clerical level you are most qualified.

Entry-Level Clerical Skills
____ Touch typing ability
____ Basic spelling skills
____ Basic reading skills

More than Entry-Level Clerical Skills
____ Average typing skills
____ Computer literacy
____ Knowledge of word processing
____ Good communications skills
____ Attention to details
____ Willingness to be a team player

Advanced Clerical Skills
____ Advanced typing ability
____ Proficiency in a variety of computer software applications
____ Proficiency in oral communication
____ Proficiency in grammar, punctuation, and spelling
____ Aptitude for numbers
____ Adaptability and versatility
____ Organizational ability
____ Initiative
____ Office experience

IN CONCLUSION

When you have completed this chapter, answer the following questions:

1. What is the employment outlook for clerical jobs through the year 2005?

2. What are the job duties and qualifications of a medical assistant?

3. What are the job duties and qualifications of a secretary?

REVIEW AND APPLICATION

 CHECK YOUR KNOWLEDGE

1. What number of job openings are expected to increase in administrative and support occupations between the years 1994 and 2005?
2. List two reasons why replacement openings occur.
3. What is causing slow demand for postal service clerks?
4. Define service-producing industries.
5. List examples of service-producing industries.
6. What is the projected increase of opportunities for receptionists and information clerks through the year 2005?
7. What is meant by civil service jobs?
8. How many hours per week do full-time employees usually work?
9. What should an employment advertisement contain that helps the ADA?
10. For what types of companies do adjustment clerks work?
11. What two types of equipment do order clerks frequently use?
12. What typing ability is required of most adjustment clerks and order clerks?
13. When he or she is not busy with callers, what duties might a receptionist perform?
14. List three types of office equipment that a general office clerk might use.
15. List five types of software programs that secretaries might use.
16. What does CPS represent and how is it obtained?
17. How can individuals gain experience in the health care field?
18. Which skills do employers consider most important for customer service representatives?
19. Give one example of an interpersonal skill.
20. Give one example of a listening skill.

 REVIEW YOUR VOCABULARY

On a separate paper, supply the missing words by choosing from the new Office Terms listed below.

1. Banking, insurance, health care, and education are considered _____ industries.
2. The needs to fill job openings because people leave occupations is known as filling _____.
3. Jobs with very little or no public contact are known as _____.
4. In some states the unemployment department is known as the (EDD) _____.
5. Government jobs are also known as _____.
6. The _____ is a handbook published by the Department of Labor.
7. In most jobs, a standard forty-hour week is considered a _____.
8. Workers who work for short periods of time, at various companies are _____.

a. back-office jobs
b. civil service jobs
c. Employment Development Department
d. full-time work schedule
e. *Occupational Outlook Handbook*
f. replacement needs
g. service-producing
h. temporary office workers

DISCUSS AND ANALYZE AN OFFICE SITUATION

1. Margarita was excited because she had two job offers. She knew she would like the work on both jobs. However, she was a little confused about which job to accept.

   The first job paid $28,000 per year but offered no benefits. The second job paid $26,000 per year and included full medical benefits.

   Which job should Margarita take? Why?

PRACTICE BASIC SKILLS

MATH

1. Albert has had two job offers. One company pays $1,800 per month. The other company pays $20,000 per year. Which job has the highest salary?

2. Winston takes public transportation to work. He pays $1.80 one way. How much does he pay for five round-trips per week? for twenty round-trips per month?

3. Five workers go to lunch. The total bill is $56.25. How much must each person pay if the bill is split equally?

4. The following are Aurora's work expenses each day for one week. How much did she spend for the entire week?

Monday
Transportation	$2.30
Lunch	5.90
Breaks	0.60

Tuesday
Transportation	$2.30
Lunch	6.50
Breaks	2.00

Wednesday
Transportation	$2.30
Lunch	12.50
Breaks	1.75

Thursday
Transportation	$2.30
Lunch	7.35
Breaks	0.90

Friday
Transportation	$2.30
Lunch	7.00
Breaks	1.25

5. Kurt was told he would receive a raise of $75 twice a month. How much of a raise will he receive for the year?

6. Compute the net pay (gross pay minus all deductions) for the following employees. (Note: FICA stands for Federal Insurance Contributions Act.)

EMPLOYEE	GROSS PAY	FEDERAL TAXES	FICA TAXES	OTHER DEDUCTIONS	NET PAY
Sofia	$2,245	$525	$190	$125	$ _____
Kirsten	2,000	475	170	190	_____
Bon	2,800	590	225	175	_____
Pablo	1,900	400	150	35	_____
Marina	2,300	550	200	235	_____
Walter	2,245	500	190	140	_____

ENGLISH

1. *Rule:* Use the pronouns *I, he, she,* and *they* as the subjects (the entities that perform the action) of a sentence.
   Examples: They came to class every day. He was the best student in the office skills class.
   Practice Exercise: Rewrite the following sentences, choosing the correct answer for each:
   a. (They, Them) were working hard.
   b. (We, Us) are learning how to use the computer.
   c. My friend and (I, me) like to study together.
   d. (He, Him) and his wife have their own business.
   e. (She and I, Her and me) were in the same class.

2. *Rule:* Use the objective form of personal pronouns—*him, her, them*—as direct objects, indirect objects, or objects of prepositions.
   Examples: The teacher taught them well. The interviewer asked her some hard questions. The responsibility was passed from him to her.
   Practice Exercise: Rewrite the following sentences, choosing the correct answer for each:
   a. The teacher recommended (she, her).
   b. The assignment gave you and (they, them) a lot of trouble.
   c. Give (we, us) the typing assignment.
   d. Are you talking about (we, us)?
   e. He likes (she, her), but does not like (him, he).

PROOFREADING

Retype the following letter, correcting all errors. Also change all contractions to full words.

Ms. Vanessa Jackson
360 Glen Springs Drive
Dallas, TX 75243
Dear Ms. Jackson:
   Now's your chance, and our chance.
   You've been a subscriber for the Dallas Independent for nearly a year. Now's your chance to tell us

how we're doing. and her's our chance to get you to reneu.

If you like what you're getting for your investment, you'll reneu you subscription to the Dallas Independent. If you don't like what you're getting, (thousand of business leds and the latest in breaking and in-depth news on area business every week), tell us so we can do better. This reneual notice is inclosed along with a business reply envelope for you convenience. Send this right away so you can get uninterrupted delivery. Also use this opportunity to sen me your coments and suggestions so we can provide the coverage you want. Go ahead, tell us.

We're here to help your make money.

Sincerely,

James Boland, Editor

APPLY YOUR KNOWLEDGE

1. An order clerk's information processing cycle is:
   receives order by phone and enters into a personal computer;

   cost is calculated by the computer;

   the total is saved in the company's computer network;

   total cost and delivery instructions are printed.
   Refer to the information processing cycle chart in Chapter 1. Using the graphics or tables feature of your software program, prepare a chart for the order clerk's cycle.

2. Read the want ads from a local newspaper. Choose an ad for a receptionist and list the qualifications required. Compare them with the ones in this chapter. Which qualifications are the same? Which are different?

3. Do the same for an advertisement for a secretarial position.

USING THE REFERENCE MANUAL

Retrieve the file CH2REF on the data disk. Use the grammar section of the Reference Manual at the back of the book to help you correct the sentences. Save and print.

1. The committee meeting is on Fri., January 24.
2. The 9:30 pm showing of the play has been cancelled due to lack of ticket sales.
3. Prof. Grace Lee is a very difficult teacher.
4. Be sure to address the letter 600 Spring St. in Los Angeles.
5. The F.B.I. requires some knowledge of accounting as part of the qualifications.
6. The Made in U.S.A. tag is on most products manufactured in the United States.
7. The plural for brother-in-law is brother-in-laws.
8. The ten deputys on the Sheriff's Department got special recognition for the arrests.
9. Mister Watson is on the program to give the opening address.
10. Send the package Federal Express to 485 So. Cedar in Prescott.

CHAPTER
3

Your Attitude and Work

OBJECTIVES

After completing this chapter, you will be able to do the following:

1. List and describe at least five reasons people work.
2. Describe the effects on others of a positive versus a negative attitude.
3. Explain how to change a negative attitude into a positive one.
4. List five attributes that all employers expect of their employees.

NEW OFFICE TERMS

esteem	self-talk
negative attitude	values
positive attitude	work
self-concept	work ethic
self-realization	

Your satisfaction and success in the world of work will depend to a considerable extent on your attitude toward work and toward other people in your work setting. This overall *work attitude* will, in turn, depend somewhat on your attitude and feeling about yourself—your self-concept. If you enjoy your time on the job and feel that you are doing something worthwhile, you will receive satisfaction from your work. You may actually look forward to going into the office to start a new project or to complete one on which you've been working.

If you get along well with other workers in the office, you will look forward to seeing them—and you will probably have conversations with them during breaks. You will enjoy sharing stories about how you and they spend time away from the office.

Your attitude about work will significantly affect your overall happiness even when you are not at work. In fact, your work will probably become the central activity in your life.

What is Work?

The Random House Dictionary of the English Language says that work means "exertion or effort directed to produce or accomplish something; labor; toil."

Ralph Waldo Emerson, in defining the meaning of life as purpose, said, "The purpose of life is not to be happy. It is to be useful, to be honorable, to be compassionate, to have it make some difference that you have lived and lived well." Emerson's statement implies a choice. We choose to be purposefully engaged. We choose to work.

The dictionary suggests that work must be difficult; exertion and effort are a part of an activity or it is not work. On the other hand, Emerson sees the purpose of life as being or doing something useful, which is a different way of viewing work.

Do you think that what Wolfgang Mozart, Marie Curie, or Benjamin Franklin did was work? When you look at these special people and their accomplishments, you begin to see that work can have many connotations. Can you imagine any of these famous people *not* working?

Buddy Ebsen, who has had several starring roles on TV, was asked during an interview when he intended to quit working. He replied that he never intended to quit. "Working is my life," he said. He was in his eighties.

Bette Davis continued making movies after she was eighty and a severe stroke had left her face partially paralyzed. In a TV interview, Barbara Walters asked Davis, "What keeps you going?" The famous actress replied, "Really and truly—what keeps me going is work." The driving force that kept her alive and happy was accomplishing something worthwhile.

Margaret Mead, a renowned anthropologist, said she might die someday but she would never retire!

Work doesn't have to be an unpleasant activity. If you enjoy what you're doing, it can seem nearly effortless and will be an important, vital part of your life and your existence as a creative human being.

Work, then, is any useful activity or purposeful, creative endeavor.

What Motivates People to Work?

Some jobs aren't very pleasant—yet somebody has to do them. The necessities of life require that we work to earn a living. We need shelter from the elements, clothing to keep us warm, and food to keep us healthy. Generally, the way to acquire these things is to get a regular, paying job.

MONEY

What do you suppose is the primary motivation for people to work? It is money, of course. Would you work if you were not receiving money for doing so?

People want money for many different reasons. Basic needs, such as food, clothing, and shelter, are obvious reasons for working. Those needs, all together, are part of a larger human need for security. Having enough money to meet your obligations brings security and independence. For example, if you don't know where the next rent payment is coming from, you can suffer enormous stress and anxiety.

Perhaps you've already had some work experience. Many young people work part-time or during the summers at jobs such as bagging groceries, cashiering, helping out at the neighborhood swimming pool or at a youth camp, or baby-sitting. If you have done so, you have felt the kind of independence earning your own money brings. Having money in your pocket to buy what you choose feels good.

Eventually, you may have the responsibility of a family. Having enough money to meet your family's expenses and obligations will make you feel secure and safe.

Most people enjoy and take pride in having a home, so they spend time and money painting and repairing their living spaces. Many people spend part of their earnings on major home improvements and comfortable, attractive furniture.

Many people save part of their earnings for the larger expenses of educating their children, covering unforeseen medical bills, and traveling.

Ethics on the Job

You have been hired as a file clerk in a company that designs and produces sports clothing. You are very happy to have this job because you will have many opportunities to learn about the business. You hope, too, that you will meet people who will possibly help you to advance within the company.

You begin to socialize with Robert, one of the young designers. The two of you become good friends.

One evening you share some drawings of bicycle clothing that you have made. Robert is very impressed and encourages you to enroll in some clothing design classes.

At work a few weeks later you come across a series of drawings that are very similar to the ones you showed to Robert. You learn that he has submitted these drawings to his manager for consideration as part of a new line of bicycle clothing. Your discovery is affecting the way you feel about your work.

1. Will you talk to Robert about the drawings?

2. Will you speak with Robert's manager about Robert's designs?

◆ *Many teenagers' first work experience is cashiering in a fast-food restaurant.*

People also want money for leisure-time activities. Some people work even if they don't enjoy their jobs, primarily to earn money to support their hobbies. Younger people, especially, who don't have the responsibility of marriage and family, spend a large part of their earnings on consumer goods such as automobiles, TV and stereo equipment, and fashionable clothing. They also spend money on social and leisure activities such as parties, concerts, movies, and sports. The list of things you might buy and the ways you might spend your money is endless.

In some circles, a person's worth is gauged by how much money he or she earns. Money can bring power and influence. Some people work very hard for years to acquire things and accomplish goals that are materially based simply because it makes them feel important.

Is it vital to you to make a lot of money? If so, earning a lot of money will require you to spend long hours on the job instead of doing other things in your leisure time.

CREATIVE SATISFACTION

The work of Mozart, Curie, and Franklin satisfied a need for them that most people have: to be creative. Some people have very special talents and decide to follow wherever those talents take them. Writers, dancers, musicians, and artists work to utilize their special abilities. You probably have something you do especially well. For example, maybe you have a wonderful speaking voice. Even if you never become a news broadcaster, you can be a receptionist. Your good voice quality will be an asset as you greet others in person and on the telephone in an office.

Workers aware of the final result of their work take pride in knowing that a task was completed, a goal accomplished. Anything from a small report, carefully and neatly prepared, to a new automobile design can bring creative satisfaction.

CONTACT WITH OTHER PEOPLE

The companionship that comes from your job is an important benefit of working. While you're in school, you probably have all the friendships and social contacts you need.

When you leave school, though, work will be your primary source of social contact. You will meet people with whom you will socialize, and they will introduce you to their friends. As you broaden your circle of acquaintances, you will also broaden your life experiences by discovering new ideas and new activities.

You may find people at work whom you don't like and with whom you'd rather not spend much time. These people will provide you with lessons in tolerance and teach you something about how to get along with all co-workers, whether or not you like them.

You and the people you work with will accomplish things together. It can be gratifying belonging to a team of this kind, which sets and accomplishes goals that are important. Consider the people who work for the National Aeronautics and Space Administration (NASA) on the space shuttles. They always appear elated when one of their missions goes well. You've probably seen them on TV shaking each other's hands, clapping, patting each other on the back, and hugging. Something about this kind of working relationship is very satisfying. Accomplishing important things with people at work is a wonderful experience.

◆ *Supervisors and more experienced workers will be major sources of information to help you learn to do your job better.*

FEELING OF IMPORTANCE

Influence comes, in part, from accepting responsibility. Those who are most often present when the work is being done are usually also present when decisions are being made. The more you're willing to work, and the greater responsibility you're willing to take, the greater influence you will have. You are also likely to earn more money.

Some people work primarily to gain this feeling of importance and influence, and they often become leaders. They take initiative and responsibility and are most happy when doing so.

Many people, though, don't choose to accept that kind of responsibility. They don't choose to be a boss, and they don't choose to make the required investments of time. Yet they feel important because they fulfill their own particular role in a project, whatever it may be.

INTERESTING CHALLENGES
AND INTELLECTUAL STIMULATION

Suppose you inherited a lot of money. Would you continue working? Many people work not because they need the money, but because they find work interesting and stimulating. Work brings meaning and pur-

Susan learned to sew when she was very young, making dresses for her dolls. As she grew up, she began to draw pictures of dresses, coats, and outfits for girls to wear. She enjoyed sewing and drawing, but she didn't realize that there might be a career for her associated with what she considered to be only a hobby.

In school, Susan learned word processing and later accepted a job as an office services assistant in a large office. She found her work interesting but something was missing from her job. She wasn't sure why, but she knew she wasn't completely happy.

Susan's office was in a large building that also housed a dressmaking firm. The building had a cafeteria where she met and had conversations with some people who worked for the dressmaking company. Susan discovered that a word processing job would soon be available in the dressmaking company, so she applied for the job and was hired.

Though her duties were essentially the same, Susan was so happy in her new environment that she had a wonderful attitude and looked forward to going to work every day.

Susan eventually learned how to design and create clothing with the computer. Her new office responsibilities incorporated dress designing with her word processing and other computer skills. Now she had an active role in an industry that she loved.

1. *What effect did the work environment have on Susan's attitude toward work?*

2. *If you were Susan, and the building you worked in did not include the dressmaking company, would you continue working at the same job or look for something else?*

pose to their lives. Even if money is not an important motivator, they continue going to work every day.

Some jobs and careers are especially fascinating, requiring research, problem solving, invention, product creation, or other intellectual activity. Some people work just because of this intellectual stimulation.

Even if your job isn't inherently interesting, you can nearly always make it interesting by being concerned about the people you work with and taking special care to complete the tasks that are assigned to you. Your attitude about what you do can make it either very dull or very interesting.

The Work Ethic

The United States, through the agricultural age and the industrial revolution, was built on the idea that everyone should do his or her share and make a contribution to society through working. This is known as the **work ethic.** Individual contributions need not be huge, but each person should do his or her share to promote the common good.

The industrial revolution made jobs possible for everyone. Some of these jobs were dangerous, and workers were treated cruelly by some employers. Labor unions were formed that helped make it possible for everyone to work reasonable hours under safe conditions.

Some people perform jobs that are clearly designed to promote the common good. Mother Teresa, a nun who has spent her life tending the

OFFICE TIP

You must believe that going to the office is important—and what you are doing in the office is important—if you are going to be responsible and have a good attitude on the job.

poor in India, is an example. Such people have chosen to work in serving professions that provide the satisfaction of doing something good for someone else.

Many kinds of organizations serve the common good, such as churches, nonprofit community organizations, and social service agencies. These organizations offer diverse and interesting jobs, including office work of all types.

Your job may not directly serve the community, as do those mentioned above. However, everyone who works makes a contribution by providing the goods and services needed for the economic survival of society.

People work for many different reasons. Different jobs interest different people, and most people work for a combination of reasons.

Recall Time

Answer the following questions:

1. What are two definitions of *work*? List and discuss them.
2. People are motivated to work because of their own personal needs. What are four reasons people want or need to work?
3. Some people work for *creative satisfaction*. What does this term mean to you?
4. Briefly, what is meant by the term *work ethic*?

Your Attitude

The reasons you work will affect your attitude toward a job. When people feel they have choices about the type of work they do, they demonstrate a better attitude on the job.

Those who feel obligated to work at dull jobs often feel trapped. Their feelings are reflected in their attitude at work.

Regardless of the job, you can make it interesting by finding new and better ways of doing it, learning to do additional assignments, and helping co-workers to become more efficient.

It is to your advantage to have a good attitude about working. You will probably work about two thousand hours a year for about forty years of your life. That's a total of about eighty thousand hours. If you do not have a good attitude toward your work, the hours and years will drag by, offering neither creative satisfaction nor any other sort of gratification. Your feelings of worth will suffer and you could feel like a failure.

◆   *This worker resents being interrupted by customers calling to ask questions. Is her attitude positive or negative?*

Do you have a classmate who has a bad attitude about school? How does this student behave? Can you name some of the traits of a bad attitude?

NEGATIVE ATTITUDE

What is commonly called a bad attitude is usually a negative attitude, and it can take many different forms. Who suffers from one person's bad attitude? Everyone who comes in contact with that person, but especially that person herself or himself. Furthermore, the worker with a negative attitude will probably not remain on the job very long.

Workers with a **negative attitude** are unpleasant, are indifferent, and rarely smile. They seldom say good morning to their co-workers, don't often have a good word for their associates, and may never offer to assist others in the office.

A negative attitude is further characterized by constant complaining about nearly everything. Complainers grumble about the boss, about co-workers, about the conditions in the office, about the weather, about their salaries, and on and on. In the process of complaining, they are critical of the people with whom they work, and they rarely have anything positive to say about their associates. These complainers are tiresome to be around, and other workers will make a point of avoiding them.

People with negative attitudes usually have low self-esteem and blame others for their own mistakes and shortcomings. They constantly make excuses and never admit their own failures. They seem unable to see things from any perspective but their own and are generally concerned only about advancing their own well-being. They even attempt to force their opinions on others.

OFFICE TIP

Training yourself to have a positive attitude in the office is not too difficult. Just catch yourself when you do something that you don't admire in someone else and change it.

FIGURE 3.1 ◆ Examples of Positive and Negative Attitude Traits

POSITIVE ATTITUDE TRAITS	NEGATIVE ATTITUDE TRAITS
◆ Shows consideration for others	◆ Thinks only of self
◆ Respects other opinions	◆ Forces own opinions on others
◆ Smiles often and with ease	◆ Almost never smiles
◆ Complains very little	◆ Complains all the time
◆ Admits making mistakes	◆ Blames others for own mistakes
◆ Helps to solve problems	◆ Expects everything to go wrong
◆ Looks other people in the eyes during conversations	◆ Avoids eye contact during conversations
◆ Almost never criticizes others	◆ Frequently criticizes others
◆ Accepts change or suggestions from others	◆ Unwilling to make changes
◆ Has many interests	◆ Has few interests

INDUSTRY FOCUS

Molly Lopez
Executive Secretary
The Clorox Company

Q. Ms. Lopez, how important is a good attitude for an office worker?

A. A positive attitude in an office environment is probably one of the most important characteristics you can bring to your job, especially in today's world where the demands are much greater and employers are much less tolerant than they were just a few years ago.

Today, supporting multiple bosses is generally the rule rather than the exception, and adjusting to the different work styles and personalities can make your job so much more difficult if you don't approach it with a positive attitude. Even the best of jobs will have certain tasks that are not as enjoyable as others; identify them, accept them, and tackle them when you are at your peak.

Q. Have you seen any examples of workers being promoted because of a great attitude?

A. Yes, two employees were candidates for a promotional opportunity in the Executive Offices. Both had excellent skills. One, however, had the reputation for going the "extra mile" in everything she did. She, of course, received the promotion.

Q. Have you seen any examples of workers who have been terminated because of a poor attitude?

A. Yes, there was a man with impeccable technical skills. His work was of the highest quality. His negative attitude, however, was felt by the entire office. Within a year of his employment, his "I was looking for a job when I found this one" attitude resulted in his termination.

Do you have any of the qualities that typify a negative attitude? The wonderful thing about attitude is that it can be changed. You can decide that having a negative attitude will not serve you well, may cause you to lose jobs, and certainly will cause you to lose friends. Then you can set about fixing your attitude.

◆ *Helping out with tasks that might not be part of your job description shows you've got the right attitude.*

POSITIVE ATTITUDE

Do you know someone who always seems to have a positive attitude about school? How does this person behave? Can you name some of the traits of a positive attitude?

Generally, people with a **positive attitude** have a high level of self-esteem, are pleasant to be around, and have lots of friends and many interests. They smile easily and go out of their way to greet their co-workers, offer to assist in small ways, and help make life easier and more pleasant for those around them. They are considerate, and they know how to compromise. When appropriate, they willingly change their own ideas and behavior for the good of their associates.

Those with a positive attitude seem unflappable, and very little appears to trouble them. They rarely complain when things go wrong around them. They willingly take responsibility for the mistakes they make and for their own shortcomings. They don't blame others when things get difficult.

You will seldom hear these people criticize their co-workers or their bosses. They are loyal and able to see things from another person's perspective because they respect other people's views.

Take some time to list your own negative and positive traits. Which word—*negative* or *positive*—do you think more accurately describes you? Check the negative traits that you want to change, and plan how you will go about making them positive traits.

Behavioral scientists believe that our attitudes toward other people, including both positive and negative attitude traits, are based primarily on our genetic makeup. However they can be, and often are, influenced considerably by cultural influences. These include the influences of our parents, other family members, friends, and the larger society. Usually, personality—including our attitudes toward others—is fairly well set by the time we reach our early twenties. So how do you go about changing negative traits into positive ones? Obviously, we can't change our heredity. But many of our attitudinal traits are habitual. That is, we act and react the same way so often that it has become a habit. If the habit is a negative one, then conscious and repeated effort to act or react in a more constructive way can eventually turn the habit into a positive one. This is similar to behavioral modification, which is a structured approach to changing one's attitudes by first changing behavior.

OFFICE TIP

Schedule the most difficult tasks in the morning, unless you are most energetic later in the day—if so, do them then.

Your Responsibilities

One important aspect of any job is responsibility. Even if your job doesn't require you to accept total responsibility for the outcome of a project, you will be responsible for your portion of it and for your personal conduct. Your attitude will be reflected in your willingness to meet your responsibilities.

Your employer will have certain expectations of you, and it will be your responsibility to fulfill these expectations. There will probably be times when you aren't sure what your employer wants you to do. When you feel unsure, ask what he or she expects of you.

COOPERATION

Your employer will expect you to be cooperative. You will probably not be working alone, so it will be important for you to cooperate with other workers. Some people feel their responsibilities are limited to an established set of tasks. Usually this is not the case, and the work of different people may overlap from day to day. Sometimes other workers will need your assistance, and you should offer it willingly.

In addition, sometimes you will be given an assignment that you feel is not part of your job—a task that doesn't fit your job description. Whether you see the request as a regular part of your job or not, you will be expected to take on the assignment willingly, without complaining. You may be asked to do some jobs you just don't like, but your supervisor will see it as your responsibility to be cooperative in doing these jobs agreeably and with a positive attitude.

HONESTY

Businesses lose huge sums of money every year to theft by their employees. It is your responsibility to understand what is yours and what belongs to the company. Some people think it's all right to take home stationery, pens, postage stamps, pencils, or paper clips. Some act as if these are perks (benefits) of the job. This is not usually the case. In fact, taking such items is usually considered grounds for dismissal. If it is not clearly stated that you are entitled to help yourself to office supplies, then all supplies should stay in the office to be used for official business.

On full-time jobs, your employer is paying you for a full day's work. Standing around the watercooler is not working. Talking on the company telephone to family and friends is not working. Give your employer an honest day's work—that is what you are paid to do.

Your supervisor will expect you to be honest when asked about different aspects of your work. Don't make up stories and excuses for things that are being questioned. Just tell the truth. Your supervisors will appreciate and respect you for it.

Honesty is your responsibility and an obligation you have to your employer.

DEPENDABILITY

Dependability means that you are on the job every day and that you arrive there on time. Continual tardiness can be grounds for dismissal.

If you are ill and cannot go to work, call your employer or supervisor and explain why. The earlier you call, the more likely it is that she or he will be able to find someone to take over your responsibilities for the day, so call no later than your usual arrival time.

Missing a day at work without a legitimate reason or not calling is also grounds for dismissal. Some people just decide to sleep in and don't call. This is irresponsible behavior and reflects a negative attitude.

◆ *This young man makes lengthy personal calls from his job. He thinks it's all right if the calls are all local. What do you think?*

HUMAN RELATIONS

Mary Ann was hired as a front desk clerk in the office at the Young Men's Christian Association (YMCA). She was interested in physical fitness and was delighted to get the job. She was efficient and did all that was required of her neatly and on time. She liked her job, came to work promptly each day, and left at quitting time.

However, Mary Ann rarely smiled and did not seem to have fun with her co-workers and the YMCA members. People got the impression that she was indifferent and did not care about her work. The YMCA is a place where people go to relax and have a pleasant time at their leisure. Even though Mary Ann was good at her job, people complained about her attitude.

Actually, Mary Ann was a conscientious young woman, and she wanted to do her best. She was unaware that she had an unpleasant manner. When it was time for her performance review, her supervisor explained that members were unhappy about her behavior. Mary Ann was eager to know how to improve the situation, and her supervisor gave her some ideas about how to behave more pleasantly.

First, her supervisor suggested that Mary Ann smile more often. Second, she suggested that Mary Ann make sure she understood what the members wanted. Third, she asked Mary Ann to try to meet the members' needs by acting interested in their concerns.

Mary Ann's behavior improved, and her co-workers complimented her on her efforts. Several members spent more time with her and seemed to like her much better. Though she had been unaware of her problem, her willingness to change demonstrated a positive attitude—and she was even happier with her job.

1. *What would have happened if Mary Ann's supervisor had not explained her effect on co-workers and others?*

2. *What if Mary Ann's supervisor had been negative in her criticism?*

3. *What if Mary Ann had not been willing to change?*

Dependability also means that you can be counted on to complete your work, that you can be expected to do what you are told to do, and that you are reliable. Dependability is an important attribute in any relationship. Your friends and family appreciate it if they can count on you to do what you say you'll do. Your employer and co-workers will expect it and appreciate it, too.

WILLINGNESS TO LEARN

When you accept a position with a company, you are responsible for learning what the job entails. You may be learning new things about the job for many months. As you master one aspect, you will find others to learn. Your willingness to take direction and to learn all aspects of your job is your responsibility when you accept employment. Show initiative by learning more than your own assigned tasks, and you will increase your probability of being promoted.

You will also be expected to listen to constructive criticism from your supervisor about how you are performing your job. This may not always be comfortable, but it will be to your advantage. Remember Mary Ann and her job at the YMCA? She willingly took suggestions from her supervisor about her behavior. Mary Ann was not aware of her problem. But when her supervisor pointed it out, she readily listened and made some changes.

ACCEPTABLE PERSONAL CONDUCT

You will be expected to act in a businesslike manner in the office. That is, you must dress appropriately, be clean and neat, and refrain from cursing, talking loudly, carrying food around, or using other bad manners around customers or co-workers.

Every office has rules. For example, some companies don't object if you eat at your desk. In that case, it's all right to bring your lunch or a snack. Most offices don't allow smoking inside the building, and some have designated smoking areas. If you smoke, do so only where permitted.

Learn the rules of personal conduct and follow them. If things are unclear to you, ask your supervisor so you won't find yourself doing something you're not supposed to do.

If you have a personal problem, such as alcohol or drug abuse, family dysfunction, or emotional difficulties, it is your responsibility to seek help. These problems affect your job sooner or later. Many companies have an industrial nurse or psychologist with whom you can talk. Your discussion will be completely private and confidential. This person will help you or will make it easier for you to get the help you need. If no such person is available in your company, seek answers from your minister or from your county's department of mental health.

Some positions require special off-the-job conduct. For example, if you work in the office of a public figure, such as a politician, you will be expected to be an upright citizen at all times. If you work for the school system, there will be certain expectations about your behavior off the job because of your contact with children.

Can you think of any other jobs that would have requirements about how you behave off the job?

Any job brings with it responsibility. Just as you are now responsible and accountable to your teachers through tests and grades, you will also be responsible and accountable to your employers through your duties and behavior on the job.

Recall Time

Answer the following questions:

1. What are the characteristics of a negative attitude? What are the characteristics of a positive attitude?

2. When you accept a job, you accept responsibility to the job, to your employer, and to your co-workers. What might be included in taking responsibility on the job?

3. An employee is responsible for his or her personal conduct. What does this statement mean?

Attitudes and Self-Concept

For many years, psychologists have studied human behavior, attempting to determine how and why people behave the way they do. Attitude is demonstrated in behavior, and attitude has roots in how we feel about ourselves, our **self-concept.**

Self-concept is developed through a complex and ill-defined process. An ongoing argument about nature versus nurture is involved. Do we act the way we do because of our genetic inheritance or because of our environments and the way our parents and families cared for us?

It is believed that our parents influence our self-concept to a large degree. Some of us were reared by parents whose expectations were difficult for us to live up to. When we did not measure up, and our parents disapproved of what we did, our self-concept suffered. Some people learn early that they are "not okay."

Several years ago, Dr. Thomas Harris explained in his book *I'm Okay, You're Okay* that many of us get the message early in life that we're not at all "okay." Unfortunately, this "not okay" message has far-reaching effects. We carry this belief, this negative baggage, around with us for most of our lives until we actively work to dispel it. Not only do we carry it around, we make it stronger in the ways we talk to ourselves.

Some people are so demanding of themselves that they are never quite satisfied with what they accomplish. These people talk to themselves in a negative manner, saying, "I'll always be stupid," "I'll never be able to do this," "I'll never succeed," and so on. Some people speak to themselves this way all the time.

Self-talk is made up of all the negative and positive thoughts we have about ourselves. These thoughts are stored in our subconscious minds and affect our behavior.

Another concept, related to self-talk, is called a *self-fulfilling prophecy.* This means that what you say about your chances of success or failure influences the outcome. When you believe certain things about yourself—about your abilities and personal characteristics—you tend to become the person you believe you are.

How do we change these negative feelings about ourselves? One way is by changing the way we talk to ourselves. A popular book by Shad Helmstetter, Ph.D., called *The Self-Talk Solution* discusses how we can begin to change negative ideas about ourselves by changing the things we say to ourselves. The idea is that when you feel a negative idea coming on, you quickly change it to a positive one.

For example, suppose a boy notices a girl at school and is interested in her. He may be telling himself that she would never be interested in him. But if he can change the message to himself, he may feel there is a chance she will like him. He might say to himself something like, "I'm an interesting person; the girls think I'm cute and appealing."

With this kind of self-talk, your attitude about yourself can change so that your self-confidence is evident. Self-confidence is generally an attractive trait in everybody.

The same kind of ideas can help you with a positive attitude on the job. If you tell yourself you are likable and capable and competent to do your job, you set yourself up for success.

ESTEEM

The need for esteem is one reason people work. **Esteem** can be how highly you regard others, but it is also how you feel about yourself—part of your self-concept. It is also how people in your environment see you. Esteem implies that you are valued by yourself and by other people. Everyone likes to be liked. Esteem needs are met through accomplishment, good attitude, and values.

Self-realization is esteem at its highest level, according to Abraham Maslow, a noted psychologist. Self-realization means that you have realized (that is, accomplished) all the important goals and aspirations in your life. It means that you have become the best that you can be. Self-realization is hard to attain, but those who do accomplish it generally do so through their work.

If you go through life without your needs for recognition and esteem being satisfied, your self-concept will suffer.

The process for developing your self-concept is complicated, but the ideas in this section can be helpful when you begin to sort out how you feel about yourself.

VALUES

As children grow and develop, they begin to incorporate values into their self-concepts. **Values** are the things that each person believes to be true and important. They could be such things as honesty, integrity, family, friends, industry, and success. Your values are often reflected in your attitude. If working is not important to you, it will show in your attitude and in your work performance. If taking your share of the responsibility is not one of your values, that will also affect your attitude and performance on the job.

Your self-concept also affects your attitude—in work, in school, and in your social and family relationships. A positive attitude is important for your success on the job and for your happiness in all of life.

If your self-concept tells you that you're capable of meeting the responsibilities of your job, chances are your attitude will generally be positive.

Recall Time

Answer the following questions:

1. Self-concept means how we see ourselves. What are some ways our self-concept is developed?

2. Self-talk is a way to undo negative thinking about ourselves. What is self-talk?

3. We all have things that are important to us. These are our values. What sorts of things come under the heading of values?

4. What are some of your values?

Summary

The way work is viewed and the things that motivate people to work affect attitudes on the job. Ralph Waldo Emerson said that the purpose of life is not to be happy, but to be useful. For a lot of people, work is being useful.

People work for many reasons. For most, the main reason is to earn a living. People spend money for various things, from necessities like food, shelter, and clothing to leisure-time activities. Most people save some of what they earn for larger expenses like medical bills and education for their children. Security and independence are probably the biggest motivators behind working to earn money.

People also work for creative satisfaction and the social benefits of being with other people engaged in common goals. Some people work to feel important and strive to earn more money while taking more responsibility in their work. Others work for the intellectual stimulation.

The work ethic means that everyone should work to do her or his share and make a contribution to society. Nearly every job contributes something to society.

Attitudes of different people range from extremely positive to extremely negative. While most of us fall somewhere between these extremes, nearly everyone could benefit by having a more positive attitude. A positive attitude is characterized by a smile, pleasantness, and willingness to be helpful and learn on the job. People who have a positive attitude usually relate well to others, make new acquaintances easily, and have many interests. They are loyal, tend not to be critical, and rarely complain. They seem to enjoy life.

A negative attitude is characterized by an unpleasant demeanor, a complaining nature, a practice of blaming others for one's own errors, and a habit of making the job more difficult for everyone. People who have a negative attitude seem unable to see things from any point of view other than their own and generally are not enjoyable to be around. They have fewer friends and a narrower range of interests.

You will notice, on the job, that the people who tend to have good attitudes are also willing to take on the responsibilities that are part of agreeing to work in an office. These responsibilities include being cooperative, honest, dependable, and willing to learn and take direction.

Acceptable personal conduct is an important responsibility. Good manners, appropriate language, appropriate dress, and general good conduct on and off the job are some areas of personal responsibility.

People's attitudes about work are directly linked with their attitudes about themselves. This is our self-concept, or how we view ourselves. The development of our self-concept is complex and involves both our environments and our genetic inheritance. Sometimes we learn as young children that we are "not okay" and we carry that knowledge around with us as we grow up. If we feel "not okay," we act "not okay"—thus, we have a negative attitude.

You can change these "not okay" feelings by using positive self-talk and eliminating negative self-talk messages that you might be giving yourself throughout the day.

Our attitudes also reflect our values—the things we consider to be important as we conduct our lives. Some values are honesty, integrity, family, friends, industry, and success.

Your attitude on the job thus develops from many other aspects of your life. Having a better understanding of those areas will help you to be happier and more positive about working.

When you are considering how to improve your attitude on the job, answer the following questions:

◆ Do I like the job I am doing?
◆ What are the reasons I want to work?
◆ Would I work if I did not receive money for it?
◆ Do I demonstrate a positive attitude?
◆ Do I demonstrate a negative attitude?
◆ Am I taking responsibility for the activities and events in my life, such as school, family, job, and other relationships?
◆ How do I talk to myself, with positive or negative messages?
◆ What do I consider important in my life? What are my values?

IN CONCLUSION

When you have completed this chapter, answer the following questions:

1. Why do people who have no need of further income often continue to work?

2. What is the effect of a self-fulfilling prophecy and what is the reason for this effect?

3. How can your thoughts change a negative attitude into a positive one?

REVIEW AND APPLICATION

✔ CHECK YOUR KNOWLEDGE

1. How does the dictionary define *work?*
2. Did our greatest composers and artists work?
3. List several different reasons people are motivated to work.
4. What are considered basic needs?
5. What is creative satisfaction?
6. How does work make people feel important?
7. Define the term *work ethic.*
8. List the attributes of a negative attitude.
9. List the attributes of a positive attitude.
10. List some ways an employer expects an employee to be responsible.
11. Honesty means more than simply telling the truth. What else does it mean?
12. Describe some ways you are responsible for your personal conduct.
13. List some things you could say to yourself that would enhance your own positive attitude.
14. How do your values relate to your attitude at work?

📖 REVIEW YOUR VOCABULARY

On a separate piece of paper, write the letter of the vocabulary word that is described below.

____ 1. esteem at its highest level
____ 2. mental position or emotional posture resulting in behavior that is unpleasant, indifferent, seldom smiling
____ 3. all the negative and positive thoughts we have about ourselves
____ 4. concept implying that you are valued by yourself and others
____ 5. mental position resulting in behavior that is pleasant, interested in others, and often smiling
____ 6. what we believe about ourselves
____ 7. idea that everyone should do his or her share and make a contribution to society through working
____ 8. things a person believes are important
____ 9. exertion or effort directed to produce or accomplish something

a. esteem
b. negative attitude
c. positive attitude
d. self-concept
e. self-realization
f. self-talk
g. values
h. work
i. work ethic

🟫 DISCUSS AND ANALYZE AN OFFICE SITUATION

1. Barry has a job as a computer operator in a busy office. He likes his job and is punctual, honest, willing to learn new things, and in other ways responsible. But Barry spends weekends drinking with his friends, and some Monday mornings he finds it difficult to get to work on time. A nondrinking friend suggests that perhaps Barry's drinking is becoming excessive and a problem, even though Barry is generally functioning well on the job. What should Barry do?

2. Susan is an accountant for a large corporation. She likes her job and generally demonstrates a high level of competency and an excellent attitude. However, problems arise when people speak to her about her work. She becomes defensive and argumentative, making it difficult for her supervisor to approach her with any suggestions.

   Susan's supervisor takes Susan aside to discuss these problems with her. The supervisor discovers that Susan comes from a family where her mother was disapproving and criticized Susan for the smallest mistakes, causing Susan to develop a negative self-concept.

   How might Susan begin to fix her negative self-concept?

PRACTICE BASIC SKILLS

MATH

1. Jerry is part of a single-parent family, so he wants to assist with expenses at home. He searches for a job that matches the computer skills he learned while in school. The job he thought he would like doing doesn't pay as much as some of the others. To help him make his decision, he creates a monthly budget for himself to clarify what he needs to earn to help his family the way he wishes.

   Create a monthly budget for Jerry with some of the following categories:

   ◆ rent
   ◆ utilities
   ◆ gasoline
   ◆ auto insurance
   ◆ lunches
   ◆ other food
   ◆ clothing

   What other items will Jerry need to purchase or pay for? If you have a checking account, review your own check register to recall how you have recently spent money. Fill in the figures for Jerry's budget, and add them up.

ENGLISH

1. To maintain a high level of self-esteem and therefore improve your attitude, you must speak and write standard English. Rewrite, or key in, the following paragraph, correcting all examples of nonstandard English.

   I can type really good and groove on doing telephone work. If you decides to hire me, I can be an asset to your office because I know how to rap with people real good. I think this is a rad job and I will enjoy be'n a part of this here office. Thank ya a lot.

PROOFREADING

1. In your office job, you may be asked to do some minor editing for your supervisor. You will want to respond to this request with a positive atti-tude. Rewrite or key in the following letter, correcting the misspelled words, nonstandard language, and punctuation errors.

Dear Mr. Brown:

I'd like to take this oportunity to speek to you about a business mater in our last shipmat we received several more peaces than we had ordered. We wood hope that you would be willing to adjust our billing of May 3 deducting the cost of the merchandise, a list of the items we didnt order is atached.

   Thank you.

                                    Yurs truely,

                                    Mr. John Green

APPLY YOUR KNOWLEDGE

1. Make a list of the kinds of things you might say to yourself if you were practicing positive self-talk. Try saying these to yourself for a few days, then write about the results.

2. It is important that you become aware of negative ideas and attitudes that you may be demonstrating. Make a list of the negative attitudes you suspect in yourself. Then ask your friends for candid ideas about how you could improve your negative attitudes. List them and attempt to put them into practice.

3. One of the first steps in learning to work with people from cultures different than our own is to identify our preconceived ideas about their cultures. Think about the people with whom you work. Make a list of the various cultures you think these people represent. Then, using your word processing program or typewriter, list both negative and positive ideas you have about each of these cultures. Think about your preconceptions as you work with these people. Compare what you observe about your co-workers with your expectations. Complete your list by comparing your preconceived ideas with your actual observations. What did you learn?

USING THE REFERENCE MANUAL

Retrieve the file CH3REF on the data disk. Use the punctuation section of the Reference Manual at the back of the book to help you correct the sentences. Save and print.

1. Tina received B grades in the following classes; English, Spanish, and Western Civilization.
2. There are three ways to study for this test, read the chapter, study the summary points, and review your notes.
3. Dear Mr. Scott; etc., etc.
4. The activity began at 5;00 p.m. Mountain Standard Time.
5. The doctor recommended only one third the normal dosage.
6. My post office box number is 3345.
7. The manager insisted on state of the art technology in his offices.
8. The ex President of Babbitt Corporation had no comment.
9. Part of the requirements in computer applications class was to re do the assignment until it was mailable.
10. Can we ignore that there are twenty five students that haven't been assigned classes?

CHAPTER
4

Getting Along with People

OBJECTIVES

After completing this chapter, you will be able to do the following:

1. Use human relationship skills in the office to work as a team member.
2. Be supportive of co-workers in the office.
3. Maintain a professional appearance in the office.
4. Acknowledge the good work and ideas of others.
5. Understand and deal with difficult people.
6. Accept criticism gracefully and admit your own mistakes.
7. Rid yourself of your own unhappy feelings.
8. Be assertive without being aggressive.
9. Accept assignments willingly and set priorities.
10. Keep your boss informed of your progress on your assignments.
11. Maintain high ethical standards in your office relationships.

NEW OFFICE TERMS

aggressive communication
assertive communication
assertiveness
body language
co-workers

human relations
interpersonal relations
passive communication
seniority

Rose: How about watching the basketball game on TV?
Anders: Na, not tonight.

This can get depressing. After a while, most people choose not to be around a person like Anders. The same thing happens at work. People will seek out your company and your opinion if you have a positive, enthusiastic attitude.

When you arrive at the office, greet people with a smile. A smile on your face will help you have a pleasant attitude—and you feel better when you smile. Keep your emotions under control; don't have temper tantrums, and save tears until you get home. Emotional outbursts in the workplace cause people to be uncomfortable, and hinder the business at hand.

MAINTAIN A SENSE OF HUMOR

Having a sense of humor doesn't require you to crack jokes constantly. That can be disruptive. However, you should be able to see the lighter side of matters, have fun at work, and laugh with your co-workers.

Don't take yourself too seriously. Laugh at yourself and encourage co-workers to laugh with you when you do something awkward or make a minor mistake. No one is perfect. Being able to laugh with others at your blunders will help you cope with stressful situations.

On the other hand, recognize that you are important to the company and to each project on which you work. Don't underestimate the contribution you make or your value as a team member. You are a vital part of whatever project is underway.

In the following example, Ramona is able to maintain her sense of humor at a stressful moment:

Ms. Parkins, the president of the company, is expected in the office any minute. People are scurrying around getting things ready for her visit. Ramona is the receptionist, and her desk is immediately inside the main entrance. She is preparing a bouquet of flowers for the front of the office and goes out to get some water. Just as Ramona reenters the office, Ms. Parkins comes in. Ramona bumps into Ms. Parkins, sending water flying. Fortunately, Ms. Parkins is able to avoid most of the water, which lands on the carpet.

"I'm so sorry," Ramona says. "May I help you?" Ramona has never met Ms. Parkins, so she doesn't realize that the important guest has arrived. Ms. Parkins laughs. "Perhaps a paper towel. Then you can tell Mr. Black that Ms. Parkins is here."

"Oh, no, I can't believe it. I wanted things to be so nice," moans Ramona.

"Things are very nice, and the flowers are beautiful. That was quite a greeting." Ms. Parkins laughs again.

Ramona laughs, too.

ACKNOWLEDGE THE GOOD WORK AND IDEAS OF OTHERS

In the 1989 movie *Working Girl*, a secretary's boss stole one of her ideas and used it as though it were the boss's own. Ultimately, the boss's scheme backfired and the movie had a happy ending, with the secretary receiving the recognition she had earned.

Always give credit where credit is due. It's all right to use someone else's idea if you have her or his permission, but be sure to mention who thought of it.

DON'T BE A WORRIER

It is unsettling to work with people who constantly worry. Act with mature assurance that everything will get done on time and correctly, and that disaster does not lurk around every corner. Energy spent worrying could be better spent working toward solutions.

KEEP A BUSINESSLIKE, PROFESSIONAL ATTITUDE

Offices can get hectic with busy telephones, interruptions from supervisors, heavy workloads, and deadlines. You will find times to laugh and have some fun, but remember where you are and act appropriately.

Being businesslike means being calm, courteous, helpful, efficient, and knowledgeable. Being knowledgeable does not mean that you have to know everything, but that you know how and where to find the answers to questions you're not sure about.

Your co-workers will have confidence in you if you project a professional attitude. Remember, too, that you are a representative of your company; your presenting a businesslike image gives the public confidence in the company.

MAINTAIN A PROFESSIONAL APPEARANCE

People begin to form opinions about you based on your appearance even before you begin your first assignment. Take pride in your personal hygiene, dress, and overall appearance.

Some businesses have dress codes that don't allow mustaches or beards for men, require stockings and high-heeled shoes for women, and so on. Most companies, though, leave style of dress to your discretion. Don't underdress or overdress. Avoid faddish styles; they detract from your professional image. For instance, skirts should not be too short or too long. Wear conservative jewelry; for example, don't wear heavy bracelets that clank and thump.

Keep your work space neat and clean, too. Clutter in your area detracts from the looks of the entire office. Don't have too many personal items—pictures, figurines, stuffed animals—on your desk. You need room to work.

Try to break nervous habits such as humming, whistling, muttering to yourself, drumming your fingers, chewing gum, twirling your hair, or swinging your foot. You will be working closely with many people, so try not to distract them from their work. This is simply being courteous and considerate of others.

OFFICE TIP

Look around you and notice what other people are wearing to work. See what you think looks best—professional, neat, attractive, and so on. Then dress accordingly. The way you dress makes the statement that you take your job seriously (or that you do not!).

REVIEW AND APPLICATION

✔ CHECK YOUR KNOWLEDGE

1. Give two reasons that personal and human relations are important in the workplace.
2. What one word is the key to a successful team of co-workers?
3. Define *expectations*. Give an example of an implicit expectation your co-workers might have of you.
4. How would you regard someone who has seniority?
5. Describe some ways that you could show support for your co-workers.
6. What is the difference between thoughtful conversation and gossip?
7. A worker who is able to adjust to changes rapidly and cheerfully is demonstrating what essential attribute?
8. Why is it valuable to attend office social functions?
9. If you have a consistently positive attitude, your co-workers will want your company and advice. Why is this so?
10. Why are temper tantrums inappropriate in the office?
11. A sense of humor can be vital to the office atmosphere. Give an example of humor that might be appropriate at work. Then give another example that might be inappropriate.
12. How would you put together the best possible wardrobe for your position?
13. What are some characteristics of a professional, businesslike attitude?
14. What is the difference between hearing and listening?
15. A co-worker says, "It took you three hours to do that! I could have done it in one." To which category of difficult people does this person belong?
16. Define *empathy*. Why is it a good strategy for dealing with difficult people?
17. Your boss stares out the window while you are speaking with her. What does her body language tell you?
18. What is gained by being pleasant to someone to whom no one else will speak?
19. Why is it counterproductive to make excuses about what you've done?
20. When a boss or co-worker is angry, it is tempting to take it personally. What can you do when that temptation arises?
21. Give a simple definition of *assertiveness*. Describe the aggressive and passive forms of communication.
22. What is a hierarchy?
23. If you were a boss, how would you like to be treated by your employees? How should they respond when you give them assignments?
24. What is a first-in, first-out policy?
25. Rather than problems, what do supervisors want from their workers? Phrase your answer in one word.
26. To what are you being true when you have high ethical standards?

📖 REVIEW YOUR VOCABULARY

On a separate piece of paper, write the letter of the vocabulary word that is described below.

____ 1. nonverbal communication through physical actions
____ 2. term meaning how people get along with one another
____ 3. people who work together in a cooperative effort
____ 4. characteristic of having worked on a job longer than others
____ 5. way of overstating what you want, being bossy, not considering the needs of others
____ 6. way of not saying what you want, or being apologetic and feeling guilty
____ 7. way of saying what you want clearly and directly, without animosity, and being firm yet considerate of others' needs

a. aggressive communication
b. assertive communication
e. interpersonal relations
f. passive communication

c. body language 　　　　　g. seniority
d. co-workers

DISCUSS AND ANALYZE AN OFFICE SITUATION

1. William realizes too late that he left out an important section of a report when he prepared it for mailing to a big client. Not wanting to lose the respect of his co-workers or face his supervisor's criticism, he searches his mind for a logical and believable excuse to give them.

   How could William best gain support and approval from his co-workers?

2. Emily has decided that her boss is a hopelessly difficult person. He is always angry, nothing is ever perfect enough or on time, and he never thanks her for her work. She avoids speaking with him whenever possible and has begun complaining about him to her co-workers.

   What type of behavior is the boss demonstrating? Is Emily being assertive? What strategies might Emily employ to improve this situation?

PRACTICE BASIC SKILLS

MATH

1. Ginger has finally achieved a position of seniority in her office. The company has presented her with a choice of options for greater pay. She may choose a simple raise of 15 percent of her present salary, which stands at $1,600 per month, or she may opt for another plan with a base salary plus commissions.

   If she chooses the latter plan, she will receive a base salary of $1,700 per month plus 6 percent of her gross sales for the month. Presently, Ginger's monthly gross sales are averaging $4,000. Which plan should Ginger choose?

ENGLISH

1. The following office memo needs revising. Rewrite it, or key it in, correcting all examples of nonstandard English, which are inappropriate in the business world.

TO: My boss
FROM: Gloria
RE: dweeby co-workers

Ms. Banks,
　I finally have to tell you this cause I know you are cool and can catch my drift. Like I am so weirded out by these jerks who share my office. Gee, I could really like scream, you know? Please do something before I croak.

PROOFREADING

1. Retype or rewrite the following paragraphs of the report, correcting all errors.

　In anilyzing the profit and loss figures for last quarter ending in august we can see that the shoping center is doing well. Its important to note that sales have gone stedily up since doors open in january However We have yet to, review which stores are the biggest gainers.

　What we can see is is that the biggest gross sales take place on week ends simply because more people are in the mall then; studies show, that people will spend simply because they are their. This is called impulse buying. Later is this report' we will address the subject of advertizing aimed at: impulse buyers.

APPLY YOUR KNOWLEDGE

1. Describe an actual experience you have had with another student or co-worker that involved human or interpersonal relations. Based on what you know now, how might you have handled the situation differently?

2. You have come up with a great idea for increasing production in your office, and you are anxious to share it with your supervisor. When you enter her office, you find that she has just received some bad news. Do you proceed to tell her your idea or do you decide to wait until later? Why?

3. Invite the manager of a local office to speak to your class on the subject of human relations in the workplace. Ask him or her to address the particular problems faced by people of diverse cultures working together. Using your word

processor or typewriter, prepare a list of questions you would like to have the speaker discuss.

USING THE REFERENCE MANUAL

Retrieve the file CH4REF on the data disk. Use the punctuation section of the Reference Manual at the back of the book to help you correct the sentences. Save and print.

1. We met in August of 81 at the Golden Gate Bridge.

2. How many Cs did Mario get on his report card?
3. Rudy is very upset because he lost Tonys' coat.
4. Wont we ever be done with this project?
5. The community college drive was launched in April of 89.
6. The two girls father could not be found in the snow storm.
7. The Meatcutters Union meets every third Wednesday of the month.
8. Under the circumstances, there isnt anything we can do.
9. How often are the childrens' play schedules interrupted each day?
10. The neighbors dog is friendly and smart.

CAREER PORTFOLIO

PART ONE: YOUR PLACE IN THE MODERN OFFICE

Introduction

The primary purpose of a student career portfolio is to demonstrate what you have learned in a given class or during a certain part of your school career. Your portfolio might include samples of a process or procedure you have mastered, an effort you have made, or specific knowledge or skills you have acquired.

Student portfolios don't have to be limited to classroom experiences. You might also include samples of items that demonstrate learning things on your own or using your skills outside of school. For instance, you might show how you applied communication skills on the job or how you used ideas from course readings and discussions to better understand people who are different from you.

In the Career Portfolio feature at the end of each of the five parts in this textbook, you will be asked to prepare two or more items for your portfolio showing ways you have used office technology and techniques. How will your portfolio be used? Instead of just showing up with a résumé at a job interview for a position as an executive secretary or administrative assistant, you will come with a portfolio showing *evidence* of your skills in the form of spreadsheets and charts done in spreadsheet applications, a newsletter you designed, samples of office memos and letters to customers, or procedures you will follow to complete typical office activities.

General Instructions for Portfolio Projects

1. After you create your student portfolio item, be sure to give it one final proofing for (a) spelling errors, by running the spell-check program, and (b) grammar errors, by running the grammar-program. In addition, refine the content of your document by using the thesaurus feature in the word processing program you are using.

2. Print out a clean copy of your document and insert behind the appropriate tab in your Career Portfolio binder. You will want to purchase an inexpensive but professional-looking binder from an office supply store and set up the sections with the following five tabs:

- ◆ *Your Place in the Modern Office*
- ◆ *Technical Skills and Knowledge*
- ◆ *Office Support Skills*
- ◆ *Communication and Problem-Solving Skills*
- ◆ *Employment Skills*

Specific Activities to Complete

Select at least two of the following items for inclusion in your Career Portfolio, using the information from Chapters 1 through 4.

1. Keyboard a list of at least four reasons you would like to work in a particular office environment, such as law, education, medical, travel. Save and print this list. (Be sure you proof according to the instructions given above.) Insert this list as the first item in your Career Portfolio binder behind the first tab, entitled "Your Place in the Modern Office."

2. Keyboard a list that summarizes the types of attitudes and human relations skills you will need on the job you've chosen. Create the list so that it meets your needs.

3. Describe a situation in which you used the material presented in Chapters 3 and 4 about your attitude and getting along with people. It should be a situation in which you feel you did the right thing and got recognized for it. (It's OK to recognize and document the right things you do!) Save, print, and insert this list behind the first tab.

PART II

Technical Skills and Knowledge

CHAPTER
5
Office Computer Systems

OBJECTIVES

After completing this chapter, you will be able to do the following:

1. Describe the relationship between a management information system and a computer system.
2. List the four classifications of computers and describe the differences between them.
3. Identify the major components of a computer system.
4. Distinguish between the terms *memory* and *storage* and list examples of each.
5. Describe the function of hardware peripherals such as the mouse, modem, and scanner.
6. List examples of system software and describe a major advantage of using each.
7. List six types of application software and describe the function of each one.

NEW OFFICE TERMS

compact disk read-only memory
  (CD-ROM)
computer
computer system
database management
desktop publishing (DTP)
Disk Operating System
gigabyte
Graphic User Interface (GUI)
graphics
hard disks
integrated software
mainframe computers
management information
  system (MIS)
microcomputers
minicomputers
modem
monitor
mouse
peripherals
random-access memory (RAM)
read-only memory (ROM)
scanner
software
spreadsheets
supercomputers
word processing

Computers are clearly the greatest advance in technology since the printing press. They provide countless benefits to almost any organization. Industries that have been downsized by global competition can use computers to maximize productivity and ensure superior customer service. A single office worker using a computer can handle most levels of operations, from data entry and document production to complex customer service transactions. Today, successful organizations expect employees to be able to use technology, analyze information, and complete routine office activities in the course of their everyday duties.

Management Information Systems

Organizations use information to effectively manage operations, people, and resources. One of the most effective tools that can help meet these information needs is a management information system, also known as an MIS. A **management information system** is an integrated system that is usually computer based and which provides information and aids in decision making critical to an organization's continued profitability and operations.

Though an MIS is typically tailored to each organization's needs, its functions are primarily used for planning and controlling the routine activities that most organizations perform. For example, MIS can help plan projects and control inventory levels, as well as assist in the performance of such critical functions as monitoring the production, quality, environment, and budgets of all types of businesses.

What is information? Information is data that has been processed. It helps decision makers by increasing their knowledge and reducing uncertainty. In order for computer-generated information to be trustworthy for decision making, it must possess six characteristics:

◆ *Accessibility.* Information must be easily obtainable without excessive effort.
◆ *Relevance.* Information must be meaningful and pertinent.
◆ *Clarity.* Information must be specific, obvious, and in an easily understandable format.
◆ *Accuracy.* Information must be precise, accurate, and error free.
◆ *Objectivity.* Information must be unbiased (not slanted by the views of particular parties).

◆ *Timeliness.* Information must be available when needed and sufficiently up-to-date to aid its users.

Computers have been used for many years to perform routine and repetitive operations formerly done by hand; for example, payroll preparation and sales order writing. Today, computer systems operate more efficiently if they are customized for the needs of different businesses. This is because each organization is unique, and the types of information that can be provided by a computer system are as diverse as each organization's use of that information. A management information system is helpful because it ensures that computer-processed information is useful by focusing on the information needs of the particular company.

Computer Systems

Computer systems should always be purchased with a knowledge of how they will be used and what type of components are needed. Buying a computer system is one of the most important decisions an organization makes. It requires thinking about future needs so that existing systems can be updated and adapted to those needs.

THE COMPUTER SYSTEM

A **computer** is an electronic device which operates under the control of instructions stored in its own memory. Computers can accept data as input in the form of words and numbers, process that data arithmetically and logically, produce usable output from the processing, and store the results for future use.

A **computer system** is a group of computer devices that are connected, coordinated, and linked together in such a way that they work as one to complete a task. Depending on the office setting, you can find relatively small and simple computer systems, composed of only one or two small computers serving an entire office, or large computer systems which store huge amounts of data and information that each person in an organization can access by using a keyboard-type device at his or her desk.

CLASSIFICATIONS OF COMPUTERS

Computers are useful because they are fast, accurate, and able to store vast amounts of data. Typically, computer systems are classified according to their physical size, memory capacity, speed, and cost. There are four classifications of computers: microcomputers, minicomputers, mainframe computers, and supercomputers.

Microcomputers   The microcomputer is the smallest in size, has the least amount of memory capacity, is slower than the other three types of computers, and costs the least. The **microcomputer,** also called the personal computer (PC), is the type used by most office

OFFICE TIP

Do not eat food or drink beverages around any computer system. An unexpected spill or food particle could damage the computer, the mouse, or a crucial computer disk. More important, such a mishap could prevent workers from completing an important job on time.

workers. These computers can sit on desks or be as small as a notebook and held on one's lap. They range in price from several hundred dollars to over $10,000.

There are several categories of microcomputers. The five primary ones are workstation, desktop, laptop, notebook, and palmtop. A brief description of each follows.

Workstation   The high-powered workstation computer has almost as much processing power as a minicomputer. The workstation can be a multi-user system that controls a small client-server network, or a stand-alone computer. As more application software is developed for workstations, their use will increase. They can be either desktop or floor mounted and cost between $6,000 and $10,000.

Desktop   The standard desktop computer is still the most widely used PC in the business world. It is typically a single-user device capable of being utilized for two or more different applications at one time. In terms of applications and processing power, desktop computers fall somewhere between the more powerful workstations and the smaller, portable microcomputers that will be discussed next. They range in cost from hundreds of dollars to $5,000 and, as their name implies, sit on a desktop.

Laptop, Notebook, and Palmtop   These last three types are often called portable computers, range in weight from less than one pound to twelve pounds, and cost from under $1,000 to $3,000. They range in size from that of a small calendar able to fit in a purse or pocket to that of a small suitcase. Portable computers are compact and lightweight enough to be transported easily from place to place. Businesspeople use them when they travel or commute to the office, stay at a hotel, visit branch offices, attend conferences, or work at home. Students use them in class and at the library. They are versatile and can even be

◆ *Workstations, such as the Hewlett-Packard 9000 Series 700 Model 712/60, frequently are used in computer-aided design.*

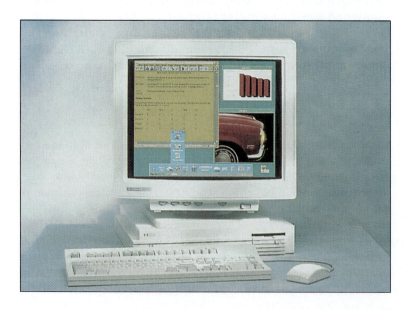

(a)

(b)

◆ *a. A desktop microcomputer. (Power Macintosh 6100/66), b. In today's world, portability is an important consideration. Gateway 2000 Colorbook 2 (Copyright 1995 Gateway 2000, Inc. Reprinted with permission.)*

connected to larger desktop PCs or other computers. Most portable computers are almost as powerful as desktop micros and use conventional software.

Minicomputers **Minicomputers** are often larger than desktop microcomputers and similarly can be used with standard electrical outlets, with no environmental controls necessary. They are used for multi-user applications, such as numerical control of machine tools in manufacturing operations and industrial automation robotics. They range in cost from a few thousand dollars to hundreds of thousands of dollars.

Mainframe Computers **Mainframes** are very fast and powerful; they are freestanding multi-user units and larger than most minicomputers. Unlike microcomputers and minicomputers, mainframes require special wiring and environmental controls to operate efficiently. Because these systems operate twenty-four hours a day, they are used primarily by large businesses and government. They range in cost from approximately $200,000 to millions of dollars.

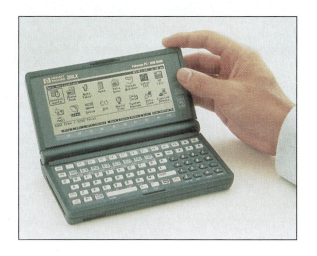

◆ *Among the smallest computers for business use is the palmtop. (Hewlett Packard Company's 200 LX-1MB Palmtop PC)*

◆ *Today, machines build machines under the direction of a computer! Some minicomputers are used in automobile factories to control robots that assemble parts of the car bodies.*

◆ *Mainframes are the largest computers commonly used in large companies. Banks use mainframes to keep track of the enormous amount of financial information that they must store.*

◆ *Supercomputers are true "number crunchers," with some being able to do hundreds of billions of arithmetic operations every second.*

Supercomputers   **Supercomputers** are the largest, fastest, and most expensive computer systems available. They can cost up to $20 million and are used primarily for scientific applications requiring complex and lengthy calculations, such as weather forecasting. The demand for and use of supercomputers will probably increase.

Table 5.1 provides a comparative summary of the users of and applications for each of the four categories of computer systems.

TABLE 5.1 ◆ Comparison of Users and Applications for Computer Types

CLASSIFICATION	USERS AND APPLICATIONS
Supercomputer	Government agencies in designing weapons, rockets, and military devices; businesses and universities for commercial and scientific applications.
Mainframe Computer	Large businesses and government agencies, such as banks, airlines, insurance companies for customer and organizational information processing.
Minicomputer	Small businesses or divisions of large companies. Used by engineers, architects, commercial artists for speedy "number-crunching" and graphics.
Microcomputer	Used extensively in businesses, the home, and educational institutions for day-to-day document processing.

Recall Time

Answer the following questions:

1. Define the term *management information system.*

2. What are the four classifications of computers?

3. What are the five primary categories of microcomputers?

Components of a Computer System

When purchasing a computer, the first and most important question to ask is, "What do you want the computer to do for you?" With the answer in mind, it will be easier to decide which processor, keyboard, monitor, and hard disk to buy; how much memory you need; and what type and size disk drives will be the most useful. To understand how to determine computer needs wisely, study the information that follows.

HARDWARE, MEMORY, AND STORAGE

The basic hardware devices for business computer systems include those items you can physically touch, such as a monitor, a keyboard, a printer, and a computer system unit containing memory chips and storage disk drives.

Hardware Devices   The following are considered the *essential* hardware devices for every system.

Monitor   The **monitor** resembles a television screen that displays information. Monitors range in cost from less than one hundred dollars to several hundred dollars depending on their size and features. The more expensive monitors have additional niceties such as color and high resolution, which produce more attractive and clearer images.

The purpose of the monitor is to show you what you are doing as you use the computer. Your choice of monitors will depend on your preferences as well as your budget. You can choose monochrome or color, screen sizes varying from thirteen inches to seventeen inches or larger, and even two-page monitors.

Keyboard   In the office, the primary input device is the basic keyboard. Different keyboard models are available, with keys located in different places and with varying numbers of keys. Most keyboards consist of three distinct sections: the typewriter (or alphanumeric) keypad with function keys at the top, the cursor movement area, and the numeric keypad. As you enter or type data on the keyboard, it is

OFFICE TIP

Computers and their peripherals become just "nice to have" gadgets unless adequate and continued training ensures their maximum use each day.

OFFICE TIP

Turn the monitor off, dim the screen image, or activate a screen saver if you plan to leave the computer. Otherwise, the document will not be confidential from others in the office.

◆ *An extended keyboard*

◆ *A modular keyboard*

◆ *An ergonomic keyboard*

simultaneously displayed on your monitor screen and stored in the computer's main memory. The newest ergonomically designed keyboards slant naturally in a soft V-shape and are becoming popular among both office and at-home workers.

Printer   Printers produce paper output in the form of text and graphics copy. Numerous types of printers are available, with price tags ranging from one hundred dollars to many thousands of dollars. Most office printers today are nonimpact, which means they do not print characters by striking the paper. Some common types of nonimpact office printers are desk-jet, laser, and xerographic ones.

◆ *Hewlett-Packard Company's LaserJet 5MP and 5P printers.*

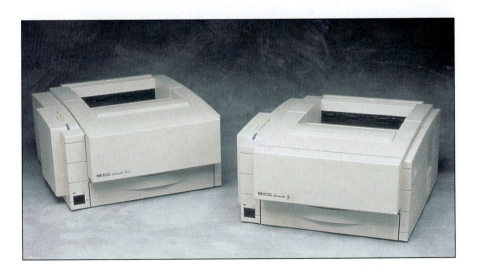

The printer of choice for most offices is the laser printer. Laser printers can usually produce a number of different typefaces, or fonts, of various designs and sizes. Many laser printers can turn out more than 120 pages per minute. Although companies like IBM and Apple manufacture excellent printers, Hewlett Packard continues to dominate both the low and high ends of the laser printer market.

Computer System Unit   The system unit in a typical personal computer usually includes a microprocessor, which is a single silicon chip containing the central processing unit (CPU) and a small amount of special purpose memory. In addition, the system unit contains one or more memory chips mounted on a main circuit board called the motherboard. The microprocessor, with its increasing speed and processing power and continually decreasing prices, has helped revolutionize the way companies do business. Major manufacturers of microprocessors are Intel, IBM, and Motorola.

Memory and Storage   The storage capacity of memory chips has been doubling every three to four years. Two of the most common memory chips used in computers today are the ROM and RAM chips. Hard drives, floppy disks, and optical disks, such as compact disk read-only memory (CD-ROM), are the most common computer storage devices.

Read-Only Memory   **Read-only memory (ROM)** chips are used for the permanent storage of certain instructions, most frequently parts of the computer's operating system software that checks the hardware when you turn on your computer. Instructions stored on ROM chips cannot be written over or altered and are not lost when electric current is disrupted or turned off. Some leading manufacturers of memory chips are Motorola, NEC, Toshiba, and Texas Instruments.

◆ *The Pentium® Chip contains more than 3.1 million electronic components on a single slice of silicon.*

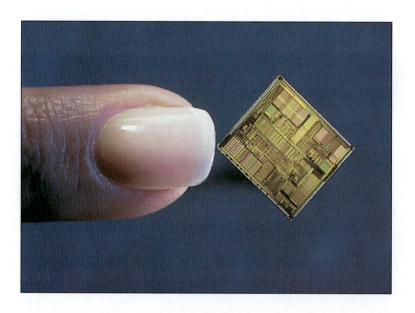

Random-Access Memory **Random-access memory (RAM),** also called main memory or primary storage, resides in the system unit. This high-speed memory area is where your programs and documents are stored while you are working on them. Computer memory is measured in bytes. A byte is the space required to store one character (a letter, digit, or symbol). The minimum recommended amount of RAM on microcomputers is 8 to 16 megabytes (MG), or approximately 8 to 16 million bytes. However, most users working in the Windows environment prefer 32 MG of RAM or more.

RAM is different from ROM in that it is active only when the computer is on. Therefore, RAM depends on the flow of electric current. If the current is turned off or disrupted by a power surge, a brownout, or electrical interference generated by lightning or nearby machines, whatever is stored in the RAM memory will be lost.

For this reason, RAM memory is said to be volatile, or temporary. Fortunately, there is storage that is not volatile—the hard disk and diskette. Computer operators should routinely save their work frequently; that is, they should save the document on the screen from RAM to a diskette or the hard disk.

Hard Disks In contrast to RAM, **hard disks** provide nonvolatile storage. In other words, when the power is off, the software and documents stored on the hard disk remain on the disk. Hard disks are thin, rigid metallic platters coated with a substance that allows data to be recorded in magnetic form.

Some hard disks are a permanent part of a hard disk drive encased within the system unit and cannot be removed. Because hard drives have many moving parts, they are more susceptible to failures than most other parts of a computer system; therefore, it is very important to back up, or make a duplicate copy of, the data stored on a hard disk drive.

A crucial question to ask when you buy an office microcomputer system is, "How large a hard disk do I need?" You should buy as much hard drive storage as you can afford that meets your company's current and projected needs. Just like computer memory, hard disk size is measured in megabytes. Most offices today need 1 gigabyte (GB) to 2 gigabytes or more of hard disk space. A **gigabyte** is a measure of computer storage capacity that equals approximately 1 billion bytes.

Optical Disks Optical disks are an important form of storage media. Created by the same kind of laser technology as the compact disks (CDs) that have revolutionized the music business, these disks have had a similar impact on the computer industry. Optical disks can provide tremendous storage capacities at a relatively low price.

The **compact disk read-only memory (CD-ROM),** the most familiar type of optical disk, is prerecorded. A single CD-ROM can hold up to 660 MB, equal to 330 high-density floppy disks. In other words, a CD-ROM can hold about 300,000 pages of information. Because of their capacity to store large quantities of infrequently updated information, CD-ROMs are suitable for storing reference materials like encyclopedias and catalogs. Their large storage capacity also makes

OFFICE TIP

Disks are sturdy enough to be used and reused many times, but you must treat them with care. Follow the "do's and don'ts" printed on disk boxes and disk envelopes. A disk itself is not valuable, but your time to rekey the contents certainly is! In addition, the lost information may be impossible to reconstruct unless backed up.

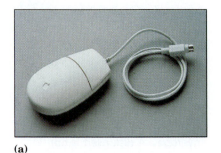

(a)

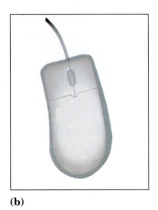

(b)

(c)

◆   *There are many different types of mice. (a) Apple Desktop Bus Mouse II, (b) Microsoft's IntelliMouse, (c) Logitech's MouseMan Sensa*

CD-ROMs a good choice for storing both sound and images, so they are frequently used for multimedia applications.

The technology used to create CD-ROMs is filtering down to the desktop. CD-recordable drives, now available for under $2,000, allow the user to write data onto a specially manufactured disk that can then be read by any standard CD-ROM drive.

PERIPHERALS AND ACCESSORIES

In addition to the major hardware components, computer operators also use peripheral devices.

Hardware Peripherals   **Peripherals** are hardware devices that are not required for operation of the basic unit. Some examples of peripheral computer hardware are the mouse, modem, and scanner.

Mouse   In order to move around in the Windows environment, which is visual rather than text oriented, you will be working with a mouse. The **mouse** is a device used for moving the cursorlike insertion point around the text and for pointing. It has a small ball on its underside that rolls around as you move the mouse across your desk. Basic mouse functions include point, single-click, press, drag, double-click, and shift-click. Computer users find that the mouse is more efficient, easier to learn, and quicker to use than the keyboard.

Modem   A **modem** is used to link a computer to telephone lines, so that communicating with other computers is possible. Today, businesses are depending more on being able to move electronic information efficiently from point A to point B. To do so, businesspeople rely on the computer and the phone; the modem is the link that joins these two tools.

The modem is ideally suited to certain tasks. Through modems, files in computer form can arrive at their destination in minutes, rather

◆ *Courier v. Everything is an external modem by U.S. Robotics.*

than the hours previously required to send a disk by overnight mail. With modems, users can conduct instant online research, gathering information from virtually any publication. Moreover, modems provide answers to computer or business questions from a pool of online experts through networking with other computer users. Major considerations in choosing a modem are:

◆ *Internal vs. external.* Internal modems come in the form of add-in boards that are installed inside your computer; external modems are stand-alone units that plug into a port at the back of the system unit and require a small amount of desk space.
◆ *Speed.* Presently, modem transmission speed is 28,800 bits per second (bps). A faster modem (33,600 bps) may be worth the extra cost if you plan to frequently transmit large files.
◆ *Fax capability.* Increasingly, modems are combining fax capabilities with standard data transmission as more workers travel with portable computers.

Scanner   A **scanner** is an input device that acts like a miniature photocopy machine connected to a computer, copying graphic images into the computer and allowing typewritten pages to be scanned and entered without retyping. A scanner does this by converting the image into a pattern of dots and transmitting the results to the computer, where it is stored as a graphic file on the hard disk. The images then can be viewed, altered, or enhanced through the use of various graphics programs.

Scanners include both handheld and desktop models. One measure of the quality of a scanner is the number of dots per inch (or resolution) it produces when converting the image. The greater the resolution, the better the control will be over the gray levels, colors, contrast, and brightness of the transferred image.

Computer Accessories   Hundreds of computer accessories have been developed to complement desktop systems and eliminate clutter. Several companies offer products designed to help employees organize

◆ *The HP ScanJet 4c scanner offers high resolution, color and grayscale. (Photo courtesy of Hewlett-Packard Company)*

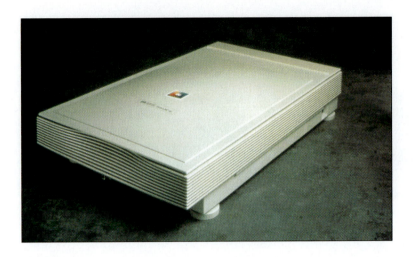

their spaces; for example, under-the-desk storage units and keyboard trays that slide out from under the table or desk.

Recall Time

Answer the following questions:

1. What essential hardware devices should every computer system have?
2. What is a major difference between RAM and ROM storage?
3. List three examples of hardware peripheral devices.

SOFTWARE

Software, also known as a program, is a group of instructions executed by the computer. Business and office software used on microcomputers or PCs is categorized as either system software or application software.

System Software   One of the first software decisions you must make when buying a computer system is to choose the operating environment in which you will work. The three most popular choices for system software are Disk Operating System, Graphic User Interface, and Windows 95. However, office professionals will also find Windows NT, OS/2 Warp, and UNIX operating systems in the business office environment.

Disk Operating System   **Disk Operating System,** or DOS, is the program that manages the resources and operations of the computer. It enables your computer to communicate with an application program such as LOTUS or WordPerfect that uses text-based commands. Software applications designed to work under DOS each have their own interfaces, and learning each one is a different and unique experience for the software user.

Graphic User Interface   **Graphic User Interface (GUI),** on the other hand, does not use text-based commands to instruct the computer; it uses a visual or Windows environment approach. The operator uses icons, or symbolic pictures, to represent programs, files, and common operations. This approach of using graphics, or pictures, and menus makes working with the computer simpler. Similar functions (save, copy, move, edit) in different programs are executed in the same way. The goal of GUIs is to create a system that the novice computer user can turn on and operate right away without any prior training or the need to refer to manuals or remember commands.

GUIs usually feature information windows or dialog boxes that can be layered on top of one another, like file folders on top of a desk. Most windows contain certain elements, including a menu bar along the top of the screen that shows basic command options, scroll bars that move parts of the document into view if the entire document cannot fit within the window, and buttons that will make the window larger or smaller. Typical icons within a window include file folders, alignment buttons, or an artist's color or style palette. Sometimes a dialog box will appear that requests information about the task you are performing or supplies information you might need.

The Windows operating environment is so named because the screen is divided into rectangular areas called *windows*. Each application, or program, runs in its own window. At any one time, there may be only one window or multiple windows on the screen. Regardless of the number of windows open simultaneously, only one window can be "active" or used at a time.

Windows 95   Microsoft's Windows 95 and its several upgrades are quickly growing in popularity. Windows 95 boasts many features, such as an end to the 640K base memory limitation, an improved interface with Mac-like ease of use, true plug-and-play capability when adding new peripherals, enhanced multimedia support for smoother video and more lifelike performance, a brand-new online network built right into the operating system, and more.

Upgrading a PC's operating system is not a minor undertaking, and for most organizations, whether to upgrade to Windows 95 will be one of the most important computer decisions they will make in the next few years. Microsoft recommends a 486 or Pentium-based PC with 16MB of RAM for good performance.

Most new microcomputers include Windows 95 preloaded on the system, and popular application software packages now have Windows 95 versions. This is important, because not all applications created for DOS and GUI will be able to run under Windows 95. Further, even those that do run under Windows 95 may not perform any better than under the old operating system. For now, only those applications created specifically for Windows 95 benefit from its added speed and power.

Table 5.2 on page 111 compares the characteristics of DOS, GUI, and Windows 95 operating systems.

MAKING OFFICE DECISIONS

The office workers at Company X are excited about the possibility that the firm is purchasing Windows 95. From the employees' standpoint, there is no reason not to upgrade all fifty computers to this new operating system, at a cost of less than $100 per computer.

From management's viewpoint, however, phasing in Windows 95 or any other new operating system is not that easy. There is new software to buy, retraining to be done, and so on.

1. *How should a business decide when to make a dramatic upgrade in its computer system?*

2. *What types of issues should be considered?*

Windows NT   Like Windows 95, Windows NT is also a complete operating system designed to take advantage of the speed of 32-bit microprocessors. Windows NT can run most applications programs designed for DOS, Windows GUI, and OS/2 and is designed primarily for businesses, particularly as an operating system for high-performance workstations and network servers. It requires a fast and powerful microprocessor with at least 32 MG of RAM or memory and several gigabytes of hard drive storage.

OS/2   IBM's OS/2 is another operating system designed to work with 32-bit microprocessors. Though it is not as popular as other operating systems, the OS/2 system is used primarily in the business environment, particularly in the financial services industry, because it can continue operating even if an application program crashes.

Unix   Unix is a popular portable operating system developed at AT&T Bell Lab in 1969. Unlike other operating systems, Unix allows application programs to work across the full range of platforms—from microcomputers to supercomputers—and across manufacturers' lines. Unix supports multi-tasking, multi-user processing, and networking and is commonly used on workstations, mainframes, and minicomputers.

Application Software   Application software is productivity software that allows office workers to use a computer to solve a specific problem or perform a certain task. Today, numerous application software packages exist for computers of all sizes—from supercomputers to microcomputers—with the greatest variety available for microcomputers. Offices are the biggest market for application software and the uses for microcomputers are as varied as the businesses that employ them. However, creating documents, such as correspondence and reports, and managing finances are the two tasks for which computers are most commonly used in an office.

The six types of application software most often used to process office data and convert it into usable information are word processing, spreadsheet, database management, graphics, desktop publishing, and integrated software and software suite packages.

TABLE 5.2 ◆ Comparison of Operating Systems for Microcomputers

DOS	GUI (WINDOWS 3.1)	WINDOWS 95
1. The most popular operating system for 16-bit microcomputers.	1. A graphical user interface that is intended to be easier to learn and use than DOS.	1. Introduces a new 32-bit operating system to microcomputer users.
2. A very large selection of application software for business is available.	2. Allows programs to use more than 640K of memory.	2. Applications will have to be upgraded and habits from using GUI will have to be relearned.
3. Limits programs to the use of 640K of memory.	3. Supports multiple programs running at the same time.	3. Includes changes to the Windows interface with more folders, icons, and a task bar to help organization.
	4. The number of application software packages have increased as GUI has gained popularity.	4. Improved memory handling; enables true plug-and-play peripheral installation for multimedia.

Word Processing A word processor makes writing and editing all documents, from a brief memo to a novel, much easier and faster. Using **word processing** software allows you to create, edit, format, print, and save letters, memos, reports, and other text with greater ease and efficiency than using a typewriter.

The real strength of word processors is their ability to edit previously stored material, as well as to format documents and arrange text so it is presented attractively on a page. Printing features can create headers, footers, and page numbers. In addition, most word processing packages contain a spell-check feature, a thesaurus, a grammar-check program, and a mail-merge option, as well as features for drawing, creating tables, and helping the operator use the software.

Selecting a word processing program depends on personal preference and individual budgets. Some popular full-featured word processing programs are Word for Windows by Microsoft, WordPerfect by Corel Systems, and MacWrite by Claris Corporation. As you should do when purchasing most software, always try to obtain the most current version; for example, Word 7 for Windows 95.

OFFICE TIP

Important documents should be proofread two or three times for accuracy. A good technique is to proof a document with a co-worker, especially if large amounts of money are involved.

Rosa Lee Saikley works part-time at Crescent Oil Company and goes to school. Although the company has over fifty employees, she knows most of them and tries to be friendly with them all. Recently, a new employee, Parker, was hired who is co-chairperson of the city's Citizens' Environmental Task Force.

One day, Rosa Lee and four others were in the lunchroom when Parker walked in, voicing rather loudly, the following three complaints:

◆ Crescent Oil Company is wasting too much paper and nobody cares.

◆ The computers are not being used efficiently and most of them are left on all night and all day.

◆ The chemicals used in the company's manufacturing process are being disposed of unlawfully and will eventually adversely affect the city's environment.

1. *Does Parker have a negative attitude or "chip on his shoulder"? Or do you agree that he is expressing valid concerns?*

2. *As Parker's co-worker, what can or should Rosa Lee do to either oppose or support him?*

Spreadsheets   **Spreadsheets** are financial planning programs that perform mathematical calculations and are used by businesses both large and small, as well as nonprofit organizations, scientists, professors, and private individuals in their homes. Spreadsheet programs have the power to record, organize, analyze, and present all sorts of financial and statistical information.

A spreadsheet software program makes it easy to calculate depreciation, prepare financial statements, track and analyze financial results, develop a budget, manage cash flow, and examine alternatives. When businesses need to compute and analyze figures quickly and easily, they use spreadsheet programs like Excel by Microsoft, Lotus 1-2-3 by Lotus Development Corporation, and Quattro Pro by Borland International.

Database Management   **Database management** software computerizes and manages record-keeping and information tasks by helping you store, organize, and retrieve information much more efficiently than using paper file folders in cabinet drawers. In fact, this software is often referred to as an electronic file cabinet. Database management involves using a computer rather than a manual system to store, manipulate, retrieve, and create reports from data and information.

Data managers allow you to enter information once, perform a complex calculation or sorting routine on that information, and then produce, for example, three different reports based on the results. Databases can store almost any type of information and ensure accurate and up-to-the-minute reports on which to base critical decisions.

Two types of application software have been developed to work with data stored in database files: file managers and database management systems. A file manager enables you to retrieve and work with files, but only one file at a time. For smaller organizations, a file manager may be all that is needed. But the inability to work with more than one file simultaneously can be a significant limitation as a business grows.

For example, suppose you want to send a collection letter to customers who are more than thirty days late with their payments. Billing information is collected in an invoice file, while customer data is stored in another file. This is an application that is tailor-made for a database management system (DBMS). DBMS software allows you to construct a database environment for a set of related files and to quickly access and manipulate the information located in several separate files. A DBMS reduces data redundancy and confusion because information can be more easily shared across department and division lines. When information needs to be updated, for example, you need to do so in only one place.

Popular file manager software programs include PC-File by ButtonWare and FileMaker Pro by Claris Corporation. DBMS software programs commonly used today include Access by Microsoft, Paradox by Borland International, and Visual FoxPro by Microsoft.

Graphics **Graphics** software presents data clearly and quickly in visual form on a computer. There are two basic forms of business graphics software: analytical graphics software and presentation graphics software. Analytical graphics software allows you to take data from an existing spreadsheet or database file and create, view, and print charts and graphs.

When more professional-looking charts and graphs are needed—for example, to accompany an oral presentation—presentation graphics software is appropriate to use. This type of program allows you to make charts and graphs, diagrams, and other visual aids from scratch.

Business professionals use graphs to define and analyze problems, summarize and condense information, and spot trends or trouble spots. Further, business reports that summarize ideas graphically are more interesting to read, easier to understand, and more persuasive with customers.

Organizations should buy graphics software according to their needs. Simple charting programs are included as part of many popular spreadsheet and database software programs, such as Excel and Access. If a company plans to use individualized graphics, however, two good presentation graphics and drawing packages are PowerPoint by Microsoft and CorelDraw! by Corel Systems.

Desktop Publishing **Desktop publishing (DTP)** means using a microcomputer to assemble words and illustrations on pages and to print them on a high-quality printer, such as a laser printer. Desktop publishing software allows you to produce professional-looking newsletters, reports, manuals, brochures, advertisements, and other documents that incorporate text with graphics. Desktop publishing helps businesspeople to present ideas powerfully and dramatically.

Using desktop publishing within a company is much less expensive and allows more control than going to an outside printer. With desktop publishing, charts, diagrams, drawings, and even photographs can be easily added to documents to enhance and clarify their messages. Today, the technology for producing desktop published documents is a part of the total integration of information systems in the office.

Large Office / Small Office: What's Your Preference?

COMPUTER SOFTWARE AND EQUIPMENT

Large offices at one time used mainframe computers extensively. Now, however, with the abilities, speed, and memory of microcomputers increasing while the prices are decreasing, many large offices use microcomputers more than ever before. This is partly because office productivity software, such as that for word processing, spreadsheets, and database management, is widespread and many more office workers now know how to do a number of computer applications than ten years ago.

In the next chapter, we will discuss networked systems. This will further explain how so much technology is available to most employees in large offices at a fraction of the cost of the microcomputer systems that are usually found in small offices (which may have only one or two office workers).

If you are interested in a computer-related career, will you apply to a large or small company for employment? Why?

Even though desktop publishing can be done with high-end word processing packages such as Word for Windows or WordPerfect, the most popular complete desktop publishing software packages sold include PageMaker by Adobe, Ventura Publisher by Ventura, and Publish It! by Timeworks.

Integrated Software and Software Suites   **Integrated software** combines several independent software packages—such as word processing, spreadsheet, graphics, and database—for coordinated use in one package. Integrated packages have several advantages compared to individual software applications purchased separately. They generally cost less, require less RAM and disk storage space, and are easier to use because all the different modules within the package share the same interface and command structure. Their main disadvantage is that the modules within an integrated package offer fewer features and less versatility than their stand-alone versions.

More full-featured versions of each type of software are also on the market. These are similar to integrated packages and are called software suites. For example, Microsoft Office 97 is a collection of full-featured products that perform alike and work together as if they were a single program. They are superior to the usual approach at providing ease of use, integration, and custom solutions.

The Microsoft Office 97 Pro package includes Microsoft Word, Microsoft Excel, Microsoft PowerPoint, and Microsoft Access, as well as several other applications. These applications in Microsoft Office 97 have standardized tool bars and consistent menus, commands, and dialog boxes. Users find that once they learn one application, learning

Ethics on the Job

You have just installed the new software package called Microsoft Office 97 Pro on your office computers. You are tempted to "borrow" a copy over the weekend (because nobody would know) and install it on the hard drive of your home computer.

Would you?

TABLE 5.3 ◆ Application Software in the Office

TYPE	POPULAR PACKAGES	OFFICE APPLICATIONS
Word Processing	◆ Word for Windows ◆ WordPerfect ◆ MacWrite	letters, memos, reports, contracts, multipage documents
Spreadsheet	◆ Lotus 1-2-3 ◆ Quattro Pro ◆ Excel	budgets, financial statements, what-if analysis, statistical information
Database Management	◆ dBASE III+ or dBASE IV ◆ FoxPro ◆ Access ◆ R:Base ◆ Paradox	customer listings, personnel listings, inventory items, vendor information
Graphics	◆ PowerPoint ◆ CorelDraw! ◆ Harvard Graphics ◆ Freelance Graphics	graphs, charts, draw and paint projects
Desktop Publishing	◆ PageMaker ◆ Quark X-Press ◆ Ventura Publisher ◆ Publish It!	brochures, advertisements, newsletters, price lists, catalogs
Integrated Software and Software Suites	◆ Microsoft Works *Suites:* ◆ Microsoft Office ◆ Lotus SmartSuite ◆ Corel OfficePro	unlimited applications most of the above

the others is easy. Other popular office software suites are Lotus SmartSuite and Corel Office Pro.

Table 5.3 lists some of the most popular software packages in offices today and how they are used to produce specific office documents.

Recall Time

Answer the following questions:

1. What is one major difference between DOS and GUI?
2. What characteristic do Windows 95, Windows NT, and Unix operating systems have in common?
3. List the six types of application software packages.

Summary

Computers are affecting the way office specialists work. For that reason, developing computer skills and knowledge is imperative in order to be prepared for jobs today and in the future.

Computer systems are classified into four types: supercomputers, mainframes, minicomputers, and microcomputers. Microcomputers are further categorized as workstations or supermicros, desktops, and laptops or portable units.

The basic hardware devices for most business computer systems include a monitor, a keyboard, a printer, and a computer system unit containing memory chips and storage disk drives. In addition to major hardware components, computer users also employ peripheral devices and can purchase various computer accessories to embellish their workstations.

Software, also known as a program, is a group of instructions executed by the computer. Business and office software used on microcomputers or PCs can be categorized as either system software or application software. Examples of system software are DOS, Windows 95, and Windows 3.1. The main function of system software is to manage the operations of the computer and resources.

Application software, on the other hand, is specific to a particular problem or task. Although there are many kinds of application software, the six types used in most offices today include word processing, spreadsheet, database management, graphics, desktop publishing, and integrated software and software suites.

Can you recall the following points mentioned in this chapter?

◆ Management information systems provide an integrated computerized approach to supply managers with the right information at the right time for appropriate decisions.
◆ The computer system should match the needs of the individual and organization; decisions must be made regarding how the system is to be used in order to design the best one.
◆ Two common memory chips used in computers today are the ROM and RAM chips.
◆ Examples of peripheral computer hardware are the mouse, modem, and scanner.
◆ Unlike DOS, the graphic user interface (GUI) does not use text-based commands to instruct the computer; instead, it uses icons and menus selected with a mouse.

IN CONCLUSION . . .

1. What might a computer system in an office look like?

2. What is the difference between system software and application software?

REVIEW AND APPLICATION

✔ CHECK YOUR KNOWLEDGE

1. Distinguish between the four classifications of computers.
2. Name three types of nonimpact printers that are often found in computer systems.
3. What is the major difference between RAM and the hard disk drive?
4. Describe the basic mouse techniques that computer users must master.
5. Describe the function of a modem in a computer system.
6. What types of office documents can scanners process?
7. Why are GUI operating systems preferred to DOS operating systems?
8. In your opinion, which types of application software are most used in today's business offices and why?

📖 REVIEW YOUR VOCABULARY

On a separate paper, match the following by writing the letter of each vocabulary word next to the number of its description.

___ 1. used for multi-user applications, such as numerical control of machine tools and industrial robotics
___ 2. using a microcomputer to assemble words and illustrations on a page
___ 3. equal to approximately 1 billion bytes
___ 4. a device used for moving the cursorlike insertion point around the text and for pointing
___ 5. shows you what you are doing as you use the computer
___ 6. thin, rigid metallic platters that are coated with a substance that allows data to be recorded in magnetic form
___ 7. computerizes and manages record-keeping and information tasks and is sometimes referred to as an electronic file cabinet
___ 8. an integrated system that is usually computer based and provides information critical for decision making
___ 9. financial planning tools that perform mathematical calculations on financial and statistical information
___ 10. used to link a computer to telephone lines
___ 11. allows you to create, edit, format, print, and save office documents like letters and reports
___ 12. also called a personal computer or PC
___ 13. a group of computer devices that are connected, coordinated, and linked together
___ 14. fast and powerful freestanding multi-user units which are larger than the minicomputer
___ 15. the largest, fastest, and most expensive computer systems available
___ 16. prerecorded and can be an optical disk
___ 17. an input device that acts like a miniature photocopy machine connected to a computer

a. compact disk read-only memory
b. computer system
c. database management
d. desktop publishing
e. gigabyte
f. hard disks
g. mainframe computers
h. management information system
i. microcomputers
j. minicomputers
k. modem
l. monitor
m. mouse
n. scanner
o. spreadsheets
p. supercomputers
q. word processing

DISCUSS AND ANALYZE AN OFFICE SITUATION

Conditions in the temporary employment services industry have been changing so quickly that it's been hard for Benson's Personnel Specialists to keep up. President J. Michael Benson recently hired an executive assistant, Beth, who has previous experience working on management information systems (MIS). Beth knows and has commented that with an MIS system in place, Mr. Benson would have information at the right time to make decisions with greater confidence.

Mr. Benson is concerned with the expense of changing the firm's current decentralized computer system, as well as the best way to approach his twenty-five employees about an MIS system; he hopes to install one within the year.

1. Why do you think employees might feel threatened by the placement of an effective management information system in their organization?
2. What, in your opinion, can management do to calm those fears?

PRACTICE BASIC SKILLS

MATH

Think like a computer. Do the processing steps necessary to correctly complete the following problems. Remember that a computer will do first the calculations within parentheses, then any multiplication or division tasks, and finally addition or subtraction tasks. Also, "+" means to add, "−" to subtract, "*" to multiply, and "/" to divide.

a. $37+22-16=$
b. $45-30+15=$
c. $10*4+12=$
d. $40/8+13=$
e. $(2+2+2)*6=$
f. $4+(72/9)=$
g. $(5*8)*2=$
h. $(100-60)*(30-20)/2=$
i. $200*(18/6)+72+33=$
j. $(1+2)*(4/2)+(55-35)/2=$

ENGLISH

Rule: when the day follows the month, do not include the ordinal ending *st, nd, rd,* or *th.* When the day precedes the month or stands alone, use the ordinal ending or write the date in words.
Examples: We plan to get together before June 15. The 8th of January is Jimmy's birthday.
Practice Exercise: For the following, if a sentence is correct, write OK beside its letter on a separate paper. If a sentence is incorrect, rewrite it correctly.
a) My birthday is on the 11 of December.
b) Spring break begins March 12th.
c) You must buy tickets before Monday, July 23.

d) Tommy is scheduled for his health exam on October 20th.
e) Graduation is scheduled for the 6th of June.
f) Gina will be inducted into the National Honor Society on Monday, April 22.
g) November 5 is my nephew's birthday.
h) Ice skating lessons for Charles Patrick are scheduled to begin on November 26th.

PROOFREADING

Rewrite or key in the following letter, correcting misspellings and incorrect punctuation.

February 3, 19—

Ms. Midnight Katzen
12 Ricardo Huch Strasse
Poppenweiler-Ludwigsburg
Germany

Dear Ms. Katzen:

Thank you, for your inquiry concernning the World Wide Web (WWW). I hope the folllowing informatin will be helpfull.

The WWW is a vast, groowing collection of online documents and information formated in Hypertext Markup Language and idstributed overr the Internet. The Web incluuds shoping malls filled with virtual retail outlets, private and public repositories of software, libraries, maggazines, news papers; online meeting spotts, and much more. Created in 1989 in Geneva, Switzerland, a scientist developed the Web to faccilitate the sharing of scientiffic documents and data.

Let me know if I can be of futher help.

Truely yours:

Dennis Clinger

APPLY YOUR KNOWLEDGE

1. Part of being comfortable operating a computer comes from understanding its parts. Visualize a computer and indicate on a separate sheet of

paper whether each of the following components is located on the outside or inside.

a. RAM	e. Diskette
b. Printer	f. Hard disk
c. Monitor	g. Control unit
d. Keyboard	h. Hard copy

2. ***Debate the Issue:***

"We live in a society fraught with information overload. Before long, we will become so paralyzed by all this information, it will be impossible to sort out what we need from what we don't."

Instructions: React to the above statement by quickly jotting down on a piece of paper three or more ideas you have supporting and refuting the statement. Prepare to role-play either point of view in a mock in-class debate.

USING THE
REFERENCE MANUAL

Retrieve the file CH5REF on the data disk. Use the letter styles section of the Reference Manual at the back of the book. Use block style and open punctuation. Save and print.

(Use Current Date)

Inside Address: Mr. Matthew D. Saikley
                    Computer Systems Supreme
                    120 East El Caminito
                    Pacific Grove, CA 93941

I am interested in a portable computer system that I can use while attending college. Since I will be majoring in business administration, I will also need to purchase appropriate business software.

Please send me any brochures or catalogs you have along with pricing information. I plan to make a buying decision within the month.

Sincerely

(Use Your Name as Signee of Letter)

Network Systems and Telecommunications

OBJECTIVES

After completing this chapter, you will be able to do the following:

1. Explain how local area networks are set up.
2. List several benefits to organizations of using local area networks.
3. Describe the role of electronic mail in today's offices.
4. Describe the benefits of using groupware in organizations.
5. Identify five technologies that help workers conduct productive meetings in physically distant locations.
6. Describe the importance of automated workflow in an office that has an effective computer system.
7. Describe the purpose of online information and database services, such as the Internet, CompuServe, America Online, and Prodigy.
8. Describe virtual organizations that use virtual workers.
9. Forecast trends that office workers can expect to develop from cyberspace.

NEW OFFICE TERMS

computer network
computer system
connectivity
electronic mail (e-mail)
groupware
Internet
local area network
network operating system (NOS)

node
server
system
telecommunications
virtual workers
virtual organizations
workflow automation

BEFORE YOU BEGIN . . .

1. Describe a networked system in the office.

2. How do businesses use the Internet?

B usinesses have long sought to improve the ways their employees work together, gain access to information, and operate outside the office. It is not financially practical for an organization to maintain all the resources its employees might like or need. When files, devices, and programs are shared among employees through networking, organizations can benefit from time and cost savings.

Networked Systems in the Office

The trend today toward acquiring technology in the office is to develop networked systems that can be shared rather than to invest in individual PCs, programs, and printers for each worker. There are many types of networked systems. We will discuss local area networks, electronic mail, groupware, and other long-distance communication systems. First, let's define the terms *systems* and *networks*.

SYSTEMS AND COMPUTER NETWORKS

A **system** implies organization and order of a combination of elements or parts. We no longer use just one office machine to complete a task; our tasks are more complex, and various pieces of office equipment can be connected to others to become part of a system that gets things done. For example, some years ago a typewriter was used as the input device, processor, and output device to produce a three-page report. Today, a computer system can complete the activity with professional-quality results in a fraction of the time.

A **computer system,** such as that shown in Figure 6.1, is a group of computer devices that are connected, coordinated, and linked together in such a way that they work as one to complete a task. Through the use of a computer system, the three-page report referred to above would be input with a computer keyboard, processed by editing and other tool features of a word processing software program, and then output to a laser printer.

The future of document processing will not be *paperless* but will consist of new documents and document management that can truly capitalize on networked microcomputers. A **computer network** is made up of several devices (computers, terminals, or other hardware devices) connected together by an electronic communications system.

Even small organizations that network two or three computers together benefit because as files and resources are shared, the costs of

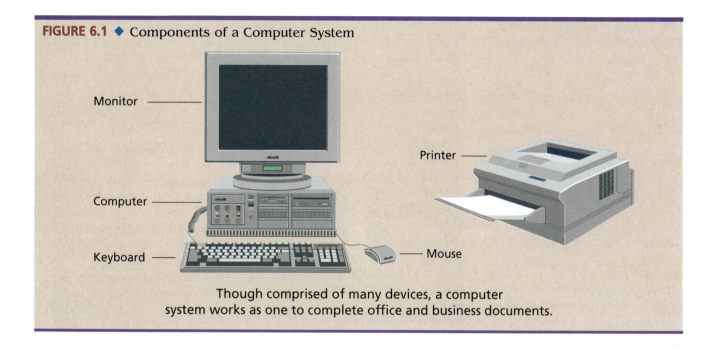

FIGURE 6.1 ◆ Components of a Computer System

Monitor

Printer

Computer

Keyboard

Mouse

Though comprised of many devices, a computer system works as one to complete office and business documents.

operation are reduced significantly. Linked computers may be scattered throughout a city, state, or country, or they may be located within a single office building.

The most current concepts in the computer area are networking, network management, and downsizing. Most employers are downsizing to personal computers (PCs) and then networking those PCs with other PCs instead of using a minicomputer or mainframe computer system.

To be employable, future office workers should have a working knowledge of the PC and of basic networking concepts. Employers need flexible, creative employees who are able to troubleshoot, solve problems, and find innovative ways to complete tasks using networked technology and systems-oriented procedures.

CONNECTIVITY AND GEOGRAPHIC COVERAGE

American business is attempting to provide connectivity resources to give people access to the tools they need to work better. Connectivity can enhance access to data that are important for completing tasks. **Connectivity** gives equal support to members of a workgroup, a client, or a customer, regardless of geographic location. In other words, connecting people and computers is the key to delivering cost-effective services in today's business environment. The concept of connecting with colleagues over a network, wherever they are, is becoming rapidly widespread.

Such new forms of communication and cooperation go by various names, from "virtual networking" and "telecommuting" to "spider-web organizations" and "virtual employees." With the advantages of connectivity and computer networks like e-mail and local area network

Ethics on the Job

You and five other workers in your office have recently had network cards installed in your computers and were given a brief training session on how to access and use the company network system. Since then, one of your co-workers keeps interrupting you with questions on how to obtain and handle information in the companywide customer database. Although you have helped her more than six times in the past three days, she still doesn't understand. You simply don't have time for this, as your own work is becoming backlogged. You find out that she is on a three-month probation because her last job evaluation was not very good.

Do you continue to help her, or tell the supervisor?

◆ *LANs are used by groups of people who need to work with one another, sharing their resources and data.*

(LAN) systems, more businesses favor workstyles that are flexible, less bureaucratic, and receptive to new ideas.

Networks can be categorized based on their geographical coverage and connection lines. A computer network using leased lines from telephone company vendors over a wide geographical distance, for example, is called a wide area network (WAN). A network extending over a few miles or within a city is a metropolitan area network (MAN). LAN systems extend only within a building or group of buildings and use physically wired connection lines. Figure 6.2 illustrates the three geographical types of networks.

LOCAL AREA NETWORKS

Low costs, versatility, ease of use, and the convenience of thousands of options and application programs make LANs a popular choice in large and small companies as well as educational institutions and schools. A **local area network** is a computer and communications network that covers a limited geographical area, allows every node to communicate with every other node, and does not require a central node or processor. A **node** is a workstation, terminal, computer, or other device in a computer network. Growing companies can benefit greatly from LANs; even an office with only two or three PCs can enjoy the advantages of local area networking at a relatively low cost.

Networks work well because of a special control program called a **network operating system (NOS)** that usually resides in a server within a LAN. The NOS is critical to LAN operations because it handles the request for data from all the users or workstations on the network. A **server** is a computer device and part of the LAN that allows for sharing of peripheral devices, such as printers to produce output copies and hard disk units to store files and applications. A server is

OFFICE TIP

The office professional should take advantage of every opportunity to attend additional training sessions, workshops, and seminars in telecommunications, because future job opportunities will depend on knowledge of this kind.

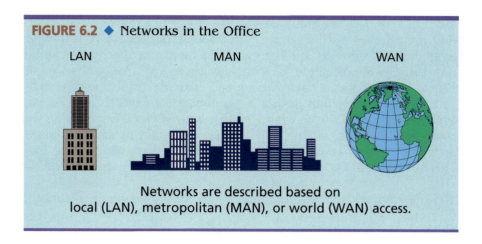

FIGURE 6.2 ◆ Networks in the Office

LAN   MAN   WAN

Networks are described based on
local (LAN), metropolitan (MAN), or world (WAN) access.

usually a microcomputer or minicomputer with the following characteristics: fast CPU speed, large RAM, large disk storage capacity, fast disk-access speed, plenty of expansion slots available, reliable hardware, and an operating system that is compatible with standard drivers such as network, disk, and video drivers. Figure 6.3 shows how LANs work between workstations with access to file servers.

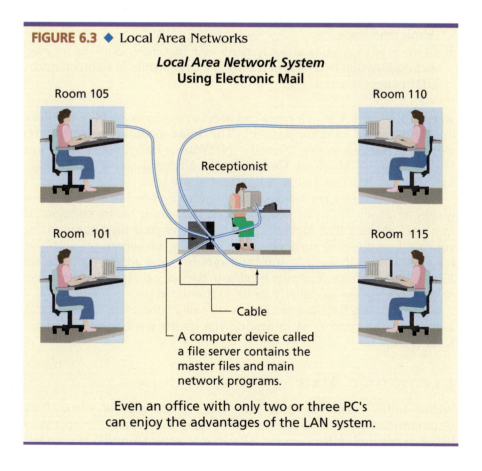

FIGURE 6.3 ◆ Local Area Networks

Local Area Network System
Using Electronic Mail

Room 105   Room 110

Receptionist

Room 101   Room 115

Cable

A computer device called
a file server contains the
master files and main
network programs.

Even an office with only two or three PC's
can enjoy the advantages of the LAN system.

Benefits of LANs Many companies are replacing minicomputers and mainframes with PCs connected to LANs because of the wider availability of software and the speed and memory capacities available now through microcomputer technology. From just about anywhere on Earth, you can use a modem-equipped computer and remote-control software modem to dial in to a computer on your office LAN. As you type (or key in) data from wherever you are, you can do everything you could do if you were sitting at your desk, and you can see it all on the screen in front of you. Organizations use LAN systems because they offer several benefits and make good business sense. Specifically, LANs:

1. Improve work-related communications among people in a workgroup.
2. Make the sharing of information easier, with less wasted time.
3. Provide access to a variety of printers, thereby avoiding the purchase of an expensive printer for each group member.
4. Offer easy, low-cost access to fax facilities.
5. Allow group members to use office resources while at home or on the road.
6. Share selected application software, such as a word processing program, for consistency of presentation and ease of editing, upgrading, and maintenance.
7. Have a common database available to all members of the group.
8. Furnish a method for scheduling meetings, group resources, and employees' time.
9. Connect all varieties of equipment—for instance, allowing for easy communication between normally noncompatible Macintosh and IBM personal computers.

Server-Based LANs Servers can access resources for files, printers, applications, or communications. The most popular central-server software packages are Novell's NetWare, Banyan's Vines, and Microsoft's LAN Manager. Currently, Novell dominates the LAN market, with an estimated 60 to 75 percent share.

How do you use a server-based LAN office system? It is usually necessary to attach or "login" to the central file server before engaging in any LAN activity. The login command employs your user name to find your user profile and authorized privileges in the server, prompts you for a password, if needed, and then sets up your access rights to the file server resources. You may be able to use only certain database files or printers during specific times on particular days.

When you are finished working with the system, you must log out. Log-out is the process of unlinking the user's workstation from the LAN system.

ELECTRONIC MAIL

Within today's organizations, little takes place without team effort. Communication tools such as electronic mail make cooperation between team members easier. **Electronic mail (e-mail)** is a system

OFFICE TIP

Take advantage of every new work situation. Consider each a growth opportunity. If possible, round out your office experiences by volunteering to work in varied environments.

The marketing department has called a special meeting due to complaints from the three sales secretaries. The secretaries' concern is that the staff is not using the e-mail system effectively. They report that only three out of the twelve sales representatives check their e-mail on a regular basis.

The secretaries are to interface by phone or in person with customers if a sales representative is not available, and to send an e-mail message to the representative regarding the customer's concern. In the past week, twenty irate customers have called and complained that their sales representatives never contacted them.

1. *Do you think the secretaries are overreacting?*

2. *What are some areas of concern in using e-mail?*

3. *What steps can an organization take to ensure the proper use of e-mail systems by office and sales staff?*

used to send messages between or among users of a computer network and the programs necessary to support such message transfers. E-mail or similar messaging systems can facilitate communication among co-workers at different locations or on different shifts.

Suppose you are administrative assistant to the human resources manager; she asks you to set up a meeting with seven company employees to discuss an upcoming change in the medical insurance plan. With e-mail, you could send a message scheduling the meeting with all of the employees simultaneously. You could also send a survey form requesting strategic departmental information at the same time. The human resources manager could then receive those completed surveys (employees could e-mail them back) prior to the meeting. E-mail makes it easy to send, receive, save, respond to, delete, or print messages.

Today's electronic mail systems are not simply replacements for intra-office memos. E-mail also provides access to shared fax resources, allows accounting and other software systems to send automatic alerts to appropriate officers, furnishes a means for distributing reports, and allows the transfer of files among co-workers.

You should, however, keep one warning in mind. Although communication networks offer widespread telecommuting and personalized media access, they also threaten individual privacy and increase the potential for information discrimination. Ethics should be an important consideration of users and designers of network systems.

GROUPWARE

Workgroup software, frequently called groupware, is one of the fastest-growing computer applications available today. **Groupware** is a combination of electronic technology and group processes that allows individual computer users to be part of a team and share information. Lotus Notes has quickly become the "gold standard" of groupware.

Groupware keeps all documents online and current, serving as a storage area for an organization's vital information. When employees

Gail, the administrative assistant to the Dean of Instruction, requested connection so she could have access to e-mail and the Internet, she was told to write a memo asking her manager to authorize funds to pay for a line drop to her workstation and the purchase of a computer network card at a cost of approximately $100.

Other employees are resentful that Gail is requesting special treatment. They, too, would like to be connected to the network.

a) How should organizations decide who should be on the network initially and who will be phased in later?

b) What can the organization expect if this situation is allowed to continue? Could this problem have been avoided? If so, how?

PRACTICE BASIC SKILLS

MATH

Help Scotty compute his summer budget as an electronic spreadsheet would. Calculate the totals and savings amounts where the question marks are.

	June	July	August	Total
Revenue				
Park job	200	200	200	?
Allowance	50	50	50	?
Baby-sitting	100	50	100	?
Total revenue	?	?	?	?
Expenses				
Snacks	75	75	75	?
Clothes	100	25	75	?
Movies	30	30	30	?
Vacation	—	150	—	?
Gifts, misc.	50	50	50	?
Total expenses	?	?	?	?
Savings	?	?	?	?

ENGLISH

Rule: Can implies ability; may indicates permission.
Examples: Can you prepare a budget using Excel?
May I help you proof your term paper?
Practice Exercise: Apply the rule to each of the following sentences. If a sentence is correct, write OK by its letter on a separate paper. If a sentence is incorrect, rewrite it correctly.

a. Can I go with you to the computer demonstration?
b. Gina Ann may not be allowed to go to the show because she is grounded for a week.
c. Can you figure the payroll this week?
d. May I put the headings in boldface type?
e. I can run the spelling check using Word software.
f. Can you organize your work in the next five minutes?
g. May we have your name printed legibly on the form?
h. Scanners can be used as an input method.
i. Can I be trained at the same time you are?
j. Can you proofread and edit accurately?

PROOFREADING

Rewrite or key in the following letter, correcting misspellings and incorrect punctuation.

Ms. Sherol Hines
20543 E. Sunshine Way
Sun City, AZ 85000

Dear Ms. Hines-

Youve asked me what the Internet is and I am happy to to reply. The Internet is too words: information and communication. The Internet is nothing more then a countless number of files stored on comptuers around the world and an agreed methud on how to share them. Every Internet program, from the primative (e-mail) to the addvanced (World Wide Web) began with a few people devicing a protocol for sharing computer files over existing communications net works.

Now on the Web, we can download files (pages) with grafics and bvackgrounds and links to other pages. Let me know if you need more informatoin.

Cordilly yours,

Marion E. Jones
Computers in Cyberspace

APPLY YOUR KNOWLEDGE

1. Brainstorm five examples of e-mail communications that an office worker could send to others in the course of doing his or her job.

2. *Debate the Issue*

"The computer and easy access to the Internet is becoming an intruder in many homes because it negatively affects the quantity and quality of family communication, in much the same way that television has."

Instructions: React to the above statement by quickly jotting down three or more ideas you have supporting *and* refuting the statement on a separate paper. Prepare to role-play either point of view in a mock in-class debate.

USING THE REFERENCE MANUAL

Retrieve the file CH6REF on the data disk. Use the punctuation section of the Reference Manual at the back of the book to help you correct the sentences. Save and print.

1. The software had a 'bug' in it.
2. The manager said, "All overtime is cancelled as of this Friday".
3. The child asked, "When will Santa come back"?
4. I will give you ten dollars, $10, if you will teach me the basics of racquetball.
5. "Where will the next workshop on Word Perfect be conducted" asked Angela Johnson.
6. The top scholastic student in senior class—Arlo Riddle—did not get the Kiwanis scholarship.
7. Chapter sixteen was called, "Anne and Her Disappointment".
8. The most difficult-to-use software, and the most fun, was being used by all students.
9. "Are there ideas you have for the newsletter" Habib asked?
10. "Which parcel was lost?" Charelle asked?

Computer and Equipment Issues

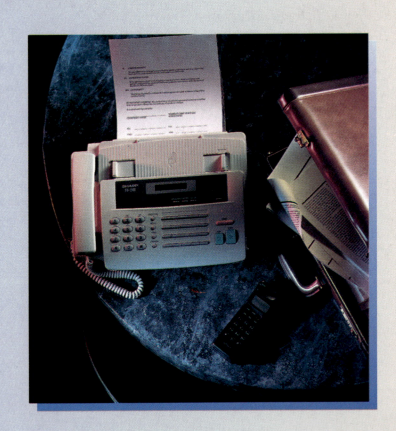

OBJECTIVES

After completing this chapter, you will be able to do the following:

1. List the qualifications computer users need.
2. Cite examples of computer monitoring.
3. Define computer hacking and piracy relative to ethics.
4. Discuss ways to prevent computer injuries.
5. Describe the relationship between computers and the wise use of energy.
6. Distinguish between centralized and decentralized copying systems.
7. Describe how automated office equipment such as facsimiles, shredders, typewriters, and dictation machines are used in today's businesses.

NEW OFFICE TERMS

computer monitoring
document imaging
facsimile (fax)

just-in-time hiring
shredders

BEFORE YOU BEGIN . . .

1. How much energy do computers use?

2. What causes computer-related injuries?

Computer-Related Employment Issues

Before ending our discussion of computers, we should acknowledge some concerns. Office professionals should have certain qualifications to be competent computer users, be aware that their work performance may be monitored by a computer, and should practice ethical behavior when using a computer.

QUALIFICATIONS FOR COMPUTER USERS

As permanent jobs become more and more temporary (through downsizing and layoffs), temporary jobs are becoming more and more permanent. Just-in-time hiring is becoming routine for many companies and qualified computer operators are in high demand. Recent recessions have helped to create **just-in-time hiring** (employing temporary workers to complete only a specific project) because there is a large pool of experienced, unemployed people who can go to work on a temporary basis on short notice without a training period. The growing use of this hiring practice will provide improved future employment opportunities for workers who have many different abilities, including computer skills.

The rate at which job functions are computerized continues to accelerate, and employees and businesses must learn to adapt quickly. That is the conclusion expressed in *Managing Today's Automated Workplace*, a 1995 report published by the Olsten Corporation which surveyed more than 1,400 executives. These are some of the other findings:

◆ Many companies have personnel who are inadequately qualified to use advanced technology profitably.

◆ Higher productivity, better communication, quality improvement, and lower administrative costs were some of the benefits of increased reliance on automated computer systems.

◆ Seventy percent of companies surveyed reported that computer users need basic keyboarding skills, such as data entry and word processing.

◆ Word processing and spreadsheet programs are the most widely used software applications in offices today.

◆ Computerized databases and records-management systems are also popular in offices.

OFFICE TIP

Ask questions of others when you receive a new office assignment. Try to determine if a similar assignment has been completed before. If so, you might save time and effort by using an already good plan or idea and adding your own creativity. Remember, work smarter, not harder.

Ethics on the Job

In your opinion, is the increased use of temporary workers by business morally right? In forming your opinion, consider that the temporary worker often works for a lower hourly wage, generally has no benefits package, and has no job security.

◆ Other capabilities in demand include desktop publishing, graphic design, and the management of network communication.

COMPUTER MONITORING

The idea of **computer monitoring** sounds threatening to most office workers, but in the future computer monitoring may be beneficial to them. For example, a computer that counts keystrokes and identifies errors might not reprimand the employee and tattle to the boss, but instead suggest that the computer user take a short breather. Other monitors could act as prompters, reminding the office worker of special details when talking with customers, or as coaches, giving tips on improving performance.

Advanced computer systems will be able to make suggestions based on information entered by the employee. Based on this added information, the computer will be able to help employees do their jobs more effectively. Overall, the use of prompts will be positive, for employees will not have to worry as much about remembering countless details.

Monitoring can be done humanely if employees are guaranteed several rights—including access to all information gathered through monitoring. Furthermore, organizations are recognizing that giving employees personal access to this information motivates them. Why? Information given to the supervisor often becomes a weapon; but when it goes directly to the worker, it can improve performance. By the end of the decade, as many as 30 million people may be constantly monitored on the job.

ETHICAL USE OF COMPUTERS

There are several ethical issues surrounding the use of information technology. Ethical choices are more complex and difficult when laws do not exist or when their applications to new situations are unclear. Today's office workers are faced with such complications; rapid technological development has left many "gray areas" not yet defined by law.

Specific ethical concerns regarding office computer use include the security and privacy of data, employee loyalty, and the copying of computer software.

1. *Hacking* is a term used to describe the activity of computer enthusiasts who enjoy the challenge of breaking computer security measures. Hacking is a crime, and gaining unauthorized access to another's computer files can be as serious as breaking into someone's home.
2. Because the field of information processing is a dynamic environment with a shortage of qualified workers, there are many job opportunities. Although court rulings differ, it should be noted that most employers expect some degree of duty or loyalty on the part of the employee. In other words, changing jobs should be done in an ethical fashion. Software packages and company secrets should not be carried to your new job.

OFFICE TIP

When you start a project, try to visualize what you want the final product to look like. Or, try to imagine how good you will feel when you've finished the project and you know it looks good. Often, the hardest part of getting a job done is just beginning it and convincing yourself that it is worth doing.

MAKING OFFICE DECISIONS

Cody Keene, a customer relations specialist at a large hotel in Scottsdale, is extremely upset. For the past month, the hotel has been monitoring his activities and performance using a computer. He has just finished reading his computer-generated performance evaluation and disagrees with just about everything in the report.

For example, he feels he was "written up" because when he spoke with five customers about making reservations, the computer showed he forgot to mention promotion packages that could have improved the chances of getting the customers' business. When Cody contacts the administrative office manager about the report, she says that he misunderstands the purpose of computer monitoring. Its purpose is to help employees do their jobs better. In fact, she tells him that, starting next month, prompts will appear on the computer screen to remind employees of promotional offers, along with the details of each.

1. *Do you feel that the information given Cody will reassure him that computer monitoring is intended to be helpful?*

2. *What might be some reasons Cody distrusts this new approach that is intended to "help" him?*

3. Software copying, or *piracy,* is the unauthorized copying of a computer program that has been written by someone else. Whether done for personal use or to sell for profit, software piracy is a crime. Most software manufacturers give purchasers authorization to legally make one copy of a program; anything more is a violation of copyright law.

Health Factors and Energy Issues Related to Computer Use

Computers, by their very nature, make it prudent for users to exercise caution and have a general awareness of their effects. Practicing good techniques can prevent computer injuries as well as minimize energy usage associated with office and home computing.

PREVENTING COMPUTER INJURIES

The increased use of personal computers for word processing, data entry, personal organizers, and other business tasks has focused attention on workplace ailments that can reduce employee productivity and increase a company's costs for workers' compensation. Two common maladies resulting from computer use are eyestrain and repetitive stress injury, both of which can be controlled in several ways.

Eyestrain   The most common computer-related health problem is eyestrain, estimated at 10 million cases a year by vision expert James Sheedy of the VDT Eye Clinic in Berkeley. What causes eyestrain?

VDTs (video display terminals) do not emit rays that are harmful to the eyes; however, staring at small letters and numerals on a screen for hours on end can create visual fatigue. Eyestrain can also be caused by the glare of an overbright or badly placed light that reflects off a VDT screen.

A regular eye examination is important for any computer operator. A number of eye specialists recommend following the 20-20 rule: keep your face at least twenty inches from the screen, and pause every twenty minutes to look around the room. Exercising your eyes can also help reduce eyestrain.

Repetitive Stress Injuries Pain in the neck, back, shoulders, arms, wrists, and legs can be minimized by movement. Move away from the computer workstation or desk periodically and take regular full-body stretches. Workers often forget how long they have been sitting in one position. As a result, some muscles may tighten and connective tissue may strain.

Shifting the body or changing its relation to the screen and keyboard helps. Repetitive strain injuries, such as carpal tunnel syndrome and tendinitis, are caused by poor keyboarding position, such as elevated elbows or bent wrists, and by excessive pounding of the keyboard.

Preventing Injuries In his 1994 book entitled *ZAP! How Your Computer Can Hurt You—and What You Can Do About It,* Don Sellers offers these suggestions for avoiding computer-related injuries.

◆ *Carpal tunnel syndrome occurs when the lining of the tendons passing through the carpal tunnel in the wrist swells, putting pressure on the median nerve and causing pain, tingling, and numbness in the hand.*

1. Correct ergonomic problems promptly. The longer stresses continue, the more difficult the damage is to repair.
2. Minimize the strain. If possible, intersperse computer work with other tasks. Type with less force.
3. Move. Every fifty minutes or so, get up. Walk down the hall. Move your hands, wrists, and arms. Bend and stretch. Rotate your shoulders. Turn your head.
4. Rest your eyes periodically. Take a fifteen-minute rest break every two hours for moderately demanding computer work. During the break, make phone calls, file, or do pencil-and-paper planning.
5. Invest in special glasses designed for computer use. Make the design correct for the distance and angle at which you view the monitor.
6. Balance the lighting. When you look at your computer screen, there should be no "hot spots" of bright light behind or around it.
7. Position your monitor eighteen to twenty-four inches from your eyes. Adjust the angle to eliminate reflections, and clean the screen regularly.
8. Sit in a chair that fits you. Have a co-worker check your posture when you are sitting at your computer.
9. Adjust the surface on which the keyboard sits so that your wrists are not forced into unnatural positions (bent up or down).
10. Work defensively. Sit directly in front of your keyboard.

COMPUTERS AND ENERGY USE

Computers are increasing the use of electricity more than any other new business development. In the last ten years, computer-related energy consumption has increased fivefold. Computer use now accounts for 5 percent of all commercial electrical consumption. The U.S. Environmental Protection Agency (EPA) warns that this figure could jump to ten percent by the year 2000 if nothing is done to reverse this trend.

TABLE 7.1 ◆ Strategies for Energy-Efficient Computing

1. **Turn off your computer and/or peripherals when they are not in use.** A moderate amount of turning computer equipment on and off will not harm it.

2. **Do not run computers continuously (unless they are in constant use).**

3. **Look for ways to reduce the amount of time your computer is on without adversely affecting your productivity.**

4. **Break the habit of turning on all your computer equipment as soon as you enter the office each day.** Turn on each piece of equipment only when you are ready to start using it.

5. **Group your computer activities informally and try to do them during one or two parts of the day, leaving the computer off at other times.**

6. **Do not turn on your printer until you are ready to print.** This especially applies to laser printers, since they consume a lot of electricity even while idling.

7. **If for some reason you must leave your computer on while you are not working on it, turn off your monitor to reduce energy consumption.**

8. **Turn off your entire computer system (CPU, monitor, and printer) when you go to lunch or will be out of the office for a meeting or errand.** Rebooting when you resume computer work usually just takes a minute.

9. **Do not use the "power strip" master switch (which turns on simultaneously all equipment plugged into it) if you do not need all of your equipment all the time you are working on your computer.**

10. **Be an energy educator and tactfully remind your co-workers and colleagues to save energy by changing their computer habits.**

Adapted from "Green Computing" by Walter Simpson, *The Secretary,* April 1995, 20–21.

Each year, more computers are purchased and put to use. It is not just the number of computers, however, that drives energy consumption upward. The way we use computers also adds to the increasing energy burden. Research reveals that most desktop personal computers are not being used most of the time they are running. In addition, 30 to 40 percent of personal computers in the United States are left on continuously.

When buying computer equipment, make decisions with energy conservation in mind. Consider these suggestions:

1. Buy only as large a monitor as you really need. A seventeen-inch monitor uses 40 percent more energy than a fourteen-inch one when in active mode.
2. Buy only as much resolution as you need. Higher-resolution monitors use more energy.
3. Choose an ink jet printer. These printers are slower than laser printers but use 80 to 90 percent less energy.
4. Purchase retrofit power-management devices. These devices power-down computer equipment when they are not actively in use.
5. Request that packaging materials used by your computer vendor are recycled, recyclable, or biodegradable.

The fundamental technique for saving energy by any type of equipment is to turn it off whenever possible, as stated in the first entry of Table 7.1, which lists ten strategies for energy-efficient computer use.

Recall Time

Answer the following questions:

1. Name one advantage and one disadvantage of computer monitoring.
2. List two ways office workers can prevent computer-related injuries.
3. Describe three ways computers use energy.

Other Automated Office Equipment

Because so much is said about computers today, it is easy to forget that other automated systems are just as vital in helping an office run smoothly. You can expect to use equipment other than computers to process office information. On the job, you might use a copier to duplicate information onto paper copies, a fax to send a letter to a customer, a paper shredder to safeguard personnel and financial records, an elec-

◆ *In a busy office with a centralized copy center, one or two employees can do most of the copying for everybody.*

OFFICE TIP

Photocopy only what you will use. Office workers often make "just a few extra copies" to be sure to have enough. Most of the time, these extra copies are not used. Suppose that 150 people make three or four extra copies each during a week. By the end of the week, a whole ream of paper (500 sheets) may have been wasted.

Ethics on the Job

How do you feel about workers who take home small amounts (fifty sheets, for example) of copier paper for their personal use, or copy personal documents without permission on the company copier?

tronic typewriter to fill in preprinted forms, and a dictation unit to speak your thoughts when creating business letters and reports.

REPROGRAPHIC (COPIER) SYSTEMS

Offices can set up copier systems either by having a centralized copy center where copier specialists do all the work, or by having several decentralized copiers that employees can use on demand.

Centralized Copying   Centralized copy centers can save organizations money by limiting the number of individual copiers needed and by reducing per-copy costs, although up-front costs may be higher due to the price of machines designed to handle high-volume photocopying. Advantages of this system include increased security via access codes and the opportunity to review printing statistics for a specific department or organization. Convenience, storage and work space requirements, and location are issues to consider when installing a centralized copy center.

Decentralized Copying   In a decentralized reprographics environment, copiers are strategically and conveniently located throughout a company's offices. With copies becoming less expensive and equipment more sophisticated, many businesses are purchasing additional individual copiers, allowing employees to make copies whenever they need them, without having to walk a long way to reach the machines.

This kind of "on demand" system works well in small offices where the volume of copies does not justify a centralized system. The biggest advantage of the decentralized approach is convenience, while the major disadvantage is lack of control.

Whether a copier system is centralized or decentralized, the use of copier controls is growing as companies strive to keep costs down and reduce waste. It is estimated that over 600 billion copies are made annually and 25 percent of these copies are unnecessary. By using copier controls, a company can determine if any machines are being used too little or too much.

Several methods of copier control have been developed to help eliminate copier abuse and misuse. One technique is to assign a number to each user so that every time he or she uses the copier this preassigned number is entered and serves to track usage. Another way is to issue each employee a magnetic stripe card that authorizes use and activates the copier.

A new monitoring technique uses telecommunications technology to collect information about all copier activity. A phone line, PC, modem, and software now permit a central computer terminal to generate reports of all copier activity within a company, and costs per copy can be attributed to specific users or departments.

Which features should you buy on an office copier? It depends on the needs of your particular organization. Table 7.2 describes popular copier features.

TABLE 7.2 ◆ Features of Copier Systems

FEATURE	EXAMPLES OF FUNCTIONS
Copy Size	Can accommodate from 5½" × 8½" to 11" × 17"
Originals	Can be sheets, books, 3-D objects
Speed	Can run from 28–80+ copies per minute
Collating & Stapling	Can assemble copies in order and staple top left corner of set, if desired
Duplexing	Can make two-sided copies
Reducing & Magnifying	Can make image smaller or larger
Other Features:	front-loading paper drawers, image shift, book copy, automatic paper selection, automatic magnification selection, auto tray switching, large-capacity cassette tray, dual original copying, 20+ bin sorter, color units, energy save, help screens, usage counters, multiple copy countdown system

What does the future hold for reprographic systems? The role of photocopiers is becoming increasingly important with the use of digital technology for document imaging. **Document imaging** is performed with a personal computer that is linked to a copier, scanner, or fax machine. With this setup, the user can scan or create a document and send it to a copier to be duplicated. Additional advances in copier technology include improved copy quality, reliability, and affordability. Many businesses have been hesitant to pay for expensive color copiers, but as new software programs and color printers become available, demand for them will increase and prices will come down.

FACSIMILES

The fax revolution is underway in offices around the world. A **facsimile (fax)** is a machine that translates copies of text or graphics documents into electronic signals, which are then transmitted over telephone lines or by satellite.

Uses of the Fax   Facsimile machines are permanently changing the way office workers place orders and corporate headquarters acquire data from field offices, altering the very nature of business. Today an office without a fax machine is as rare as one without a computer.

The fax is gradually replacing the U.S. Postal Service and overnight express mail services for delivery of business communications. With the convenience of a phone call, fax machines speed up business interactions in a relatively inexpensive way. As previously discussed, an

◆ *Dial carefully when sending a fax, especially if you must send confidential material.*

emerging trend is to install modem/fax cards inside the computer and use fax software to send and receive paper messages.

Low-end fax units still use slippery thermal paper, but you can now purchase feature-packed models that offer ink jet or laser printers. The high-end machines can receive faxes at 300 dots per inch (DPI) and can store messages in memory if they run out of paper.

Concerns Regarding the Fax   The widespread use of fax machines is causing some concern about proliferation and security issues.

Proliferation   As businesses and institutions rely more on faxes, questions about product speed and quality, training and usage, and cost containment take on a new urgency. Fax machines provide speed and convenience, however, most offices currently lack the organization or discipline to control this powerful technology by establishing clear, simple guidelines for its use. For example, these guidelines might clarify who is authorized to fax documents, what types of documents are too confidential to fax, and when fax transmission should occur to lower cost.

Security   Security is becoming an increasingly worrisome problem. The sheer number of fax machines in use increases the chances of sending confidential information to a wrong number. As more fax machines are connected to networks, unauthorized tapping becomes more possible. Cellular phones are particularly vulnerable to eavesdropping, making mobile faxing especially risky as well.

SHREDDERS

Office paper **shredders** provide document security and, at the same time, help the environment. Many companies use shredders to destroy

OFFICE TIP

Using all the electronic wonders on the market today—from special telephones to laptop computers to fax machines—can indeed free your time. An overindulgence or overdependence on machines, however, can waste more of your time than those machines can save.

sensitive material to ensure that it stays confidential. Shredded paper is easier than unshredded to recycle and more biodegradable when placed in a landfill.

Paper shredders, the sales of which are increasing each year, vary greatly in productivity and price. Some models fit over wastebins; however, larger machines placed in central locations are generally more powerful and can handle more paper. When buying a paper shredder, you should consider the materials you will be destroying and overall capacity in terms of your current and future needs. Paper shredders range in cost from $50 desktop models to heavy-duty ones priced at over $100,000.

Some companies are paying for paper shredders, which used to be considered a luxury, by selling the shreds to recycling centers and to animal breeders, who use them for bedding. Also, innovative office workers now reuse paper shreds as packing material for fragile items.

PRINTER-BASED DEVICES

Printer-based devices can be called multipurpose machines. They can print, fax, copy, and sometimes scan. Many models introduced recently are priced at under $1,000, making them affordable. Can this device be the "everything machine" for every office? Perhaps, depending on individual needs, but the trend is toward these all-in-one machines, especially for the smaller office.

TYPEWRITERS AND DICTATION MACHINES

The increased use of computers among office workers has had a great impact on the use of typewriters and dictation machines. Employees

◆ *Many offices use paper shredders to maintain the confidentiality of the information contained on discarded papers.*

◆ *The H-P OfficeJet 1150C Color printer-copier-scanner delivers color inkjet printing, color copying and color scanning demanded by small businesses, full-time home-office professionals and corporate telecommuters. (Photo courtesy of Hewlett-Packard Company.)*

in modern offices seldom use either of these pieces of equipment that were so prevalent a decade ago; nevertheless, they are still found in many offices and used by some workers.

Typewriters   Electronic typewriters are often more convenient than personal computers for tasks such as printing mailing labels and index cards, addressing envelopes, and filling in multipart forms. Typewriters range in price from $150 for a basic machine to $6,000 for a high-end model with video display and internal memory. When selecting a typewriter, you should determine how you will use it and investigate the cost of supplies.

Dictation Machines   A dictation machine is a device used to quickly capture thoughts on magnetic voice media. The use of dictation machines, however, has decreased in recent years. This decrease can be directly attributed to the advent of portable computers and a lack of trained transcriptionists.

Recall Time

Answer the following questions:

1. What does "on demand" copying mean?
2. What are two advantages of using the facsimile machine?
3. Why do companies shred documents?

Summary

Several employment issues related to computers affect how office workers will perform on the job. Office professionals must be qualified computer users, practice good ethics when using the computer, and be aware that in an office setting, their work or even the messages they send using e-mail may be monitored by a computer.

An office worker should also exercise caution when using computers to prevent injuries, and know how to minimize energy usage in the office.

Other types of automated office equipment help businesses run smoothly. These include copier systems, facsimiles, shredders, printer-based devices, typewriters, and dictation machines.

Recall the following specific points from this chapter:

◆ Ethical considerations that influence office computer use include the security and privacy of data, employee loyalty, and the copying of computer software.
◆ Some common ailments resulting from computer use are eyestrain and repetitive stress injuries.

◆ Make computer-purchasing decisions with energy conservation in mind and remember to turn the computer off when not in use.

◆ In the office, you might use a copier to make paper copies, a fax to send a letter to a customer, and a paper shredder to safeguard personnel and financial records. In addition, you may have an electronic typewriter and a dictation machine.

◆ Office copier systems can be either centralized centers or decentralized "on demand" copiers located throughout the company's area.

◆ Fax users should be aware of some concerns, such as proliferation and security issues.

◆ Printer-based devices are multipurpose machines that print, fax, copy, and sometimes scan documents.

IN CONCLUSION . . .

1. How much energy do computers use?

2. What causes computer-related injuries?

REVIEW AND APPLICATION

 CHECK YOUR KNOWLEDGE

1. How does just-in-time hiring relate to the qualifications of future office workers?
2. If a person does not want to be monitored by a computer, do you think he or she should have a choice in the matter?
3. Why is computer hacking and piracy an ethical issue in business?
4. If you know people who suffer from carpal tunnel syndrome or tendinitis, describe their symptoms.
5. List five ways to conserve energy when using or purchasing an office computer.
6. What is the major advantage and disadvantage of the decentralized copier approach?
7. What is the purpose of the facsimile machine?
8. Do you believe the typewriter and dictation machine will totally disappear from the business office in the twenty-first century? Why or why not?

 REVIEW YOUR VOCABULARY

On a separate paper, match the following by writing the letter of each vocabulary word next to the number of its description.

_____ 1. provide document security and, at the same time, help the environment
_____ 2. is performed with a personal computer that is linked to a copier, scanner, or fax machine
_____ 3. is possible because there is a large pool of experienced, unemployed people who can go to work on a temporary basis on short notice without a training period
_____ 4. is the use of computers to help employees do their jobs more effectively
_____ 5. is a machine that translates copies of text or graphics documents into electronic signals, which are then transmitted over telephone lines or by satellite

a. computer monitoring
b. document imaging
c. facsimile (fax)
d. just-in-time hiring
e. shredders

DISCUSS AND ANALYZE AN OFFICE SITUATION

Tracy Koch has just been hired as a computer operator in an established real estate office in town. She wants to do her best and learn as much as she can on the job. Tracy hopes someday to get her real estate license and sell residential properties herself. She views the job as a way to learn the business from the ground up.

Almost immediately, Tracy senses something is wrong when she asks the other three office workers questions to clarify her assignments and the office procedures. Two of them, Roxanne and Randy, seem to withhold important information from her intentionally. It appears to Tracy that they are telling her only the minimum that is needed. The third person, Denise, is more helpful. Tracy finds herself feeling closer to Denise and using her as a role model.

1. Why do some office workers have the attitude that they must keep, rather than share, certain knowledge and special procedures?
2. Roxanne and Randy's behavior can lead to human relations problems. What are some other outcomes when employees have negative attitudes?

 PRACTICE BASIC SKILLS

MATH

Calculate the percentages and totals where the question marks are in the table below to determine monthly costs and usage.

Copying Item	Cost/Month	% of Monthly Total
Toner	$ 250	?
Paper	350	?

Operator time	1,000	?
Copier rental	400	?
Total	$?	100%

ENGLISH

Rule: Whenever possible, avoid dividing a word at the end of a line. When word division is unavoidable, divide at a point that will least disrupt the reader's understanding of the word. Divide words only between syllables. If unsure, consult a dictionary.

Examples: automation   au-to-ma-tion

information   in-for-ma-tion

Practice Exercise: Apply the rule to each of the following words. Set up a separate paper with the alpha letters for the words. If a word is divided correctly, write OK next to its letter. If it is divided incorrectly, rewrite it correctly.

a. facs-im-ile
b. pho-tocopy
c. busi-ness
d. cal-cu-la-tor
e. off-ice
f. tele-phone
g. in-te-gra-ted
h. gra-phics

PROOFREADING

Rewrite or key in the following fax transmission, correcting misspellings and incorrect punctuation.

Apprill 27, 19—

TO: Robin Scott, RAS & Co.
FAX #   (520) 555-2211

FROM: Raymond at the Youth Hockey Office
(520) 555-1122

Thank you for agreing to do the 20 trophies we wil need for the end-of-season ice hockey recognition banquett. Attacched is a list with the inforrmation you will need to engrav the trofies. Let me know if you need further information and if there is any problm in picking them up by May 15.

APPLY YOUR KNOWLEDGE

1. Which office system would you use to process each of the following office tasks? On a separate paper, next to the letter of each description, write the letters EM if it is electronic mail, FAX if facsimile, or RPG if reprographics.

____ a. pie chart sent from Los Angeles to Chicago
____ b. notice of sales meeting sent to ten sales representatives in the building
____ c. order for ten office chairs sent to a vendor 100 miles away
____ d. memo about business ethics sent through a LAN
____ e. request for six copies of fifty pages to be collated and stapled
____ f. request for six overhead transparencies of a sales presentation

2. *Debate the Issue*

"We live in a society fraught with information overload. Before long, we will become so paralyzed by all this information, it will be impossible to sort out what we need from what we don't need."

Instructions: React to the above statement by quickly jotting down three or more ideas you have supporting *and* refuting the statement. Prepare to role-play either point of view in a mock in-class debate.

USING THE REFERENCE MANUAL

Retrieve the file CH7REF on the data disk. Use the grammar section of the Reference Manual at the back of the book to help you correct the sentences. Save and print.

1. Class begins at eight fifteen in the morning.
2. Is the glass ½ full or ½ empty?
3. There are 3 checks left in the checkbook.
4. The parade through downtown was over in 45 minutes.
5. The secretary of the Outdoor Club lived at 1151 9th Street.
6. Do you want 2 or 3 5" by 8" cards?
7. 44 new students joined the All-City Chorus.
8. Twilight has grown eleven inches in the past two years.
9. Cats are said to have 9 lives.
10. The speed limit sign said fifteen miles per hour.

PART TWO: TECHNICAL SKILLS AND KNOWLEDGE

Specific Activities to Complete

Select at least two of the following items for inclusion in your Career Portfolio using the information from Chapters 5, 6, and 7.

1. *Keyboard descriptions of the types of software packages you might use in your selected office work environment. Beneath each description, briefly list the abilities of each software package. Save and print this list. (Be sure you proof according to the instructions given previously on page 92.) Insert this document as the first item in your Career Portfolio binder behind the second tab, entitled "Technical Skills and Knowledge."*

2. *Keyboard descriptions of five situations in which you as an office professional will use networked systems. Save, print, and insert these descriptions behind the second tab as well.*

3. *List and describe four or five Web site home pages you might use as an office professional to locate up-to-the-minute information needed to perform your job. Save, print, and insert this list behind the second tab.*

4. *Describe at least three ethical practices office workers should demonstrate when using computers and other office equipment. Save, print, and insert these descriptions behind the second tab.*

PART
III

Office Support Skills

Telephone Procedures

OBJECTIVES

After completing this chapter, you will be able to do the following:

1. List and explain the important qualities of a good telephone voice.
2. List and explain the steps necessary to answer, place on hold, and transfer a business telephone call.
3. List and explain the steps used to screen calls in a business office.
4. List what is needed to record telephone messages for another person.
5. List and explain the types of outgoing telephone calls made in a business office.
6. List and explain the special features of telephone equipment used in a business office.

NEW OFFICE TERMS

call screening   time zone
conference call   WATS

BEFORE YOU BEGIN . . .

Answer the following questions to the best of your ability:

1. How important is the telephone in the business world?

2. What are the differences between using the telephone at home and in a business office?

Did you know that at this very minute, millions of office workers are using the telephone? Did you know that the telephone is used in approximately 95 percent of all business transactions? It is estimated that more than 100 million business calls are made each day. A customer calls to get information or to place an order. A customer service representative uses the telephone to service accounts and to sell products.

Did you make a business call recently? Maybe you called to get your car repaired and an office worker made an appointment for you. Perhaps you called to ask what time a store closed. These are all business calls. Did you get a polite answer?

Many people are not hired because they cannot talk properly on the telephone. Sometimes when you answer an advertisement for a job, the preliminary screening is done over the telephone. Individuals may pass all a company's tests, yet not be hired for the position because of their telephone manners.

Some people lose jobs because they cannot handle business calls on the telephone. A fast typist might be hired for a job, but be terminated if he or she cannot follow proper telephone procedures.

Effective telephone use is crucial to the success of your employer. No company wants to lose business because of its employee's improper telephone techniques. If you appear rude or unconcerned, that will be the impression you give of your company. However, if you express enthusiasm and confidence in your telephone conversations, callers will view your firm in a positive way.

Potential clients make judgments about your competence and your company's attributes based on how you handle their calls. It is important that these potential clients feel valued and appreciated when you are handling their telephone calls. Do you remember being treated poorly when you made a doctor's appointment or when you called for information about a movie or a restaurant? Do you also remember being treated nicely when you made other calls? How did you react?

In a speech to a group of business students, a personnel manager stated that all office employees frequently use the telephone. Are you prepared to use proper telephone techniques on the job?

OFFICE TIP

Always use generally accepted common courtesies in any business situation.

Proper Procedures

Answering the telephone in a business office is easy if you know the right procedures. The correct methods involve what you say and how you say it.

When the telephone rings, even before picking up the receiver, prepare yourself for the caller. You can do this as follows:

◆ Stop any work you are doing, so you can concentrate entirely on the caller.
◆ Always have a message pad or notepaper and pen or pencil ready.
◆ Set aside the problems of the day and have a positive attitude.

Did you know that the way you hold the telephone can affect the sound of your voice? Do not rest the telephone on your shoulder or chin. This will make your voice sound muffled. The listener may have to ask you to repeat or to speak louder. Hold the telephone about one inch from your lips and speak directly into the mouthpiece.

One important aspect of proper telephone procedures is concentrating on having good voice quality. A caller will not be able to see you smile or see your friendly expressions. You must rely entirely on your voice and good telephone manners to create a positive impression for your company. Here are a few steps to take to have a good telephone voice:

◆ Speak distinctly. Use clear, unmistakable words and sentences.
◆ Speak with a normal tone. Do not shout at the caller, but speak loud enough to be heard.
◆ Speak naturally. Let your pleasing personality show.
◆ Speak politely. Be considerate and respectful to the caller.
◆ Speak courteously. Talk in a manner that will please the caller.

How you speak on the telephone in an office is quite different from the way you do at home. Talking to a client is not like talking to your friend or neighbor. When you speak on the telephone at work, remember the following:

◆ Never use slang. Avoid words such as *ain't* or *huh.*
◆ Never have something in your mouth. Avoid chewing gum.
◆ Never run words together; for example, not "Whadidya say?" but "What did you say?"

You should use standard English when speaking on the telephone in an office. For more information on standard English, refer to Chapter 19.

◆ *The impression you make over the telephone is determined entirely by your voice and good telephone manners.*

Recall Time

Answer the following questions:

1. What are three ways an office worker can prepare to answer the telephone when it rings?

2. What are four important qualities of a good telephone voice?

3. Ari, an officer worker, receives a call from a new customer who wishes to place an order. Ari has a radio on very softly broadcasting a football game so the customer cannot hear it.

(Continued on next page.)

Recall Time continued

The customer begins giving the order, but Ari interrupts and puts her on hold because he cannot find anything to write with. Since the customer has a heavy accent, Ari talks very loud and almost shouts at times. He also needs to say "huh" quite frequently during the conversation. Ari concludes the transaction by saying, "Thanks for placing the order."

What would you have done differently if you were Ari?

4. Make a telephone call to inquire about clerical job openings at a local business. Ask for the personnel department and request that job descriptions be sent to you. After you place the call, answer the following questions:

   a. Did the employee at the personnel department appear to be concentrating on your conversation? If not, why not?

   b. Did he or she have a good business telephone voice—distinct, polite?

   c. Did he or she not use slang expressions and avoid running words together?

Receiving and placing calls in an office are also different from at home. The following are business procedures for receiving and placing calls.

INCOMING CALLS

Let's now look at the mechanics of answering a telephone in a business office. The following techniques can be used whether you are answering a telephone system with many lines or a standard business phone on your own work desk with just a few lines.

The main parts of the telephone that you will encounter on a job are the handset, the hold button, the transfer button, and the incoming and outgoing lines.

Most telephones in a business office have more than one line for incoming and outgoing calls. As this type of telephone rings, the button for the incoming call will begin to flash. To answer the call, pick up the handset and push down on the button that is flashing.

Most businesses follow certain procedures when answering incoming calls, such as the following:

- Answer the call promptly; preferably after the first or second ring.
- If the call was first answered by a receptionist, answer by giving the department name and then identifying yourself.
- If the call was not answered by a receptionist, answer by first giving the company name and then identifying yourself.
- If you are answering your boss's telephone, identify your boss first, and then yourself.

Ethics on the Job

You have been working in the production department of a large oil company for two years. Part of your job requires that you put the daily mail through the postage meter and take it to the post office. Some days there are over 200 pieces of mail to process.

You are active in a church group that will be holding a fund-raiser at the end of the month. You could easily mail the church flyer from work without anyone knowing.

Since it is for such a worthy cause, should you use the work postage meter for the mailing?

For example, when customers call Rudy Yee, a receptionist answers the phone, then transfers the call to Rudy. He answers like this: "Payroll Department, this is Rudy Yee."

When clients call Margo Gonzales, the calls go directly to her desk. She answers like this: "Good morning; Transworld Company, Margo Gonzales speaking."

Hugh Scott's boss usually answers her own phone. However, when she is away, Hugh answers like this: "Ms. Lopez's office, Hugh Scott speaking."

Some companies have their own procedures to follow when answering the telephone. It is best to review company policies when beginning a new job.

HOLD OR TRANSFER CALLS

Once you have answered an incoming call, the next step may be to hold or transfer the call. If the call is for another person, say to the caller, "One moment, please" or "One moment, please, I will ring her office." Then press firmly on the hold or transfer button and release it.

If you have a hold button, after you press it, the line button for the line or extension you were speaking on will begin to flash on and off. Always remember to push the hold button, or your connection to the caller will be broken.

If you have a transfer button, after you push it, you simply key in the extension to which you want the call transferred. The call will ring on that person's telephone. When he or she answers, the light will stop flashing.

Keep these points in mind when holding or transferring calls:

◆ Ask permission before placing a caller on hold.
◆ If you return to a call, thank the caller for waiting.
◆ Never leave a caller on hold for more than thirty or forty seconds before returning to check on the caller.
◆ When transferring, give the caller the name and number of the person to whom you are transferring the call.

Cora is an administrative assistant for a travel agency. This is an example of how she would transfer a call: "Good morning. GO Travel Services, Cora speaking . . . . That would be handled by our international division. May I transfer you to that department? . . . In case you get disconnected, I am transferring you to Harold Price at 4217."

Have you ever been left on hold for a long time? This is annoying. Leaving someone on hold for an extended period is a common mistake made by many office workers. Do not make the same error; keep checking back with a caller who is on hold. You can tell a caller is still on hold if the line continues to have a flashing light. Get back to him or her and say, "Do you still wish to hold or may I take a message?"

Many executives want their calls screened before a transfer is made. This means they want you to find out who is calling before you put that person on hold. It is important that you screen calls in a polite way so you don't offend a caller. Some common phrases used for

◆ *Use your best telephone manners when screening calls or taking messages.*

◆ *Many office employees must answer and screen calls for their bosses. That is why verbal communication skills are so important for office workers.*

call screening are "May I ask who is calling, please?" and "May I tell Mr. Partel who is calling, please?" Check with your employer to see if calls should be screened.

MESSAGES

Many times, your boss will not be able to take a telephone call. In these cases, politely tell the caller why your boss is unavailable. Then ask if you can take a message or transfer the caller to voice mail if your office has it. For example, say, "I am sorry, she is not at her desk right now. May I take a message or transfer you to her voice mail?" or "I am sorry, Ms. Chavez is out of the office today. May I take a message or transfer you to her voice mail?" It would also be helpful to say when your boss is expected back and to ask if you or someone else can be of help.

Never say, "She is busy right now." This may offend the caller by implying that he or she isn't important. Your company does not want to insult any customers.

Sometimes, your boss will be available, but will not wish to speak to a particular caller. In that situation, you may use the same phrases you would use if your boss were unable to take the call: "I am sorry, he is not at his desk right now. May I take a message or transfer you to his voice mail?" or "I am sorry, he is out of the office. May I take a message or transfer you to his voice mail?"

One executive secretary in an advertising firm has a special method of screening calls for her boss, Mr. Perkins. Mr. Perkins is particular about which calls he answers. The secretary handles it this way:

Caller: May I speak to Mr. Perkins?

Secretary: I am not certain if Mr. Perkins has returned from his meeting. Let me check. May I have your name, please?

In this situation, the secretary can tell Mr. Perkins the name of the caller and he can decide if he wishes to speak to the person. If he does not, the caller will be told Mr. Perkins has not returned from the meeting. This is a good way to avoid offending a caller.

If you need to take a telephone message, you can use a standard form (see Figure 8.1). This type of form is available as a telephone message pad. The format may vary a little, but you will always need to record who the message is for, the date, the time, who the message is from and the name of that person's company, a return phone number, the message itself, and your signature or initials.

FIGURE 8.1 ◆ Sample Page from a Telephone Message Pad

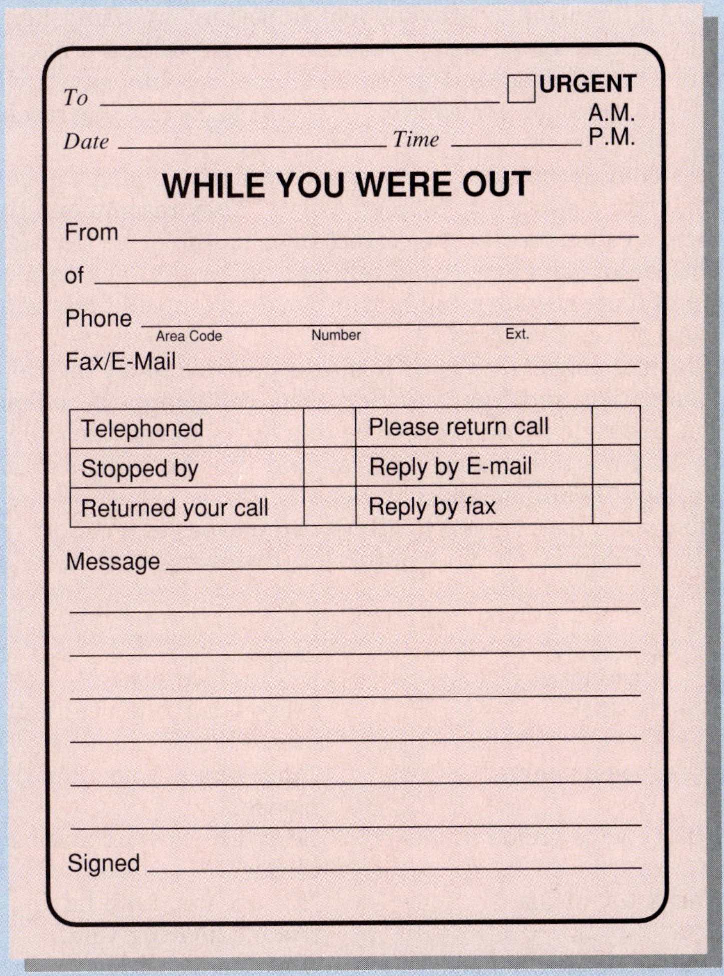

Recording the correct information is very important. Here are some helpful hints:

◆ If you cannot hear, ask the caller to speak louder.
◆ If you do not understand, ask the caller to repeat.
◆ Always get the caller's telephone number. This saves looking it up.
◆ If you cannot spell the caller's name, ask him or her to spell it for you.
◆ Before you hang up, read back the information to the caller. This will ensure that your message is accurate.

Have you ever answered the telephone at home and the caller said, "Sorry, I dialed the wrong number"? Well, maybe he or she was given the wrong number. It is extremely important to record the correct telephone number onto the message pad. Too many wrong numbers could mean a loss of business for a company. It could also mean the loss of a job for you.

It never hurts to be especially polite when taking messages. For example, you can make a caller feel important by using her or his name during the conversation. Assume you are taking a message for Ms. Huff. The caller is Mr. Carver. To be really polite, say, "I will give Ms. Huff the message, Mr. Carver" or "I will be certain she receives the message, Mr. Carver."

Professional administrative support staff care enough about their jobs to put extra effort into helping callers. They recommend that you try to help a caller receive the correct information or be transferred to the right person who can. Avoid telling a caller that you cannot be of any help. If it is necessary, tell him or her that you will find the answer and return the call yourself.

Finally, it is considered good business practice to let the caller end the conversation and hang up first. The caller may be offended or think you are rude if you seem to be in a hurry to end the call. This is also a good time to practice courtesy and use the caller's name. For example, say, "Thank you for calling, Ms. Harris."

The following list is given to all new employees at a county office in northern California. It is helpful for reviewing tactful telephone phrases.

◆ *The caller will have a good impression of you and your employer if you are courteous and helpful.*

Do not say . . .	Do say . . .
"Who is this?"	"May I ask who's calling, please?"
"What's your name?"	"May I have your name, please?"
"What's your phone number?"	"May I have your number, please?"
"Speak up, please."	"Excuse me, I am having trouble hearing you."
"You didn't talk to me."	"I cannot remember talking with you."

"What do you want to
talk to him about?"

"May I ask what your call is in
reference to?"

OUTGOING CALLS

When you work in an office, you will not only receive calls, you will
also have to place them. First, prepare yourself for placing the call. To
do this:

◆ Make a checklist of subjects you wish to cover.
◆ Have all the necessary information needed to ask or answer
  questions. This may include file folders, notes, and a calendar.
◆ Be certain to have the correct phone number. If in doubt, look it up.
◆ Be aware of the time, especially if you are calling someone in
  another time zone. Try to call during business hours and avoid
  lunchtimes.

Now you are ready to make the outgoing call. Remember that when
the buttons on a telephone are lighted, it means someone is talking on
those lines. Therefore, when placing an outside call on some phone
systems, you must find an unlighted button on your telephone.

Once you have found an open line (one that is not lighted), pick up
the handset, push down on the button for that line, and key in the
number you are calling. Give the person enough time to answer—eight
or ten rings.

When the party answers, identify yourself before starting the conversation. In some cases, it will save a lot of time if you also identify
your company. For example, when the party answers, you could say:
"This is Saul Neal calling. May I speak to Ms. Lew?" or "This is Sally
Perez from Fresno Travel Service. Is Mr. Allen in, please?"

Sometimes, your boss may want to speak to someone but will ask
you to place the call and get the person on the telephone. If this happens, be certain your boss is close by and ready to talk to the person
when you have him or her on the line. For example, Mr. Castle asks
his executive secretary, Kay, to get Ms. Butler of Invest Savings on the
phone for him. Kay keys in the telephone number. Ms. Butler answers
and the conversation is as follows:

Kay: Ms. Butler, this is Kay West from Castle & Curl. Bill Castle
     would like to speak with you. May I put him on the line now?
Ms. Butler: Yes, please do.
Kay [As she signals her boss]: Here he is, Ms. Butler.

Another time-saver when making outgoing calls is to spell uncommon words or names when leaving a message. If your name or your
company's name is easily misunderstood, it is best to spell it. For example, Orv is an administrative assistant at the law firm of Weinberg and
Heller. When people hear the name Weinberg, they may think
Wineberg, or Weinburg, or another spelling. When Orv must leave messages, he says the following:

OFFICE TIP

Sometimes your boss or another
office employee is on the
telephone when you wish to
speak to him or her, so you must
wait. Stand far enough back so
you do not hear the conversation.
If it is a private office, stay
outside the office until the call is
finished.

MAKING OFFICE DECISIONS

Olga works as an administrative assistant for a public relations firm. She enjoys word processing and finds it interesting to type the proposals for new clients. She works for three bosses and is kept busy most of the day.

In this company, all the administrative assistants must take turns relieving the receptionist at lunchtime one day each week. During this period, the telephones are very busy, so there is no time for any other work.

Tuesday is Olga's day to relieve the receptionist. One Tuesday, the receptionist says she has an important lunch date, so she must leave on time. On that same Tuesday, one of Olga's bosses gives her a proposal that must be typed and sent to a client by 1 p.m. At noon, when the receptionist wants to leave, Olga still has a few pages to complete.

Olga begins to get nervous. She must finish the proposal, yet it is her turn to relieve the receptionist.

Explain at least three actions that Olga could take in this situation.

"This is Orv Fletcher from Weinberg and Heller. I would like to leave a message to remind Ms. Reiser of our meeting . . . . Yes, Orv F-l-e-t-c-h-e-r of W-e-i-n-b-e-r-g and Heller. Thank you very much."

Other Important Procedures

Most offices follow similar procedures regarding the use of the telephone.

PERSONAL CALLS

All companies have a policy on personal telephone calls. Most companies do not allow them, except in an emergency.

Current technology allows companies to identify calls made from all telephone extensions. This lets employers charge calls to departments or special accounts. This also allows employers to separate business calls from personal calls and trace each one to the person who made it.

Check company policy on personal calls. It is considered good business ethics not to make personal calls from work.

DISCONNECTED CALLS

Have you ever been disconnected when talking on the telephone? When this happens in a business office, it is customary for the person who made the call to call back immediately.

WRONG-NUMBER CALLS

It is not uncommon for a person to get a wrong number when making a call. If this happens on a long-distance call, find out what number you actually reached, and hang up immediately. You may then dial the

Ralph has been an office support person for an architect's firm for three years. His attendance record is good and the quality of his work is excellent.

Ralph comes from a family of seven brothers and sisters. The brothers and sisters are always having problems and relying on Ralph for advice. Therefore, Ralph is constantly on the telephone at work answering calls from his siblings.

Ralph was raised with a strong family commitment, so he believes all the personal problems can be given attention during work time. Besides, his production tasks are always done with few errors.

1. What do you think of Ralph's attitude?

2. Should family calls be allowed at work? Is there a limit?

3. Should other personal calls be allowed?

operator and request that the company not be charged for the call. You will have to give the operator the number you reached in error.

TELEPHONE COVERAGE

If you are a receptionist or in charge of answering many lines, it is crucial that you arrange for phone coverage when you are away from your desk. Always ask someone to answer the phones for you.

Recall Time

Answer the following questions:

1. What are the four major parts of a telephone?

2. You are an employee working for Alex Auto Supplies. When calls come to you, they go directly to your phone; there is no receptionist. How should you answer the calls?

3. You are an employee in the accounting department of Garcia Advertising Company. All calls are first answered by a receptionist and then transferred to your desk. How should you answer your calls?

4. Your boss is Ms. Seville. She is not available, so you answer her telephone. What do you say when you answer, and what do you tell the caller?

5. Your boss, Mr. Woo, wants all his calls screened. What does this mean, and how do you do it?

6. What are seven items of information that need to be recorded when taking telephone messages?

Conference Calls

A **conference call** allows three or more parties to participate in the call from several locations. The caller first tells the receptionist the names and phone numbers of those taking part in the conference call and the time of day he or she would like to set up the call. Conference calls may be local or long distance.

Before placing long-distance calls, make sure your company permits them. Also consider the time of day. This is important because long-distance telephone calls are cheaper at certain times. It is also important because times differ across the United States. You want to make calls only when you know people are in their offices.

It is helpful to refer to a **time zone** map before placing long-distance calls. The United States is divided into four time zones: Eastern, Central, Mountain, and Pacific. Time changes by one hour as you move through the zones. Figure 8.2 is a sample of a time zone map. The map is used in the following way:

When it is . . .	it is . . .
4 a.m. in Wyoming	6 a.m. in New York
10 a.m. in most of Kansas	11 a.m. in New York
7 p.m. in Nevada	10 p.m. in Massachusetts
9 p.m. in Virginia	7 p.m. in Arizona
11 a.m. in Texas	9 a.m. in California

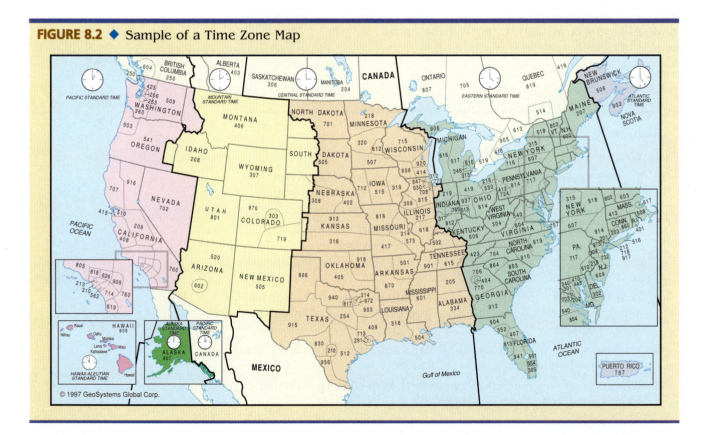

FIGURE 8.2 ◆ Sample of a Time Zone Map

© 1997 GeoSystems Global Corp.

As you view the map in Figure 8.2, notice that in addition to time differences, it lists the various three-digit area codes. This is handy when you need to place a call to a number outside your area code.

Directory assistance is sometimes necessary when you cannot find a number in your telephone directory. To call directory assistance outside your area code, key in the number 1, then the area code, and then 555-1212. If you do not know the area code, you can refer to the time zone map:

For directory assistance in . . .	dial . . .
New Mexico	1-505-555-1212
Maine	1-207-555-1212
Duluth, Minnesota	1-218-555-1212
Springfield, Missouri	1-417-555-1212

Reference Materials

You will find the telephone books in an office are the same type that you keep in your home. In addition, most offices have several local directories, copies of the Yellow Pages for various geographic areas, and other directories related to their type of business.

When you want to find the phone number for an individual, a company, or sometimes a government agency, you refer to the White Pages of the telephone book. The names are listed in alphabetical order. Most telephone books also have a separate section for government agencies—divided into classifications of federal, state, county, and city. For example, to find a phone number for the Navy, you would look under United States Government, Navy Department.

The local telephone directory Yellow Pages contain an alphabetic listing of businesses only. The businesses are arranged by subject area or according to the service they provide or the product they sell. For example, to find the number of the local Hyatt Hotel, you would look in the Yellow Pages under hotels.

Company telephone directories list the telephone numbers or just the telephone extensions of employees within a company. They list the various departments and the employees within each department. They also contain an alphabetic listing of all employees. In Figure 8.3, you will find the telephone number for Gene Ott by looking under Marketing.

Telephone Equipment

The computer-controlled telephone equipment used in businesses today is very sophisticated. It is set up in various networks and can provide a variety of features for both large and small companies.

Most businesses use equipment that allows incoming calls to go directly to the individual being contacted. However, companies using this system have one general number listed in telephone books in case a caller does not have an individual employee's number. These general

FIGURE 8.3 ◆ Sample Company Telephone Directory

Brimmer & Associates Employee Directory   *PAGE 1*

NAME	MAIL CODE	PHONE	NAME	MAIL CODE	PHONE
ACCOUNTING DEPARTMENT			Darwin, Bette	D1-22E	8433
Adams, Randell	D2-75	8521	Davis, Vickie	D1-18	8036
Arthur, Elaine	D1-13	8668	Easton, Jane	E6-21	8771
Balach, Carole	D7-67B	8621	Hodsdon, Roger	D7-63	8611
Dollison, Lee Anne	D5-18	8737			
Miller, Jeff	D2-55F	8780	**COMPUTER DEPARTMENT**		
Thomas, Joseph	C2-17	8071	Allred, James		
			Anderson, Julie	D5-19	8738
ADVERTISING DEPARTMENT			Biggers, Betty	D6-50	8710
Aune, Kelly	E1-50	8717	Collins, Danny	E8-09	8009
Aws, John	B6-04	8028	Enz, David	B1--2	8776

Ethics on the Job

Bernice is in charge of all the supplies for her department. This includes ordering the supplies, placing them in the cabinets, and taking inventory.

Bernice does freelance computer work at home on weekends for small companies that do not have office help.

Bernice takes small supplies—Post-It notes, paper clips, pens—from her job and uses them at home. Since the supplies are so inexpensive, she thinks it is all right to do this.

Do you agree with Bernice? Why or why not?

calls are usually answered by a receptionist. With this system, employees place outgoing calls directly—they do not need to go through a company operator.

Some firms prefer that all calls first go to a receptionist, who transfers the caller to the proper employee. This system is used when companies want to screen all callers or when executives believe this method provides better customer service.

When calls are transferred and an employee is not at his or her desk, calls are often answered by the employee's voice mail. Voice mail is similar to an answering machine except there is no need for the machine; computer-controlled telephone equipment provides the service.

Companies that receive frequent calls from within their own network of telephones may purchase a liquid crystal display (LCD). This is a display terminal that can be connected to telephone sets. This feature displays the names of callers from within the office.

SPECIAL FEATURES

Once the equipment is installed, a company may subscribe to one or more of the following services:

Automatic Callback   When you call a busy number, the automatic callback feature "remembers" the number and dials it for you automatically after you hang up.

Example: You dial a number and it is busy. Your preset program will continue to redial until the line is clear.

Call Forwarding–Busy Line–Don't Answer   The call forwarding–busy line–don't answer feature automatically reroutes calls to a designated answering station if your line is busy or if you do not answer after a certain number of rings.

Example: Your phone rings five times (the number of rings you have preset); no one answers. The call is automatically transferred to another person's desk.

Call Hold   The call hold feature lets you put a caller on hold and make another call. It also allows you to switch back and forth between on-hold calls. It is different from the hold button because it gives you access to the dial tone while a call is held.

Example: You are speaking to a party on the telephone. You need to get some information for the person. You press a special key to put the person on hold. With the same line, you now place a call to another department to get the information.

Call Waiting   The call waiting feature lets a caller reach you even when your line is busy. A gentle signal alerts you to an incoming call.

Example: You are speaking on the telephone. You hear a soft beep in your ear. This means another call is coming in. You can depress the receiver button to answer the call; your first caller is automatically put on hold.

INDUSTRY FOCUS

Edward Gibson
Senior Clerk, Emergency Registration
Merrithew Memorial Hospital

Q.   Mr. Gibson, some students think that good computer skills are all that is needed for a job. Is this true? What other skills do you use on your job?

A.   No, while computer skills are extremely valuable, they are not all that is needed. Critical thinking and the ability to solve problems are just as important. The most important skill to possess is the ability to interact effectively with co-workers and customers—both in person and on the telephone.

Q.   What advice would you give to a student preparing for a career as a clerk in a hospital setting?

A.   ◆ Take as many courses as possible in developing good interpersonal skills.
    ◆ Have a genuine concern and compassion for people.
    ◆ Be a volunteer in a hospital and try to get as much overall knowledge of how departments operate and how the clerical staff interrelates.

9

Filing and Managing Records

OBJECTIVES

After completing this chapter, you will be able to do the following:

1. List the purposes for maintaining records.
2. Give examples of classification of records.
3. Give examples of filing systems.
4. List the steps taken to file a record.
5. List paper storage systems.
6. List electronic storage systems.
7. List advantages of electronic storage systems.
8. Give examples of basic indexing rules.
9. Give examples of basic alphabetizing rules.
10. Give examples of a record retention system.

NEW OFFICE TERMS

alphabetic filing system
centralized filing system
chronological filing system
cross-reference
electronic files
geographic filing system
hard copy
indexing

lateral files
mobile files
numeric filing system
open files
rotary files
subject filing system

BEFORE YOU BEGIN

Answer the following questions to the best of your ability:

1. What are the four basic filing systems? Explain them.

2. What are three examples of equipment used for filing records?

3. Name three types of electronic storage.

H ave you heard of the paperless office? Does one really exist? Will one ever exist?

In the 1980s, personal computers became commonplace in businesses and employers began to talk about the paperless office. Many people thought that storing information in a computer would eliminate the need for paper.

So far, this has not proven true. Individuals still want to see information on a hard copy. **Hard copy** means information printed onto paper, as opposed to saved on a computer disk.

What are all these pieces of paper that people expected to disappear? Here are some examples:

◆ a purchase order for a new desk
◆ the mortgage papers on a building owned by a business
◆ personnel records of all employees
◆ all financial papers for tax purposes
◆ advertisements

◆ *As you can see, the paperless office has not arrived for most businesses. Missing or misfiled documents can mean hours of wasted, unproductive time.*

◆ copies of letters
◆ copies of contracts
◆ copies of memorandums

It is important for a business to maintain records to function effectively. Records are also kept for legal reasons, such as for tax reports or to comply with state and federal labor laws.

For example, consider a rental agreement between the owner of a small business that rents an office and the owner of the office building. This record will be used for tax purposes, for rent increases, and to prove who is responsible for maintaining the property.

Records should be stored and maintained in an orderly fashion so that information can be located and used when needed. Storing and maintaining records is known as records management.

Records management involves developing a filing system that will meet the needs of a particular office. This system must allow you to store records. It must also allow you to retrieve them easily when needed.

Many office workers say that the simpler the filing system, the more efficient it will be. For the rental agreement described above, the easiest method would be to file the agreement under the address of the property, because more than one tenant occupies the building.

Filing Systems

The basic filing systems used in offices are alphabetic, subject, geographic, numeric, and chronological. Some offices use just one system. Other offices use a combination of two or more.

ALPHABETIC

The **alphabetic filing system** is the most conventional and widely used system. It consists of arranging files in order beginning with *A* and ending with *Z*. Files may be records for individuals, businesses, or government agencies.

The following is an example of names listed in alphabetic filing order:

Acme Bread Company
Andrews, Harold
Danford Hauling and Storage
Justine's on the Park
Kirk, Ronald

SUBJECT

The **subject filing system** involves arranging files by topic or by subject. An office worker should be careful when establishing this type of system. It is important to choose meaningful topics or subjects.

FIGURE 9.1 ◆ A Sample Cross-Reference Sheet

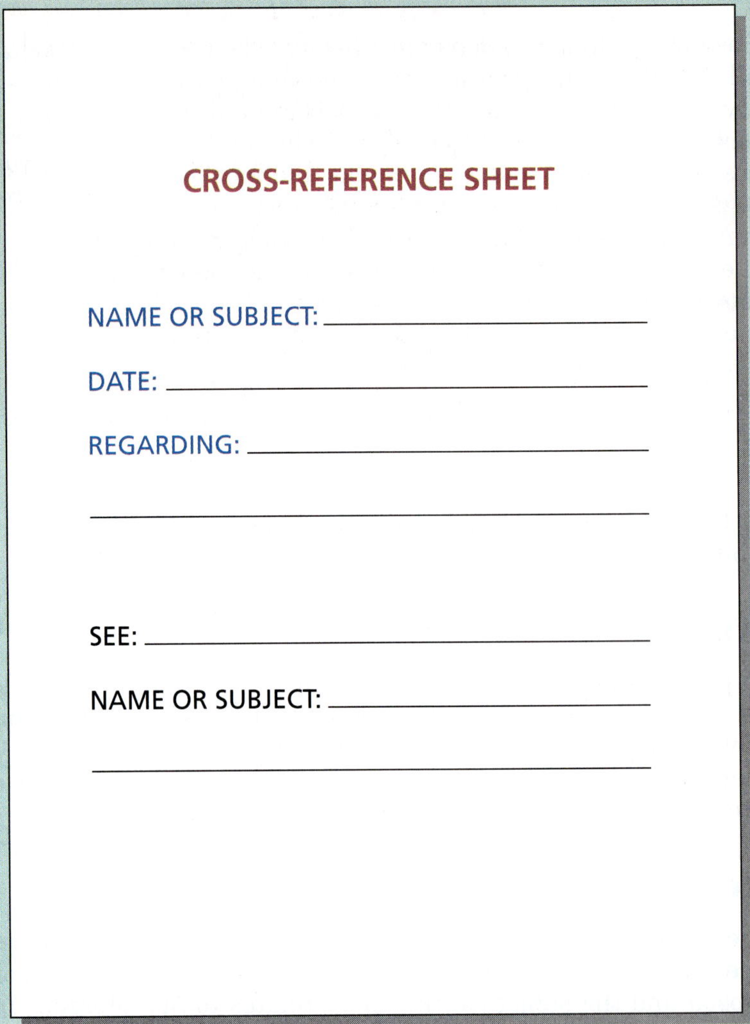

CROSS-REFERENCE SHEET

NAME OR SUBJECT: _____

DATE: _____

REGARDING: _____

_____

SEE: _____

NAME OR SUBJECT: _____

_____

Classification and Retention

Carole was not aware that there was so much to know about filing until she began working for the graphics company. She soon realizes that companies have many different kinds of records. Some are vital to keep, some are important to keep, some are useful to keep, and some need not be kept at all. For example, Carole discovers the following:

◆ The graphics firm owns the building in which it is located. The mortgage papers are *vital records* to keep.
◆ Businesses must pay taxes, just as do individuals. All files relating to taxes are *important records* to keep.

Large Office/Small Office: What's Your Preference?

MAINTAINING RECORDS

Most large offices use a **centralized filing system** for their records. This means that a company's general files are stored in one central location. Under this system, employees are hired to work exclusively in the centralized filing area. These employees are responsible for maintaining all the centralized files including developing a method to know where the records are at all times. Large offices with a centralized filing system use lateral or open filing equipment instead of vertical files.

Small offices may also use a centralized system, but it is more common for them to use a decentralized one. This means that records are stored in different locations within an office. Each administrative assistant or other clerical employee is responsible for the storage and retrieval of files pertaining to her or his specialized work. Vertical filing cabinets, rather than lateral files, are most often used in small offices.

Would you like to begin your office career as a file clerk in a large office with a centralized filing system? Why or why not? If you work in a small office, will you remember to set time aside for filing on a regular basis?

- The graphics firm recently purchased Carole a new desk. The purchase order for the desk is a *useful record* to keep.
- Carole's boss received an announcement of a luncheon meeting sponsored by a graphics club. He has an appointment that day and cannot attend. There is no reason to keep the announcement. This is a *nonessential record.*

Once Carole decides which records are vital and important to keep, her next question to her supervisor is, "Do we keep these records permanently? If not, for how long?" This decision is usually made at the time of the first filing and is based on a record retention schedule set up by each company. A record retention schedule is a listing of all the classifications of records and how long each should be retained. Carole's supervisor, Mr. Lloyd, is an active member of the Association of Records Managers and Administrators (ARMA). Thus he is able to give her an accurate answer.

Figure 9.2 is a partial listing of the results of a nationwide survey on the subject of record retention. The schedule in this figure was determined by examining the record retention schedules recommended by leading authorities on record storage and by businesses with established procedures.

The information in Figure 9.2 reflects current business thinking. However, the retention periods shown are not offered as a final author-

---

FIGURE 9.2 ◆ Partial Listing of Nationwide Survey
on Records Retention

RETENTION SCHEDULE

(P = permanent; O = optional; numbers represent suggested years)	
Accounts payable ledger	P
Accounts receivable ledger	10
Building permits	20
Government audit reports	P
Annual reports	P
Checkbook orders	O
Check records	7
Employee service records	P
Pension plan	P
Sales invoices	7

---

ity, but as guideposts. States have statutes of limitations (laws on how long records must be kept) and federal agencies have regulations that must be followed. Each company makes the final decision on how long to retain records.

Location of Permanent Records

Carole is concerned about space for all the records that must be kept on a permanent basis. She also wonders if there is enough room for records that must be kept for long periods and yet are not being used. She asks Mr. Lloyd about this.

Mr. Lloyd explains that at their graphics firm, records pass through three stages:

◆ *Stage 1.* These records are active and should be close at hand. They are referred to frequently and Mr. Lloyd must have immediate access to them.
◆ *Stage 2.* These records are only occasionally needed by Mr. Lloyd. They are semiactive and can be placed in storage.
◆ *Stage 3.* These records are no longer needed by the graphics firm but must be kept because of government regulations. They are usually held in permanent storage, often in a separate location.

Carole later learns that these procedures are followed by many other firms.

Filing Equipment

Choosing the proper equipment in which to store records is an important part of records management. Choose equipment that will protect

◆ *Businesses most frequently use vertical filing cabinets.*

the records from damage and that is efficient to use. For example, you can use vertical, lateral, open, rotary, mobile or portable, or card files.

VERTICAL FILES

Vertical filing equipment is usually made of metal, sits upright, and has one or more drawers. The files face the front of the drawer, making it easy to locate documents.

LATERAL FILES

Lateral filing equipment is also made of metal, but the drawers rest sideways. The files are arranged vertically, from side to side, inside the drawers. Cabinets for **lateral files** require less aisle space than do vertical cabinets.

OPEN FILES

Open filing equipment resembles open bookshelves. The file folders are placed on an uncovered shelf. Equipment for **open files** saves space. Many employees use color-coded files for quicker location of records.

ROTARY FILES

Rotary files may be contained in a small unit that sits on a desk or in a large one that operates on the floor. A small unit may simply be a

◆ *Businesses also commonly use lateral file cabinets.*

rotating wheel that holds various business cards. A large floor unit may be electronically operated and contain standard file folders and guides. The files rotate in a circular motion similar to that of a carousel.

MOBILE OR PORTABLE FILES

When files must be shared on a regular basis, it is easiest to keep them in portable cabinets. These portable cabinets are known as **mobile files.** They are usually one-drawer cabinets on wheels, allowing them to be moved from one location to another. The drawer normally has a lid to pull up, rather than the usual pullout style.

CARD FILES

Many office workers keep card files even when other filing equipment is used within the company. A card file is normally a small desktop box or tray that is used for quick reference of frequently needed information. Card files can also be located in a cabinet drawer when more space is needed and quick reference is not important.

Basic Indexing Rules

When preparing a new folder or card for filing purposes, you must decide in what order to type the name of the person or company. This is called **indexing.** Once you have indexed the name on the folder, then you will file the folder alphabetically with the rest of the files.

INDIVIDUAL NAMES

Individual names are indexed by first the surname (last name), next the first name or initial, and then any middle names or initials. For example:

The name . . .	is indexed as . . .
Ann E. Delgardo	Delgardo, Ann E.
T. C. O'Neil	O'Neil, T. C.
J. Linda Singh	Singh, J. Linda

COMPANY NAMES

Company names are indexed in the order that they appear. For example:

The name . . .	is indexed as . . .
Westamerica Bank	Westamerica Bank
Applied Biosystems	Applied Biosystems
C. Martin, Inc.	C. Martin, Inc.
Rita Ramos & Sons	Rita Ramos & Sons

Basic Alphabetizing Rules

Lorie started as a temporary office worker six months ago in a large midwestern city. Lorie could not type, so most of her assignments were filing jobs. Lorie began to compare the filing rules she learned in school with the systems she found on various assignments. She noticed many deviations in the filing systems used. Nevertheless, Lorie realized that secretaries all followed the same basic filing rules, modeled after ARMA recommendations.

FIRST FILING RULE

Arrange files in alphabetical order by the first word. The first word is the first one you typed when you did the indexing. For example:

Out of Filing Order	In Filing Order
Erickson, Barbara	Alioto, Martin
Clark, Tyler	Clark, Tyler
Alioto, Martin	Erickson, Barbara
Wiggins, Heloise	Wiggins, Heloise

SIMILAR NAMES OF UNEQUAL LENGTH

When two or more names are the same up to a certain letter, the shorter name is filed first. Clark is filed before Clarke. A good rule to help you remember this is "nothing comes before something." For example:

Out of Filing Order	In Filing Order
Lowe, Georg	Low, Charles
Low, Charles	Lowe, Georg
Smithe, Lucy	Smith, Sara
Smith, Sara	Smithe, Lucy

HYPHENATED NAMES

Hyphenated names are treated as one word. Debbie Wilson-Tobin is filed under Wilson-Tobin. For example:

Out of Filing Order	In Filing Order
Lee-Harris, Shelly	Harris, Carol Lee
Harris, Carol Lee	Lee-Harris, Shelly
Perkins-Millan, Inez	Millan, Flora
Millan, Flora	Perkins-Millan, Inez

ABBREVIATIONS

Abbreviations are considered one unit. For example:

OFFICE TIP

Schedule fixed blocks of time for group projects. For example, do a batch of filing all at one time. Do a batch of photocopying all at one time. Type a group of labels or envelopes all at one time. This is more efficient. It also provides longer periods of concentration on one project, which aids accuracy.

Out of Filing Order	In Filing Order
Portillo, Wm.	Burrell, Chas.
Burrell, Chas.	Pembroke Rental Co.
St. Veronica's School	Portillo, Wm.
Pembroke Rental Co.	St. Veronica's School

SURNAMES WITH PREFIXES

If an individual surname is compounded with prefixes, it is treated as one word. For example:

Out of Filing Order	In Filing Order
O'Neil, Richard	Del Rosario, Rima
Del Rosario, Rima	D'Martini, Christine
D'Martini, Christine	Los Robos Lodge
Los Robos Lodge	O'Neil, Richard

ARTICLES, PREPOSITIONS, CONJUNCTIONS

Articles, prepositions, and conjunctions are considered separate filing units. The exception is if the word "the" is the first word of a company name. For example:

Out of Filing Order	In Filing Order
The Fashion Center	Fashion Center (The)
Hospice of Marin	Haswell Group (The)
Top of the Bay Hotel	Hospice of Marin
The Haswell Group	Top of the Bay Hotel

NAMES CONTAINING NUMBERS

When a name contains a number that is spelled out, index it as a word in alphabetical order. When a name contains a number written as a digit, index it as a digit in ascending order. The digit numbers precede all alphabetic words. For example:

Out of Filing Order	In Filing Order
50 Sutter Place	9 Months Only
One Market Plaza	50 Sutter Place
9 Months Only	First American News
First American News	One Market Plaza

Recall Time

Answer the following questions:

1. What is the marking process when records are prepared for filing?

(Continued on next page.)

Recall Time continued

2. When is a cross-reference sheet used?

3. What is the difference between indexing and filing?

4. What is the result when you index the following?

> Donald Hammond
> Stephen Wong
> J. Alice Goldstein
> Sunrise Hill Associates
> Union City Tire & Brake

5. What is the result when you arrange the following in alphabetic order?

> Garcia Bakery
> Cox, Ben
> Day Hour Mini Mart
> Apple Annie's
> Cox, Chas.
> Smith-Hawkins, Paula

6. What is the result when you arrange the following in alphabetic order?

> The Kraftsman Group
> Del Rose, Teresa
> 25 Moller Plaza
> Society of Brothers

Preparation of Filing Supplies

Blanche is excited. She has been hired as a receptionist by an architect who has been in business for only a year but who has a good reputation and quite a few clients. Since the architect's business is new, not much work has been done in setting up files for the clients. Blanche decides to attack this as one of her first projects. She first purchases a new vertical filing cabinet. She then purchases a secretary's handbook from a local bookstore, reviews the section on record management techniques, and begins to set up the files. Her procedure involves preparing folders and labels, inserting correspondence, and placing folders into a file drawer.

PREPARING FOLDERS AND LABELS

Blanche sets up a business-size 8½×11-inch manila folder for each client. She types a label for the folder, using the largest type possible, by typing in uppercase letters. When Blanche has worked at the firm a few months, she is going to suggest that the company purchase computer software that will print labels from a template.

While preparing the folders, Blanche is faced with the following problems. She is able to solve them with help from her office handbook.

◆ She finds two clients with the exact same name. Her solution is to use labels of different colors for these two clients. In this way, she can more quickly identify the folders.

◆ She discovers that one client already has so many reports that they cannot all fit into one folder. Her solution is to prepare two folders for the client and separate them by date headings.

INSERTING CORRESPONDENCE

Once the folders are prepared, Blanche gathers all the correspondence for each individual client. She arranges the correspondence in the appropriate folder by date, with the latest date on the top. She is extra cautious that the right papers go into the right file folders. She remembers that her boss told her that new business prospects can be lost if the necessary papers are not available when needed for clients.

PLACING FOLDERS INTO A FILE DRAWER

Blanche places the folders in alphabetic order in a drawer of the vertical file cabinet. She then refers to her office handbook and reads the section on file guides. File guides divide the file drawers into sections, making it easier to locate a folder. For example, one guide can be labeled A and all the folders behind it can begin with the letter A. If you have only a few clients, the guide can be labeled A–D and all the folders behind it can begin with the letters A, B, C, and D. Both examples are primary guides because they represent major divisions within the drawers.

Blanche completes the project by setting up the primary guides. She also reads about secondary guides, which divide the folder even further into subdivisions. However, she does not think this procedure is necessary for her situation. She does not yet have enough files to make subdivisions useful.

Refer to Figure 9.3 for an example of a file drawer with both primary and secondary guides. File guides may be purchased at stationery stores.

Where's the Folder?

No matter how efficient your filing system, it will not work if you cannot find a folder when you need it. One cause of misplaced folders is another employee taking them from the file drawer from time to time. In this case, some notation must be made stating which employee has a particular folder. This is done by an out card.

An out card is the same height as the file folders. It may be a different color with the word *OUT* printed in all capital letters on the top tab of the card. On the front of this out card are ruled columns for an employee to record the date, a description of the file or material removed, when the item is to be returned, the name of the person the item is charged to, and other remarks. See Figure 9.4 for a sample of an out card.

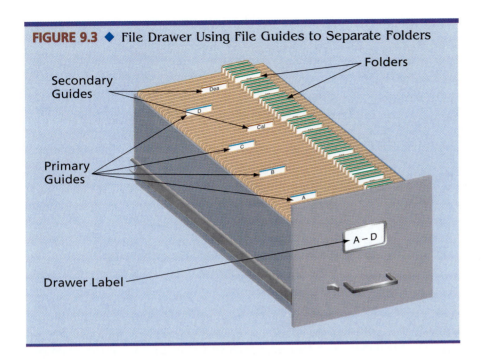

FIGURE 9.3 ◆ File Drawer Using File Guides to Separate Folders

Folders

Secondary Guides

Primary Guides

Drawer Label

A–D

The out card is placed in the exact spot from which a folder or material is removed. An office worker will not use an out card every time a file is pulled. An out card is used only when someone outside the immediate office wants a file or if an office assistant or a boss wishes to remove a file for a long period of time.

Bar Coding Files

Another method of keeping track of files that are checked out from a central location is to use bar coding. This method is similar to that used in a library or video store.

The file folders are bar coded when they are first set up. When an employee checks out the file, the file bar code and the employee's bar code are scanned into the system. When the employee returns the file, it is rescanned.

Bar coding is a fast and efficient method of keeping track of files. Some software packages have bar coding available for records management.

Electronic Storage

Most records are still stored on paper. However, **electronic files** are becoming common in the business world.

HARD DRIVES

Storing files on the hard drive of a PC is one method of electronic filing. However, on the hard drive the files can easily be deleted or

◆ *Imagine filing all the data collected by the IRS if there were no electronic files!*

FIGURE 9.4 ◆ Sample Out Card

OUT

DATE	MATERIAL	DATE REMOVED	TO BE RETURNED	REMOVED BY	COMMENTS

altered. In addition, the files use up the computer's memory. Therefore, the hard drive is adequate for short-term storage, but it is not recommended for long-term storage.

OPTICAL DISKS

Optical disks are used by businesses that want more permanent storage for their files. The optical disks may be the same size as the disk you use in your PC, but have a much greater storage capacity. The optical disk may hold several hundred thousand pages.

Some businesses prefer write-once-read-many-times optical disks because documents cannot be altered or deleted from these disks. Rewriteable optical disks are also available, but on these disks the files can be replaced.

◆ *Optical disks provide high capacity storage that is more permanent than storage on the hard drive.*

CD-ROMS

Businesses also use CD-ROMS as a permanent storage media for their files. Documents stored on CD-ROMS also cannot be altered or deleted.

CD-ROMS cost less than optical disks. CDs are also easier to duplicate.

◆ *Magnetic tape cartridges are often used to back up the contents of a computer's hard disk.*

COMPONENTS

Creating and storing electronic files is simple. However, some businesses want to convert paper files into electronic files. This procedure requires the use of other components: a scanner and scanner software. The scanner, connected to or built into the computer, is the hardware that accepts the paper copy. The software is the program required for the conversion.

ADVANTAGES OF ELECTRONIC SYSTEMS

Some of the major advantages of electronic files over paper files are:

◆ *Space.* Filing space requirements are reduced. A larger number of documents can be stored in a smaller amount of space.
◆ *Retrieval.* An employee can retrieve a document from a computer terminal. This provides immediate access to the file.
◆ *Updating.* Files can be added to the existing disk. This can be done indefinitely.

◆ *Removable cartridges such as Iomega's Zip disk can store large quantities of data.*

◆ *Longevity.*   Disks do not need any special storage facility. There is no necessity for special protection from the climate or the environment.

EXAMPLES OF NAMING ELECTRONIC FILES

For two months over the summer, Bo worked as an administrative assistant through a temporary placement service. The computer classes he had taken in high school and at a local community college had helped prepare him for the work. However, when it came to creating names for the electronic files, the real world of work was the best teacher.

Bo learned that most companies consider the following before deciding on policies for naming electronic files:

What is the topic of the file?

Who originated the file?

Who is the client?

Where is the file located—directory or subdirectory?

At one firm Bo got a better understanding of directories and subdirectories from the company's training manual, which gave the following example.

(Directory:)

Actvcli(Active Clients)

  (Subdirectories:)

    AP (Applied Biosystems)

      Proposal

      Budget

      Projects

      Press Tour

      Press Releases

      New Product

    HA (The Haswell Group)

      Proposal

      Budget

      Press Tour

    SU (Sunrise Hill Associates)

      Proposal

      Budget

      Press Tour

      Press Releases

    UN (Union City Tire & Brake)

      Proposal

      Budget

      Projects

      Press Tour

      Press Releases

Working for a small law firm, Bo created a document and stored it under the file name

  pswill.ab

He arrived at the file name by:

  client initials—Pamela Shaw

document contents—a will

attorney that originated the document—Amos Brown

Working at a twenty-five person public relations firm using a Mac network, Bo created a document and stored it under the file name

IN—sept 98 press tour

He arrived at the file name by

the client's first two initials—Internet Solutions

the topic of the document—Press Tour of the East Coast

Working at a 200-person real estate appraisal firm with a PC network, Bo created a document and stored it under the file name

f/w7/03/chart/00778/052298.bk

He arrived at the file name by:

the network directory—f

the software used—Word 7

the employee (identified by number 01, 02, 03, and so on)—03

type of document—a chart

document number—00778

document date—May 22, 1998

Bo Kline's initials—bk

Recall Time

Answer the following questions:

1. You are setting up file folders. How do you solve the following dilemmas?

    a. You need folders for two different clients with the same name.

    b. One client has too many papers to fit into one folder.

2. What are file guides used for?

3. What is the difference between primary and secondary file guides?

4. What is an out card used for?

5. What are two advantages of using an electronic filing system?

Summary

Filing is a task that all office workers perform. Some do more than others, but all workers must maintain files. Most workers use standard basic filing systems to help make filing tasks efficient.

Most office workers also use basic indexing rules. Once these rules are mastered, filing systems become fairly easy to maintain.

Some companies use electronic filing systems in addition to hard copy systems. In a few companies, electronic systems replace hard copy systems.

Look at the following list of filing methods and systems. Do you understand all of them? If not, which ones do you need to study further?

◆ alphabetic filing system
◆ subject filing system
◆ geographic filing system
◆ numeric filing system
◆ chronological filing system
◆ preparation of records for filing
◆ retention of files
◆ selection of filing equipment
◆ basic alphabetizing rules
◆ electronic filing methods

IN CONCLUSION . . .

When you have completed this chapter, answer the following questions:

1. What are the four basic filing systems? Explain them.

2. What are three example of equipment used for filing records?

3. Name three types of electronic storage.

REVIEW AND APPLICATION

✔ CHECK YOUR KNOWLEDGE

1. Would you classify each of the following as a vital record?
   a. a letter from your attorney
   b. canceled checks
   c. a copyright
   d. a tax return
2. Arrange the following in alphabetic order:
   Dearborn Poultry
   Janice's Coffee Shop
   Apple Tree Orchard
   Andrews, Harold
   Kirk, Ronald
3. How does a subject filing system work?
4. What is a geographic filing system?
5. Arrange the following in numeric order:
   345643501
   075353312
   465493344
   312455352
   129853401
6. Is it easy or difficult to find files using a numeric system?
7. Explain how a chronological filing system works.
8. List the steps in the preparation of records for filing.
9. Explain the difference between vertical filing equipment and lateral filing equipment.
10. An office has its files in a one-drawer cabinet that has wheels and is shared by several employees. What is this type of equipment called?
11. Index the following names:
    Amanda C. Parada
    C. F. Del Veccio
    J. Harding Bennett
12. Index the following business names:
    Santos Air Conditioning
    F. H. Daly, Inc.
    Acme Scale Company
    Joe Wong & Associates
13. Arrange the following names in alphabetic order:

Peter Yu
William Perry
Aileen Friedman
John Fara
Charles Fara

14. Arrange the following business names in alphabetic order:
    House of Fillmore
    Center for Creative Studies
    Bay Valley Repair
    Sure Clean Carpet
    J. Hall Associates
15. When typing a label for a new file folder, should you use small or large type? Why?
16. What are file guides used for?
17. Give an example of a primary file guide and an example of a secondary guide.
18. When more than one client has the exact same name, what could you use to make it easier to distinguish between them?
19. List two disadvantages of permanently storing files on the hard drive of a PC.
20. List two questions a company may ask when setting policy on naming electronic files.
21. What two components are needed to convert paper files to electronic files?
22. Should each of the following records be stored permanently or for a limited number of years?
    a. accounts payable ledger
    b. accounts receivable ledger
    c. check records
    d. sales invoices
    e. annual reports

REVIEW YOUR VOCABULARY

On a separate paper, supply the missing words by choosing from the new Office Terms listed below.

1. There is a document that can be filed under more than one name. You file the document under one name and _____ under the other.

2. If information is printed on paper, you have a _____.

3. A _____ system arranges records according to location.

4. A _____ system arranges names by topics.

5. A _____ system arranges records by date.

6. A large company keeps all its files in one central location. This is called a _____ system.

7. When preparing a new folder or card for filing purposes, you must decide in what order to type the name of the person or company onto the folder or card. This is called _____.

8. _____ files are contained on a wheel that rotates in a circular motion.

9. _____ files are portable and shared on a regular basis.

10. _____ files resemble bookshelves.

11. _____ files have drawers that rest sideways with the files arranged from side to side.

a. alphabetic filing system
b. centralized filing system
c. chronological filing system
d. cross-reference
e. geographic filing system
f. hard copy
g. indexing
h. lateral files
i. mobile files
j. numeric filing system
k. open files
l. rotary files
m. subject filing system

DISCUSS AND ANALYZE AN OFFICE SITUATION

1. Diane and Ruth are file clerks for a large corporation. Their entire workday is spent in the file room. They are the only two employees doing the filing.

   They have little contact with other employees except when someone calls for a lost file. The file room employees have no dress code.

   Diane has noticed a strong odor coming from Ruth the past few days. Ruth is a clean person and bathes every day. However, Diane has noticed that Ruth wears the same clothes each day. Diane is guessing the odor is coming from the clothes.

   The smell is beginning to bother Diane. Should Diane say something to Ruth? If so, how should she approach Ruth?

 **PRACTICE BASIC SKILLS**

MATH

1. Your boss asks you to total the following expenses charged to the filing department.

ITEM	AMOUNT	PRICE
Hanging folders	3 boxes	$14.79 per box
Hanging folder labels	5 packages	4.59 per package
Hanging folder frames	6 boxes	4.20 per box
Tab inserts	8 packages	1.05 per package
File jackets	9 packages	4.19 per package

2. Your boss receives a discount supply catalog. He asks you to calculate how much would have been saved if the items in exercise 1 had been purchased at the following discount prices.

ITEM	DISCOUNT PRICE
Hanging folders	$6.79 per box
Hanging folder labels	2.49 per package
Hanging folder frames	1.99 per box
Tab inserts	0.69 per package
File jackets	2.29 per package

3. Compute the total amount that will be charged to the filing department for use of temporary help during the last six months. Use the following information:

Temporary Help
Six-Months Report

January	
Advertising department	$375.00
Filing department	235.00
Accounting department	680.00

February	
Advertising department	375.00
Filing department	460.00
Accounting department	680.00

March

Advertising department	235.00
Filing department	375.00
Accounting department	680.00

April

Advertising department	800.00
Filing department	1,275.00
Accounting department	1,490.00

May

Advertising department	775.00
Filing department	1,030.00
Accounting department	1,490.00

June

Advertising department	800.00
Filing department	1,490.00
Accounting department	1,275.00

ENGLISH

1. *Rule:* Use a hyphen when *self, vice,* and *ex* are joined with another word.
   Examples: He was a self-made man. His ex-boss was in the building
   Practice Exercise: Rewrite the following sentences, placing hyphens where needed.
   a. It was viewed by all the people as self imposed exile.
   b. The woman was elected vice chair of the committee.
   c. The meeting was scheduled for 3 p.m. between the attorney and his ex wife.
   d. He has always been a self supporting person.
   e. He furnished a new office for the vice president.

PROOFREADING

1. Retype or rewrite the following, correcting all errors.

BOOKS FOR SALE

ACTIVE FILNG FOR PAPER RECORDS by Dr. Ann Bennick, CRM

Active Filing for Paper Records focuses on three bacis topics related to the managemnt of paper records: file systems development, filing equipment, and filing suplies. Implementation and conversion procedures is presented within the context of systems development techniques and ,where appropriate, as the relate to a discussion of spesific procedures, equipment, and supplies.

OPTICAL DISK SYSTEMS FOR RECORDS MANAGEMENT
By William Saffady

Optical Disk Systems for Records Management is divided into two parts. Section One provides an overview of optical disk technology. It defins the various types of storage media and breifly reviews their records management significance. Section Two provides a detailed discusion of optical filing systems, computer-based hardware and software configurations which store digitized document images on opticl disks for on-demand retreival. The discussion emphasises characteristics which influence the evaluation and selection of optical filing systems for records management applications.

 APPLY YOUR KNOWLEDGE

1. Using the tables feature of a word processing program, input, save, and print the following words. Use three columns and input in alphabetical order.

storage	geographic
chronological	numeric
lateral	digit
vertical	important
rotary	reference
centralized	business
records	retrieval
financial	folder
paperless	tabs
vital	labels
alphabetic	supplies
index	drawer

2. The CFEB Company's file drawers contain the following primary guides:

A–Cr	Jes–Me	Rx–Th
Cs–F	Mf–Pi	Ti–W
G–Jer	Pj–Rw	X–Z

Behind which guide would you file each of the following?

Solano Bakery　　　　Jerrett Pies
Yarnell Cheese　　　　Tin Recycled
Barnes Culinary　　　Kraft Dairy
Place & Place Products　McMillan Bros.
Rennett Corporation　　Modems for Less

USING THE REFERENCE MANUAL

Retrieve the file CH9REF on the data disk. Use the manuscripts and reports section of the Reference Manual at the back of the book to help you supply the correct information. Save and print.

1. Manuscripts may be _____, _____, or space and one-half.
2. The title is typed _____ and _____ on page 1.
3. For reports bound on the left side, the side margins should be set with the left margin at _____ inch, and the right margin at _____ inch.
4. Subheadings are typed at the _____ margin in all _____ letters.
5. For reports bound at the top, the first page should have a _____-inch top margin.
6. All other report pages except page 1 are numbered at the top _____ margin, _____ lines down.
7. The title page should contain the _____ and _____ of the report.
8. The Table of _____ lists main divisions and page numbers in the report.
9. A _____ is prepared in _____ order to give credit to the sources of information used in the report.
10. The bibliography is usually prepared using _____-spaced lines.

CHAPTER
10

Processing Business Documents

OBJECTIVES

After completing this chapter, you will be able to do the following:

1. List the major parts of a business letter.
2. Describe how a block letter is typed.
3. Describe how a modified block letter is typed.
4. Explain the difference between mixed punctuation and open punctuation.
5. List the major parts of a memorandum.
6. List three different styles used for memorandums.
7. Prepare business envelopes.
8. Make corrections using proofreaders' marks.
9. List the major parts of business reports.
10. List the rules for typing business reports.
11. Prepare an itinerary.
12. Prepare an agenda for a meeting.
13. List the contents of the minutes of a meeting.
14. Type legal forms.
15. Set up a tickler file.

NEW OFFICE TERMS

agenda
appendix
attachment notation
bibliography
block style
body
closing
default margins
enclosure notation
greeting
inside address

itinerary
leaders
memorandums
minutes
mixed punctuation
modified block style
open punctuation
proofreaders' marks
template
tickler file

Bibliography   The **bibliography** is a listing of all sources used to write the report. It includes books, magazines, and newspaper articles. It usually appears at the end of the report.

TYPING RULES

Office workers follow certain procedures when typing the various parts of business reports.

Title Page

◆ Center each line horizontally.
◆ Leave several blank lines between each item (title, name of person the report is for, author, company name, and date). Center the typed lines vertically on the page.

Table of Contents

◆ Center the titles and page numbers both horizontally and vertically.
◆ Depending on the size, either double- or single-space.
◆ Beginning at the left margin, first list the topic number, usually as a roman numeral. On the same line, follow with the name of the topic. On the same line, end with the page number at the right margin.
◆ Use **leaders** (periods) across the space between the topic name and the page number.

Note: Word processing software can automatically perform all these functions.

Body

◆ Usually, double-space the body of the report. However, sometimes you will space-and-a-half a report, leaving a half-space blank line between typed lines. You will seldom single-space a report.
◆ Use a two-inch top margin for the first page and a one-inch top margin for all other pages, a one-inch bottom margin for all pages, and one-inch side margins for all pages.
◆ Type the headings and subheadings at the left margin, in all capital letters.
◆ Type the page number in the center of the page, three lines up from the bottom.

Bibliography

◆ Prepare items in alphabetic order.
◆ For each item, include the name of the author, the publication, the publisher, and the publication date.
◆ Begin the first line of each item at the left margin, and indent all other lines.

◆ Single-space lines.
◆ Use the same margins as in a report.

Travel Arrangement Documents

Angelina is an administrative assistant in the corporate office of a large bank in Chicago. Her boss has to go on a business trip. This is Angelina's first experience in making travel arrangements for her boss.

Angelina learns from another employee that business executives within the company make travel arrangements through a travel agent. The company already has an account established with the agency.

Before Angelina calls the travel agent, she writes down the following information:

◆ where her boss is to go
◆ date of departure and return
◆ class of travel
◆ if hotel accommodations will be needed
◆ if a rental car will be needed

Angelina also looks in her files to learn her boss's preference for seating on the airplane.

Now Angelina is ready to prepare an itinerary for her boss. When her boss returns, she will complete an expense account form for him.

ITINERARY

An **itinerary** is a record of travel plans. It is neatly typed and includes the date and time of departures and arrivals, location of departures and arrivals, transportation means, and hotel accommodations. It may

REVIEW AND APPLICATION

✔ CHECK YOUR KNOWLEDGE

1. What is the inside address of a letter?
2. What does the word *attachment* mean when it appears on a letter?
3. Is "4/18/98" acceptable for the date on a business letter?
4. On a business letter, are the typist's initials in all capital letters?
5. What does "c" mean? Is it always part of a business letter?
6. On a block-style letter, should you type the date at the left margin and the closing in the center?
7. In mixed punctuation, is a comma allowed in the greeting?
8. If you are typing a letter with a word processing program, what margins do you use?
9. Is it acceptable to use the term *Mr.* in a memorandum?
10. When typing a memorandum, how many blank lines are left between the subject and the body?
11. If you are typing with a word processing program, which feature is suggested to be used with the file name?
12. What is a template?
13. If the word *confidential* is to appear on an envelope, where should it be typed?
14. In what format does the post office prefer envelope addresses typed?
15. Does the bibliography come at the beginning of a business report?
16. In a business report, where do you most often find a table that is supplemental to the report?
17. What person is often contacted when making travel arrangements for a business trip?
18. Does an itinerary usually include the price of an airline ticket?
19. List the major headings of an itinerary.
20. List the major parts of an agenda for a meeting.
21. Do the minutes of a meeting usually include the names of the people attending the meeting?
22. Should minutes of meetings be signed?
23. Do all states have the same rules for the typing of legal documents for their courts?
24. How many folders are needed to set up a tickler file? Why?

REVIEW YOUR VOCABULARY

On a separate paper, supply the missing words by choosing from the new Office Terms listed below.

1. A _____ has all parts of the letter typed at the left margin.
2. A _____ has the date and closing typed at the center.
3. In word processing, _____ means to use the margins preset in the program.
4. The main part of a business letter is the _____ of the letter.
5. The word *Sincerely* is used in the _____ of a business letter.
6. The word *Dear* is used in the _____ of a business letter.
7. The word _____ typed on a business letter means you are enclosing something with the letter.
8. In a business report the _____ lists the sources used to write the report.
9. In a business report the _____ contains supplementary information.
10. A _____ contains the words *To, From, Date, Subject.*
11. An _____ is a record of travel plans.
12. Periods that are used in a table of contents to separate topic name from page number are called _____.
13. A _____ is a file that is set up by dates.
14. Using _____ in a business letter means to put a colon after the greeting and a comma after the closing.
15. Using _____ in a business letter means to put no punctuation after the greeting or after the closing.
16. What is to take place during a meeting is listed on an _____.

17. What actually takes place at a meeting is recorded in the _____ of the meeting.
18. A _____ is an electronic file that contains the company's standard format for a particular type of correspondence.

a. agenda
b. appendix
c. attachment notation
d. bibliography
e. block style
f. body
g. closing
h. default margins
i. enclosure
j. greeting
k. inside address
l. itinerary
m. leaders
n. memorandum
o. minutes
p. mixed punctuation
q. modified block style
r. open punctuation
s. proofreaders' marks
t. template
u. tickler file

DISCUSS AND ANALYZE AN OFFICE SITUATION

1. It is Pierre's first day on the job and he is given some letters to type. Pierre wants to impress his employer by not asking questions and just getting the work done. He types the letters in block style because he remembers his teacher in school saying, "All companies use the block style for letters."

   At the end of the day, Pierre is told by his supervisor that the company does not use block style for letters because of the setup of its letterhead. Pierre is asked to redo the letters.

   How could this have been avoided?

PRACTICE BASIC SKILLS

MATH

1. Your boss is planning a meeting for all company supervisors that will be held at a local hotel. Refer to the hotel's Conference Price List given below as you answer these questions:
   a. How much should the breakfast budget be if you order the following?
      2 gallons of coffee
      1 gallon of tea
      40 whole wheat muffins
      3 trays of fresh fruit
   b. How much should the evening budget be if you order the following?
      25 petits fours
      3 dozen Danish cookies
      10 mud pies
      30 soft drinks
   c. You can get 12 slices from the zucchini bread. How much is saved by ordering 4 loaves of zucchini bread instead of 48 whole wheat muffins?
   d. A gallon of coffee serves 16 cups. How many gallons would you order to plan for 70 cups?
   e. A pitcher of orange juice serves 12 glasses. How many pitchers would you order to plan for 90 glasses?

Conference Price List		
MORNING COMBINATIONS		
Item	Quantity	Price
Coffee	Gallon	$20.00
Tea	Gallon	20.00
Orange juice	Pitcher	16.00
Fresh fruit	Tray	19.50
Date nut bread	Loaf	17.50
Zucchini bread	Loaf	17.50
Whole wheat muffins	Each	2.25
EVENING COMBINATIONS		
Item	Quantity	Price
Fresh fruit	Bowl	$15.00
Petits fours	Each	1.50
Soft drinks	Each	1.75
Danish cookies	Dozen	8.00
Fruit punch	Gallon	18.00
Mud pies	Each	1.75

ENGLISH

1. *Rule:* Use a comma to separate dependent clauses.
   Examples: With your help, we will get the task completed by Wednesday. As soon as the machines are repaired, we will return to work.
   Practice Exercise: Rewrite the following sentences, placing commas where needed.
   a. For further information call the toll-free number.

b. During the committee meeting a minor earthquake rattled the room.

c. If you need any further help you may call our service representative.

d. In order to get the job done we will need to call a temporary service.

e. As mentioned last week we will need those three reports typed by 12 noon.

PROOFREADING

Mark the following exercise for corrections, using the proofreaders' marks shown in Table 10.1 on page 231. Then retype it, correcting all.

EARTHQUAKE RECOVERY GUIDELINES

self-help techniques

1. Don't push thoughts and memories of the event away, it is critcial to talk about them.

2. Don't feeel embarrassed about a repetitious need to talk to people. Try family; friends, co-workers, church and social groups. As what others are doing to cope.

3. Keep your life in balance There are pracitcal thing you can do to regain a sense of control over your life.

   a. Know what practical things you can do to be prepared for on-going earthquake strss.

      1. Duck and cover

      2. Stand under a door way

      3. Know emergency routes

      4. Sleep in your clothes, put flashlihgts, wallets, shoes, etc. closeby

5. Follow emergency preparation guidelines in phone book

b. Resume your normal program of activities asquicklyas you can.

c. Pay careful loving attention to your self—eat nutritional foods, get plenty of rest, drink liquids, and increase other self-nurturing activities.

4. Write about your experiences.

5. Increase physical activity.

6. Practice relaxation, meditation or prayer activities.

APPLY YOUR KNOWLEDGE

1. Using word processing software, type and print the sample itinerary on page 224 and the agenda on page 228. Use special features of your software—outlines, graphics, fonts, and so on.

2. Using a memo template from your word processing software, type a memo to your instructor stating where to type the file name on a document and why it is necessary to include the file name.

USING THE REFERENCE MANUAL

1. Use the addressing envelopes section of the Reference Manual at the back of the book to correctly keyboard envelopes for five of your friends. Be sure to include your return address. (You may make up the addresses if necessary.)

2. Keyboard these envelopes on a regular 8½×11-inch paper; however, use the size of a legal envelope as a guide.

3. Save as file CH10REF on your data disk, and print a copy.

Accounting and Other Financial Activities

OBJECTIVES

After completing this chapter, you will be able to do the following:

1. Describe the advantages of a computerized accounting system compared with a manual accounting system.

2. List the components of a computerized accounting system.

3. List accounting and other financial activities that are performed by an office worker.

4. Discuss the purpose of a balance sheet.

5. Interpret the accounting equation Assets = Liabilities + Owner's Equity.

6. Discuss the purpose of an income statement.

7. Interpret the accounting equation Net Income = Revenue − Expenses.

8. Describe the proper banking procedures to follow in depositing, endorsing, and writing checks.

9. Describe the steps to follow in reconciling a bank statement.

10. Describe how an office petty cash fund is set up and maintained.

NEW OFFICE TERMS

accounting cycle	liabilities
assets	net income
balance sheet	owner's equity
computerized accounting system	petty cash payments
expenses	reconciliation
file	record
income statement	revenues

BEFORE YOU BEGIN . . .

Answer the following questions to the best of your ability:

1. What is a computerized accounting system?

2. What types of financial activities do office workers perform?

Business organizations of all types must keep accounting and other financial records. Salesclerks, farmers, factory workers, and owners of businesses all must keep records. Regardless of where you work or the position you accept when you graduate, you will probably have to keep some records as part of your job. Why? One reason is that the government requires businesses to keep records so that certain information is reported to the Internal Revenue Service (IRS) on a periodic basis. Another reason is that accurate records are the basis for sound business decisions.

Maintaining accounting records will probably become an important responsibility of yours at some point in your office career. You might be responsible for a range of financial activities, from taking care of the small amounts of cash needed to run an office on a day-to-day basis to helping an accountant prepare the financial statements essential to the success of a business.

The purpose of this chapter is not to teach you accounting procedures, but to describe what types of accounting systems and financial

OFFICE TIP

When you enter financial information into records, be sure to use the same abbreviations and formats each time. If there are no established procedures for entering information in a consistent manner, help your organization develop them.

◆ *Whether done by hand on ledger sheets or with a computer on electronic spreadsheets, financial records must be accurate.*

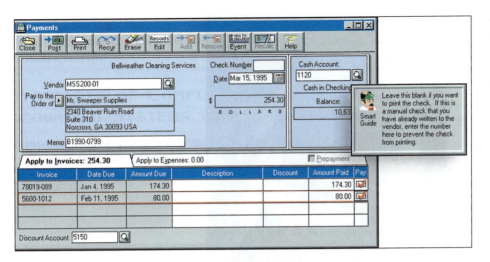

◆ *A knowledge of accounting packages such as Peachtree Accounting for Windows is useful if your job involves handling financial data.*

activities you will find in offices today and how related tasks are typically performed.

Computerized Accounting Systems

Accounting activities may be done by hand and stored on paper. But in today's fast-paced world, most accounting activities are completed with a computer and stored on disk for future updates and revisions. The same financial information is kept in either case. With manual accounting (done by hand), you perform calculations using an electronic calculator; this will be described later in the chapter.

At one time, only the largest organizations could afford computer equipment, which was very expensive. Today, even the smallest businesses can purchase a computer capable of keeping detailed accounting records and switch from their manual accounting systems to computerized accounting systems. A **computerized accounting system** is any set of organized procedures used to collect and record accounting data with the use of a computer. Although there are several accounting software packages, Peachtree Complete Accounting (PCA) by Peachtree Software, Inc., is among the most popular.

It takes a lot of time to maintain accurate business records. Even if there is only one owner-employee, it is sometimes difficult to administer all of the necessary paperwork on schedule. Accounting software helps save time and gives a detailed representation of a company's financial picture. A well-designed accounting system produces reliable information that can be used to prepare financial statements for decision making, and is flexible enough to accommodate additions as the business grows without totally redesigning the system.

To some extent, businesses that thrive maintain accurate, up-to-date records in usable form. This is because competition in business rewards maximum efficiency. Inaccurate accounting records often con-

Office Tip

Computers have reduced the amount of time office workers spend keyboarding forms, but they have not reduced the need for accuracy, neatness, and familiarity with accounting forms and related terminology.

INCOME STATEMENT

An **income statement** is a summary of all income and expenses for a certain time period, such as a month or year. It is probably the most frequently studied of all financial statements. Owners study income statements to determine how much profit they are making. Bankers study income statements to decide whether or not to approve a business loan.

Unlike a balance sheet, which presents a stationary financial picture, an income statement reflects a business's profitability over a given time period. The accounting formula for income statements is as follows:

$$\text{Net Income} = \text{Revenue} - \text{Expenses}$$

Revenues, or income, are all funds an organization raises from the sale of its goods and services. They are generally received in the form of cash payments. Cash, as used in business, may mean currency (bills and coins) or a check drawn on a business or personal checking account.

Expenses are the costs a business incurs as it buys the resources it needs to produce and market its goods and services. They are classified as the cost of goods sold (for manufacturing firms) and as operating expenses, such as salaries, rent, supplies, and utilities.

Net income is the amount of money that remains after expenses are subtracted from revenues. It is commonly called the "bottom line." If an income statement shows that revenues were greater than expenses, the company made a *net profit*. If expenses were greater than revenues, however, the company suffered a *net loss*.

Businesses detect the reasons for increases or decreases in net income by comparing current and previous income statements. This comparison is helpful in making management decisions about future operations, and money management in general.

Suppose the Cap Company has been in business for one year. Over the past year, it has ordered more caps on three occasions and sales are continuing to increase at a steady pace.

These transactions are included on the Cap Company's income statement covering the period November 30, 1997, to November 30 of the following year, as shown below.

The Cap Company						
Income Statement						
For Year Ended November 30, 1998						
Revenue:						
Sales					$1,500	00
Expenses:						
Caps Purchased		$450	00			
Advertising Expense		$ 95	00			
Postage Expense		$ 37	50			
Miscellaneous Expenses		$ 96	00			
Less: Total Expenses					$ 678	50
Net Income					$ 821	50

Recall Time

Answer the following questions:

1. Write the accounting equations for the balance sheet and the income statement.
2. What are the purposes of the balance sheet and the income statement?

Other Financial Activities

As an office worker, you can expect to complete certain types of financial activities. Among those you are likely to perform are banking tasks and petty cash fund maintenance tasks. The tool you will likely use is the ten-key calculator.

USING THE TEN-KEY CALCULATOR

The ten-key calculator has the capacity to solve numerical problems manually with great speed. Calculators can be either printing or display machines. Printing calculators print numbers on a paper tape. Display calculators display numbers as illuminated figures on a screen. It is possible to combine and use both techniques with a printing-display calculator.

When you learn to operate an electronic calculator with the touch system, the technique, speed, and accuracy you develop can easily be transferred to other machines. For example, most PC keyboards have a special ten-key section on the right side. If you were a computer data entry clerk at a local bank, you would probably be paid based on the number of keystrokes entered from a ten-key pad.

The basic rule for learning touch operation is to not look at your fingers while depressing the number keys. The ten-key pad is operated with the four fingers of the right hand. The home keys are 4, 5, and 6. These are the starting positions for any key from 1 to 9. You make your reaches up or down from the three home keys. Many businesspeople consider being able to touch-operate a ten-key pad as important as being able to touch-type at a keyboard.

Here is a quick lesson on touch operation. Place your fingers on the home keys, as shown in Figure 11.2. On most calculators and computers, key 5 has a raised dot or line, which you can easily feel. This elevation makes the starting home row position readily identified by touch.

The finger used to depress home key 4 is used to reach up to key 7 and down to key 1. The second finger is used to depress home key 5 and also to reach up to key 8 and down to key 2. And finally, the finger used to depress home key 6 reaches up to key 9 and down to key 3. On the computer keypad, the right thumb is used for the zero key.

Your accuracy and speed will naturally improve with practice, if your technique is correct and you keep your eyes on the problem.

◆ *If you work with financial records, your ability to operate a ten-key calculator or pad is as important as your skill with a computer keyboard.*

FIGURE 11.2 ◆ Correct Hand Position at an Electronic Calculator

Index Finger	Middle Finger	Ring Finger
7	8	9
4	5	6
1	2	3
0		.

Thumb

BANKING TASKS

Most businesses put cash receipts in a bank and make cash payments by check. They do this because money, consisting of bills and coins, is not as safe as many other assets. Care must be taken in handling money because it can be transferred easily from one person to another with no questions asked. Unfortunately, in most cases, ownership is determined by the person having the money.

For these and other reasons, businesses keep most of their cash-on-hand in a bank and use various banking services. Banking services are safe, convenient, and provide great accuracy in maintaining cash records for businesses. A business depends on banking services to verify accounting records, to compare the business's records of checks written with the bank's records of checks paid, and to transfer cash electronically using *electronic funds transfer* (EFT). With EFT, businesses can electronically make payments and deposits and conduct other banking transactions quickly and in a timely manner with this "paperless" transfer of funds.

Let's review some common banking terms you will encounter while processing banking tasks:

◆ Placing cash in a bank account is called *making a deposit.*
◆ A person or business in whose name cash is deposited is called a *depositor.*

At lunch one day, a discussion takes place that makes Justine feel very uncomfortable. Andy, Heather, Ron, and Shujian are sitting at her table. They are co-workers that Justine has grown to know over the past year while working at a large insurance company in Milwaukee.

The four co-workers are laughing and joking about how easy it is these days for employees to steal from companies and supplement a small paycheck. Heather says she heard on TV of how a computer programmer established a separate personal checking account that received all the half-cents and lesser amounts from payroll checks. This programmer made more money than he could have imagined.

Shujian tells about a friend who works for a charity organization. This friend told Shujian that periodically, when cash is received through the mail, she will pocket the donation. Shujian agrees with her friend that this practice isn't bad because the amounts are only $5 and $10 and too small to help out anyway.

Other examples are shared during lunch in Justine's presence. That afternoon, Justine can't get the discussion off her mind. It really bothers her.

1. *Would the discussion have bothered you as it did Justine? If you were Justine, would you have said anything to the four co-workers about how you felt?*

2. *What are some results of this behavior for organizations? Are these attitudes commonplace in today's society? Explain your response.*

◆ A bank account from which payments are ordered by the depositor is called a *checking account.*
◆ A *check* is a business paper used to make payments from a checking account.
◆ *Endorsing a check* is signing your name or a company's name on the back of a check in order to transfer the check to a bank or to someone else.

In an office, you may perform three common banking tasks. These tasks are depositing checks that have been properly endorsed, writing checks, and reconciling monthly bank statements.

Preparing Deposits   To prepare deposits, you follow three steps: (1) endorse all checks to be deposited, (2) fill out the deposit slip, and (3) record the deposit in the check register.

When you deposit a check in a checking account, you must transfer it to your bank by signing your name on the back of the check. This procedure is called endorsing the check. You can use three endorsements: blank, restrictive, or full. A *blank endorsement* is a signature-only endorsement. A *restrictive endorsement* restricts the use of the check. Many businesses and individuals write "for deposit only" to ensure that the check amount will only be deposited and not cashed. A *full endorsement* names the party to whom a check is transferred. Figure 11.3 shows examples of acceptable endorsements.

When you deposit a check, you must list it on a deposit slip along with any bills and coins for deposit, as shown in Figure 11.4. Be sure

FIGURE 11.3 ◆ a) Paycheck for Patrick Reynolds
b) Sample Check Endorsements

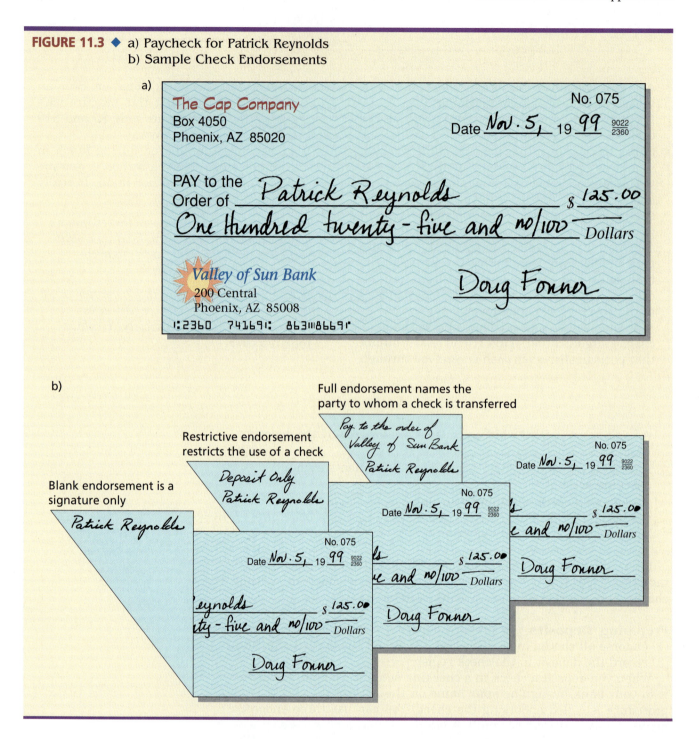

to enter the total amount of the deposit in the check register and add it to the old balance to find your new checkbook balance.

Writing Checks   Some checks have two parts: the stub or NCR (no carbon required) tissue copy, which remains in the checkbook, and the check itself, which is sent to the person to whom you owe money. The

FIGURE 11.4 ◆ Sample Deposit Slip with a Check Listed

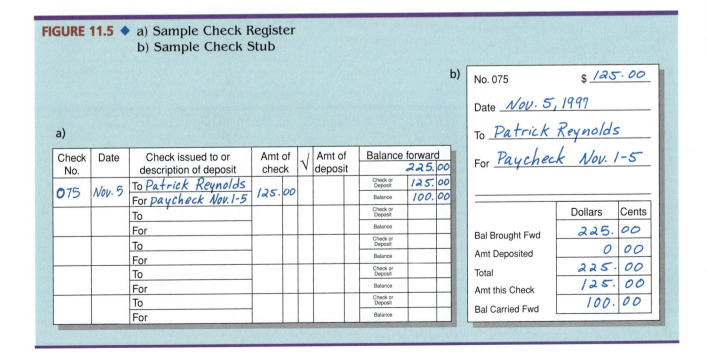

stub or copy gives a record of the important facts about a check. The tissue copy shows all the information; however, if your check has a stub, always fill out the stub first before writing a check so that you will have a clear record of the check. Some checks do not have stubs; you can also keep track of the details of checks you write by using a check register (see Figure 11.5). A check register contains a listing of each check that was written and each deposit made.

If a business writes many checks, it's a good idea to use a machine known as a check writer or check protector. This machine prints the

FIGURE 11.5 ◆ a) Sample Check Register
b) Sample Check Stub

OFFICE TIP

If you are unable to locate errors while reconciling a bank statement, you can call the bank for assistance. If you find the bank has made an error in entering amounts of money, notify the bank as soon as possible.

amount on a check in a way that makes changes to the check amount impossible without being detected. Today, businesses are increasingly preparing their checks using computerized systems.

Reconciling Bank Statements   Reconciling a bank statement is a common task for an office worker. The purpose of this procedure is to bring your company's checkbook balance and a bank statement balance into agreement.

Usually, the bank sends a monthly statement that summarizes all checking account transactions. It lists all checks processed and paid by the bank, all deposits recorded, and any service fees charged.

When you receive a bank statement, compare either your check stubs or your check register entries to the bank's summary. This procedure is called **reconciliation.** Banks usually provide a reconciliation form on the back of the monthly statement. Figure 11.6 shows a sample reconciliation form for the Cap Company. Here are the steps to follow to reconcile a bank statement:

1. Compare the amounts of all deposits shown on the bank statement with the deposit amounts you recorded on the check stubs or in the check register.
2. Arrange the canceled checks (if they have been returned to you) in numerical order by check number.
3. Compare the amounts of the canceled checks with the amounts entered on the stubs or in the check register. Make a small check mark on the stub if a canceled check has been returned and the amounts agree. Stubs that are not checkmarked represent checks that were not returned by the bank. These are called outstanding checks.
4. Prepare the bank reconciliation form (usually on the back of the monthly bank statement). Outstanding checks and any service

FIGURE 11.6 ◆ Sample Bank Reconciliation Form

The Cap Company Bank Reconciliation Form December 31, 1999					
Checkbook balance	525	00	Bank balance	607	00
			Less: o/s checks		
			#129	525	00
Adjusted chkbk balance			Adjusted bank bal	82	00

fees should be deducted from the total and unprocessed deposits added to give a true picture of what is in the account.

PETTY CASH FUND MAINTENANCE TASKS

Businesses must keep careful records of all money they spend. This is true for payments made both by check and with currency. Although businesses prefer to make payments by check, it is often necessary (and easier) to pay with currency. If you buy postage stamps for the office or gas for a company delivery truck, for example, you may have to use currency. Because these payments are in small, or "petty," amounts, they are called **petty cash payments.**

A business normally keeps all its cash in a checking account. Thus, the currency needed for these petty cash payments is usually obtained by writing and cashing a check. The amount of the check is an estimate of how much money will be needed for a certain time period, such as a week or month. After cashing the check, the office places this currency in a container called a *petty cash box.*

Let's assume you work for Ms. Larson and she puts you in charge of the petty cash fund. Ms. Larson starts the petty cash fund by cashing a check for $75. Here are the steps you, as the petty cash clerk, will follow in handling a typical transaction.

Al, your company's delivery person, comes to you and needs $10 to fix a flat tire on the delivery truck. You first fill out a *petty cash voucher.* This is a receipt that verifies that Al received $10 in cash. When Al returns with a receipt for the tire repair, you staple the petty cash voucher and the tire repair receipt together. At the end of the day, you count the currency, total the petty cash vouchers in the box, and enter the information in the petty cash book. A petty cash book records receipts and disbursements. With Al's transaction, your petty cash balance will look like this:

Total of vouchers in box	$10
Plus cash in box	$65
Equals original fund	$75

This simple example balances, but sometimes the petty cash fund does not. A *cash shortage* occurs when the actual currency in the petty cash box is less than the balance shown in the petty cash book. A *cash overage* occurs when the actual currency in the petty cash box is more than the balance shown in the petty cash book. The goal is to make petty cash balance. If it doesn't, then something is wrong—you have accounted for either too much or too little money. If this happens, you should record any discrepancies in the petty cash book and correct the balances.

When the petty cash fund runs low, you remove all vouchers from the box, add them, and give them to Ms. Larson. She then gives you enough cash to replenish the fund back up to the regular amount of $75.

Ethics on the Job

Suppose you are in charge of the petty cash fund for a company and your best friend, who works at the same company, is down on her luck and needs $20 for a few days. She asks you to loan it to her out of petty cash. No one will likely find out about it.

What will you do?

REVIEW AND APPLICATION

✔ CHECK YOUR KNOWLEDGE

1. How is using a computerized accounting system similar to using a manual accounting system?
2. Relative to computerized accounting, what are records and files?
3. Describe what *business assets, liabilities,* and *owner's equity* mean in reference to the preparation of a balance sheet.
4. Describe what revenue and expense items might include when preparing an income statement.
5. When might an office worker use a ten-key calculator?
6. What steps must be followed to deposit and endorse checks properly?
7. Briefly describe the steps involved in reconciling a bank statement.
8. What is the procedure to set up and maintain an office petty cash fund?

 REVIEW YOUR VOCABULARY

On a separate paper, match the following by writing the letter of each vocabulary word next to the number of its description.

____ 1. is the claim that an owner has against the firm's assets
____ 2. is any set of organized procedures used to collect and record accounting data with the use of a computer
____ 3. shows the financial condition of a business at a particular time
____ 4. involves recording, classifying, and summarizing financial information
____ 5. is a summary of all income and expenses for a certain period of time, such as a month or year
____ 6. is the amount of money that remains after expenses are subtracted from revenues
____ 7. is the comparison of either the check stubs or the check register entries to the bank's summary of activity

____ 8. cash payments for small amounts made from an office fund
____ 9. are a business's financial obligations or debts
____ 10. is comprised of fields and stores information about one employee, one inventory item, one account, and so forth
____ 11. all funds an organization raises from the sale of its goods and services
____ 12. everything of value that a company owns
____ 13. is a group of records
____ 14. are the costs a business incurs as it buys the resources it needs to produce and market its goods and services

a. accounting cycle
b. assets
c. balance sheet
d. owner's equity
e. computerized accounting system
f. expenses
g. file

h. income statement
i. liabilities
j. net income
k. petty cash payments
l. reconciliation
m. record
n. revenues

 DISCUSS AND ANALYZE AN OFFICE SITUATION

Cecilia is a new secretary in the accounting department at Federated Foods. This is her third job this year. She is sure this is a nice place to work because the people here seem to like her.

Cecilia uses a PC to do word processing tasks for the first two weeks on the job. She is looking forward to entering accounting transactions using the general ledger accounting software.

Mr. Ziede is manager of the accounting department. He is concerned, because almost one-fourth of the correspondence Cecilia has completed so far has been returned because of spelling or general typing errors. What is most perplexing to Mr. Ziede is that Cecilia doesn't see any problems with her skills. It almost seems that she doesn't care. Cecilia's normal response is that mistakes are easy to fix with a computer, and if she doesn't see an error, someone else will point it out to her.

Mr. Ziede is sure that he will not permit Cecilia to enter accounting data in the computer. But the immediate problem is whether he should keep her on the job. Cecilia is a nice person, but she is unobservant and fails to recognize errors or problems. Mr. Ziede knows that this attitude cannot be allowed in the accounting department.

1. If you were Mr. Ziede, what actions would you take?
2. If Mr. Ziede decides to counsel Cecilia, what should he say?

PRACTICE BASIC SKILLS

MATH

1. Complete the bank reconciliation form below on a separate paper. (Follow the instructions on page 258 and note Figure 11.6.)

Cookies by Blanche			
Bank Reconciliation Form			
May 31, 1998			
Checkbook balance	$5	92	25
Less: service charge		5	60
Adjusted checkbook balance		?	
Bank balance	$6	74	25
Add: outstanding deposits	1	05	00
Less: outstanding checks			
#152	$	90	00
#155	$1	02	60
Total outstanding checks		?	
Adjusted bank balance		?	

2. Practice the touch method by adding the following columns of figures using an electronic calculator. A good way to check each answer is to add the numbers again in the opposite direction. Write your answers on a separate paper.

(1) 45 (2) 55 (3) 656 (4) 333 (5) 444 (6) 7878
     33   66   333   222   234   5896
     65   35   456   654   699   4485
     58   47   699   411   544   8644

ENGLISH

Purchase orders often use abbreviations to save space on forms. Write the meanings of the following abbreviations next to their letters on a separate paper. Refer to an office reference book if you aren't sure of a meaning.

(a) c/o
(b) COD
(c) dept
(d) doz
(e) gal
(f) pkg
(g) ea
(h) @
(i) min
(j) max
(k) qty

PROOFREADING

Find and correct misspellings and incorrect punctuation in the following letter. Rewrite it on a separate paper.

David James
15208 N. 25th Place
Monterey, CA 94039

Dear Mr. James;
    I appreciate the information you sent and that I recieved yesterday. In replay to your inquery about activitey tickets, you may contact the following people and they may be able to help you;; Brooke, Kristy & Daniel.
    If I can be of furrther service to you, please call me.

Sincerly yours

Melissa Christine

APPLY YOUR KNOWLEDGE

1. Below are examples of balance sheet items. On a separate paper, write next to the letter of each example the letter *A* if it is an asset account and the letter *L* if it is a liability account.

(a) office supplies
(b) cash
(c) notes payable (City Bank)
(d) accounts payable (Smith's Furniture)
(e) merchandise
(f) office equipment
(g) accounts receivable (May Johnson)
(h) accounts receivable (Della L. Fry)
(i) accounts payable (Republic Supply Company)
(j) FICA tax payable

2. Below are examples of income statement items. On a separate paper, write next to the letter of

each example the letter *R* if it is a revenue account and the letter *E* if it is an expense account.

(a) advertising expense
(b) secretarial fees collected
(c) sales of office supplies
(d) salary expense
(e) advertising expense

(f) sale of caps
(g) postage expense
(h) miscellaneous expenses
(i) selling expenses
(j) attorney fees collected

USING THE REFERENCE MANUAL

Retrieve the file CH11REF on the data disk. Use the grammar section of the Reference Manual at the back of the book to key the rule for each sentence underneath it. Save and print.

1. There are three 5¼" disks left over.
2. Pick me up by 7:30 a.m. so I won't be late.
3. The project took a total of fifteen hours from start to finish.
4. Nine persons were present for the committee meeting on school spirit.
5. There will be hundreds of spectators at the parade.
6. My sister lives on Ninth Street, but my brother lives on 83rd Avenue.
7. Do you see the glass as one-half full or one-half empty?
8. The room measured 16 feet by 24 feet.
9. The deficit is in the billions.
10. The class must have three more students to make full enrollment.

Sending and Receiving Mail

OBJECTIVES

After completing this chapter, you will be able to do the following:

1. List and explain four procedures for sorting mail in an office.
2. Describe how to arrange mail before presenting it to an employer.
3. List and explain the major classifications of outgoing mail.
4. List and describe postal equipment used in an office.
5. Use a ZIP code directory to locate ZIP codes.

NEW OFFICE TERMS

annotating mail
bar code sorter (BCS)
centralized mail department
confidential mail

priority mail
routing mail
sorting mail

At 9 a.m. in a city on the East Coast, Vivian starts her day by sorting the mail in the mail processing department of a large corporation. At the same time in a town in the South, Maynard begins to sort the mail for his three bosses in the accounting department of a small firm. Vivian is a mail clerk and Maynard is an administrative assistant. Both know the procedures for processing mail. When you begin to work in a business office, you also must know the procedures for processing incoming and outgoing mail.

In a large company, mail may be processed in a **centralized mail department.** The employees in this department are responsible for all the mail that comes in or goes out of the company. At various times during the day, they distribute incoming mail to all the company personnel and pick up mail that is to be sent out. They also distribute interoffice correspondence (mail sent to and from offices within the company).

A small company may not have a centralized mail department. In this case, an office employee receives the mail when it is delivered each day by a postal carrier. Once the mail is received, certain procedures are followed for processing it.

Incoming Mail

The procedures for processing incoming mail include the following:

◆ sorting the mail
◆ opening the mail
◆ date and time stamping the mail
◆ reading and annotating the mail, if your boss prefers
◆ other helpful procedures
◆ arranging the mail for your boss

SORTING THE MAIL

In office terms, **sorting mail** means arranging or separating mail according to the kind it is and who is to receive it; for example, separating letters from magazines, and the manager's mail from the supervisor's mail.

◆ *This is what the mail room for a large company might look like. Notice the wooden mail slots where the mail is put for each department or person.*

Before you begin the process of sorting the mail, clear a work area on your desk. You do not want the mail to be lost or mixed up with other papers. Push all clutter aside and concentrate on this one project.

You may handle the mail for more than one boss or for more than one department. If so, first sort the mail for each person or for each department. It is easy to do this by sorting into individually marked folders or trays. Once this is done, sort the mail within the individual trays by grouping it into piles of correspondence, advertisements and circulars (papers intended for wide distribution), and magazines and newspapers.

As you are sorting, you may notice mail that has been delivered to your company in error. First, check with your boss to see if the mail belongs to anyone within the company. If not, cross out the incorrect address, write "Not at this address" on the envelope, and put it into the outgoing mail. Only first-class mail will be forwarded without adding extra postage. *First-class mail* is mail that will generally be delivered overnight to locally designated cities and in two days to locally designated states. These areas are selected by the post office.

OPENING THE MAIL

Many office workers are asked to open the mail for their bosses. This does not necessarily mean they are to read the mail. At some companies, an office worker uses a letter opener to open the mail and then places the mail on the boss's desk. At other companies, an office worker is required to remove the contents from the envelope. It is always best to check company policy for the proper procedure.

Before beginning to open the mail, separate all letters that say Confidential or Personal. These letters are **confidential mail** and should be opened only by the person to whom they are addressed. It is a good

idea to assume that a letter written in longhand is personal and should also be opened only by the person to whom it is addressed. If you open a personal letter in error, be certain to write on the envelope "Sorry, opened by mistake." Sign your name or initials and tape the letter closed.

It is helpful to have all necessary supplies ready before opening the mail. You will need a letter opener, a stapler, a pencil, and some paper clips.

Once you have opened the mail, your boss may want you to remove the contents from the envelopes. If so, do the following:

◆ If the address of the sender is not on a letter, staple or paper clip the envelope to the letter.
◆ Check the bottom of each letter for the words *enclosure* or *attached*. If you see one of these words, check to see that the material is included. If not, make a pencil notation on the letter that the enclosures were not in the envelope when it was opened.
◆ Use a paper clip to attach enclosed material to the back of the letters.
◆ Put all the envelopes aside until you have finished sorting the mail. You may have to check for overlooked contents or addresses.
◆ If a letter is undated, write the postmarked date from the envelope onto the letter.

DATE AND TIME STAMPING THE MAIL

Have you ever received an announcement of an event after it had taken place? This may have happened because the letter was temporarily lost during transit or because the announcement sat unopened in your house for a few days.

Mail is sometimes received late in a business office. For this reason, companies ask the person who processes the mail to put a date and time on the letters to show when they were received. This is usually done with a rubber stamp, but it can also be done with a pen.

Why are companies concerned with the exact date the mail is received? One reason is to prove if a payment is late, or a person has not met a payment deadline. A time difference may exist between the date a letter was received and the date the letter was typed.

Another reason is to prove if a person has met the application deadline for a job. Many civil service jobs have deadlines by which applications must be received. If a person does not meet the deadline, she or he will not be considered for the job.

READING AND ANNOTATING THE MAIL

Chiara Briganti is a busy executive for a management consulting firm. To save time, she has her administrative assistant read and annotate the mail each day. **Annotating mail** means underlining important facts and making comments or special notations in the margin of a letter. Examples of facts to underline are model numbers, prices, and

Large Office/Small Office: What's Your Preference?

MAIL

If you did a survey in your area, you would find that some large offices have their own mail rooms where all the processing of the mail takes place. You would also find that the duties of the mail-room employees include only the processing of incoming and outgoing mail and the distribution of interoffice mail. Since many pieces of mail must be handled daily in these large offices, you would find automatic letter openers and sorting equipment in addition to the standard postage meters and scales.

A survey of small offices would give you a slightly different view of the role of office workers in the handling of mail. In a small office, the mail processing is done by a variety of office support staff, who handle the mail in addition to their other clerical duties. Your survey would show the receptionist, office support worker, secretary, and other clerical employees processing the mail for themselves and for their bosses. It would also show that the postal equipment in a small office is usually limited to a postage meter and scale.

Would you like to begin your office career as a mail-room clerk for a large company? Why or why not? Do you like the idea of having someone else handle your mail for you, or would you prefer making occasional trips to the mail room to process your own mail?

meeting dates. An example of a notation you may write in the margin is that you verified that your boss has no other meetings on the date in question.

See Figure 12.1 on page 273 for a sample of an annotated letter. Note how Ms. Briganti's administrative assistant underlined the date, time, and place of the luncheon meeting. She also made a notation in the margin that no conflicting appointments were scheduled on this date. Can you see how valuable this process could be for a busy executive?

Recall Time

Answer the following questions:

1. What are three duties of the employees in a centralized mail department?

2. What are the procedures for processing incoming mail?

3. Alexandra is an office support person for a small firm. One of her duties is opening her bosses' mail. She opens a letter that is marked Confidential. What should she do?

(Continued on next page.)

Recall Time continued

4. If you were sorting the mail into piles, what three groupings might you use?

5. You open a business letter for your boss. The letter does not have a return address on it. What should you do?

OTHER HELPFUL PROCEDURES

Office workers use many other procedures to help their bosses process the daily mail. Some examples are attaching related materials, using action-requested slips, saving advertisements and circulars, keeping an outgoing mail record, routing mail, and accepting special mail.

Attaching Related Material   Frequently, before your boss can respond to or take action on a particular piece of correspondence, he or she will need to see other documents. In these cases, you will be helping your boss a great deal if you attach any related material to the letters. You may attach previous correspondence or the file folder that correlates with a letter.

For example, Ken is an insurance clerk for an automobile insurance company. A client writes to his boss concerning an accident. After opening the letter and before giving it to his boss, Ken will attach the client's file folder to the letter.

Using Action-Requested Slips   If you process and forward lots of mail for your boss, it is helpful to use action-requested slips. You can either purchase these from a stationery store or create them yourself. A sample is shown in Figure 12.2 on page 274. You simply check the action you wish to be taken.

Saving Advertisements and Circulars   It may be advantageous to save some of that so-called junk mail. This is a good way for you and your boss to notice trends in new products. These circulars may be particularly helpful to the advertising department, which is always looking for new ideas and also wants to see what the competition has to offer.

If you or your company is concerned about helping save the environment, you may also put this junk mail in a special box. When the box is full, you can deposit it at a recycling center. You can recycle other items in addition to advertisements. Call your local recycling center for more information.

Keeping an Outgoing Mail Record   Many companies have found it helpful to keep a daily record of all the mail they send out that requires another person outside the company to take action. The office support staff can refer to this record on a regular basis and do any necessary follow-up when action is supposed to occur.

Ethics on the Job

Tomeko works as a "floater" in a large law firm. Because of her excellent computer skills, she works in various departments when needed. One day while working in the law library, she deleted a file from the company database by mistake. Since she only occasionally works in this department, no one will know she deleted the file.

If you were Tomeko, would you tell your supervisor that you had made an error and deleted the file? Why or why not?

FIGURE 12.1 ◆ Sample Annotated Letter

Stonehill Chamber of Commerce
345 Alpine Terrace
Stonehill, NH 03062-6211
(333) 543-9876

May 15, 1998

Chiara Briganti
HiTech Associates
45 Tower Place
Stonehill, NH 03062-3252

Date O.K.
no conflict

Dear Ms. Briganti:

Congratulations! You have been selected to receive our annual
Woman Of the Year Award for your dedication to the business
community. All our members agree that you deserve this award.

The award will be presented to you at our annual luncheon
awards meeting Thursday, June 25, 12 Noon at the Pines
Conference Center. Please confirm that you will attend by
contacting Rose Perez.

Sincerely,

Rosylin Thomas

Rosylin Thomas
Awards Committee

cb

Figure 12.3 on page 274 shows a sample of an outgoing mail register. In the Description column, you will record the name of the company to which each letter is going, the subject of the letter, and the actual date of the letter. The date column is for the date of the entry (usually the date mailed).

Routing Mail   It may be necessary for certain magazines, reports, and special documents to be seen by more than one person in the company. The most efficient way to handle this situation is by routing the mail. **Routing mail** means attaching a routing slip to correspondence and then having each person initial the routing slip after she or he has read it.

A routing slip is usually a preprinted form that is commonly used by businesses. See the sample in Figure 12.4 on page 275.

FIGURE 12.2 ◆ Sample Action-Requested Slip

☐ For your approval

☐ For your comments

☐ Please forward

☐ Please return

☐ Note and file

☐ _____

Accepting Special Mail　Mail is sometimes delivered by express mail, by a messenger, or by a private delivery service. If the mail is delivered to you and it is your job to sign the required receipt for it, you should be certain the addressee (person to whom the mail is addressed) works for your company, sign the required mail receipt, and bring the mail immediately to the addressee. This type of mail delivery denotes important information.

FIGURE 12.3 ◆ Sample Mail Register

MAIL REGISTER

DATE	DESCRIPTION	TO WHOM	ACTION TO TAKE	FOLLOW UP
6/25	Perry Walker Brothers	Perry Walker	Confirm	

FIGURE 12.4 ◆ Sample Routing Slip

ROUTING SLIP

(initial after reading)

Foster, J. ———

Morales, E. ———

Prentice, B. ———

Shapiro, W. ———

Bala, M. (last) ———

Arranging the Mail for Your Boss

Before putting the mail on your boss's desk, arrange it according to importance. Check your boss's preference; the following arrangement is acceptable for most executives. The first item listed is on the top of the stack and the last item listed is on the bottom of the stack.

◆ confidential and personal letters
◆ correspondence from outside the company
◆ interoffice correspondence
◆ advertisements
◆ newspapers and magazines

The mail is usually placed in the boss's in-basket and any parcels are put in a separate pile on the desk.

Outgoing Mail

Office workers use many procedures for processing outgoing mail. A few examples are assembling the mail, selecting classifications for the mail, using the U.S. Postal Service, using private delivery services, using postal equipment, following mailing guidelines, and packing for mailing.

ASSEMBLING THE MAIL

No letter should be mailed from a business without the proper signature. One of your responsibilities might be to prepare outgoing mail for your boss. Since getting the boss's signature on letters is one of the last steps of the procedure, you should have the envelopes ready as well when you present them to him or her. Place the flaps of the envelopes over the front of the letters and attach paper clips over the flap of each.

Most employers want their mail to get out as quickly as possible, so place any letter needing a signature on your boss's desk in an area where it will easily be seen. Check back on a regular basis to see if the letter has been signed so that you can proceed with the next step.

Once a letter has been signed, bring it back to your desk and prepare it for mailing. However, before you proceed, double-check the following:

◆ Has the letter been signed?
◆ Are enclosures included with the letter?
◆ Is the address on the letter the same as the address on the envelope?
◆ Make one last check—did you miss any errors or did your boss make any further changes?

Once all this has been confirmed, fold the letter and insert it into the envelope. Figure 12.5 shows how to fold a full-size ($8\frac{1}{2}$-×-11-inch) letterhead into a legal-size (long) envelope.

If you have enclosures to go with a letter, do the following: If the enclosures are the same size as the letter, fold and insert them with the letter itself. If they are smaller than the letter, staple them to the top left of the letter. If they are bigger than the letter, mail them in a large manila envelope with the letter unfolded and inserted as the first page on top of the enclosures.

SELECTING CLASSIFICATIONS FOR THE MAIL

Melanie has just been employed as a mail clerk for a large law firm. She is quite confused about which classification to use for all the outgoing mail. Her supervisor explains that the final decision is based upon which way is most efficient. She should make this decision for each particular piece of mail by asking, Should this item be delivered to the destination as quickly as possible, or can money be saved by using a slower, but less expensive, means of delivery? Melanie's supervisor also tells her that she can better understand mailing classifications by reading the U.S. Postal Service's *Consumer's Guide to Postal Services and Products*. In this guide, an office worker can find information on the various classifications of mail: First Class, Priority, Express Mail, Standard Mail (A), Standard Mail (B), and Periodicals.

First Class   Use first-class mail for letters, postcards, and postal cards. First-class mail must weigh twelve ounces or less. If first-class mail is not letter size, make sure it is marked First Class.

FIGURE 12.5 ◆ Steps Office Workers Use to Fold and Insert Outgoing Mail

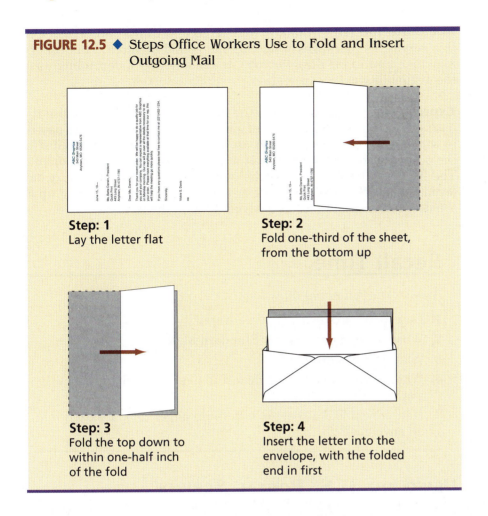

Step: 1
Lay the letter flat

Step: 2
Fold one-third of the sheet, from the bottom up

Step: 3
Fold the top down to within one-half inch of the fold

Step: 4
Insert the letter into the envelope, with the folded end in first

First-class mail will generally be delivered overnight to locally designated cities and in two days to locally designated states. Delivery by the third day can be expected for the remaining outlying areas.

Priority   **Priority mail** is first-class letter mail and packages weighing more than twelve ounces. The maximum weight for priority mail is seventy pounds. Free priority mail stickers are available from your local post office.

Periodicals   Only publishers and registered news agents who have been approved for Periodicals mailing privileges may mail at the periodicals rates of postage. This classification allows them to send large mailings at a reduced rate.

Standard Mail (A)   This classification is also referred to as bulk business mail or advertising mail. It may be sent by anyone, but it is used most often by large mailers. Nonprofit agencies such as chambers of commerce or church groups may also use it. This class includes printed material and merchandise weighing less than sixteen ounces and requires a minimum of 200 pieces per mailing.

Standard Mail (B)   Standard Mail (B) is also called parcel post. Use this service for packages weighing one pound or more. This service may take up to nine days for coast-to-coast delivery, depending upon the availability of transportation.

Express Mail   Express mail is the fastest mail service. It is also the most expensive one. Express mail guarantees delivery the next day, or in some cases, the same day. To use it, take the item to be mailed to the post office by 5 p.m. or deposit it in an express mail collection box. The item will be delivered to the addressee by 3 p.m. the next day (even if it is a Saturday, Sunday, or holiday), or it can be picked up at the destination post office as early as 10 a.m. the next day.

Recall Time

Answer the following questions:

1. How fast is first-class mail delivered?
2. What is another name for Standard Mail (A)?
3. What is Standard Mail (B)?
4. What is the name for the fastest mail service? Explain how it works.
5. How do you fold a sheet of letter-size paper to be inserted into an envelope?

USING THE U.S. POSTAL SERVICE

In the *Consumer's Guide to Postal Services and Products,* Melanie reads about the other options available through the postal service. These include certificates of mailing, certified mail, collect on delivery, return receipts, insurance, registered mail, international mail, and other services.

Certificates of Mailing   A certificate of mailing proves an item was mailed. It does not provide insurance coverage for loss or damage.

Certified Mail   Certified mail provides a mailing receipt, and a record of delivery is maintained at the recipient's post office. For an additional fee, the sender can also buy a return receipt to provide proof of delivery. Certified mail can be applied only to first-class or priority mail.

Collect on Delivery   Use collect-on-delivery (COD) service if you are sending merchandise and you want to collect the money owed for its purchase when it is delivered.

Return Receipts   A return receipt is a sender's proof of delivery. It shows who signed for an item and the date of delivery.

MAKING OFFICE DECISIONS

Mike is working as an administrative assistant to the vice president of the legal department of a large corporation. In his department are five other clerical workers—an office services assistant, a researcher, and three general office clerks. Mike's status as an administrative assistant is much higher than the status of the other office workers. He has more responsibility and gets paid more money.

It is late Thursday afternoon, and Mike has his usual work to get done. He has no urgent work, but enough to keep him busy.

A general office clerk is stuffing and sealing envelopes for a large mailing that must be in tonight's mail. The clerk is complaining that the mail may not get done in time.

Should Mike help with the envelopes, or should he continue with his own work? Explain your answer.

Insurance   Insurance can be purchased on registered mail up to a maximum replacement value of $25,000. It is also available up to $600 for Standard Mail (A and B).

Registered Mail   Registered mail is the most secure option offered by the postal service. It provides added protection for valuable and important mail. Registered articles are controlled from the point of mailing to delivery. First-class or priority mail postage is required on registered mail.

International Mail   Airmail and surface mail can be sent to virtually all foreign countries. Five types of international mail are provided: letters and cards, other articles, parcel post, express, and global priority mail. Limited registry service and insurance are available. Information on international mail regulations can be found in *The International Mail Manual,* sold by the U.S. Government Printing Office.

Intelpost   Intelpost (International Electronic Post) is an international facsimile message service available between the United States and more than forty foreign countries. A black and white image of the document (text and/or graphics) is printed and delivered in the destination country. The document you are sending can be hand-delivered to the postal service or sent by fax or computer. Depending on your choice of delivery option, your facsimile message is delivered either the same day or the next day.

Easy Stamp Services   The Postal Service has made it more convenient than ever to buy stamps with EASY STAMP services. Businesses now can choose from the following options to purchase stamps: by mail, by phone, from vending machines, and by computer. Prepackaged stamps are also now sold at the checkout line of many stores, such as pharmacies, grocery stores, gift and card shops, and independent mailing services.

Other Services   Other services available through the U.S. Postal Service include passport applications, money orders, and postage meters.

Customer Service   If you have questions that aren't answered by the *Consumer's Guide to Postal Services and Products,* you can call the customer service line at the National Postal Center, 1-800-275-8777. With this number you can get ZIP codes, rates, hours of local post offices, and tracking and ordering information. Certain questions can be answered through their automated phone system, and others will be handled by a real live customer service representative.

Information on the Internet   A wealth of information is available at your fingertips when you visit the Postal Service Web site on the Internet at http://www.usps.gov. You can look up ZIP+4 codes, get information on the latest postal rates, and find answers to frequently asked questions.

USING DELIVERY SERVICES

◆ *Private delivery services such as these companies are frequently used by businesses. The services include convenient pickup and delivery.*

Many office workers have found that it is sometimes more convenient or cost effective to use a private delivery service. These companies deliver parcels by truck within a city or by airplane to other cities or countries. Firms that specialize in delivery services usually offer the convenience of pickup and delivery. You can locate these firms by looking in the Yellow Pages of your telephone book. Examples of companies that you might find are United Parcel Service (UPS), Federal Express, Airborne, and DHL Worldwide.

In large cities, private messenger services are used even to go short distances—a few buildings or a few blocks. These are often bicycle messengers. Messenger service is expensive, but the fast delivery is worth the cost to the company. These messenger services also can be found in the Yellow Pages.

A secretary or administrative assistant will keep a file of frequently used private delivery services. The file should be updated regularly. The telephone numbers for those most frequently used can be coded into a company's system for speed dialing (see Chapter 8 in this text).

It may be advantageous to open a company charge account with frequently used delivery services. After doing this, when you have a letter or item to send, you will need only telephone the service and request a pickup. The delivery service will ask you for your account number and will bill your company at a later date. This way, you can save time by not having to repeat company information whenever you call and by making payments less frequently, which saves on check writing and processing.

Another reason a business may want to use this type of delivery is to use specialized software. Some delivery services offer free software that allows a business's computer to prepare shipments, create labels, maintain an address book of customers, print receipts, track packages, and keep an accurate history of all shipments. The Internet can be used to track packages through the Web sites of some delivery service companies.

Recall Time

Answer the following questions:

1. What is the maximum amount of insurance available on registered mail?
2. What is the maximum amount of insurance available on Standard Mail (A) and (B)?
3. Are the following statements true or false?
   a. Passports are available through the U.S. Postal Service.
   b. Federal Express delivers overnight for the U.S. Postal Service.
   c. Money orders can be purchased at a local post office.

USING POSTAL EQUIPMENT

Special postal equipment used by office workers helps to process the mail efficiently. Equipment includes scales, meters, and other items.

Scale and Meter Whether you work for a large or small company, you will find that a postage scale and a postage meter are the basic pieces of equipment needed to process outgoing mail. The scale can be purchased at any office supply store. The postage meter must be obtained from a manufacturer that has a product approved by the U.S.

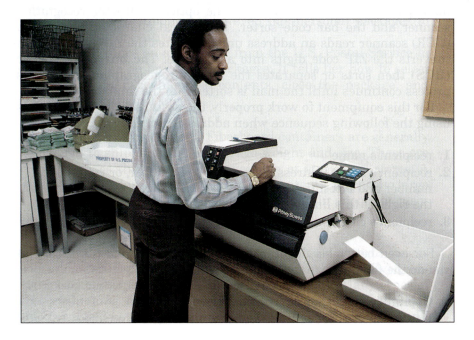

◆ *This office worker is using a postage meter and scale to process his boss's mail before leaving the office at the end of the day.*

Court on the same page. The letter *B* means that both even- and odd-numbered houses have the same ZIP code, 75240-7681.

No, all these numbers are not a waste of time to use. The ZIP codes are necessary for efficient use of optical character recognition scanners. The scanners read the numbers and sort the mail into the right piles by the number locations. Using the 75230-2825 ZIP code as an example, the first three digits, 752, represent a major geographic area, either a section center (for example a block with many buildings) or a large city. The next two digits, 30, represent the local post office in that area.

The postal service encourages businesses to use ZIP+4 for their mailings. This system adds four extra digits at the end of a ZIP code. An example is 94114-0929. The number 09 represents a group of streets or several blocks, and the number 29 represents a building or floor or department within a building.

Unauthorized Use of Postage and Supplies

Businesses do not allow their employees to use postage or postage supplies for personal mail. This includes using the postage meter, or taking company envelopes, stationery, labels, or stamps for personal use.

Over a period of time, a business can lose lots of money if employees misuse postage meters or use company postage supplies for private use. Some companies consider this practice to be stealing.

Recall Time

Answer the following questions:

1. What information can you get from an electronic postage scale?
2. What does a collator do?
3. Where can you get an up-to-date brochure on requirements for addressing mail?
4. What are three types of materials used for cushioning items in a package?

Summary

An office worker has to know a lot of information to process incoming and outgoing mail efficiently. When you begin working in an office, it is important that you remember this information in order to follow proper procedures for processing mail.

Use the following list to see if you are prepared to handle the processing of mail in an office environment:

◆ Once I receive the mail, I know the procedures to follow for processing it.

◆ Before putting the mail on my boss's desk, I know how to arrange it according to importance.

◆ Before the outgoing mail is sealed, I know the procedures for getting signatures, checking for enclosures, and addressing envelopes.

◆ Before putting postage on the outgoing mail, I know how to determine which class of mail to use.

◆ After determining which class of mail to use, I know how to use postal equipment to determine the cost.

◆ If items need to be packed for mailing, I know the most efficient way to do this.

◆ If addresses need ZIP codes, I know how to use reference materials to locate the proper ZIP codes.

IN CONCLUSION . . .

When you have completed this chapter, answer the following questions:

1. What are at least three classifications of mailing? Explain why each one may be used.

2. In what order should an address be typed on an envelope? Create a sample.

REVIEW AND APPLICATION

✔ CHECK YOUR KNOWLEDGE

1. Describe a centralized mail department.
2. Explain the process of annotating the mail.
3. List the column titles commonly used for an outgoing mail record.
4. When is a routing slip used?
5. How are enclosures inserted into an envelope when processing outgoing mail?
6. Name a U.S. Postal Service booklet that will help you better understand mailing classifications.
7. What is the maximum weight for priority mail?
8. Who uses Periodical rate?
9. If you use Standard Mail (B), what is the maximum number of days expected for coast-to-coast delivery?
10. Explain certified mail.
11. Explain the function of the U.S. Postal Service customer service line.
12. Is UPS part of the U.S. Postal Service?
13. Name the two most common pieces of postal equipment used for mail processing in an office.
14. List and explain the two pieces of special equipment used at postal sorting centers.
15. List the sequence to be used when addressing mail.
16. If your office does not have a ZIP code directory, where can you quickly find one?
17. Explain ZIP+4.
18. Create a routing slip for six teachers in your school.
19. List four ways a businessperson can purchase stamps from the U.S. Postal Service.
20. List two reasons a business may want to use computer software to connect with a private delivery service.
21. What is the name of the international facsimile service available through the U.S. Postal Service?
22. What does the postal service recommend that you do to the following address to bring better service?

Brandon Cash
134 Whipple Drive
Dallas, TX 75303

23. Rewrite the following address in proper sequence:

69 Keyport Way
Rachelle Mertz
Huntington, NY
11745-2325

📖 REVIEW YOUR VOCABULARY

On a separate paper, supply the missing words by choosing from the new Office Terms listed below.

1. In a large company the processing of mail may be done in a _____ department.
2. An office worker may _____ into individual trays for more than one supervisor.
3. _____ is first-class mail weighing more than twelve ounces.
4. The secretary was underlining important facts in the letter; she was _____ the letter.
5. BCS stands for _____.
6. An administrative assistant should not open _____.
7. A routing slip is used for _____ to more than one person in a company.

a. annotating
b. bar code sorter (BCS)
c. centralized mail department
d. confidential mail
e. priority mail
f. routing mail
g. sort mail

DISCUSS AND ANALYZE AN OFFICE SITUATION

1. Henrico is an office worker for a construction company. He also is the chairperson of a fund-

raiser for his church. Henrico has fifty letters to mail for the church; he is trying to decide if he should put them through the company postage meter and not tell anyone. This way he would save money for the church.

What would you advise Henrico to do? Explain your answer.

PRACTICE BASIC SKILLS

MATH

1. You go to the post office for your boss. It costs $13.90 to send the mail. How much change do you receive from a $20 bill?
2. At Lucas Advertising, the employees must record mail charges for each client. What is the total monthly charge for Levis on the following mail expense register?

MAIL EXPENSE REGISTER FOR APRIL

Charge To	Amount	Charge To	Amount
Levis	$14.89	Chevron	$8.90
HewPac	7.13	Levis	2.90
Levis	43.90	Cal Milk	0.75
Levis	0.56	Chevron	3.78
PacTel	8.90	Levis	0.55
Levis	0.45	Chevron	8.90
Admin	6.60	Levis	2.67

3. You need to reimburse petty cash up to $40. You have used $8.90, $3.45, $15.78, and $0.35 for postage. How much needs to be reimbursed?
4. You mail a package costing $13.50 and a letter at $0.65, and you purchase a sheet of stamps for $12.50. How much change do you receive if you give the postal clerk $30?

ENGLISH

1. *Rule:* For the possessive form of a noun that does not end in *s*, add *'s.*
   Examples: cat's paw, men's hats, clerk's pay, children's lunch
   Practice Exercises: Rewrite the following sentences, placing apostrophes to form the possessive where needed.
   a. One customers last name was omitted from the mailing list.

b. Ms. Chins secretary attended the workshop on data bases for mailing labels.
c. Why is the receptionists letter opener sitting on that managers desk?
d. The mail operators position was eliminated because of all the new PCs.
e. Invitations were mailed to each members supervisor in order to gain new members.

PROOFREADING

1. Retype or rewrite the following memo, correcting all errors.

April 5,

TO: Office Staff
FROM: Orin Martin
SUBJECT: EXPRESS MAIL
Teh following informtion was recieved from the US Postal Service concerning Espress Mail.
Express mail has always been a great value. Now that we've introduced our new overnight letter rate, you can fly with the Eagle for less than ever before.
For a low rate, you can send up to eight ounses throughout the US overnight. Thanks to our ovrnight reliabelity, your get guaranteed before-noon delivery between all major markets.
And the conveniences of 13,5000 Express Mail boxes, 2,6000 Express Mail post offices and 265,000 letter cariers. More drop-off points than all our competitors combined.
So whether you've got an overnight letter or package, why not soar with the Eagle.

APPLY YOUR KNOWLEDGE

1. Using the tables or the columns feature of a word processing program, type the following handwritten names and addresses as they would appear for mailing. Use uppercase and no punctuation. Place in alphabetical order.

a. kate roper
   tristate
   115 montebello rd
   jamaica plain ma 02130-6372

f. bette waller
   san lorenzo high school
   1719 grange circle
   longwood fl 32750-3803

b. judy wan
   aaa hauling
   85 whipper lane
   stratford, ct 06497-8251

c. doro gutierrez
   gunn hotel
   350 rockingstone ave
   larchmont ny 10538-3400

d. karl wolfe
   us air
   1313 gardner blvd
   norton oh 44203-2525

e. oscar rosa
   calistoga water
   3607-4th avenue
   minneapolis mn 55409-0404

g. daryl lee
   lee catering
   115 upper terrace
   vicksburg ms 39180-9574

h. roger fine
   fine word processing
   2246 flossmoor rd
   flossmoor il 60422-1306

i. harriet gandi
   calstate
   4515 dromedary rd
   phoenix az 85018-8432

j. marilee fong
   amador appliance
   543 sonoma ave.
   livermore ca 94525-9618

2. Using a computer software program, input and print the following chart. Use various features of the software program to produce an appealing chart using landscape printing (11×8½-inch paper).

	WORLDPOST (U.S. Postal Service International Services)						
KIND OF MAIL	INTELPOST 0 to 1 Days	EXPRESS 2 to 3 Days	PRIORITY 3 to 7 Days	SURFACE AIR LIFT 7 to 14 days	AIRMAIL 4 to 7 Days	SURFACE 4 to 6 weeks	BUSINESS REPLY 4 to 7 days
Hand-Delivered Fax	XXX						
General Correspondence		XXX	XXX		XXX	XXX	
Business Reply Mail					XXX		XXX
All Printed Matter		XXX	XXX	XXX	XXX	XXX	
M-Bag Option				XXX	XXX	XXX	
Merchandise Shipments		XXX			XXX	XXX	

USING THE REFERENCE MANUAL

Use the Post Office abbreviations section of the Reference Manual at the back of the book. Keyboard the two-letter abbreviations for the following 20 states. Save as file CH12REF on your data disk and print a copy.

States:

1. Minnesota
2. Georgia
3. North Carolina
4. Ohio
5. Vermont
6. Washington
7. Arizona
8. Hawaii
9. Alabama
10. California
11. New Mexico
12. New York
13. Florida
14. Nevada
15. Tennessee
16. Texas
17. South Dakota
18. Massachusetts
19. Colorado
20. District of Columbia

Managing Office Activities

OBJECTIVES

After completing this chapter, you will be able to do the following:

1. Organize your desk and work area so you can work efficiently.
2. Use a calendar and tickler file to arrange appointments and plan upcoming events.
3. Plan business meetings and conferences.
4. Plan business trips for executives and other travelers.

NEW OFFICE TERMS

agenda

itinerary

priorities

time management

BEFORE YOU BEGIN . . .

Answer the following questions to the best of your ability:

1. How would you organize your pens and pencils?

2. What type of work activity would you plan for the first project in the morning?

3. How would you handle interruptions?

4. What are five steps you would follow in planning a business meeting?

5. What are the first several steps in planning a business trip?

6. What would you schedule for an executive on the first day after he or she returns from a business trip?

It has been said that great minds love chaos, that they love to go about organizing and straightening things to make them work better. This may be true for a few people, but most of us need order and organization in our lives to be efficient and effective.

You need to be organized in an office environment because you will be receiving, sorting, rearranging, and communicating vast amounts of information. This environment can be overwhelming unless you have systems of classifying and storing details so nothing gets lost or forgotten.

There are several helpful systems that can make your job easier and less chaotic. This chapter details many current ideas about how to organize your space, time, and duties in ways that can help you do your job efficiently.

Organizing Yourself

YOUR DESK

You will be spending much of your work time at your desk or work area. You will accomplish more in less time if you have all your work within easy reach. An efficient way to organize your work is to use a desk organizer.

Two types of desk organizers are available. One has horizontal slots in which you can place documents upright so tabs can easily be read. The other type is made up of several stacked trays. Trays can be different colors, making it easier to identify their contents. Label each section or tray with what it will contain. For example, labels that say In Mail, Out Mail, In Work, Out Work, Mr. Jones, Ms. Wong reflect what you need to process.

Keep tools that you use often on your desk. These tools usually include pens and pencils (in an upright container), cellophane tape, paper clips, a stapler, and a pad for phone messages and notes. If you use a computer and store magnetic diskettes on your desk, do not use magnetic paper clip holders, as they may damage data stored on your diskettes. You will want your calendar or plan sheet within easy view. Some people also like a few reference items on their desks, such as a dictionary, an index containing frequently used telephone numbers and addresses, or a user's manual for the computer or other office machines that they use on a regular basis.

You will probably have a telephone. Place it close enough that you can reach it easily and jot notes while you talk. If you're right-handed, your telephone might be to the upper left, so you can answer it with your left hand, freeing your right hand to write. The opposite would apply if you're left-handed.

Different tasks will require different tools. Before you begin a task, decide which tools you will need and place them on the top of your desk. You can store some of these tools in your desk drawers until you need them. A drawer organizer will keep these items separated so they are easy to locate when you need them.

You will also keep stationery, envelopes, typing paper, and other supplies in your drawers. Keep them neat and tidy so you can easily access the items you need.

If you use a PC, you can save a lot of desk space by placing it on supports beside your desk. Several types of supports will allow you to do this. Some microcomputers are housed in *tower cabinets* (which are vertical rather than horizontal) and have built-in floor supports. You can also place your PC monitor on a swing-away arm that will allow you to push it out of the way when you need your desk space for other work.

YOUR MATERIALS

Your supervisor or office manager will provide small quantities of supplies that you keep on your desk and in your drawers. In addition, most offices have a central storage area for large quantities of supplies, such as computer diskettes, oversized envelopes, large quantities of paper, stationery, file folders, labels, ribbons, and pens and pencils.

If you work in a small office, you will probably be expected to keep supplies stocked by reordering them from an office supply store as they run low. This can be tricky with company stationery because it requires printing time. So keep track of the materials on hand and reorder early enough that new stock can be delivered when needed. Put newly received supplies behind or under older supplies so the older ones are used first.

YOUR RESPONSIBILITIES

To be well organized and efficient, you will need to understand thoroughly what is expected of you and what your duties entail, not only for a day at a time but for the week, subsequent weeks, and coming

These materials might include folders with copies of special information developed by those planning the meeting. You may distribute pens or pencils and pads for the participants' convenience. In a large meeting where people are not familiar with one another, you will want to provide name tags to make communication easier and help participants avoid the difficulty of having many names to remember.

You may place these materials on the tables where individuals will be seated or distribute them as participants sign in. Other pieces of literature and handouts may be displayed on the table so participants may examine and take what they wish.

Participation   Your role in the meeting should be clearly defined beforehand by your supervisor. As the person who made the arrangements, it may be your responsibility to continue monitoring the meeting to ensure that all goes smoothly. Perhaps you will greet people at the door. If so, greet them with a smile and a pleasant attitude so they will feel welcome and comfortable. Keep the water and coffee supplies replenished and attend to participants' other needs, such as requests for photocopies of specified documents.

Discuss Ideas   Apart from the role you play as assistant and organizer, you may be asked to share your own ideas or to state your opinion about what others have to say. If so, then participate in that way. However, if your supervisor limits your participation to planning the meeting and taking minutes, do not attempt to join in the discussion of ideas.

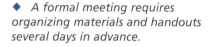

◆ *A formal meeting requires organizing materials and handouts several days in advance.*

Take the Minutes A role often delegated to secretaries and assistants is recording the events and actions of the meeting by taking minutes. The minutes are the official record of the meeting and concisely document facts about it, though statements and events are not recorded verbatim (word for word). The minutes should provide a clear, accurate accounting of what transpires at the meeting.

Various formats for minutes are acceptable, but minutes will always contain the following:

◆ the date, time, and place of the meeting
◆ the name of the organization or group sponsoring the meeting
◆ the name of the person conducting the meeting
◆ a listing of the people present—and if others were expected to attend, a listing of absentees

In general, if the meeting is conducted according to the agenda, the minutes will take that general form—call to order, roll call and introductions, minutes of the last meeting, treasurer's report, and so on.

Your minutes might begin like the following:

On June 8, 1998, the meeting of the Sunbeam Corporation Board of Directors was convened at 7 p.m. at the Red Lion Inn. Ms. Dunlop, the chief executive officer, called the meeting to order. . . .

As you are recording the minutes, recognize that actions are more important than what the participants say. Write the minutes clearly, ensuring that you don't lose any crucial information about business conducted at the meeting.

Correct the Minutes Part of the agenda for the meeting will be reading and correcting the minutes of the previous meeting. Someone may disagree with what has been recorded as having taken place. If the correction or addition is small, you may cross out the error and write in the correction. If the correction requires more writing, cross out the mistake and attach another page to record the correct information. Index the correction by placing a reference number next to the crossed-out section, directing the reader to the new page and new information.

After the minutes have been approved by the attending participants, don't add anything to them.

Follow-Up Several tasks will require completion after the meeting. If these tasks are assigned to you, do them as soon as possible, demonstrating efficiency to all parties involved. These tasks may include paying bills, preparing correspondence, or completing reports determined by the business conducted at the meeting. The sooner you do these, the better, while the events of the meeting remain fresh in your mind.

Prepare and Distribute the Minutes Sometimes the person who takes the minutes at the meeting is not the person who prepares and distributes them. Therefore, you may have to prepare minutes that

OFFICE TIP

Locate files according to activity. Locate files used daily in a desk file drawer or a small cabinet next to your desk. Locate other often-used files in a larger cabinet nearby. Place inactive files in a storeroom.

someone else has written. This means neatly typing them according to the format upon which the group has agreed. If you are not sure about a word or phrase because of unclear handwriting, question the person who took the minutes to avoid any misunderstandings.

Distribute the minutes according to the group's wishes, either mailing them immediately or mailing them along with the next meeting notice.

Prepare Related Correspondence   Your supervisor may ask you to prepare correspondence directly related to the meeting. This might include requests for more information, thank-you notes to participants or speakers, and follow-up information about ideas discussed at the meeting. These tasks should be completed as soon as possible after the meeting is held.

Recall Time

Answer the following questions:

1. What are the main differences between formal and informal meetings?
2. What is an agenda? How is it prepared and how is it used?
3. Several tasks are required when making arrangements for a meeting. What are four of them?
4. How are minutes taken? What information must be in them, and what format is used?
5. A meeting is not over when it's over. You may be responsible for many activities after a meeting. What are some of them?

Handling Travel Arrangements

You may be asked to make arrangements for your managers to travel to a meeting or for participants to come to one. Your company will give you guidelines to follow about company policy regarding travel. As soon as you learn that you will be responsible for making these arrangements, prepare a travel folder.

Consider the following questions when planning travel for someone else:

1. What are the exact destinations, and on what dates does the traveler want to leave and return?
2. How does the traveler wish to get from one place to another? Some people are uncomfortable flying and would prefer to go by train.
3. Does the traveler have special requests, such as a specific time of day to leave and return or, if traveling by plane, a preferred seating assignment? Some people insist on an aisle seat, whereas

others want to look out the window. Is a certain airline preferred? Does the traveler have any special food requirements?

4. Will someone at the destination be driving, or will a car rental be required?
5. Does the traveler have a favorite hotel in the destination city or a favorite hotel chain that he or she feels provides good service in most cities? Does the traveler require a specific type of accommodation? Will the traveler require a meeting room at the hotel?
6. Does your manager want you to arrange any other detail of preference or special request?

When you know the answers to these questions, you can plan and complete the travel arrangements.

PLANNING

Travel can be complicated and exhausting if not properly planned and orchestrated. You will discover that in any business activity, proper planning in the beginning saves valuable time in the end.

Early Preparations Begin your trip folder as early as possible so you don't have loose papers lying about; this might cause you to over-look helpful details. Your trip folder will be a file folder that contains all the information relevant to a particular trip. Prepare separate travel folders for different trips.

When you first learn the approximate dates of a trip, make some notes about the time frame for planning; that is, how long do you have to make all the arrangements, and when must you accomplish each task? Make notes about the various aspects of planning the trip and about the tasks and responsibilities assigned to you.

Outline the trip, including the meetings to be attended during it. If possible, do this initial outlining and planning in consultation with the person who will be traveling. The outline will keep you focused on what you need to accomplish and the status of matters as your plans proceed.

Final Preparations Prepare a checklist to use as you make the final preparations. After your outline is complete and the designated tasks are accomplished, prepare your traveler's final itinerary. The **itinerary** is an outline that includes flight numbers, departure and arrival times and places, and information on hotel accommodations and car rentals. If you use the services of a travel agent, you should receive a final itinerary of the travel arrangements from her or him.

Confirm Appointments Call each person with whom your supervisor plans to meet and confirm the appointments. Recheck the times, dates, and places of all activities.

HUMAN RELATIONS

Louise is an administrative assistant in the home office of a large manufacturing company. Louise understands quite well most of the computer programs used in the office. Word processing, spreadsheet, and database programs all seem simple to her. So simple, in fact, that she cannot understand why many of the new workers frequently have difficulty comprehending how to use these programs.

Arnold is a new employee in the office. He spent four hours one morning reading manuals and trying to understand how to use a database program, but he couldn't figure it out. He was feeling frustrated, a little bit stupid, and angry when he walked into the staff meeting. Although using computer programs was not on the agenda for the day, Arnold announced that he wanted this item added to the agenda. Louise, who was chairing the meeting, agreed and added it as the first item for discussion.

Arnold, still frustrated and angry, began by saying, "This company must use the worst programs on the market—the one for database management is terrible!"

Louise, who not only understood the programs well but had personally selected the database management program, was not sympathetic. She replied, "We have the best programs on the market. The database management program is simple and easy to learn for anyone of average intelligence."

Feeling he had just been insulted, Arnold said, "Excuse me," stood, and walked out of the meeting.

For the past two days neither Arnold nor Louise has spoken to the other.

1. *What would have been a more effective way for Arnold to share his frustration about the computer program?*

2. *What could Louise have said that would have promoted more effective human relations?*

3. *What should Arnold and Louise say to each other now?*

Make Reservations   Make any reservations that have not previously been made. A travel agent may have made most reservations, but with the final setting of the itinerary, some of these might have to be changed.

Prepare an Itinerary   When you have your outline, your reservations are made, and your meetings are confirmed, you can prepare the final itinerary for your traveler. The itinerary contains a calendar of meetings and hotel and travel reservations with addresses and telephone numbers. Include any instructions about special considerations.

Ask the traveler, who will probably be your boss or supervisor, who else should receive a copy of the itinerary. She or he may need several copies—one to carry, one to stash away in the baggage, and one to leave with the family.

Assemble Related Items   Place with your boss's itinerary the tickets, travel money, hotel confirmations, and forms for recording expenses.

Early in the planning process, your supervisor began to think about materials to take along. Gather those materials and prepare them in the appropriate manner.

By planning carefully early on, following your checklist, and preparing a detailed itinerary, you can create an easy, well-organized, successful trip. Your boss will be able to accomplish much more on the trip because of your careful work; she or he can spend energy on conducting business instead of tending to other details.

USING TRAVEL AGENTS

Your company may not expect you to personally arrange travel plans. You may be dealing with a travel agency that can make all the arrangements, from booking flights to making hotel and car rental reservations.

Travel agencies are paid a commission for booking hotels and air travel, and they have access, through computers, to arrival times, departure times, and ticket prices for most airlines. Therefore, they can efficiently take care of these details for you. Even if you do work with a travel agency, you will need the information listed above to ensure a comfortable, enjoyable trip.

Before you begin searching for a travel agent, ask your supervisor if the company ordinarily uses a particular agency that has provided satisfactory service in the past. If not, you may ask other people for references to a good agency. Using one that specializes in business travel will probably be your best bet.

Before you contact an agency, determine company policy regarding paying for the trip. Is the travel agency to bill the company for expenses, or will you be given a credit card number to give to the agency? When you call the agency, have your trip folder in front of you with all the information the agent requires. You will need to give the agent as many specific details and instructions as possible.

As soon as the agency completes the arrangements, it will send you the tickets along with a computer printout of the itinerary it has arranged and an invoice listing charges. Check this information carefully, then ask your supervisor or the traveler to check it, too. Make needed corrections with the travel agent without delay to ensure a convenient and pleasant trip.

ARRANGING TRIPS YOURSELF

Sometimes you may be required to make travel arrangements yourself. For example, if a rush trip comes up suddenly, you may not have time to enlist the aid of a travel agent. Though this will be less convenient, you should be able to handle the plans adequately.

Scheduling Air Travel You will need to do a bit of research when booking airline tickets yourself. If you will be doing a lot of scheduling, subscribe to one of the many periodicals that help people make travel arrangements. You can find these as well as books about travel in your local library.

If you live in a large city, you will have several airlines from which to choose. Your supervisor might have a preference for one airline. Most airlines provide updated timetables with the following information:

- ◆ arrival and departure times
- ◆ days each flight is available
- ◆ flight numbers
- ◆ special services and features of each flight
- ◆ toll-free number where more information can be gathered and reservations can be made

Obtain the best price for tickets as well as the most convenient departure and arrival times. You must call airlines and ask questions to accomplish this. Use the airlines' toll-free numbers so you can make the calls without paying long-distance fees. Be sure to consider any special programs for frequent flyers or business travelers.

As soon as you decide which airline to use, book the flight. Before you call, place your trip folder in front of you so you can make the special arrangements requested by your traveler. You will need to know how you will be paying for the tickets. The airline may prefer a credit card number. You can make arrangements to pick up the tickets and pay for them in person, or request that the airline bill your company for the tickets.

You will probably not have time to have the tickets mailed. So, unless you plan to pick the tickets up ahead of time, arrange for your traveler to pick them up at the airport on the day of departure.

Car Rental   Whether your traveler needs a car at her or his destination or will be making the entire trip by automobile, arrangements have to be made in advance. If you're using a travel agency, it will take care of car rental details as part of its service to you.

If you will be making the arrangements, do some research to secure the best rates. The rates will depend on the size and model of car, the destination, and the length of time the car is needed. The cost will include a daily rate plus an additional charge for miles over a certain daily allotment. Most of these details are negotiable and vary from agency to agency.

You can look in the Yellow Pages of your telephone directory to locate the rental agencies in your area. Several are usually located at major airports, and most medium-sized towns also have several from which to choose.

Hotel and Motel Accommodations   Your traveler may have to spend the night or several nights at her or his destination. A travel agency will be able to book accommodations for you.

Your traveler may have hotel or motel preferences if she or he is acquainted with the town to be visited. Ask before you begin your search. The chamber of commerce in the destination community can help you with finding and arranging accommodations. Most large hotels have toll-free numbers for bookings.

USING THE INTERNET AND ONLINE SERVICES

The Internet and all major online services, such as America Online, Prodigy, and Compuserve, can be very helpful in planning trips. For

INDUSTRY FOCUS

Ralph A. Prater
*Team Member, Contributions and
 Programs*
Chevron Corporation

Q. Mr. Prater, students hear that businesses are becoming more global than in past years. What is meant by this?

A. Yes, that is true. It means that companies are conducting or seeking to conduct business all over the world. In the past, U.S. companies did the majority of their business in this country. That is no longer true for many businesses. Recently I read that because of the global economy, the number of Americans working for international companies has more than doubled since 1980, to nearly 5 million.

Q. What advice would you give to a future office worker concerning working in a global economy?

A. An office worker in a global economy must be knowledgeable of foreign customs, practices, and nuances of a particular country on any given day in which business is being conducted.

A good starting point for students is to become acquainted with specifics of other countries. For example, learn how to determine currency exchange rates, how to fax or telephone a foreign country, and how to determine the time difference in these countries.

example, you can check current airline fares and prices of hotel accommodations on your computer. You can even purchase airline tickets, reserve hotel rooms, and rent a car using these services. The Internet and online services are being updated constantly, so check this out on your own by "surfing the Net," talking with friends, or asking questions at your local computer software store.

CONTINUING YOUR WORK WHEN THE EXECUTIVE IS AWAY

You may feel that your work will be disrupted while the boss is out of town, but for the most part, you can continue your work as usual. Sometimes you will accomplish more with your boss away and therefore unable to create as many interruptions.

Keep careful track of events in the office, visitors, incoming mail, and phone calls, so you can report them to your boss. Don't set any

OFFICE TIP

When you have the choice, it's often better to send out some jobs, such as a big photocopying job, than to get mired down for days and get behind on other important work.

appointments on the day your boss is due to return to the office. You both will have a lot of catching up to do.

FOLLOWING UP WHEN THE EXECUTIVE RETURNS

When your boss returns, a lot of follow-up work will be necessary. You will need to write thank-you letters to people who provided services or assistance. You will also need to prepare other correspondence associated with the business conducted during the trip.

You may have to prepare detailed reports showing what was accomplished on the trip. You and your boss will have your hands full for several days after she or he returns.

Managing activities and duties in a busy office can appear complex and sometimes nearly impossible, but you can learn some systems that make it easier for you. After you have been working in the office for a while, you may be surprised at how routine all this will become.

Recall Time

Answer the following questions:

1. Whether you make your supervisor's travel arrangements or leave the details to a travel agency, you need to consider several things before you begin. What are these considerations?
2. Usually, people use travel agencies for their travel needs. How do travel agencies work and what can they do for you?
3. If it is up to you to schedule your supervisor's air travel, you will have to do some research. What kinds of information will you seek?
4. How do you rent an automobile?
5. How do you arrange hotel or motel accommodations?

Summary

You may have heard the phrase, "Time is money." This is especially true in business. In a busy office, you may quickly become overwhelmed and waste valuable time if you do not get organized. Think through every item, from how you will organize the tools on your desk to setting up conferences and planning trips.

The first step in getting organized is to understand your new job. Someone may train you for a few days, or you may be given a procedures manual. After you clearly understand your responsibilities, you can begin to organize matters so that you can handle them.

Managing your time will be crucial to your success. This requires planning your day carefully. Set priorities, assign each task a time for completion, and follow your plans as nearly as possible while continuing to be flexible.

Design ways of managing details. These include using files and folders, and writing notes to yourself. Details have a way of disappearing if they are not managed correctly and systematically.

You can often work on just one task at a time until it is completed. However, be prepared for interruptions. They are part of the job, so schedule time for them in your daily work plan. Adjust your schedule so that the intensity of your work does not last all day. Schedule easier tasks between more difficult ones.

Part of organizing a busy office is keeping a calendar. List all upcoming meetings, events, and appointments. You may be asked to schedule your supervisor's appointments. If so, you will be the "keeper of the calendar." You will block out time for recurring events, handle cancellations, and coordinate your calendar with others in the office.

A tickler file is a follow-up file that alerts you to tasks you need to do. Using a tickler file in conjunction with your calendar, you should be able to deal with all the events of a busy office.

Much of the business of a company is conducted in formal or informal meetings. You may be responsible for making arrangements for formal meetings. These will include reserving a room, organizing equipment and refreshments, and preparing materials. Begin your planning by setting up a folder in which to keep details, recording all information that crosses your desk about the meeting, notifying participants, and preparing an agenda.

An agenda is an announcement and listing of what will be discussed at a meeting. Minutes are an accounting of the meeting. You may be asked to take minutes, then prepare and distribute them after the meeting is over. Other follow-up activities will be completing correspondence, such as thank-you notes, and perhaps conducting further research on a project and preparing follow-up reports.

Your boss may attend meetings out of town, and it may be your job to make travel arrangements. If so, make a list of your boss's preferences and special needs before you make any plans. A travel agent can schedule flights, book hotel rooms, rent cars, and take care of other details for you. Most businesses today use travel agencies because of their access to information about arrivals, departures, costs, and so on. If it is up to you to make the travel arrangements, with a little research you can do the same things the travel agent does.

While the boss is away, take care of business as usual. When the boss returns, you will need a few days to catch up, and you may have follow-up tasks that have been generated by the trip.

Plan, plan, plan. Managing office activities is about careful, thoughtful, systematic preparation and planning so time will be used profitably.

Managing office activities will include some or all of the following tasks:

◆ Organize the top of your desk and its drawers.
◆ Organize the purchase and storage of materials and supplies.
◆ Clearly learn and understand your responsibilities in the office.
◆ Manage your time.
◆ Set priorities.

◆ Plan your work for the day before beginning.
◆ Create a system for managing details.
◆ Whenever possible, work on one task at a time.
◆ Learn to cope with interruptions, which are part of any busy office.
◆ Schedule time to relax.
◆ Keep a calendar, handling appointments and cancellations.
◆ Learn to keep a tickler file.
◆ Plan, schedule, and make arrangements for meetings.
◆ Take minutes, and prepare and distribute them.
◆ Make travel arrangements yourself, or with the assistance of a travel agent.

IN CONCLUSION . . .

When you have completed this chapter, answer the following questions:

1. How would you organize your pens and pencils?

2. What type of work activity would you plan for the first project in the morning?

3. How would you handle interruptions?

4. What are five steps you would follow in planning a business meeting?

5. What are the first several steps in planning a business trip?

6. What would you schedule for an executive on the first day after he or she returns from a business trip?

REVIEW AND APPLICATION

✔ CHECK YOUR KNOWLEDGE

1. Describe the importance of getting organized.
2. Describe how you might organize your desk. List the materials and tools and where they would be placed.
3. Training for a new job can take several different forms. Can you name some of them?
4. Explain how to set priorities for different duties.
5. Discuss the many ways to sort and store details.
6. When should your day be planned and how do you do it?
7. By law, you are entitled to a lunch break and two fifteen-minutes rest breaks throughout the day. Describe other ways you can schedule in relaxation time.
8. Describe the different types of calendars and their use.
9. Handling appointments can be tricky. What information should you have from your boss if you are expected to set her or his appointments?
10. Describe a tickler file and its use.
11. What are the basic differences between formal and informal meetings?
12. List some steps in preparing for a formal meeting.
13. What are minutes and how are they prepared?
14. What is the easiest and most efficient way to deal with travel arrangements?
15. How would you begin making travel arrangements?
16. What things should you know about your traveler before you begin to make her or his arrangements?
17. How would you arrange for airplane tickets? hotel accommodations? car rental?
18. What is an itinerary and what information might be on one?
19. What are some last-minute details that may need attention when your boss is leaving on a business trip?
20. How do you deal with the boss's being out of the office?
21. What kinds of activities might take place when the boss returns?

REVIEW YOUR VOCABULARY

On a separate piece of paper, write the letter of the vocabulary word that is described below.

____ 1. preferences in the order of work activities, usually decided according to levels of importance
____ 2. a list of topics to be covered during a meeting
____ 3. the art of knowing what you need to do in a given time frame, setting priorities for projects, and completing projects in the time allotted
____ 4. an outline that includes flight numbers, departure and arrival times and places, and hotel accommodation and car rental information

a. agenda   c. priorities
b. itinerary   d. time management

DISCUSS AND ANALYZE AN OFFICE SITUATION

1. Fred has accepted a new job in a new company. The person he is replacing left the job in a hurry because of a health emergency. The boss has given him a little time, but she is busy and training Fred is not her main priority. Other people in the office have similar jobs and are helpful to some extent. Still, Fred is not sure what his duties are and does not clearly understand his responsibilities. If you were Fred, what would you do?

2. Gretchen was in the habit of scheduling her boss's appointments and carefully keeping a calendar of events. One day, Gretchen woke up with a terrible cold and felt she should not go to the office. She called her boss and explained. When she returned to the office, someone else had been doing the scheduling. That person had set some overlapping appointments and had not blocked out time for a special meeting. How can Gretchen fix the confusing calendar?

PRACTICE BASIC SKILLS

MATH

1. It is your job to rent an automobile for your boss's trip. He will be driving to a city 300 miles away and back. He will need the car for three days and you estimate that he will drive it about 100 miles while in his destination city. He requested that you rent a four-door sedan. You research the matter carefully, asking people what company to use and calling companies in the Yellow Pages. You discover that different companies charge different rates:

- ◆ Company 1 charges $34.99 per day for the rental fee and allows 150 free miles per day. Each mile over 150 will cost $0.20.
- ◆ Company 2 charges $39.95 per day for the rental fee and allows 100 free miles per day. Each mile over 100 will cost $0.15.
- ◆ Company 3 charges $36.95 per day for the rental fee and allows 120 free miles per day. Each mile over 120 will cost $0.25.

Calculate which company offers the best price for renting a car.

ENGLISH

1. You may be called upon to welcome meeting participants as they arrive. Rewrite on separate paper the following greeting, remembering that you are representing your company, correcting words and phrases that are inappropriate because they are rude or simply not standard English.

Hey there, how ya doin'? Where would you like to set it down? This will be a pretty cool meet-ing, don't ya think? If you want coffee ya gotta get it yourself. Over there on the table below that ugly picture. You'll find it. Hope you dig on the meeting, and have some laughs.

PROOFREADING

1. If it is your responsibility to record and prepare the minutes of a meeting, you will want to proofread them carefully so they contain no spelling or punctuation errors. Rewrite the following minutes on a separate paper, correcting any errors.

The metting was called to orden at 7:00 pm by the President, Mrs. Brown. Then Mrs. Brwon led the fleg slute. The secretary red the minites from the last metting and thee wear approvd as red.

The tresurer gave her reprot and a discussion follwed.

Old buesness include discusion about the water problum.

There was no newer business.

The meetin was ajourned at 8:00 PM

APPLY YOUR KNOWLEDGE

1. Using your school day as an example, carefully plan your day. Set priorities for events and activities, and assign times to each item on your list.
2. Prepare a calendar for yourself, detailing all the activities you have planned for the month. Give everything a time value. See if this kind of planning helps you keep your activities organized.
3. Plan a business trip. Select a city, an airline, a hotel, and a car rental company, and determine the cost of each service you will require. Refer to maps, airline schedules, American Automobile Association (AAA) books, and any other references you can locate. For guidance, you may discuss your trip with a travel agent, if you wish.

USING THE
REFERENCE MANUAL

Retrieve the file CH13REF on the data disk. Use the proofreaders' marks section of the Reference Manual at the back of the book to help you correct the paragraph. Save and print.

Meetings plan an important rolein the comunication of information in every kind of business. they are held to conduct business, to follow up on a Previously discussed activity, or simply to communicate information to an individual or to a group Careful planing and prepration are the keys to eficiently run, worth while meeting.

CAREER PORTFOLIO

PART THREE: OFFICE SUPPORT SKILLS

Specific Activities to Complete

Select at least three of the following items for inclusion in your Career Portfolio, using the information from Chapters 8 through 13.

1. *Keyboard a list of the five most important telephone tips you will need to remember on your first job. Save and print this list. (Be sure you proof according to the instructions given previously on page 92.) Insert this list as the first item in your Career Portfolio binder behind the third tab, entitled "Office Support Skills."*

2. *Keyboard a list of five important rules to remember when you are responsible for filing and managing records in an office. Save, print, and insert this list behind the third tab as well.*

3. *Keyboard some examples of accepted formats for a letter, a memorandum, and an envelope. Show your documents to a fellow student and incorporate any suggestions that may improve the appearance of the documents. Save, print, and insert these documents behind the third tab.*

4. *Keyboard a balance sheet and income statement using the examples in Chapter 11 as a guide. Save, print, and insert these documents behind the third tab.*

5. *Keyboard five important reminders for office workers when they send and receive mail in the office. Save, print, and insert these reminders behind the third tab.*

6. *Keyboard a list of how you will go about managing your time while efficiently performing expected office activities on your first job. Save, print, and insert this list behind the third tab.*

PART IV

Communication and Problem-Solving Skills

Essentials of Office Communication

OBJECTIVES

After completing this chapter, you will be able to do the following:

1. Describe the communication process.
2. List examples of nonverbal communication.
3. Discuss how filtering negatively affects the communication process.
4. Explain the importance of feedback in the communication process.
5. Describe the difference between upward communication and downward communication.
6. Explain the positive and negative aspects of the grapevine as an informal communication channel.
7. Explain the difference between literacy and workplace literacy.
8. List the five competencies and three-part foundation skills that the SCANS report refers to as basic workplace know-how.
9. Describe techniques and steps workers can use to read, write, and speak more effectively in business activities.
10. Describe several communication behaviors of active listeners.

NEW OFFICE TERMS

active listening
communication
downward communication
feedback
filtering
grapevine
lateral communication

previewing
Secretary's Commission on
   Achieving Necessary Skills
   (SCANS)
upward communication
workplace literacy

BEFORE YOU BEGIN . . .

Answer the following questions to the best of your ability:

1. What are some typical office communication networks?

2. Which communication skills should office workers be able to demonstrate?

The Communication Process

Communication is the basis of all our relationships. Without it, each of us would live dreary lives in isolation. We need other people, and our connections to others are forged by communication. Yet, because we learned to communicate gradually, as we grew up, most of us have never really thought about this valuable skill.

Although most of us take communication for granted, its importance cannot be overestimated. According to experts in this field, we spend about 70 percent of our waking hours communicating—speaking, listening, reading, and writing. Further, in the office setting we can choose the most appropriate communication medium—face to face, telephone, electronic mail, written memos, or video.

Simply put, **communication** is the exchange of messages. Messages can be verbal, using spoken or written words; or they can be nonverbal, using symbols, gestures, expressions, and body language. For communication to take place, there must be a sender, a person who transmits the message, and a receiver, a person who gets the message. Whether it is one-way or two-way, effective communication occurs when the sender and the receiver have the same understanding of the message, as shown in Figure 14.1.

ONE-WAY COMMUNICATION

In one-way communication, the sender transmits a message, the receiver gets it, and the process is complete. For example, an employee calls in to report she is ill and will be out for the day. The person receiving the call understands the message, makes note of it, and hangs up.

TWO-WAY COMMUNICATION

In two-way communication, the sender transmits a message, the receiver gets it, and subsequently the receiver responds with another message. The process may continue with the sender and receiver alternating roles, giving each other feedback. Office conversations and business correspondence are examples of two-way communication.

OFFICE TIP

When communicating, try to keep your temper even when faced with unfair resistance. To lose your temper is to lose an opportunity to share your message.

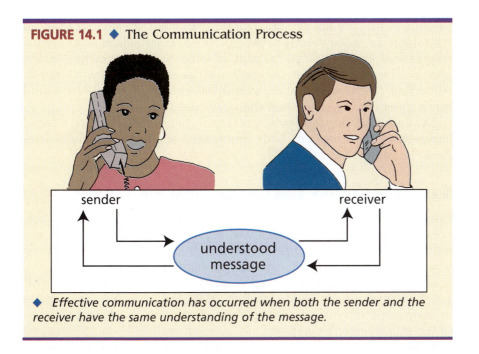

FIGURE 14.1 ◆ The Communication Process

sender   receiver

understood message

◆ *Effective communication has occurred when both the sender and the receiver have the same understanding of the message.*

NONVERBAL COMMUNICATION

Most of us think of words as our chief means of communicating. Being clear, concise, and courteous in your choice of words is important. However, studies of face-to-face communication have shown that 80 to 90 percent of the *impact* of a message comes from nonverbal elements, such as facial expressions, eye contact, body language, and tone of voice.

Communication experts point out that in face-to-face communication, 55 percent of what we communicate is in our body language, 38

◆ *Nonverbal communication can carry a much greater impact than the words that are being spoken.*

percent in how we speak, and 7 percent in what we say. Further, on the telephone, we have only between 15 and 30 seconds to make a good impression. Only 10 to 20 percent of what we communicate on the phone is based on what we say; 80 to 90 percent is in how we say it. According to these statistics, nonverbal communication can reveal much more of a message than the words used.

Examples of the four areas of nonverbal communication—facial expressions, eye contact, body language, and voice qualities—are given in Table 14.1.

COMMUNICATION FEEDBACK AND FILTERS

Communication and feedback in business are important to reach corporate goals and to maintain good morale. **Feedback** is verbal and nonverbal responses that the receiver gives by further communicating with the original sender or another person.

It is not easy to give feedback in such a way that the receiver will not feel threatened. To successfully give feedback requires you to develop sensitivity to other people's needs and be able to put yourself in the other person's position.

Filtering is the tendency for a message to be watered down or halted completely at some point during transmission. Both speakers

TABLE 14.1 ◆ Nonverbal Communication

TYPES	EXAMPLES
Facial Expressions	Smiling, frowning, and raising your eyebrows are facial expressions which communicate feelings.
Eye Contact	Making eye contact when speaking with someone is usually desirable. In the United States, for example, people who o not meet your eyes during conversations are thought to be hiding something. This, of course, differs in other cultures.
Body Language	Nodding your head, shrugging your shoulders, gesturing with your hands, or shifting your weight from side to side are examples of body language. Body language can indicate a wide range of emotions, from boredom (yawning) to impatience (tapping your fingers or feet).
Voice Qualities	A person's voice can be loud or soft, high or low pitched, fast or slow, pleasant or harsh, monotonous or interesting. Not only can a voice tell a lot about how one feels in a particular situation, but perhaps more important, it tells much about how the person is feeling physically and psychologically at the moment.

◆   *Misunderstandings occur when the message gets blocked or distorted as a result of barriers in either sending or receiving information.*

and listeners have communication "filters," or barriers, through which messages must come. In other words, the speaker sends a message through his or her filters; the listener receives the message through his or her's. As you can see, total and accurate communication is very difficult to achieve.

Some examples of filters that cause people to misunderstand each other occur when the speaker and/or listener

◆ do not listen or do not want to listen
◆ do not understand the "language of feelings"
◆ do not say enough, or are not given the chance to say enough
◆ get mixed up in definitions; for example, a speaker often assumes that the listener understands what he or she said
◆ fail to indicate to each other that they understand and that it is not necessary to continue the dialog
◆ give information too fast
◆ are generally unwilling to ask questions
◆ experience personality conflicts or differences between each other
◆ jump to conclusions
◆ fail to read nonverbal messages

Office Communication Networks

Communication networks in organizations are unique and reflect, to a large degree, the organizations' mission to customers and vision to achieve it. One way to view communication networks is through upward, downward, and lateral communication; another way is through formal and informal communication channels.

Regardless of which network or channel is used, effective communication occurs when the right people receive the right information in a timely manner. If any of these three conditions are not present, communication will be ineffective.

UPWARD, DOWNWARD, AND LATERAL COMMUNICATION NETWORKS

Upward communication is feedback of data or information from lower levels in the organization to upper-management levels. This type usually deals with problems, clarifications, attitudes, ideas, and accomplishments. Managers use suggestion systems, attitude surveys, team meetings, complaint procedures, and committees to encourage upward communication from workers.

Downward communication, on the other hand, follows the organization's formal chain of command from top to bottom. This type covers procedures, policies, goals, assignments, and directives. A concern with downward communication is that the message decreases in accuracy as it passes through the chain of command. For that reason, managers use written materials such as employee handbooks, policy manuals, organizational newsletters, bulletin boards, videos, and meetings to clearly communicate downward within the organization.

Lateral communication, also known as horizontal communication, occurs between departments or functional units, usually as a coordinating or problem-solving effort. Organizations can set up short-term task forces so colleagues can discuss unique projects, or they can set up long-term committees so that co-workers can get together and discuss a particular organizational concern or issue on an ongoing basis.

◆ *Managers use handbooks, newsletters, bulletin boards and other clear means of conveying messages downward through the chain of command so that all employees receive accurate information.*

HUMAN RELATIONS

James Frederick, president of a computer consulting firm, has just entered the company's conference room to meet with his staff of twenty-five consultants, administrators, and office workers. He explains that he is about to make a decision about buying out a competitor that specializes in international business consulting.

If he does so, the staff will increase by fifteen persons, ten of whom are from other cultures and speak languages such as German, Spanish, Japanese, and Russian. He has asked everyone in attendance for their input on his decision. If you were an employee, how would you respond to the following questions?

1. *In what ways can this merger be a positive move for the company?*

2. *In what ways can this merger be a risky move for the company?*

3. *If you were Mr. Frederick, what would you do?*

FORMAL AND INFORMAL COMMUNICATION CHANNELS

In addition to communication networks in offices, there are also communication channels. These are different from each other and are usually referred to as formal and informal communication channels.

Formal Channels Formal communication channels are the officially prescribed means by which messages normally flow inside organizations, and are similar to downward communication. This is also called "following the chain of command"; this means the correct channel to follow is to discuss issues or concerns with your immediate superior first before going over his or her head to a higher-level manager.

Informal Channels The chain of command does not take into account informal communication between members. Informal communication channels convey messages along channels other than those formally designed by organizations. Informal interaction helps people do their jobs more effectively. The best-known types of informal communication within an organization are "the grapevine" and rumors.

The Grapevine The **grapevine** involves transmission of information by word of mouth without regard for organizational levels, and often provides a great deal of useful information. Unfortunately, however, the grapevine can also distort information, create resentment between and among workers, and counteract organizational plans and objectives.

One example of grapevine chatter is talking about an unpopular directive from the boss. Cliques of co-workers gather in the cubicle corners of every office across the country. Organizational psychologists say such talk is usually harmless. Some feel that the grapevine is an effective way to alleviate subordinates' sense of helplessness and strengthen bonds among colleagues.

◆ *The office grapevine can strengthen bonds between employees, but can also distort information and cause discontent due to misunderstandings.*

Rumors Generally, a person's best strategy is to let office rumors slide. Trying to refute gossip usually gives it more credence. However, the best approach to follow when clarifying rumors is to attack the source. Private one-on-one conversations with the perpetrators of gossip usually squelch further rumors.

Table 14.2 recaps these communication networks and channels.

Workplace Literacy and SCANS

Do you feel you are a literate person—a person who can read, write, and do basic math? A major concern for organizations today is the difficulty of locating and hiring a worker who is literate; specifically, one who is able to function in a literate way while performing routine work-

TABLE 14.2 ◆ Communication Networks and Channels

Communication Networks	**Upward Communication Is . . .** feedback of data or information from the lower levels of the organization to upper-management levels. *Examples are: suggestion systems, surveys, team meetings, complaint procedures, and committees.*
	Downward Communication Is . . . feedback of data or information that follows the organization's formal chain of command from top to bottom. *Examples are: employee handbooks, policy manuals, organizational newsletters, bulletin boards, videos, and meetings.*
	Lateral Communication Is . . . feedback of data or information that occurs between departments or functional units, usually as a coordinating effort. *Examples are: short-term task forces or long-term committees.*
Communication Channels	**Formal** Communication that follows the formal chain of command as represented on the company's organizational chart.
	Informal Communication that allows for informal interaction between workers to help them do their jobs more effectively.

place activities. **Workplace literacy** is the aspect of functional literacy related to employability and skill requirements for particular jobs.

The foundation for this is a combination of traditional literacy and the ability to pull together the information obtained from reading and calculations and *apply* it in real-life situations. This application of knowledge requires information processing, logical reasoning, and critical thinking capabilities together with basic reading, writing, and mathematics skills.

The need for a high degree of workplace literacy reflects the reality that the basic skill levels that used to suffice are now inadequate for employees faced with sophisticated quality control systems, team-based work, and participatory management practices. What degree of reading, writing, communication, and personal skills should you attain and be prepared to demonstrate on your first job?

READING SKILLS

Today's office professional must be able to read well enough to understand correspondence, reports, records, equipment manuals, directories, charts, and graphs. Reading is the primary method used to locate information needed to make decisions or recommend courses of action. For example, when a new software package or upgrade version is purchased, employees are expected to have the ability to teach themselves through reading and understanding instructions in documentation and other reference material.

WRITING SKILLS

Composition and grammar skills are becoming critical as more writing responsibilities are assumed by the office professional. While word processing software can check spelling, word usage, and grammar, it cannot edit for content or completely proofread. Office workers must be able to use a wide variety of reference books to fine-tune their thoughts and produce professional office documents.

OTHER COMMUNICATION SKILLS

The authors of the book *Workforce 2000* predict that 41 percent of new jobs will require high-level communication and problem-solving skills. The abilities to listen carefully to customers and co-workers and speak well enough to convey one's point of view clearly and effectively are essential. The office professional must be able to communicate with customers both in person and by telephone, understand customer concerns, explain schedules and procedures, relay messages accurately, work as a team player, teach others, reason logically while probing for hidden meanings, and solve problems.

Clearly, the degree of preparedness *expected of all workers* is rising dramatically. Many of the skills expected of a typical worker today were those expected only of managers a decade or so ago.

To be competitive, organizations must either employ literate workers or upgrade the literacy levels of current workers. Table 14.3 com-

◆ *Perhaps the most important skill to take to a new job is the ability to read and comprehend well.*

TABLE 14.3 ◆ Literacy vs. Workplace Literacy

Literacy	In general, the ability to read and understand a wide range of material, as well as the ability to write clearly and coherently.
Workplace Literacy	The aspect of literacy related to employability and skill requirements for particular jobs. In general, workplace literacy requires information processing, logical reasoning, and critical thinking capabilities together with basic reading, writing, communication, and mathematics skills.

EXAMPLES OF ON-THE-JOB WORKPLACE LITERACY SKILLS

Reading	Locates, understands, and interprets written information in documents well enough to perform tasks. These documents could be manuals, graphs, schedules, reports, or proposals.
Writing	Communicates thoughts, ideas, information, and messages in writing. Checks for complete and accurate information and edits for correct information, appropriate emphasis, form, grammar, punctuation, and spelling.
Problem Solving	Discovers a rule or principle underlying the relationship between two or more items and applies it in solving a problem. Uses logic to draw appropriate conclusions from available information.

pares the concepts of literacy and workplace literacy and gives examples of on-the-job workplace skills needed for office-related reading, writing, and problem solving.

SECRETARY'S COMMISSION ON ACHIEVING NECESSARY SKILLS (SCANS)

"AMERICA 2000: An Education Strategy," initiated by President George Bush, is a comprehensive plan to revitalize and reinvent America's schools. One major element of this strategy is the work completed by a commission, appointed by the U.S. Department of Labor, known as the **Secretary's Commission on Achieving Necessary Skills (SCANS).** Advanced by the secretary of labor, SCANS was formed in February 1990 and consisted of thirty-one representatives from business, unions, government, and schools. The commission was charged with the task of defining the know-how needed in the modern workplace and considering how this know-how is best assessed.

The SCANS report, entitled *What Work Requires of Schools,* identifies the eight areas (five competencies and a three-part foundation) considered essential preparation for all workers, whether they are going directly to work after high school or are planning further education. All eight competencies and foundations are highly integrated and require students and workers to be able to draw on *multiple* skills *simultaneously*.

Although the SCANS outcomes are not typically discussed among or even readily recognized as such by most businesspeople, their impact is enormous for business. When searching for productive employees, it is these SCANS-identified outcomes that are most often required and demanded by employers. As a result of SCANS, the business world has formally directed the schools—kindergarten through university—to teach the needed skills. By the same token, it has indicated that students equipped with these globally competitive skills will be hired.

SCANS's Five Competencies   The first part of SCANS, workplace competencies, states that effective workers are able to productively use resources, demonstrate effective interpersonal and information skills, and work well with systems and technology. Briefly, each of the five competencies are described below.

1. *Resources.* All workers know how to identify, organize, plan, and allocate time, money, materials, space, and staff.
2. *Interpersonal Skills.* All workers can work on teams, teach others, serve customers, lead, negotiate, and work well with people from culturally diverse backgrounds.
3. *Information Skills.* All workers can acquire and evaluate data, organize and maintain files, interpret and communicate, and use computers to process information.
4. *Systems.* All workers understand social, organizational, and technological systems; they can monitor and correct performance; and they can design or improve systems.
5. *Technology.* All workers can work with a variety of technologies to select equipment and tools, apply technology to specific tasks, and maintain and troubleshoot equipment.

Table 14.4 provides a clearer understanding of these five competencies by citing typical office tasks performed for each competency.

SCANS's Three-Part Foundation   The second part of SCANS states that competent workers in the high-performance workplace need the following three foundation skills.

1. *Basic skills*
   ◆ Reading—locates, understands, and interprets written information in documents such as manuals, graphs, and schedules
   ◆ Writing—communicates thoughts, ideas, information, and messages in writing; and creates documents such as letters, directions, manuals, reports, graphs, and flow charts

TABLE 14.4 ◆ Secretary's Commission on Achieving Necessary Skills (SCANS)'s Five Competencies

COMPETENCY	FOR EXAMPLE, AN OFFICE WORKER EFFECTIVELY TAKES THE FOLLOWING ACTIONS:
Productively Use Resources	1. Prioritizes one's own activities according to the manager's preferences, external environment, and target dates by selecting goal-relevant activities, ranking them, allocating time, and preparing and following schedules 2. Acquires, stores, allocates, and uses materials or space efficiently
Demonstrate Effective Interpersonal Skills	1. Participates as a member of a team—contributes to group effort by assisting other office professionals in preparing for a board meeting 2. Teaches others new skills 3. Exercises leadership by communicating ideas to justify position, persuading and convincing others by responsibly challenging existing procedures and policies
Demonstrate Effective Information Skills	1. Acquires and evaluates information from multiple sources 2. Organizes and maintains information such as a computerized storage of information 3. Uses computers to process information
Work Well with Systems	1. Understands how social, organizational, and technological systems work and operates effectively with them 2. Monitors and corrects performance—distinguishes trends, predicts impacts on system operations, diagnoses deviations in systems' performance, and corrects malfunctions
Work Well with Technology	1. Chooses procedures, tools, or equipment including computers and related technologies to enter and modify final reports in the computer 2. Applies technology to tasks and understands overall intent and proper procedures for setup and operation of equipment

Adapted from "Skills and Tasks for JOBS: A SCANS Report for AMERICA 2000," the Secretary's Commission on Achieving Necessary Skills, U.S. Department of Labor, Washington, D.C., 1992.

◆ Arithmetic/mathematics—performs basic computation and approaches practical problems by choosing appropriately from a variety of mathematical techniques
◆ Listening—receives, attends to, interprets, and responds to verbal messages and other cues
◆ Speaking—organizes ideas and communicates orally

2. *Thinking skills*
◆ Creative thinking—generates new ideas
◆ Decision making—specifies goals and constraints, generates alternatives, considers risks, and evaluates and chooses the best alternative
◆ Problem solving—recognizes problems and devises and implements plan of action
◆ Seeing things in the mind's eye—organizes and processes symbols, pictures, graphs, objects, and other information

3. *Personal qualities*
   ◆ Responsibility—exerts a high level of effort and perseveres towards goal attainment
   ◆ Self-esteem—believes in own self-worth and maintains a positive view of self
   ◆ Sociability—demonstrates understanding, friendliness, adaptability, empathy, and politeness in group settings
   ◆ Self-management—assesses self accurately, sets personal goals, monitors progress, and exhibits self-control
   ◆ Integrity/honesty—chooses ethical courses of action.

Implications of SCANS for New Workers and Employers If SCANS recommendations are followed by educators, student assessment in school will be transformed on the theory that multiple-choice, paper-and-pencil tests cannot evaluate students' ability to apply knowledge to real-world problems. SCANS recommends that in its place, every student should establish a student competency portfolio beginning in sixth grade. This portfolio will include several items such as a personal résumé, evidence of competence in specific areas of study, work history, extracurricular experience, and a record of community services.

If completed in a professional manner, your portfolio will tell the story of your progress in a given area. Therefore, when you begin your job search, you can adjust the portfolio to demonstrate you have the qualities and skills for which the employer is looking. It would be up to the employer to decide how much weight to give elements in the portfolio, using the company's own needs as a guideline.

Recall Time

Answer the following questions:

1. Describe three examples of nonverbal communication.
2. How is workplace literacy different from traditional literacy?
3. Is the grapevine a formal or informal channel of communication? Explain.

Effective Reading, Writing, and Speaking Skills in the Office

In your opinion, are good communication skills critical to attaining success in life? Many people feel that how well you communicate can make your daily activities either easy and pleasant or difficult and upsetting. The ability to communicate effectively is a skill that you can acquire just like any other skill. For example, the same practice and awareness of basic principles that are needed to become a good volleyball player are needed to become a good communicator.

To be good communicators in business, it is important that workers practice effective reading, writing, and speaking skills (as well as listening skills, which will be discussed later in the chapter).

EFFECTIVE READING TECHNIQUES

You may have discovered in preparing for exams that time spent reading can be either well spent or lost. Whether preparing for an exam or on a job reviewing a business report, you can get more out of your time, energy, and efforts by following a few basic steps. The basic steps in reading for information are previewing, questioning, and reviewing. This method is sometimes called the PQR system.

Previewing   Experienced readers preview the material before they start to read for comprehension. **Previewing** means scanning the selection, looking for main points, and discovering how the material is organized. To preview a report, for example, skim the preface, then turn to the table of contents and examine it to see how the main ideas are related to one another, and finally leaf through the report to get a feel for what is there. If there is a summary, read it. If not, read the first and last paragraphs of each major section to get a general idea of what the report is about.

Questioning   Become an active reader by taking a questioning approach to the material. Ask yourself, Why am I reading this? How will this material meet my needs? What do I already know about this topic? Asking and answering questions as you read helps you master the material and keeps you focused.

Reviewing   Most of the time, reading something once is not enough. You review what you read to fix it in your memory. You do this by using three processes—seeing, saying, and writing. First, go back over the material, skimming each section of the article. As you *see* the material, *say* the answers to your questions aloud. Then *write* brief reference notes that summarize the main points. This review method helps you remember by organizing and repeating the material.

EFFECTIVE WRITING TECHNIQUES

The skill of writing business documents is directly related to reading office letters, memos, reports, and other paperwork. Researchers estimate that American businesses generate over 30 billion pieces of original writing each year. Workers on average spend one-third of their time on the job writing letters, memos, and reports.

Much of the writing, however, is unnecessary; most of it is poorly written, and all of it has to be read. A great deal of time is wasted not only by the millions of people who have to write on the job but also by those who have to read all of this writing. Table 14.5 suggests ten steps you can take to become a more effective writer.

Using the "five C's" to check your writing is an effective method. The five C's are: complete, clear, concise, coherent, and correct. When you

Ethics on the Job

Suppose you work with a person named Bob who has excellent writing skills and who willingly helps anyone in the office to draft letters, memos, proposals, and so on. Even top managers ask Bob to take a look at their work. You've noticed that Bob is never given any credit and rarely even an honest thank-you.

Would you say anything to anyone about this lack of recognition of Bob's skills?

TABLE 14.5 ◆ Ten Steps to More Effective Writing

STEPS	EXPLANATION
1. Determine the purpose of the correspondence.	Ask yourself: What is the reason for writing the letter? What response is required?
2. Decide which kind of letter or report is needed.	If you are writing a letter, should it be good news, bad news, or persuasive? If you are writing a report, should it be direct or indirect?
3. Make notes of important points to bring out.	List everything that needs to be said, in no particular order.
4. Organize the notes by topics.	Arrange the points as you want to present them.
5. Write freely.	Write as you would talk. In other words, let your writing do the talking. Don't worry about spelling, grammar, and punctuation at this point. These can be corrected later.
6. Use appropriate sentence structure and length.	Your writing should contain a variety of sentence lengths. Remember, long sentences may be difficult to read and too many short sentences may make your writing seem choppy.
7. The writing should contain several paragraphs.	Short paragraphs permit the reader to identify the facts and points of emphasis.
8. Revise.	Read the document for content. If it is not correct, revise.
9. Edit.	After writing the initial draft, you should take a break from the task of writing. After this break, you should read the draft, correcting the spelling and grammar as you read.
10. Ask for input.	Ask a colleague to read the document for you. Welcome any feedback.

Source: "Basics for Better Business Writing," by Annette Vincent, Ph.D., *The Secretary,* March 1995, 8.

fine-tune your writing effort according to these five criteria, you question your written words and ideas by asking if the writing is

1. *Complete.* Are all the reader's questions answered? Does the reader have enough information to evaluate the message and, if necessary, to act on it?

WHAT'S YOUR ATTITUDE?

Becky Contreras has been the receptionist at Atlantic Business Services for less than a year. Her attendance record is good and the quality of her work and rapport with customers is excellent.

Becky comes from a family of seven brothers and sisters. Her siblings have frequent problems and rely on Becky for advice. As a result, she receives between three and five telephone calls at work each day from her family.

Becky was raised with a strong family commitment, so she believes all these personal family problems can and should be given attention even during work time. Besides, she figures, her customers on the phone or at her desk receive her immediate attention and are her priority.

1. *What do you think of Becky's attitude and beliefs in this situation?*

2. *Should family calls be allowed during the workday? Explain.*

3. *Should other personal calls be allowed during the workday? Explain.*

2. *Clear.* Does the reader get the meaning you intended? Does the reader have to guess what is meant?

3. *Concise.* Does the style, organization, and visual impact of the message help the reader to read, understand, and act on the information as quickly as possible?

4. *Coherent.* Are the ideas presented in a logical, consistent manner that makes it easy for the reader to follow and understand, and if necessary, make a decision or conclusion?

5. *Correct.* Is the information in the message accurate? Is the message free from errors in punctuation, spelling, grammar, word order, and sentence structure?

Some additional business writing suggestions are:

1. *Be specific.* Misunderstandings usually arise when your writing lacks clarity. For example, don't write, "I will get the report to you in a couple of weeks"; write instead, "I will get the report to you by September 15."

2. *Avoid redundancies.* Many writers like to use two words with nearly the same meaning in their sentences, erroneously thinking these add emphasis to the message. Instead, these redundancies add bulk. Two examples are: pleased and delighted, help and support. Using either word, not both, gets your message across just as effectively.

3. *Be positive, even when the message is negative.* Think about it; don't you find yourself responding more to positive statements rather than negative ones? For example, instead of writing, "The budget will not cover trip expenses over $100," write, "The budget will cover trip expenses up to $100."

4. *Turn passive voice into active voice.* Readers can visualize an active statement more easily than they can a passive one. For

example, "A meeting will be held on Thursday," is better stated as, "We will meet on Thursday."

EFFECTIVE SPEAKING TECHNIQUES

From the time you get up in the morning until you go to sleep at night, you use your voice to communicate. At home you converse with your family about the events of the day. With your friends, you chat about whatever concerns you. You use the telephone to talk about business and personal matters. At school, you ask and answer questions in class and speak with other students. If you work, you give directions, explain things, ask and answer questions, participate in meetings, and talk with customers and co-workers. In addition, you may occasionally give oral presentations at school, clubs, church, or work.

When you speak, try to give clear examples, use appropriate language, repeat information, ask questions, and use your voice effectively. Remember, when we speak, our voices tell a lot about us. Some facts about your voice that you need to know are:

1. *Your voice has a vital role in confirming another person's first impression of you.* If you sound harsh and abrasive, timid and insecure, or strong and confident, you will likely be viewed that way.
2. *Your voice has a physiological effect upon your listener.* Speak rapidly and the listener's heart rate and adrenaline level increases. Shout at someone and his or her blood pressure rises. Speak calmly, and he or she feels a soothing effect.
3. *Your voice is a barometer of your physical and emotional state.* It reveals stress before other physical signs, reflects how tired you are, and gives clues to other emotions. For example, the voice of a person who is upset, tense, angry, or afraid rises.

OFFICE TIP

Stage fright in public speaking can be substantially reduced if you know *what* you want to say, *why* it is a valuable message for your audience, and *how* you will best communicate the importance of that message.

Listening and Helping Skills in Business

Good listening habits foster success on the job. Think of the times that someone has asked you a question you just answered. Or, remember the times when someone interrupted when you were trying to communicate a problem and needed someone to listen and help you through it. If this is unpleasant in casual conversation, think how annoying it is when conducting business, especially when you are the one trying to communicate to a poor listener or a nonhelping agent.

EFFECTIVE LISTENING SKILLS

Most of us do not mean to be rude or insensitive to others when we lapse into poor listening practices. Sometimes, there are roadblocks that prevent us from actively listening.

◆ *Effective listening is as important to good communication as comprehension is to reading well.*

Roadblocks to Effective Listening   There are some realistic and honest roadblocks to effective listening that all of us experience from time to time. They are:

1. Our minds will not wait; our thoughts race along four to ten times faster than most people speak.
2. We think we know already; so we listen with "half an ear."
3. We are looking but not listening. Have you ever been introduced to someone and failed to catch the person's name because you were focused on his or her clothes or mannerisms?
4. We are busy listeners; we try to do too many things while we listen.
5. We miss the big ideas; we are listening to words, not concepts.
6. Our emotions make us ignore input when someone offers opposing ideas on matters about which we have strong opinions.

Active Listening   Good listening skills in the office do not just happen. You must be aware that listening is one of the most essential business skills you can have. One technique you can develop and use is active listening. **Active listening** is a restatement of the sender's total communication (thoughts and feelings) to help the sender understand both of these aspects of his or her communication as you view them.

How do you listen actively? You do this by feeding back the underlying feelings you hear as well as the content of the message. You probably do this automatically with friends, but simply don't realize you are actively listening.

Specific examples of active listening are: "You sound upset when he uses your equipment," or "You are not pleased with the way the report is coming, are you?" Evaluate your abilities as an active listener by answering the questions in Table 14.6.

OFFICE TIP

When taking a message for someone, besides recording it accurately, the three most important things you can remember to record on the message are the date, time, and your name.

TABLE 14.6 ◆ Are You an Active Listener?

INSTRUCTIONS: Respond to each of the following questions with either a yes or no, and check your score according to the scale at the bottom of the page.

DO YOU . . .

1. Limit your talking during conversations: (You can't talk and listen at the same time.)
2. Think like the customer? Can you understand and appreciate the customer's point of view?
3. Ask questions: If you don't understand something, do you clear it up now so it doesn't embarrass you later?
4. Interrupt another speaker? (A pause, even a long one, doesn't always mean that the sender has finished what he or she wants to say.)
5. Concentrate on what is being said and practice shutting out distractions?
6. Take brief notes to help remember important points?
7. Listen for ideas, not just words?
8. Turn off personal fears, worries, and problems when dealing with others?
9. React to ideas, not the person?
10. Allow the speaker to complete sentences? Or do you jump to conclusions by mentally or verbally completing sentences for the speaker?

SCORE YOUR YES RESPONSES:

	8–10	You're a good active listener.
	5–7	You're making an effort to become an active listener.
	4 & under	Oops, have you wondered why it's difficult to get a conversation going?

EFFECTIVE HELPING SKILLS

Sometimes a friend at school or, if you work, a customer or co-worker, is upset and needs someone just to listen while he or she talks through a problem. When you perceive cues that another person is in this situation, and you *choose* to help him or her, there are a number of communication helping skills that you can use. These skills are listed in order of increasing activity and involvement on your part. They are:

1. *Silence.* Simply listening passively with accompanying nonverbal behaviors (posture, eye contact, nodding of the head, and so on) communicates your interest and concern.
2. *Noncommittal acknowledgment.* Brief expressions that encourage the person to continue talking toward an eventual solution communicate your understanding, acceptance, and empathy. Examples: "Oh, I see," "Mmm-hmm."

3. *Door openers.* Gently inviting the speaker to expand or continue his or her expressions of thoughts and feelings shows you are interested and involved. Examples: "Tell me about it." "Would you like to talk about it?"

4. *Content paraphrasing.* Putting the factual portion of the message into your own words and sending it back to check your accuracy in understanding. Examples: "So you really told your boss off"; "You're saying, if your plan works the problem will be solved?"

Recall Time

Answer the following questions:

1. What does PRQ stand for and when is it used?
2. List the five C's for effective writing.
3. Cite three examples of roadblocks to effective listening.

Summary

Communication is the exchange of messages. They can be verbal, using spoken or written words, or they can be nonverbal, using symbols, gestures, expressions, and body language. Office communication networks can take on different meanings depending on the way they are viewed—as upward, downward, and lateral communication or as formal and informal communication channels.

Organizations expect and require employees to be literate on the job. In addition to reading and writing skills, office workers need to be able to apply such personal skills as information processing, logical reasoning, and critical thinking. The SCANS report addressed this need and identified eight areas considered essential preparation for all workers, whether they are going directly to work after high school or are planning further education.

To be good communicators in business, it is important that workers practice effective reading, writing, and speaking skills, as well as listening skills. The basic steps for reading information are known as the PRQ system, which stands for previewing, questioning, and reviewing the material you read. When you write, check your writing with the five Cs, by asking if what you wrote is complete, clear, concise, coherent, and correct. Effective listening skills include recognizing roadblocks to effective listening and becoming an active listener who uses good helping skills.

Key points to recall from this chapter include:

◆ For communication to take place, there must be a sender, a person who transmits the message, and a receiver, a person who gets the message.

◆ Experts point out that 93 percent of what we communicate is in our body language and how we speak, while only 7 percent is communicated by what we say.

- Both speaker and listeners have communication "filters" or barriers through which messages must come.
- Although information travels rather quickly through the grapevine, it can become distorted and at times counteract organizational plans and objectives.
- Essential workplace competencies, according to the SCANS report, are that effective workers are able to productively use resources, demonstrate effective interpersonal and information skills, and work well with systems and technology.
- The three foundation skills that competent workers need are basic skills, thinking skills, and personal qualities such as responsibility, self-esteem, sociability, self-management, and honesty.
- In office speaking situations, try to give clear examples, use appropriate language, repeat information, ask questions, and use your voice effectively.
- Good listening skills are one of the most essential business abilities you can develop to be successful.
- Effective helping skills include silence while listening, noncommittal acknowledgment, door openers, and content paraphrasing.

IN CONCLUSION...

When you have completed this chapter, answer the following questions:

1. What are some typical office communication networks?

2. Which communication skills should office workers be able to demonstrate?

REVIEW AND APPLICATION

✔ CHECK YOUR KNOWLEDGE

1. Give an example of one-way and two-way communication in which you have participated this week.
2. Explain what is meant by the idea that both speakers and listeners have communication filters through which messages must pass.
3. Give some examples of how organizations demonstrate both upward and downward communication.
4. In your own words, define *workplace literacy*.
5. What is the reason SCANS was formed?
6. What are some suggestions to keep in mind when writing office letters, memos, and reports?
7. In what ways are active listening and effective helping skills related?

📖 REVIEW YOUR VOCABULARY

On a separate paper, match the following by writing the letter of each vocabulary word next to the number of its description.

____ 1. the tendency for a message to be watered down or halted completely at some point during transmission

____ 2. feedback of data or information from lower levels in the organization to upper-management levels

____ 3. that aspect of functional literacy related to employability and skill requirements for particular jobs

____ 4. a special commission appointed by the secretary of the U.S. Department of Labor

____ 5. the exchange of messages

____ 6. scanning the selection, looking for main points, and discovering how the material is organized

____ 7. communication that follows the organization's formal chain of command from top to bottom

____ 8. a restatement of the sender's total communication (thoughts and feelings) to help the sender to understand both of these aspects of his or her communication as you view them

____ 9. transmission of information by word of mouth without regard for organizational levels; often provides a great deal of useful information

____ 10. verbal and nonverbal responses that the receiver gives by further communicating with the original sender or another person.

____ 11. feedback of data or information between departments or functional units

a. active listening
b. communication
c. downward communication
d. feedback
e. filtering
f. grapevine
g. lateral communication
h. previewing
i. Secretary's Commission on Achieving Necessary Skills
j. upward communication
k. workplace literacy

DISCUSS AND ANALYZE AN OFFICE SITUATION

Ling Chu is secretary at Clean Sweep Janitorial Services, a good-sized cleaning service in the Houston metropolitan area. Recently, cleaning supply sales representatives who have spoken to her have told Ling how other janitorial companies are being sued because their workers have caused medical emergencies due to their inability to read and comprehend directions. Apparently, the workers cannot understand the warnings on labels of chemically based cleaning products.

Ling wonders if she should discuss this information with the president of the company.

1. Assume Ling does contact the president. What concerns should they discuss?

2. If you were the president and were apprised of pending litigation for companies like Clean Sweep, what steps might you take to deal with the workplace literacy problem?

PRACTICE BASIC SKILLS

MATH

Using the chart below, answer the following questions on a separate paper about the number of pages prepared during January and February after you have calculated the monthly totals and overall totals for letters, memos, and reports.

a. What percentage of the total number of pages for January is represented by the total number of letter pages for January?
b. What is the total number of pages typed in both January and February?
c. What percentage of the total number of pages typed is the total number of letter pages typed?
d. At a cost of $3.50 per page, what does it cost to type January's reports?

NUMBER OF PAGES				
Month	Letters	Memos	Reports	Monthly Total
January	622	433	788	____
February	533	401	790	____
TOTALS	____	____	____	____

ENGLISH

Using simpler wording, rewrite the following sentences on a separate paper.

a. We will deliver the products in the near future.
b. You should study all of the new innovations in your field.
c. Our office is charged with the task of counting supplies not used in production.
d. This condition can be assumed to be critical.
e. Our goal is to effect a change concerning the overtime pay rate.
f. I will talk to him with regard to the new policy.
g. In accordance with their plans, the company sold the land.

h. Clint is of the conviction that service to the customer has improved.
i. Losses created by the strike went over the amount of eighteen thousand dollars.
j. The consensus of opinion of the parent group is that more money is needed.

PROOFREADING

Rewrite the following memo, correcting misspellings and incorrect punctuation.

MEMO

TO: All Staff Members
FROM: John Glenn, Office Manager
DATE: Deccember 23, 19—
RE: Changes in Corespoondence Preparation

Please be awarre of the following changes that should be incorporated in outgoing mail begining the first of the year:

1. If you can not find the name, of the person you are addressing the letter to, address it to the postion (Ex., Dear Travel Agent—not Dear Sir or Dear Gentlemen)
2. If the letter is for A. Smith and you don't know if the A is for a man or a woman, you should type *A. Smith* in the inside address. Your salutation should read "Dear A. Smith"
3. Eliminate wornned out phrasess such as:
   ◆ If you have eny questions...
   ◆ In answer to your letter datted...
   ◆ In as much as...
   ◆ Enclosed you will please find...
   ◆ I feel . . . I hope . . . sorry . . . glad . . . happy . . . thanks in advance
   ◆ Eleminate sexist language

APPLY YOUR KNOWLEDGE

1. Willie Tadano, a new employee at Mountain Pediatric, works with other employees in the general office area. When a new procedure write-up comes to the department, it is sent

around to each worker. After reading it, each worker initials the write-up and passes it along. A fellow office worker, Persia Gorman, has noticed that Willie puts his initials on the materials without actually reading them. According to the other office workers, he then asks them to explain the new procedure to him.

a. What may contribute to Willie's preference not to read new information?

b. Is there anything Persia should suggest to him?

2. *Debate the Issue:*
"In today's world, communication is based on speed of the message, not the effectiveness of that message."

Instructions: React to the above statement by quickly jotting down three or more ideas you have supporting *and* refuting the statement. Prepare to role-play either point of view in a mock in-class debate.

USING THE REFERENCE MANUAL

Retrieve the file CH14REF on the data disk. Use the proofreaders' marks in the Reference Manual at the back of the book to help you correct the paragraphs. Save and print.

When you plan your written communcation, start by definig the purpose and identifying the audience. Then make a outline and revise the outline untill it represents your writing objectife.

Geting the ideas down on paper is muh easier if you've done a good job in the first step. The best way to impress your reader is with the clarity and conciseness of your messge, not with the no. of multisyllable words you use.

In the editing process, you might have to keyboard in final copy from a rough drft prepared by someone else. In those situations, you should understand the meanings of severla proofreaders marks.

CHAPTER
15

Communicating in a Changing Workplace

OBJECTIVES

After completing this chapter, you will be able to do the following:

1. Describe the role of an office worker in a reengineered and horizontal organization.

2. List some alternatives to the command-and-control hierarchy.

3. Describe the external forces which are influencing today's office communication.

4. Evaluate the impact that the quality movement and total quality management are having on the workplace.

5. Describe new attitudes in the workplace about the importance of the customer.

6. Relate W. Edwards Deming's 14 points to the way organizations strive to do business today.

7. Compare the results of applying the continuous improvement process as a means of problem prevention.

8. Describe the internal forces which are influencing today's office communication.

9. Explain how empowerment is a motivational tool and enhances office communication.

NEW OFFICE TERMS

alternative work systems
continuous improvement
   process (CIP)
cross-functional teams
customer
empowerment
horizontal organizations

portable skills
quality
quality circles
reengineering
statistical process controls (SPC)
technology
total quality management (TQM)

BEFORE YOU BEGIN . . .

Answer the following questions to the best of your ability:

1. List some external forces that affect office communication.
2. What do TQM and CIP stand for?

The Changing Office Environment

As a result of recent and future economic, political, and social realities, organizations are restructuring around new roles for information and technology. New roles for information will affect the organization's structure, forms of management, and the way office workers do their jobs.

THE CHALLENGE OF CHANGE

Successful organizations, managers, and office workers recognize the difficulties presented by change. Figure 15.1 presents several excuses each of us uses from time to time to resist change. However, change is constant. There will always be emerging trends and ideas that will require each of us to occasionally alter our thinking and behavior.

FIGURE 15.1 ◆ Common Excuses Not to Change

It will take too long.

No one asked me.   It's hopeless.

I don't have the authority.

It can't be done.

There's not enough time.

It's too ambitious.   It's not my job.

It's just a fad, I'm all for it, but...

It's too expensive.

We don't have the equipment.

We're doing OK as it is.

In the past week, how many of these statements have you used when resisting an idea that required you to change?

We have already seen that today's employees have dramatically changed their work expectations, values, and lifestyles. As a result, many organizations are responding with numerous **alternative work systems.** Alternative work systems are nontraditional working arrangements that include office sharing, job sharing, flextime, and telecommuting, which will be more fully discussed in Chapter 18.

The familiar management hierarchy depicted on organizational charts as a pyramid was a formal diagram which showed how work was divided up. More important, it clarified who in organizations reported to whom. But that mentality, which worked so beautifully a century ago, has become self-destructive these days. Few business leaders foresaw the cutthroat competition, the emergence of a more skilled and educated workforce, and the development of advanced technologies that do everything faster and smarter. They have resulted in a change in the way office workers communicate with each other, their supervisors, and customers.

BUSINESS REENGINEERING, EMPOWERMENT, AND WORK TEAMS

In 1993, Michael Hammer and James Champy's book, *Reengineering the Corporation,* informed businesses about the benefits of a new managerial idea called reengineering. The authors proposed that, when properly applied, reengineering allows companies to do much more with far less—less investment, less time, fewer people. **Reengineering** means the stem-to-stern redesign of the way a company works, from its organizational structure to its corporate culture.

Business reengineering is not about fixing anything. Business reengineering means starting over from scratch. Old job titles and old organizational arrangements—departments, divisions, groups, and so on—cease to matter. What matters is how best to organize work, given the demands of today's markets and the power of today's technologies.

How does reengineering work? Successful reengineering is based on two principal concepts: empowering employees and using cross-functional teams.

Empowerment means giving employees closest to the customer the authority and tools required to make many independent decisions. It is founded on the belief that the person doing the job knows better than anyone else the best way to do it and how to improve performance. As a result, empowerment utilizes a worker's abilities and potential to a great extent, while cutting costs and improving customer service. This eliminates shifting customers from one employee to another, speeds decision making, and decreases mistakes. Worker-empowered organizations will be covered later in this chapter.

Another reengineering approach is to use **cross-functional teams** of disparate employees working together in a way that makes them aware of changes that may affect their jobs. These teams, based around task relevance, can propel organizations to new levels of success by increasing employee enthusiasm, involvement, cooperation, and commitment to success.

For example, suppose you work for an organization that wants to develop a new product line or service. With cross-functional teams, workers from marketing, manufacturing, human resources, and administration will share information and ideas and follow this new concept from start to finish. (See Chapter 17 for a further discussion of teams.)

ALTERNATIVES TO THE ORGANIZATIONAL HIERARCHY

A major change occurring in workplaces today involves reorganizing the organizational chart. The pyramid is passé. Wheels, clusters, and inverted pyramids are in style. As a result of these new structures, the manner, methods, and modes of communicating affect the work relationships of not only the president and CEO, but also the custodian and receptionist. Figure 15.2 illustrates some of the imaginative alternatives to the pyramid style of organization that are currently surfacing. These alternatives are discussed below.

1. The *inverted pyramid,* created by Nordstroms, literally turns the traditional organizational structure upside down. This organizational structure is relatively flat. There are only a few levels, with salespeople and sales support staff on top, making the key decisions. There is, in fact, only one formal rule at Nordstroms that employees are expected to honor: Use your own best judgment at all times. The company believes that salespeople should pay more attention to their customers' needs than to those of their bosses.

2. The *cluster* organization brings groups of people from different disciplines together to work on a semipermanent basis. In a cluster organization, groups are arranged like bunches of grapes on a corporate vine; the vine is the corporate vision that connects one group—a bunch of people working together—to another.

3. The *wagon wheel* is another organizational chart redesign—a circular chart, much like a wagon wheel. It has three main parts: the hub of the wheel; a series of spokes, which radiate from the hub; and finally, the outer rim. Customers are the center hub. The spokes could be the business functions such as finance, marketing, or engineering, or they could be teams dedicated to working on new product development or customer satisfaction. Keeping it all together on the outer rim are the chief executive and board of directors, who are placed there to make sure everybody has, at his or her fingertips, everything needed to serve the customer. In this organizational design, managers are coaches and supporters, not authoritarian whip crackers.

Each of these newfangled designs has its supporters, those who claim that their pet designs are the once-and-for-all cure for everything that ails a company. Not true. Without the right mindset, supporting measures, rewards, and management, even a reengineered organization is doomed.

But if it is done right, redesigning an organization can be hugely effective in harnessing the intelligence of its present employees.

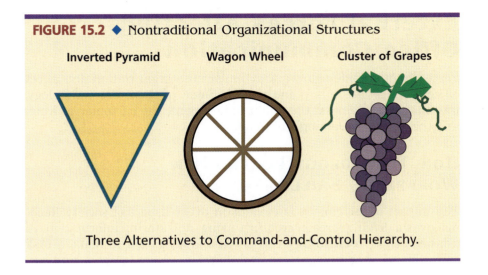

FIGURE 15.2 ◆ Nontraditional Organizational Structures

Inverted Pyramid   Wagon Wheel   Cluster of Grapes

Three Alternatives to Command-and-Control Hierarchy.

Reengineering is not the same as reorganizing, delayering, or flattening the company, although reengineering may, in fact, produce a flatter organization.

THE HORIZONTAL ORGANIZATION

Entrenched bureaucracy is a feature of the typical vertical organization, a company where staffers look up to bosses instead of out to customers. Even after these companies undergo the cutting, downsizing, and delayering designed to streamline their operations, too many layers of management still slow decision making and lead to high coordination costs.

In the quest for greater efficiency and productivity, corporate America's biggest names have redrawn their hierarchical organization charts. The trend is toward flatter, **horizontal organizations** in which managing "across" has become more critical than managing "up and down" as in a top-heavy hierarchy.

In its purest state, the horizontal organization has a skeleton group of senior executives at the top in such traditional support functions as finance and human resources. But virtually everyone else in the organization works together in cross-functional teams that perform core processes, such as product development or sales generation. The result is that the organization might have only three or four layers of management between the chairperson and the staffers in a given process.

Recall Time

Answer the following questions:

1. List some excuses people use who do not like to change.
2. Describe a horizontal corporation.

OFFICE TIP

Seize every opportunity that comes along to be trained in new technology, equipment, and work methods. Workers who do this improve their competitive edge in organizations.

External Forces Affecting Office Communication

Forces from outside sources that impact the organization and affect office workers are many and varied. Some of them are technology, international business, the quality movement, the customer as king, and the effects of Deming's 14 points.

HOW TECHNOLOGY FORCES NEW WORKPLACE SKILLS

The impact of technology is evident in every aspect of society. Technology is a driving force in creating, using, and storing information. In a broad sense, **technology** can be viewed as an aid to make a task easier by using equipment and procedures to create, process, and output information. Technology's impact is also apparent in the changing job market. Employers will hire and pay good wages to employees who demonstrate the ability to use technology effectively.

As Chapters 5 and 6 pointed out, workers must know how to use electronic information technologies to process data with computers and related equipment. These electronic information technologies manipulate text, numerics, graphics, voice, video, and sensory data.

Technology has lowered the skill levels of some jobs or eliminated them altogether, while raising the skill levels of other jobs. Technological advances also allow information and other resources to be transported faster than before. Today's workers most often need to locate, assess, communicate, and apply information as opposed to remembering it. This is because content changes and new information replaces

◆ *Today's worker must be able to adapt to new situations easily and apply current skills and previous experiences to solving new problems.*

old information at an alarming rate. Today's workers often lack skills for processing new information and integrating it with what they already know. Those processing, communicating, and integrating skills are vital in a fast-changing business world.

As a result, employees need new abilities. One is knowing how to learn effectively, so they can quickly apply strategies and tactics for mastering new tasks. They also need to develop portable skills. If you have **portable skills,** you are able to transfer what you already know to slightly new situations. Workers need to recognize when a problem is similar to something they have done before so they can use skills and previous experience to solve the new problem.

As we discussed earlier, literacy at work, unlike in school, is seldom a matter of understanding or writing whole paragraphs. Rather, it involves sets of words that relate in a restrictive way to the organization and its particular work. Workplace literacy involves the ability to use words clearly and with brevity and accuracy in the context of a given job.

The distinct language of the workplace is not academic in style; over time, workers tend to develop a highly specialized vocabulary, a language apart from the one learned in school. Though writing well is an important communication skill, researchers estimate that the typical U.S. worker spends only about 9 percent of the workday writing and 13 percent of it reading. Another 23 percent of a worker's day is spent in speaking and a significant 55 percent in listening.

INTERNATIONAL BUSINESS AND INTERCULTURAL COMMUNICATION SKILLS

It is rare to meet anyone these days who doesn't have some connections with another country. The world is indeed becoming a global village in which information and services are transmitted everywhere by fax machine, telephone, modem, and satellite. The ability to transfer information electronically has made information itself a prime export. Most countries do not have good information infrastructures and will buy information properly packaged from the United States. To succeed as employees in this global environment, workers must acquire the tools that will make their organizations internationally competitive.

International Business Skills   There is nothing mysterious about what knowledge and types of skills today's office workers need in order to become effective employees in international business. The key is not to wait, but to develop these skills in an appropriate international context according to recognizable world standards. Some international business skills include:

1. *A basic understanding of international trade and economics.* Simply put, what a country produces efficiently, it can export; what it does not, it will likely import from a more efficient foreign supplier. Organizations realize that improved trade opportunities happen when their employees demonstrate worldwide skills,

OFFICE TIP

One of the best resources for international business information is the U.S. government. Specifically, information and assistance are available through the Small Business Administration, the Office of International Trade, and the Department of Commerce in Washington, D.C.

which include knowing something about the religious beliefs, social customs, business philosophy, and family structure of other nations.

2. *Ability to manage information.* One of the driving forces behind our global economy is the revolution in communications. To be competitive, businesses and their employees must be efficient users of information, much of it electronic, whether it is from domestic or foreign sources; familiar with the primary business documents used by nations as they conduct trade with one another; and familiar with the global network communications system that makes possible the instant transmission of business correspondence, news, and vast amounts of business data to virtually any point in the world. The sources and types of information are virtually unlimited; the problem is accessing them and processing the acquired data. It is critical to be aware that effective information management is at the heart of what most businesses do.

3. *Knowledge of and sensitivity to political and cultural contexts.* Foreign government regulations must be understood and obeyed. Business culture can also vary dramatically from country to country. For example, in Muslim countries the workweek usually begins on Sunday.

Intercultural Communication   The more international business becomes, the more important it is to recognize differences among people from different cultures; these differences affect good communication. The more we take advantage of opportunities to interact outside our own cultural boundaries, the better communicators we become. For example, Table 5.1 provides some customs and tips for doing business in European nations relative to greetings, appointments, and social activities.

Intercultural communication skills play a significant role in the success or failure of U.S. firms participating in the global arena. In 1991, the *Ernst & Young Guide to Expanding in the Global Market* indicated that 96 percent of the world's population was outside the borders of the United States. This statistic translates into potential markets for U.S.

TABLE 15.1 ◆ Customs and Tips for Doing Business in European Countries

COUNTRY	NAMES AND GREETINGS	APPOINTMENTS AND PUNCTUALITY	SOCIALIZING AND GIFTS
France	Prefer to be addressed by last name; shake hands at beginning and end of meeting	Make appointments in advance; punctuality is a sign of courtesy, but up to fifteen minutes late is still acceptable	Invitation to a home is rare; but if invited, give flowers or chocolates to the host
Germany	Use titles and never refer to someone by first name unless asked to do so	Make appointments in advance; punctuality is essential	If invited to a home, bring flowers and follow up with a thank-you note
Great Britain	Use first names upon introduction; shake hands only at first meeting	Make appointments in advance; arriving ten to twenty minutes late is expected	Invitation to a home, pub, or restaurant is normal; never smoke until after the toast to Her Majesty's health
Italy	Refer to executives by their last names; handshaking and gesturing common	Make appointments in advance; being late requires an apology	If invited to a home, bring host a bottle of wine, flowers, or chocolates; exchanging business gifts is common
Spain	Use of first names occurs quickly; close friends greet with an embrace	Punctuality is not essential	If invited to a home, bring host flowers or chocolates; don't discuss business until after coffee is served

Adapted from Karen Matthes, "Mind Your Manners When Doing Business in Europe," *HR Focus,* January 1992.

goods and services and an abundance of promising international opportunities for North American firms. However, the most successful firms in the international marketplace are companies whose employees not only understand world economics and global competitiveness but who also have the ability to communicate effectively with international counterparts.

According to an April 1995 article in the *Business Education Forum,* employees in the U.S. need to study intercultural communication issues, such as:

◆ developing techniques that will overcome language barriers, both oral and written
◆ recognizing the advantages and disadvantages of using interpreters
◆ studying American negotiation strategies and how they differ from the negotiation patterns of other countries

◆ *To be successful in the global marketplace, businessmen from any culture must be able to communicate effectively with international counterparts.*

◆ understanding the impact of one's own culture on personal attitudes and behaviors, and recognizing that global workers are also molded by their cultures

◆ developing a sensitivity to intercultural differences and different value systems

◆ learning to feel comfortable using telecommunications technology, such as computer networks, electronic mail, and bulletin boards, to communicate internationally

THE QUALITY MOVEMENT

American business traditionally has had the attitude that "quality costs money." Today, however, that attitude has changed. More companies are realizing that "quality makes money." You may have noticed that quality has become a popular advertising theme for American-made products.

This claim to quality is not just idle puffery; rather, it is a desperate attempt to find acceptance in a world market that is becoming increasingly quality conscious. This new concern for quality closely follows a time when quality was taken for granted by the same organizations.

Quality has been redefined. The key issue driving the demand for quality, and one that cannot be ignored, is that in the current worldwide business arena, the product that was good enough yesterday barely squeaks by today and will be substandard tomorrow.

Quality is based on problem prevention—the concept that we can avert a problem only when we understand the *process* by which the product is produced or the service is rendered. A commitment to quality means stopping the process and fixing the problem before a customer becomes irate or a critical stage is reached. Quality further means continuously searching for improved task processes and higher product or service standards. Table 15.2 lists six of the most important beliefs of companies that emphasize quality and continuous improvement.

Total quality management (TQM) applies quality principles to everything a company does. Even the way an organization's departments work together on the inside (satisfying internal customers) is a hallmark of the TQM process. Pursuing total quality means turning each employee into a problem solver for customers and a keen observer of the bottom line. TQM embraces many organizational virtues: quality of work, quality of service, quality of innovation, quality of people, quality of company, and quality of objectives.

Quality, in this sense, is a judgment by customers or users of a product or service. It is the extent to which the customers or users believe the product or service meets or, preferably, surpasses their needs and expectations. Quality improvement, therefore, is a lifetime commitment organizations make. There is no "quick fix."

Why improve quality in the office? Because everything in an organization should be done in the best way that is humanly possible. There is no room for "good enough." Applying quality to the service side of organizations includes looking at issues such as how promptly telephones get answered, how quickly callers get the information they need, and how accurate the information is that is given to customers. Quality improvement means changing the way business is done. The aim of quality improvement is to satisfy the customer *completely.*

THE IMPORTANCE OF CUSTOMERS

In organizations, the customer has the influence of a king. As shown in Figure 15.3, a **customer** is an individual inside or outside an organization who depends on the output of its efforts. A customer may be your boss, a co-worker, or another department. In other words, a customer can be anyone who receives the work that you complete. It is

---

TABLE 15.2 ◆ Quality and Continuous Improvement Work in Companies That Hold These Beliefs . . .

1. *The customer is accepted as the most important part of the process.*
2. *Management's long-term commitment is to make the improvement process part of its management system by giving it focus, leadership, and participation.*
3. *There is room to improve, and preventing problems is better than reacting to them.*
4. *Improvement must focus on the process, not the people.*
5. *Performance standards must be zero errors.*
6. *All employees must participate, with recognition for success given both to groups and individuals.*

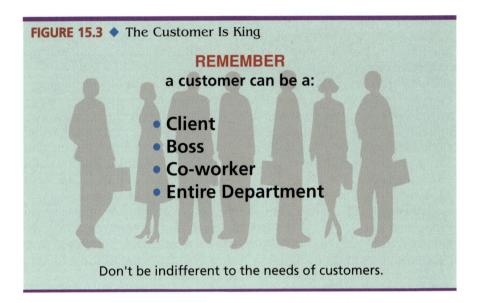

FIGURE 15.3 ◆ The Customer Is King

REMEMBER
a customer can be a:

- **Client**
- **Boss**
- **Co-worker**
- **Entire Department**

Don't be indifferent to the needs of customers.

that customer who must be satisfied with the product or service, because in the final analysis, quality is what the customer says it is.

Surveys reveal that although companies lose customers for a variety of reasons, the main one is that the people they deal with in the company are indifferent to their needs. Many workers' attitudes about the importance of customers are in need of an overhaul.

A recent four-year survey of customer service employees was conducted by Personnel Decisions, Inc. The most successful employees, they found, shared four key traits:

1. *Friendliness.* Good employees enthusiastically greeted and made eye contact with customers. They were also able to engage customers in easy and appropriate small talk.
2. *Self-control.* Employees stayed cheerful in tense situations and handled irate customers with ease and respect. In addition, they were patient with indecisive customers.
3. *Dependability and initiative.* The employees showed strong commitment to assigned duties and were highly motivated in their jobs.
4. *Effective problem solving.* Employees showed a willingness to seek help from others when necessary and demonstrated intuition in anticipating a customer's needs.

How do you defuse a customer who is angry and is directing that anger toward you? The January 1995 issue of *The Secretary* offered tips to deal with customers who are hurt, angry, or both. The following statements can be helpful:

1. *"Let me see if I understand what you are saying."* Listen carefully as the customer vents. Repeat back what you've heard and ask, "Am I getting this right?"

◆ *The main objective of a worker must be to satisfy the customer, whether inside or outside the organization.*

2. *"I'm sorry this has happened."* Never make the mistake of getting angry at an irate person. Empathy and sympathy help to calm a person.
3. *"If I could change it, I would."* You can note limits, but assure the customer that you will do everything you can.
4. *"There was no way to know this would happen."* Unpredictable events do happen, and your customer should know that you do not have total control over an outcome. It does not mean you are ducking away from responsibilities, but just pointing out circumstances that are beyond your control.
5. *"Thank you again for doing business here."* Remind the customer that you still value his or her business.

Customers are the most important people in any business. To use an analogy, customers are not the frosting on the cake—they are the cake. The frosting is an improved reputation and higher profits that result from a top-quality job. The following affirmations are an example of what one successful company believes about customers:

◆ Customers are not dependent on us; we are dependent on them.
◆ Customers are not an interruption of our work; they are the purpose of it.
◆ Customers are doing us a favor when they come in or call; we are not doing them a favor by serving them.

In reality, most customers are easy to please. They simply want us to do what we say we are going to do when we say we are going to do it. They are also pleased, and surprised, when we take the time to fol-

OFFICE TIP

Customers deserve the most courteous and attentive treatment we can give them and are the lifeblood of every business. Without them, a business would have to close its doors.

Ethics on the Job

Through a computer error, your department has overcharged a regular customer for consulting services. You tell the billing department manager, and she tells you to mind your own business. You strongly suspect she will not correct the error.

What should you do?

Charlotte Bauer and Julie Dodd were at lunch one day and were discussing the new emphasis at work on customers and how important it is to please them. Julie said something that surprised Charlotte. Julie said, "Mr. Jacobzak, my boss, pays my salary. For all the talk about serving customers, the real objective is to keep him happy."

As Charlotte drove home that evening from work, she reflected on what Julie said.

1. *If you were Charlotte and agreed with Julie, list two points you would make that would be supportive of Julie's attitude.*

2. *List two points that you would make that would take issue with this attitude.*

low up and ask if they are satisfied with the product or service they received. The idea of calling to follow up with a customer seems obvious, but its implementation is rare in today's organizations. Imagine how many compliments and good ideas for improvement an organization would receive if follow-up calls were viewed as *opportunities* rather than threats.

Recall Time

Answer the following questions:

1. List three ways to improve international communication among workers.
2. What does quality mean in the business world?
3. Who is the customer in businesses today?

DEMING'S 14 POINTS

As a basis for understanding TQM and the Japanese way of doing business, refer to Table 15.3. It explains the underlying assumptions and ideas about each of Dr. W. Edwards Deming's 14 points of management, which he taught to Japanese businesspeople in the 1950s. Deming convinced these leading Japanese industrialists that by instituting his methods, Japanese quality could become the best in the world. Though it has taken several years, this philosophy of quality is practiced in many U.S. companies today.

As the table points out, Deming's way is more than just attention to quality control. It is a managerial philosophy for achieving lower costs and higher quality. The philosophy is universal. It works not only in the factory, but in hospitals, in service industries, and even in the office.

Goals of TQM   Some companies waffle by speaking and using the vocabulary of TQM, but not adopting its principles. When this happens,

TABLE 15.3 ◆ Deming's 14 Points Explained

KEY POINT	HOW IT IS APPLIED
1. Create constancy of purpose for improvement of the product and service.	*Rather than to make money, the goal is to stay in business and provide jobs through innovation, research, constant improvement, and maintenance.*
2. Adopt a new philosophy about errors.	*Make a change in accepting mistakes and negativism; they are unacceptable.*
3. Cease dependence on mass inspection.	*Quality comes from improvement of the process, not inspection.*
4. End the practice of awarding business on price tag alone.	*Seek the best quality and work to achieve a long-term relationship with the supplier.*
5. Improve constantly and forever the system of production and service.	*Improvement is not a one-time effort, and management must continually look for ways to reduce waste and improve quality.*
6. Institute training.	*All employees need to be trained— quality cannot be left to chance.*
7. Institute leadership.	*Leading consists of helping people do a better job and of learning (by objective methods) who is in need of individual help.*
8. Drive out fear.	*Encourage employees to ask questions or take a position on issues of concern to them.*
9. Break down barriers between staff areas.	*Employees need to work as a team so they can solve or foresee problems.*
10. Eliminate slogans and targets for the workforce.	*Let people put up their own slogans.*
11. Eliminate numerical quotas.	*Quotas take into account only numbers, not quality or methods.*
12. Remove barriers to pride of workmanship.	*People are eager to do a good job and distressed when they cannot.*
13. Institute a vigorous program of education and retraining.	*All people need to be educated in new methods, including teamwork and statistical techniques.*
14. Take action to accomplish the transformation.	*Workers cannot do it on their own, nor can managers. It will take a special top-management team with a plan of action.*

Adapted from W. E. Deming, *Out of Crisis,* MIT Center for Advanced Engineering Study, Cambridge, MA, 1986.

Business
Math Skills

OBJECTIVES

After completing this chapter, you will be able to do the following:

1. Name decimal place holders.
2. Add numbers that contain decimals.
3. Subtract numbers that contain decimals.
4. Multiply numbers that contain decimals.
5. Divide numbers that contain decimals.
6. Multiply numbers that contain percentages.
7. Divide numbers that contain percentages.
8. Round off numbers.
9. List examples of how basic math is used in business offices.

NEW OFFICE TERMS

decimal place holders
dividend
divisor
floater

fraction equivalents
percentages
prorated

ENGLISH

1. *Rule:* Use semicolons to separate two independent clauses that are not joined by a conjunction. *Examples:* The plane flew low; it began to spray the plants. The new machine arrived; it was broken.

   Practice Exercise: Rewrite the following sentences, placing semicolons where needed.
   a. My little brother's toy arrived some parts were damaged.
   b. Interest rates fell sales of homes rose.
   c. The fruit ripened early the cooks made jam.
   d. Prices of food in the Philippines had gone up many people began to go hungry.
   e. Personal computers entered the workplace office productivity increased.

PROOFREADING

1. Retype or rewrite the following, correcting all errors.

CFEB COMPANY PUNCTUALITY AND ATTENDANCE POLICY

Five episodes of latness in any three month period will result in a persons being placed on written informal warning, with a copy of the warning sent to Wanda Lambert. Supervisors may, of course, verbally warn an individual before he/she reaches the fifthe latness in in a 3-month period. In fact, the supervisor who disscusses the potensial for a written warning before the number of latnesses reaches five is doing the subordinate a favor. Fail- ure to improve after being given a writen informal warning will advanced the individual to a formal warning. Formal warning are placed in the individual's permanent personel file and remain there for too years.

Five periods (frequencies) of absense in any twelve months will result in an indeviduals being placed on informal written warning, with a copy of the warning sent to Wanda Lambert. If a supervisor verbaly warns a person prior to doing a written informal warning, she/he has done that employe a favor. With attendence as with punctuality, someone whoe does n't improve adequatly after being given the written informal warning will be placed on formal warning.

APPLY YOUR KNOWLEDGE

1. Using word processing software, type the following invoice, calculating all the figures in the amount column.

Cheapie Technology Supply Company 123 East Fargo Street Reston, VA 20191-1596			
Sold to	Phase Two 151 8th Street Reston, VA 20191-1596		
Qty	Description	Unit Price	Amount
6	Quickwiz software	525.75	
3	Victory computers	2,200.25	
2	Deskjet printers	375.00	
3	24000 baud modems	95.50	
3	Cables	8.85	
	Subtotal		
	Sales Tax (7.5%)		
	Amount Due		

2. Using spreadsheet software, complete the Projected Expenses chart on page 391.
3. Recalculate the Projected Expenses chart in problem 2 using 20% off instead of 25%.

USING THE REFERENCE MANUAL

Retrieve the file CH16REF on the data disk. Use the numbers section from the Reference Manual at the back of the book to help you key a sentence that supplies an example of each rule. Save and print.

A. Spell out numbers one through ten. Use figures for numbers above ten.
B. Use figures for clock time.
C. Spell out fractions.
D. Spell out indefinite numbers.
E. For numbers of street addresses, use the basic rule of under ten spell out.
F. Spell out numbers that begin a sentence.

CHAPTER 17

Communicating in Groups and Problem Solving

OBJECTIVES

After completing this chapter, you will be able to do the following:

1. Identify the types and characteristics of groups in organizations.
2. State reasons people become part of a group.
3. Discuss the impact groupthink issues and hidden agendas have on accomplishing an organization's goals.
4. Describe the concept and application of self-managed teams in organizations.
5. List seven steps in the problem-solving process.
6. List the five conflict management styles.
7. Describe the reasons conflict in organizations may be healthy.
8. Identify the outcomes of win-lose, lose-lose, and win-win negotiating styles.

NEW OFFICE TERMS

formal groups
group
groupthink
hidden agendas
informal groups

lose-lose negotiating style
norm
teambuilding
win-lose negotiating style
win-win negotiating style

The Nature of Groups and Teambuilding Considerations

Effective organizations help their members learn how to work in groups to get results. A **group** is two or more people who interact with each other personally in order to achieve a common goal. Since much of the work in companies is accomplished through group effort, it is essential that office workers understand how groups function and how they impact both organizational and individual behavior.

TYPES AND CHARACTERISTICS OF GROUPS

When individuals associate on a fairly continuous basis, groups will form, with or without the approval of management. Individual members receive a great deal of satisfaction from being part of the group. A group can be either informal or formal.

Types of Groups   **Informal groups** arise spontaneously throughout all levels of a company and evolve out of employees' need for social interaction, friendship, communication, and status. In contrast, **formal groups** are deliberately created and set up by management in order to attain organizational goals and objectives. Two examples of formal groups are problem-solving committees (that meet on an as-needed basis and are relatively permanent), and task force groups (which usually focus on a specific issue, meet a few times, and then disband).

Characteristics of Groups   Groups have some common characteristics. For example, groups appear to set norms, instill conformity, and engender cohesiveness. Groups form with these common characteristics not only in the workplace, but also in other settings such as at school and in the family unit.

Norms   If being a member of a group is important to an individual, he or she will change personality, beliefs, and behavior to conform to the group. A **norm** is a generally agreed-on standard of behavior that every member of the group is expected to follow. For example, a norm for a dance group might be the way its members wear their hair at performances and their lively expressions. Human nature compels most

◆ *People have a need to interact with others through being part of a group. Most of us belong to several different groups simultaneously.*

◆ *Our involvement in groups begins when we are very young. We are part of family groups, clubs, classes, church organizations, and various other types.*

of us to gravitate toward groups of like-minded individuals with strong identities, so these norms ordinarily do not offend group members.

Conformity   Group pressure forces its members to conform, or comply, with the norms established by the group. Because nonconformity threatens the group's standards, stability, and longevity, pressure

FIGURE 17.1 ◆ Hidden Agendas

Let her wait till the next meeting and she won't be so great when only one or two show up!

Hidden agendas can sometimes be intentionally hurtful.

service. Team members make decisions on a wide range of issues, often including such traditional management prerogatives as determining who will perform which tasks, solving quality problems, settling conflicts between members of the team, and selecting team leaders. The team approach seems to be more an overall philosophy than a tightly defined set of rules.

◆ *An effective team is one in which every member participates and all work together toward a clearly stated, agreed-upon goal.*

Managers and workers alike participate on teams. Team members need to develop or possess skills in dispute resolution, team building, consensus building, and meeting facilitation. Team members need personal skills as well, such as the ability to keep agreements, communicate honestly, perform straightforward self-assessment, and give and receive feedback. In the current business environment, teams and self-managed groups at all levels of organizational structure are the most likely basis for fundamental reform in organizations.

What a team might look like is described in Table 17.1. Ideally, an effective team is one that is efficient, productive, and cohesive.

Teambuilding Elements   Organizations must help build effective teams because teambuilding does not just happen. **Teambuilding** is one of many interventions that are used to create change in an organization. Its purpose is the creation of a work environment that enables and promotes achievement of organizational and individual goals. Modern teambuilding efforts usually include concentration on how team members relate with each other and how work is completed.

Here are some ways to help team efforts become more effective:

1. Avoid arguing for your own viewpoint. Instead, state your point as clearly and concisely as you can and listen to others.

TABLE 17.1 ◆ What Does a Team Look Like?

Who Are Team Members?	1. A team is composed of two or more persons in the organization, usually from dissimilar departments. 2. Its members are competent and knowledgeable in the way they carry out their duties.
What Does a Team Attempt to Do?	1. The team is constantly learning and growing—adapting itself to changing requirements and multiple goals. 2. Its work is consistently superior in both quality and quantity.
How Does the Team Concept Work?	1. Problems and conflicts within the team are addressed quickly and professionally. 2. The quality of decisions made by the team is high and members share a sense of satisfaction in work accomplished.

Adapted from seminar, "Fundamentals of Teambuilding," presented by Jerry Odell, August 1993, Phoenix, Arizona.

2. If the discussion reaches an impasse, do not assume that someone must win and someone must lose. Look for a new option that is the next best alternative for everyone.

3. Never change your mind just to avoid an argument. Encourage differences of opinion among team members.

4. If an agreement comes too quickly, take another look at the issue. Various interpretations of what was agreed to may be hiding differences. Make sure that everyone fully understands the intent and content of the agreement.

5. Do not give way to other viewpoints unless you feel they have reasonable merit.

6. Avoid using conflict-reducing tricks to reach agreement, such as the majority vote, calculating an average, flipping a coin, or bargaining.

7. Make sure that every member of the group contributes.

Recall Time

Answer the following questions:

1. What motivates people at work to join groups?
2. List two potential problems associated with groupthink.
3. Describe a team in a work environment.

Decision Making and Problem Solving

Decision making is the heart of management, but it is increasingly becoming critical for all office workers to do it and do it well. Decision making is difficult. One thing is clear, however: unless you can overcome the fear of making decisions, your career may stall.

DECISION-MAKING RESPONSIBILITY

Poor decision makers may be smart and diligent, but when it comes to settling on a course of action, they resort to delaying tactics or blame others to avoid responsibility. At work, you are penalized much more harshly for not making a decision at all than for making a poor one. Avoiding this responsibility and failing to make a deadline are cardinal sins that few organizations will tolerate.

The Decision-Making Process   Decisions are based on facts, intuition, and past experience. On paper, decision making is a relatively simple process. The process starts with a need to make a decision; then at least two alternative courses of action are determined, followed by a selection of the best choice from the alternatives. In practice, how-

MAKING OFFICE DECISIONS

Tandy is the senior office assistant at Southwest Timber Company. She likes her job and has been recognized by management on numerous occasions for her outstanding work. Tandy has enthusiastically taken advantage of the many opportunities to learn and grow at her job since she was employed four years ago.

Management says that the company is growing and will add more equipment and workers to the office within the year, and will therefore hire a new office manager. Tandy feels she is a natural to get the job and is looking forward to really selling herself during the interview. She knows that, as office manager, she could make some changes that would help Southwest run more efficiently.

Tandy and two others inside the company apply for the position. In addition, four people are interviewed from other companies. When the announcement of the new office manager is made, Tandy is crushed because she didn't get the job. She is hurt that someone with prior experience as an office manager outside the company was selected. Tandy feels like quitting; she doesn't want to help the new person; she is angry at management for bringing in someone from the outside when she could have done a good job. After all, Tandy knows the company, and this new person has much to learn.

1. *If you were Tandy, would you stay with Southwest Timber Company?*

2. *How would you decide what to do?*

ever, decision making is a very conscious process that involves the future and is not needed when the outcome is inevitable.

Factors to Consider   Keep the following factors in mind when you make decisions:

1. The right person should make the decision.
2. Decisions should contribute to objectives and reflect the organization's vision.
3. Effective decision making takes time and effort but cannot be postponed.
4. Though there is seldom only a single acceptable choice, one direction usually surfaces as the best to take at the time.
5. Decision making improves with practice. The more you do it, the easier it becomes.
6. A decision may not please everyone. That is not its intent.
7. A decision begins the process for other activities to progress.

Below are questions you can use to make this task easier and guide effective office and business decisions. When making a decision, ask yourself:

1. What is the basic issue that must be addressed and resolved?
2. Is all the needed information available to make a timely and informed decision?

3. How have similar issues been handled in the past? Should anything be done differently this time?
4. If the stakes appear too high, can a compromise be settled on as a safety net?

Should decisions be made by an individual or by a group? Clearly, the trend is toward empowerment and group decision making; however, to provide some perspective, Table 17.2 lists both advantages and disadvantages of group decision making.

PROBLEM-SOLVING STEPS

People are not born with problem-solving skills; they learn and fine-tune this art over the years. Typically in a work setting, one learns the problem-solving process by observing and emulating others.

A simple technique you can use to speed a solution more quickly is to write a description of the problem you are trying to solve in the form of a question and display it in a prominent place. For example, the question, "What is the single most important thing we should do to improve document turnaround time?" displayed on a whiteboard or on a sticky note near a work area can be noticed throughout the workday.

Using the display technique helps to clearly define the problem, which is the first step to problem solving. The steps that follow represent one approach to problem solving:

1. Define the idea or problem to be acted on.

TABLE 17.2 ◆ Group Decision Making

ADVANTAGES	DISADVANTAGES
1. Provides the manager with a broad range of information	1. Holds the manager accountable for the group's decision
2. Lends a more "creative" approach to problem solving	2. Takes the workgroup's time away from other aspects of their jobs
3. Improves communication in the department	3. May result in "choosing sides" and cause morale problems
4. Creates high morale in the workgroup	4. Allows strong personalities to dominate the workgroup
5. Stresses a stronger commitment to decisions made	5. Requires more supervisory skill
	6. Is difficult to use if the decision must be made quickly

HUMAN RELATIONS

Assume you are interviewing for an executive secretarial position in your city. Surprisingly, you have been offered positions at two good companies on the same day. You feel you could be equally happy working at either one. Answer the questions below to help you decide which offer to accept.

1. *Will you use the decision-making process in deciding which job offer to select? Why or why not?*

2. *What specific criteria would you want the company you work for to meet? Consider*

managerial style, benefits, salary, size, values of the company, and so on.

3. *Would your decision-making process be different or affected in any way if your personal circumstances reflected either of the following situations?*
   ◆ *You are a twenty-eight-year-old single mother with an infant child.*
   ◆ *You are a forty-five-year-old married man with two teenage children in high school.*

---

2. Collect, interpret, and analyze information.
3. Develop possible alternative solutions.
4. Analyze the implications of selected alternatives.
5. Select the preferred alternative.
6. Implement the decision.
7. Follow up, evaluate, and modify the decision, if needed.

Conflict Resolution

As a student and as a member of a family, you deal with various conflict situations almost routinely. Organizations do, too. Why? Because no two people are exactly alike. And this uniqueness guarantees that there will always be conflict.

Since we all have our own personal values, experiences, beliefs, and perceptions, the chance that they will clash with those of someone else from time to time is very real. Conflict is an inevitable part of life, and the workplace is no exception. That is what makes effective conflict management an essential skill for any successful office professional.

Conflict, in itself, is not a bad thing. Disagreement can be a healthy and creative factor in the growth and development of an individual, team, or project. Further, conflict can ultimately strengthen work relationships. Trouble erupts, however, when conflict goes unmanaged and unresolved. Therefore, the goal should not be to eliminate all conflict, but to minimize and redirect dysfunctional discord by seeking and applying constructive solutions.

Whether the outcome of a conflict issue is positive or negative is almost totally determined by the way it is managed. Why not let individual "flash fires" burn themselves out? A thoughtful response is that they can ultimately take a tremendous physical, psychological, emotional, and financial toll on an organization and its employees.

UNDERSTANDING AND RESOLVING CONFLICTS

Until recently, conflict of any sort in the office has been unwelcome—perhaps because many people associate it with a lack of harmony, emotional pain, or destructive behavior.

Benefits of Conflict   Though it is true that conflicts can have a devastating effect on productivity, morale, teamwork, and ultimately an organization's bottom line, conflicts can sometimes actually be healthy for a business. Here's how:

1. *Conflicts produce change.* Conflict is often the first step in getting rid of outdated procedures, revising regulations, and fostering innovation and creativity.
2. *Conflict leads to unity.* Addressing rather than suppressing conflict opens the lines of communication, gets people talking to each other (instead of about each other), and makes people feel that they are part of a team that cares.
3. *Conflict promotes compromise.* People learn how to work harmoniously, come up with creative solutions, and reach outcomes that benefit everyone involved.

To resolve conflict effectively, you must keep an open mind, listen actively, and realize that a conflict situation is a problem waiting to be solved. In conflict resolution, the objective is to find the best solution for everyone.

The Conflict Resolution Process   You will find that the steps in the conflict resolution process are similar to the problem-solving procedures discussed earlier. Adhere to these steps when you need to resolve conflicts:

1. *Identify the problem.* Sometimes the problem needs only to be reframed. If you put a new frame on a picture, the picture looks different. If you put a new meaning on a problem, the problem looks different, too. For example, you can look at a glass of water as half full or half empty.
2. *Look for solutions.* Good solutions come most often from random, nonjudgmental brainstorming.
3. *Choose the best solution.* The best solution solves the problem, does not hurt anyone or interfere with his or her rights, and satisfies all parties. There should be no winner or loser; both sides should feel as if they have achieved something. This is called a win-win solution (which we will discuss more thoroughly later in this chapter).
4. *Act.* Follow through on one of the solutions.
5. *Evaluate.* If your approach turns out to be ineffective, do not look on it as a failure. It just means you have eliminated one approach and you are ready to try another. We learn by our mistakes. (Go back to step 1.)

◆ *Conflict is not necessarily a bad thing if handled well. Through effective communication and negotiation, conflict can lead to needed changes in an organization.*

At every step during the conflict resolution process, communication is important. Communication does not mean just telling someone what you want. It means *listening to* what they want. It means establishing eye contact and being sensitive to body language. It means not making demands or ultimatums, but using suggestions instead.

When conflicts become heated, and they sometimes do, follow these hints to control your impulses:

1. Be aware of your feelings. Although some people are ashamed of their angry, sad, or jealous feelings, these emotions are real and you are entitled to have them. For example, if you are angry, admit it to yourself and express your anger in a mature way.
2. Take a break if your feelings get too intense to handle. Divert yourself—do something else or go somewhere else.
3. Count to ten slowly. It will give you at least ten seconds to cool off and think about your approach.
4. Consult with someone such as a close friend, relative, or coworker who has a calming effect on you, and whom you can trust in confidence.

There is one final point you should understand about organizational conflicts. Organizations by their very nature create unique obstacles to problem solving. Be aware that the following workplace realities do at times hamper honest conflict resolution attempts:

1. Employees are afraid to criticize their bosses.
2. People are self-protective of their positions and power.
3. Technical expertise is intimidating to those with less knowledge.
4. People see problems from their own viewpoints rather than from the broader organizational perspective.

MANAGING AND NEGOTIATING EFFECTIVE SOLUTIONS

The goal of productive problem solving and conflict resolution is for the parties involved to move from some form of compromise to ultimate collaboration marked by a shared success.

Conflict Management Styles According to an article in the May 1992 *Journal of Business Ethics,* there are five generally accepted styles for dealing with conflict. Nothing is inherently right or wrong with any of these styles. In fact, each can be appropriate and effective, depending on the situation, issues to be resolved, and personalities involved. In fact, most of us from time to time have used these styles without realizing it—with our families, our friends, or in classroom situations. These conflict management styles are competing, accommodating, avoiding, collaborating, and compromising. Refer to Table 17.3 for a detailed description and understanding of each conflict management style.

Ethics on the Job

Your immediate superior has an attitude of "win at all costs" when negotiating solutions. You realize that if you approach working with others in this way, it will compromise your personal values.

Do you go along with his negotiating style to keep your job?

TABLE 17.3 ◆ Conflict Management Styles

STYLE AND DESCRIPTION	INVOLVES
Competing An aggressive and totally antagonistic style. A "competitor" pursues his or her own views at a colleague's expense. This is a power-oriented mode in which a group member uses whatever means seem appropriate to win.	Competing could mean "standing up for your rights," defending a position that you believe is correct, or demonstrating a win-at-all-costs attitude.
Accommodating An unassertive, self-sacrificing, and hospitable style that is in direct opposition to competing. Colleagues who use this approach relinquish their own concerns to satisfy the concerns of another employee.	Accommodating usually takes the form of selfless generosity or blind obedience and yielding completely to another's point of view.
Avoiding Avoiding is an unassertive, side-stepping, and retreat-oriented conflict management style. An avoider generally chooses to dodge conflict at all costs.	Avoiding takes the form of diplomatically side-stepping an issue, postponing an issue until a better time, or simply withdrawing from a situation either emotionally, physically, or intellectually.
Collaborating A more cooperative, synergistic, and multilateral conflict resolution style. Collaborators find mutually satisfying solutions as they dig into a situation to identify underlying issues.	Collaboration involves agreeing to not compete for resources or not use confrontation; instead, to find creative solutions to mutually engaging problems.
Compromising Compromising means that both parties "split the difference" in order to settle disagreements. It might mean exchanging concessions or seeking quick, middle-ground solutions.	Compromising involves finding expedient, mutually acceptable solutions that partially satisfy both parties.

Adapted from Dawn M. Baskerville, "How Do You Manage Conflict?" *Black Enterprise,* May 1993, 63–64.

When used appropriately, each of these styles can constitute an effective approach to conflict resolution. Recognize that any one style or a mixture of the five can be used during the course of a dispute to arrive at the collaboration and compromise required for ultimate agreement.

INDUSTRY FOCUS

Dan Farley
Senior Human Resource Representative
Silicon Graphics Computer Systems

Q. Mr. Farley, we often hear that decision-making skills are necessary for office support personnel. Is this true? If so, why?

A. Yes, it is very true. There are several reasons. One is that organizations now are becoming "flatter," meaning that there are fewer levels of managerial authority. Individuals are being asked to make more decisions on their own. Someone who has that ability is valuable to an organization.

A second reason is that office support personnel are often the "hub of the wheel" in an office, meaning that they serve many different customers within the organization. Someone who can make logical decisions when multiple demands are being made upon them is going to be successful.

Q. What skills do you look for when interviewing for office support positions?

A. Referring to my "hub of the wheel" comment, you need someone who is very organized and can handle multiple demands made upon them. Interpersonal communication skills are also very important, because office support personnel interact with so many different people.

Initiative is another characteristic we look for. People in offices are very busy, and having office support personnel who don't need to be asked for everything, who can anticipate demands and make improvements on their own, are invaluable.

Conflict may be unavoidable in organizations, but the anger, grudges, hurt, and blame that often ensue from it are not. Although negotiation is defined as conferring, discussing, or bargaining to reach agreements, most workers realize that in practice, negotiations involve conflict and therefore can result in win-lose, lose-lose, or win-win situations.

Negotiating Styles   An office professional should expect to spend a good portion of time negotiating with employees, suppliers, customers, or other work groups. When people bargain, they tend to back themselves into corners defending their positions, which results in a number of either win-lose or lose-lose outcomes.

OFFICE TIP

Every time we face up to a problem and resolve it, we grow by learning to get along better with others and by taking responsibility for our own actions.

Win-Lose   The **win-lose negotiating style** assumes that one side will win by achieving its goals and the other side will lose. When engaging in a win-lose negotiation, the person with the most information is in the most powerful position. A win-lose approach to negotiations is sometimes obvious and appropriate, while at other times it is less apparent and destructive.

For example, groups often set themselves up for win-lose outcomes by following the principle of majority rule—if 51 percent of the group votes one way, then 49 percent are losers. Another example of the win-lose approach is when the parties start the negotiation process by stating the specific outcomes they want to see.

When the issues involved in a conflict are trivial or when a speedy decision is required, this style may be appropriate. In organizations, it is also appropriate when unpopular courses of action must be implemented—for instance, when implementing the strategies and policies formulated by higher-level managers.

In general, use the win-lose style when:

◆ you have a clear conflict of interests,
◆ you are in a much more powerful position, or
◆ you are not concerned with a long-term relationship.

Lose-Lose   The **lose-lose negotiating style** comes into play when one party attempts to win at the expense of the other but ultimately creates problems for both parties. Two examples of lose-lose outcomes are when unreasonable union demands force companies into bankruptcy or when employers destroy the effectiveness of their workers by taking unfair advantage of them.

◆ *Often, people who are in a position of negotiating think they must win and others must lose. The best results are achieved when everybody wins.*

Mutually destructive outcomes can also arise from personal disputes among employees. For example, feuding co-workers may destroy their own careers by acquiring reputations of being difficult to work with or not being team players.

Compromise can sometimes seem better than fighting a win-lose battle and risking a lose-lose outcome. When resources are scarce or limited, compromise may indeed be the best solution.

Win-Win   The **win-win negotiating style** assumes that a solution can be reached that will satisfy the needs of *all* parties. Instead of looking at their opponents as adversaries to be defeated, win-win negotiators see others as allies in the search for a satisfactory solutions through collaborative means.

In most situations, the needs of the negotiating parties are not incompatible, they are just different. The four basic components of a win-win negotiation are:

1. Separating the people from the problem.
2. Focusing on interests, not positions.
3. Generating a variety of possibilities before deciding what to do.
4. Insisting that the result be based on some objective standard.

As you can see in Figure 17.2, there is a vast difference in results among the three styles.

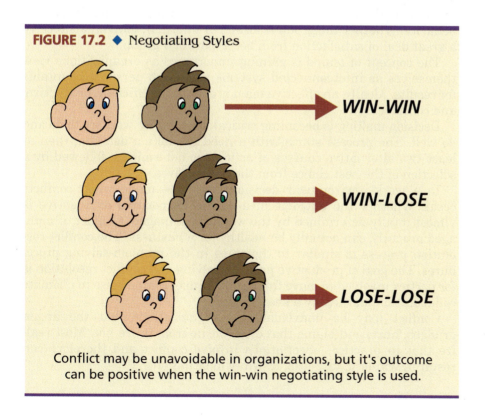

FIGURE 17.2 ◆ Negotiating Styles

WIN-WIN

WIN-LOSE

LOSE-LOSE

Conflict may be unavoidable in organizations, but it's outcome can be positive when the win-win negotiating style is used.

By focusing on the end result instead of the means of getting there, win-win solutions can frequently be found. You will want to use the win-win style when:

◆ you have common interests,
◆ power is approximately equal, or you are in a weak position,
◆ a continuing, harmonious relationship is desired.

Recall Time

Answer the following questions:

1. List five factors to consider when making decisions.
2. How is the conflict resolution process similar to the problem-solving steps?
3. Briefly describe the three negotiating styles.

Summary

Because much of the work in companies is accomplished through group effort, it is essential that office workers understand how groups function and how they impact both organizational and individual behavior. Whether the group is formal or informal, individuals receive a great deal of satisfaction from being part of a group.

The concept of teams is gaining importance as organizations view themselves as interconnected systems with each person accountable for results. Ideally, an effective team is one that is efficient, productive, and cohesive.

Decision making is becoming critical for all office workers to do and do well. The process starts with a need to make a decision; then at least two alternative courses of action are determined, followed by a selection of the best choice from the alternatives.

In a work environment decisions must be made when conflicts occur. Whether the outcome of a conflict is positive or negative is almost totally determined by the way it is managed. Conflict, if managed properly, can actually be healthy for a business. The conflict resolution process is similar to the steps in the problem-solving procedures. The goal of productive problem solving and conflict resolution is for parties involved to move from some form of compromise to ultimate collaboration marked by a shared success.

Conflict may be unavoidable in organizations, but the anger, grudges, hurt, and blame that often ensue from it are not. Most realize that in practice, negotiations involve conflict and therefore can result in win-lose, lose-lose, or win-win situations.

Here are a few essential points made in this chapter:

◆ Informal groups arise spontaneously throughout all levels of a company, whereas formal groups are deliberately created and set up by management.
◆ Groups appear to set norms, instill conformity, and engender cohesiveness.
◆ People become part of a group for the following reasons: affiliation, power, identity, and goal accomplishment.
◆ Groupthink and hidden agendas of individual group members can have negative consequences on the overall goals of an organization.
◆ Self-managed teams make decisions on a wide range of issues, often including determining who will perform which tasks, solving quality problems, settling conflicts between members on the team, and selecting team leaders.
◆ Conflict is an inevitable part of life, and the workplace is no exception. The goal should not be to eliminate all conflict, but to minimize and redirect discord by seeking and applying constructive solutions.
◆ Five generally accepted styles for dealing with conflict are competing, accommodating, avoiding, collaborating, and compromising.

IN CONCLUSION . . .

When you have completed this chapter, answer the following questions:

1. Describe the function of teams in business organizations.

2. What are three negotiating styles?

REVIEW AND APPLICATION

✔ CHECK YOUR KNOWLEDGE

1. Why would an office worker want to be identified with an informal group at work?
2. In your opinion, what is the most effective way for a leader to help a group handle hidden agendas?
3. What behaviors do you think describe a poor decision maker?
4. Why is it not a good idea for organizations to let conflict run its course?
5. Based on your experience, what percentage of time have you tried to follow most of the five steps when resolving personal conflicts? Were they effective?
6. Give an example of a win-win and a lose-lose situation you were in recently.

REVIEW YOUR VOCABULARY

On a separate paper, match the following by writing the letter of each vocabulary word next to the number of its description.

____ 1. attitudes and feelings that an individual brings to the group
____ 2. one of many interventions that are used to create change in an organization
____ 3. assumes that one side will win by achieving its goals and the other side will lose
____ 4. two or more people who interact personally with each other in order to achieve a common goal
____ 5. arise spontaneously throughout all levels of the company and evolve out of employees' need for social interaction, friendship, communication, and status
____ 6. one party attempts to win at the expense of the other
____ 7. the tendency of highly cohesive groups to lose their critical evaluative abilities and out of a desire for unanimity, often overlook realistic, meaningful alternatives
____ 8. deliberately created and set up by management for the purpose of attaining organizational goals and objectives
____ 9. assumes that a solution can be reached that will satisfy the needs of all parties
____ 10. a generally agreed-on standard of behavior that every member of the group is expected to follow

a. formal groups
b. group
c. groupthink
d. hidden agendas
e. informal groups
f. lose-lose negotiating style
g. norm
h. teambuilding
i. win-lose negotiating style
j. win-win negotiating style

DISCUSS AND ANALYZE AN OFFICE SITUATION

Assume you are a member of a strategic planning committee and the goal is to review the wording and intent of the organization's mission statement. There is one individual on the committee who exhibits the following behaviors and attitudes during discussions: "I must have everything my way." "Everything has to be perfect."

Using the five steps to resolve conflicts that were covered in this chapter, describe how you and/or other committee members should deal with this person.

PRACTICE BASIC SKILLS

MATH

On a separate paper, write the total amounts for the following purchase order:

	Quantity	Description	Unit Price	Total
1.	12 ea	Yellow pads	1.55	
2.	6 ea	HP toner cartridges	80.50	
3.	12 ea	Dry erase markers (red)	1.25	
4.	24 ea	31/2" high-density disks	1.10	
5.	12 ea	Sticky notes (3×5) yellow	2.00	
		Subtotal		
		Plus 6.5% tax		
		TOTAL		

ENGLISH

Rule: When points of the compass are used to designate specific geographic regions, capitalize them. Do not capitalize them when they are used to indicate direction.

Examples: Flagstaff is located north of Phoenix. Rapid growth is occurring throughout the Southwest.

Practice Exercise: Apply the rule to the following sentences. On a separate paper, if a sentence is correct, write OK. If a sentence is incorrect, rewrite it correctly.

a. Her travels took her to the far east.
b. Sean thought Northerners were very conservative in their thinking on this issue.
c. A second path is located just south of the main trail.
d. Proceed West on Washington Street to reach the Capitol.
e. The weatherman reported our area would receive westerly winds over the next few days.
f. The college course dealt with Western civilization.
g. Many people go south for the winter.
h. Is Portugal east or west of Spain?
i. The train was Eastbound toward New York City when the accident occurred.
j. The best restaurant in town is located just south of the public library.

PROOFREADING

Rewrite the following checklist on a separate paper, correcting misspellings and incorrect punctuation.

When you first join a group are you quiet at first? do you keep to yourselv, observing how people interract? You can sharpen your powers of analisis by asking yourself; some questions when you first encounter a group. As you observe, try to answer the follwoing questions;

◆ What are the objecrtives of the group?
◆ Are the groups goals cooperative or competetive?
◆ Does the group function as a team, or are there rivalaries among members?
◆ Does the group have a leader? Who is the leader.
◆ What are the norms o the group? Is it formal or informal?

APPLY YOUR KNOWLEDGE

1. Keep a journal for three days and note examples of decisions you make while at school, at home, at work, and with friends. Evaluate any three of the decisions according to the decision-making process steps.
   a. Did you follow the process?
   b. Identify any decisions that were faulty because you made a snap decision without enough facts, or you wanted more facts and waited too long to decide.

2. Describe two situations where either you or someone you know has successfully used two of the five conflict management styles described in this chapter.

USING THE
REFERENCE MANUAL

Retrieve the file CH17REF on the data disk. Use the proofreaders' marks section of the Reference Manual at the back of the book to help you correct the paragraphs. Save and print.

Attitude is a word that will have a ~~huge~~ *tremendous* impact on your future. It also effects to a great extent the quality of decisions you make. If you can not create and keep a positive attitude toward your job, your company, and life in general, you may find many doors closed to you and your personal life boring.

You can look at your job and focus your attention on all its negative aspects (poor working conditions, long hours, dull) or you can focus your attention on the more positive factors of the job (kind and caring co-workers, opportunity for advancement, tuition assistance). it's up to you.

CAREER PORTFOLIO

PART FOUR: BASIC SKILLS

Specific Activities to Complete

Select at least three of the following items for inclusion in your Career Portfolio, using the information from Chapters 14 through 17.

1. *Keyboard a list of the five ways you will improve your current listening and helping skills. Then relate each item on this list to on-the-job performance in an office. Save and print this list. (Be sure you proof according to the instructions given previously on page 92.) Insert this list as the first item in your Career Portfolio binder behind the fourth tab, entitled "Basic Skills."*
2. *Describe a situation in which you used the problem solving process with success. Save, print, and insert this description behind the fourth tab as well.*
3. *Describe your current international business and intercultural communication skills and areas in which you plan to improve. Save, print, and insert this description and plan of action behind the fourth tab.*
4. *Evaluate your workplace literacy skills according to SCANS. Save, print, and insert the evaluation behind the fourth tab.*
5. *Create a flyer using the desktop publishing features of your word processing package describing a seminar on Conflict Resolution. (Make up appropriate details relative to date, time, place, speaker, cost, and so on.) Save, print, and insert this flyer behind the fourth tab.*

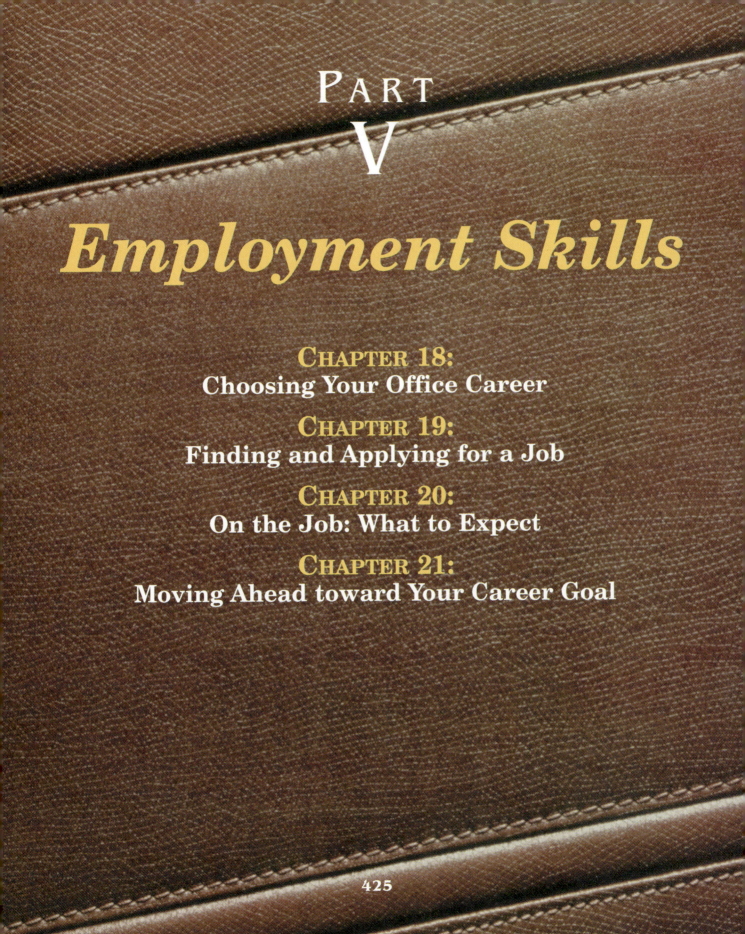

PART V

Employment Skills

Choosing Your Office Career

OBJECTIVES

After completing this chapter, you will be able to do the following:

1. Describe in detail the life you dream of having five, ten, and twenty years in the future.
2. List the eight steps in career decision making.
3. List the work values that are important to you.
4. List four topics on which you will need to gather career information.
5. List three sources of career information that are published by the U.S. Department of Labor.
6. Describe your own personal attributes.
7. Describe the responsibilities and requirements of careers in which you may be interested.
8. Develop a plan of action to reach your lifestyle and career goals.

NEW OFFICE TERMS

aptitude
Dictionary of Occupational Titles (DOT)
extrovert
flextime
fringe benefits
Guide for Occupational Exploration (GOE)
interest survey
introvert

job sharing
just-in-time hiring
lifestyle goal
Occupational Outlook Handbook (OOH)
personality
values
virtual organization
work values

BEFORE YOU BEGIN . . .

Answer the following questions to the best of your ability:

1. What personal attributes should be considered when choosing a career?

2. What types of career information should be considered when choosing a career?

3. What types of information should be included in a plan of action to reach your lifestyle and career goals?

A re you a dreamer? Do you sometimes think about how you would like to live in the future? Daydreaming is often discouraged as a waste of time. Nevertheless, this type of thinking—using your imagination— is the first step in planning anything.

As you consider how you might fit into one type of career or another, keep asking yourself how the work would affect your overall lifestyle. Chapter 2 discussed which office job classifications will most likely be available through the year 2005 and the types of companies that will provide many of these employment opportunities. It also described the duties of, qualifications for, and working conditions on jobs such as office clerk, administrative assistant, secretary, receptionist, and customer service representative. Although these job titles represent the majority of office workers, offices provide many other job opportunities as well.

Career Choice and Lifestyle

You have probably narrowed your ultimate career goal to some type of office work, but you may not have decided on the exact career or job title that you want. Even if you have already decided, you may change your mind. If you are under the age of twenty, you will probably work for about forty years. Planning for and making a career choice is extremely important, because your decision provides a direction for the rest of your life.

Most career choices are tentative—and that's good. You should feel free to change your mind about the career you want to pursue if you learn that another career is probably more appropriate for you. Office careers provide a wide variety of work, both for beginning workers and for those with years of experience. Besides differences in the types of skills used, they offer a great variety of work environments. For example, suppose you are a secretary in the racing office at Hollywood Park Race Course. You have a friend who is an administrative assistant in an office at the headquarters of IBM. You have another friend who is a secretary in a doctor's office, and yet another friend in a law office. Although your clerical and computer skills may be similar, the different environments provide great variation in these jobs.

Whatever your career choice, you must earn enough to pay for your housing, transportation, food, leisure activities, and your children's education. Thus, your work will directly affect all other aspects of your lifestyle.

If you can be happy living in a small apartment and using a bus for transportation, then you won't need to earn a lot of money. If you dream of a more expensive lifestyle—a house in the suburbs and two cars—then you need to consider future earnings when you look at possible career choices.

You will get more from work than just money. Your work will satisfy, to a greater or lesser extent, your social, psychological, and self-esteem needs. Your work will probably become the central activity around which you plan your daily life.

Making Career Decisions

Does it sound as though your work will control your life? In many ways, it will, but you may choose the type of work you do. So if there's a secret to a fulfilling life, perhaps it's choosing the type of work that will provide the lifestyle you want to live in the future. You have a right to do exactly that—and with proper planning, you can take control of your life.

◆ *Your career will most likely become the central activity around which you plan your daily life, and it will affect every other aspect of your life.*

While in high school, Recado made no plans for his future. "It's not important to think about that stuff," he thought. "I'd rather hang out with my friends or watch TV." After graduation, Recado's uncle offered him a job at his second-hand furniture store. Even though Recado wasn't particularly interested in that business, he took the job because he didn't know what else to do and that would "get him by."

1. *Will Recado's attitude of letting things happen to him lead to a fulfilling life?*

2. *What attitudes and actions will help you find a satisfying career?*

Of course, many people don't take control of their lives. They don't plan for a career. They make a choice, all right, but it's a choice to give up control—to just let things happen to them. You can make a better choice. You will most likely make an intelligent career choice if you follow a decision-making procedure.

Whether you know it or not, you follow certain procedural steps in making any important decision. Some choices are so simple that we don't even recognize the procedure. Choices about which TV show to watch are easy. Choosing which car to buy requires more thought, but you may not follow a step-by-step procedure to do so.

The following eight-step procedure is an adaptation of the decision-making process discussed in Chapter 17. These steps work especially well for career decision making.

1. *Define your need or want.* What do you want out of life? Think about your daydreams and picture your hoped-for future lifestyle. Consider your values and interests.

2. *Analyze your resources.* Your skills and aptitudes (natural abilities) are the resources you contribute to a career.

3. *Identify your alternatives.* Your alternatives are the careers about which you want to learn more. You have probably already thought about the careers or jobs that you believe would be interesting. Select at least three career fields for in-depth research, and you will have some alternatives to compare.

4. *Gather information on your alternatives.* Information on careers includes responsibilities and requirements, working conditions, benefits, and opportunities.

5. *Evaluate your alternatives.* Review all the information you have gathered on alternatives. Compare each alternative with your personal attributes. Would the work activities be interesting? Do the activities, responsibilities, and working relationships match your values? Do you have the skills required? If not, do you have the aptitudes to learn the required skills? If you will need further training and education for advancement, how will you complete them? Does this work mesh well with your personality? Can you realistically expect to earn enough to support your long-range lifestyle plans? It is likely that this field will have ample opportunities when you begin working?

6. *Make your decision.* Which alternative is best for you? Which is second best? If one alternative is clearly best, then you will probably stick with this decision. Most people, though, need to keep reviewing their career decisions for months or even years (see step 8). Things can and often do happen that make another career alternative more appealing or appropriate, so think of your initial career decision as a flexible one. No matter how certain you feel about your decision, you may want to change it later.

7. *Plan your action.* Your plan of action is an outline of what you must do to reach your career goal—and thus have your desired lifestyle. This will require setting some planning goals, which are the stepping stones toward bigger goals.

8. *Evaluate your decision.* After making your decision, continue reviewing it to determine whether it is, indeed, the best choice for you. Either you will become even more convinced that it is a wise decision or you will begin to have lingering doubts about whether it is appropriate. If the latter occurs, then review your other alternatives again. If you decide that another choice would have been better, then change your career goal. Before you change it, though, make certain that your new choice matches more closely with your long-range plans for your lifestyle.

OFFICE TIP

Don't delay decisions unnecessarily. Most decisions should be made as soon as you have the information needed to act.

Exploring Personal Attributes

Your personal attributes are your own needs, values, interests, data-people-things preferences, skills and aptitudes, and personality. Once you assess your personal attributes, you can determine which careers will match them.

An easy way to organize the information you discover about your personal attributes (and later, what you learn about career alternatives) is to record all of it in a notebook. Divide your notebook into four sections: Personal Attributes, Career Alternatives, Career Choices, and Plan of Action. As you explore your personal attributes, record this information in the first section. As you gather information about career alternatives, record it in the second section. Use the third section to record information on how your personal attributes match with each of several career alternatives. Finally, use the fourth section to develop a plan of action that will guide you toward your chosen career.

NEEDS

When you were younger, you probably began to plan your future by thinking about—daydreaming about—how you would like to live someday. Can you picture now how you would like to live five, ten, even twenty years from now? As you picture your hoped-for future life, you will probably consider the following:

◆ where you will live
◆ the type of car you will drive

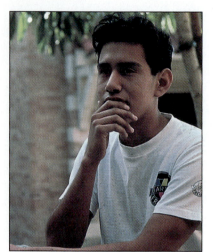

◆ *Your goals for the future are determined in large part by your values. If your values are clearly defined, you will likely have specific goals established.*

◆ how you will spend your leisure time
◆ your relationships with family and friends
◆ community, social, and religious activities
◆ the work you will do to earn a living—your career

Would you like to live the same lifestyle that your parents live? If not, how would you like your lifestyle to be different from theirs?

Your lifestyle is an expression of ideas and feelings that you believe are desirable, important, and worthwhile. These ideas and feelings are called **values.** As you daydream about the future and the lifestyle you want to live, you will picture ways you hope to express your values. Focus on different parts of your future life, and you will begin to see the whole picture of how you want to live. The way you want to live in the future is your **lifestyle goal.** You must have a clear understanding of your values to clearly picture your future lifestyle goal. If you are unsure of your own values, this picture of the future will remain blurry.

VALUES

If you have a clear set of values, you may find it relatively easy to focus on the future. You can set goals and plan how to reach them because you know where you're going.

Your values have been formed throughout your life, beginning soon after birth, and they will continue to change some as you grow older. When you were a child, your values probably mirrored those of your parents or other members of your family. When you were in elementary school, your family was still most likely the primary influence on your values. However, as you have grown older, your teachers and friends have affected them, too. The media, especially TV, have also influenced your values. As a teenager, you probably began to wonder about some of your values.

As young adults, it's easy to get confused about what is important. This is when we begin testing reality. We're unsure about a lot of things. Perhaps you're in the process of questioning some of your values now.

Consider what your family, friends, teachers, and others think is important, but decide for yourself what is important to you. As you mature, you will select values that you believe in, and they will become the guideposts in your life.

You may become more confident in your ability to plan for the future by setting and achieving goals as you develop and follow your own set of values. In the beginning, these goals don't have to be especially important ones. Achieving some small goals will build your confidence. In a year, or two or three, this confidence will help you achieve important goals.

We all have general values that define how we live our daily lives. Certain values define needs we expect to fulfill through work; they are sometimes known as **work values.** Your work values may include the following:

◆ fame
◆ economic well-being
◆ creativity
◆ religious activity
◆ prestige
◆ security
◆ independence
◆ friendships
◆ close family life
◆ humanitarianism

You will be a happier person if your work is compatible with your values than if your work demands opposing values. For example, if fame is important to you, you will likely be happier as a performer than as an accountant. If security is important, you will probably be happier as an accountant than as an aspiring but often unemployed actor.

Sometimes a formal survey is helpful in clarifying values. These surveys are called values scales or values tests. However, unlike most tests, they have no right or wrong answers. Most simply ask you to respond to a list of statements describing what people like or don't like in their work.

Values surveys are provided by the counseling office in many schools. If you think such a survey would be helpful, ask your school counselor about it.

INTERESTS

In choosing a career, the first criterion that comes to mind is to find work that is interesting. No job is all fun, but you will be happier doing work you find interesting than doing work you find boring or unpleasant. Try to match the work activities of a career with your own interests. How? Begin by listing all the activities you enjoy doing, starting with what you enjoy most. If you have some hobbies, you may be able to apply the knowledge you learn from one of them to your future work activities.

Your favorite classes in school may indicate interests that can be satisfied through a particular type of work. What in-class activities do you enjoy? Consider, especially, any activities that you might do on the job. You have probably used a computer for word processing and perhaps other applications. Do you like working with a computer? Which applications do you enjoy most?

If you like doing lots of different activities, you will find it easier to choose a satisfying career. If you haven't developed a variety of interests, you may find it difficult to decide which career would be absorbing. In that case, take time to explore some new interests, and try to relate them to various work activities.

An interest survey may help you identify work activities that you would enjoy. An **interest survey** lists statements describing a variety of activities. These surveys are called interest inventories or interest tests. Your response on one of these instruments can help you discover your level of interest in various careers. School counseling offices usually offer interest inventories, so ask your school counselor about them if you would like to take one.

DATA-PEOPLE-THINGS PREFERENCES

All jobs require working with data, other people, and things. On some jobs, such as that of an accountant, you would work primarily with data (information). On other jobs, such as that of a receptionist, you would work primarily with people. On yet other jobs, such as that of a copy machine operator, you would work primarily with things (machines).

Have you considered your data-people-things preferences? Do you like reading, writing, or doing math and working alone? Do you prefer activities involving other people? Are you fascinated by working with things, such as by building models? Your working relationships with data, people, and things will vary greatly from one type of work to another, and most work involves dealing with all three to some extent. Don't overlook this characteristic when considering careers or individual jobs.

SKILLS AND APTITUDES

An awareness of your interests and data-people-things preferences will help you choose work that you will enjoy doing. However, simply finding work that sounds interesting is no assurance of success—and you won't enjoy any career or job for long unless you are successful. You have already developed some of the general skills required for all jobs, such as being able to get along well with others. You have probably developed some of the special skills required for office work, too, such as keyboarding (typing) and using a computer for various applications. As you narrow your list of careers, it is helpful to know your aptitude for learning additional skills.

An **aptitude** is the potential for learning a skill. For example, if you found it easy to learn keyboarding, then you have an aptitude for keyboarding. Learning skills for which you don't have an aptitude will be more difficult, so it is helpful to determine what these are.

You are probably aware of some of your aptitudes. List them in your career planning notebook under Personal Attributes. Your performance in classes at school may indicate certain aptitudes. If you score high on most of your math tests, it's probably because you have an aptitude for math. You will likely be successful in accounting or other careers that require a lot of math.

An aptitude test may help you determine how much ability you have in certain areas. Some aptitude tests, such as the General Aptitude Test Battery, indicate levels of aptitude in various areas and list job titles that match your aptitudes. Your school counselor may be able to arrange for you to take one of these tests.

PERSONALITY

Your **personality** is the outward reflection of your inner self. It is apparent in how you look, speak, and act. All employers look for cheerfulness, enthusiasm, honesty, neatness, self-control, tact, and a good sense of humor.

Success in certain careers depends a great deal on specific additional personality traits. Perhaps the simplest way of categorizing personality types is to divide everyone into two groups, extroverts and introverts. An **extrovert** is a person who has an outgoing personality. If you make friends easily and enjoy the company of a lot of people, then you are probably an extrovert. You will most likely want to work where you can interact with a variety of others. You might enjoy being a receptionist in a busy office where you can greet and talk with lots of clients and co-workers.

An **introvert** is a person with a quiet personality. If you are uncomfortable in a room full of strangers and have difficulty making new friends, then you are probably an introvert. You might enjoy a job as an accountant, where you can work primarily with information and will not be interrupted frequently by other employees.

Neither personality type is better than the other, but each type is more appropriate for certain careers. As you may have guessed, most people fall somewhere between the extrovert and introvert extremes, but you are probably closer to one personality type than the other.

Just as we have measurement instruments for values, interests, and aptitudes, we have tests for personalities, too. They aren't tests in the usual sense—there are no right or wrong answers. But if you would like more information to help you define your own personality, then a personality test may help. Certain of these show how similar your personality is to that of most workers in particular careers. If you would like to take one of these tests, ask your school counselor.

Recall Time

Answer the following questions:

1. Sheila has decided on her long-range desired lifestyle. Following the eight-step procedure, what are the next steps she should take toward choosing her career?

2. When you imagine the lifestyle you would like to be living five to ten years from now, what do you see?

3. Raymond is particularly interested in a clerical job in the field of travel. Besides interest, what else is important in evaluating whether a person is "right" for a job?

4. A clerk's job at the library involves categorizing and labeling books, working alone in a back room. As the employer, what personality traits would you look for when hiring someone for this position?

INDUSTRY FOCUS

Kaycee Hale
Executive Director
FIDM (Fashion Institute of Design &
* Merchandising)*
Resource and Research Center

Q. Ms. Hale, are there certain skills that employers look for when hiring new employees? If so, what are they?

A. Today's employers (managers/supervisors) are responsible for assessing "potential" employees as human resource assets—the most valuable capital of any organization. In order to enhance one's organizational competitive edge within the "global village," managers/supervisors must evaluate an interviewee with an eye toward workplace basics, the skills employers want.

What I look for in a "potential" staff member is:

◆ computer literacy
◆ sense of humor
◆ flexibility
◆ strong work ethic
◆ willingness to embrace change
◆ service orientation
◆ enthusiasm and energy

Q. What advice about the real work world would you give to a student?

A. Start making connections. See every encounter as a possible opportunity to make your first impression a positive and a lasting one.

    Put your best foot forward in everything you do. Act as if your homework, your class participation, your in-class public speaking presentation, are dress rehearsals for your upcoming interviews and performance evaluations which might result in a promotion.

    Show interest, enthusiasm, and personality in class, in meetings, in conversation. You never know who's watching. Maintain a positive attitude with a "can and will do" attitude. Participate in group activities so that you can learn how to work effectively in a team environment.

    Expand your horizons. *Soar.* Dare to dream great dreams. Then promise yourself to make them come true!

Exploring Careers

Although your future life is sure to take some unexpected turns, the dreaming and planning for the future that you do now will leave less to happenstance and allow you to take control of your life. If you haven't yet settled on a career goal, the following information on exploring careers can help you make that decision. Even if you have already decided on a career goal, look again at some other careers—or at some specific jobs within your chosen career field. However, remember that career goals should be kept flexible, and they should be continually evaluated.

Although you can explore careers in many ways, plan to gather information on the following four topics:

◆ responsibilities and requirements
◆ working conditions
◆ opportunities and benefits
◆ emerging career options

A variety of sources for this information are available.

◆ As you explore career options and job opportunities, consider if a particular one is compatible with your own skills, values, and personality.

RESPONSIBILITIES AND REQUIREMENTS

The most important information you will need about jobs and careers is a description of the daily work activities. These are the tasks you will do if you select a particular job or career. As you explore each career and later consider individual jobs, ask yourself, "What are the duties and responsibilities?" Think about whether you would enjoy performing these duties and carrying out these responsibilities.

If the duties and responsibilities appeal to you, determine the requirements for success in this career or on this particular job. If you want to earn promotions and pay raises, you will need more than the simple entry-level skills required for a beginning position. How many of these skills have you already developed? Do you have the aptitude to learn high-level skills in this career? What additional training and education are needed for advancement? Where can you get the required training and education?

Some careers are more compatible with your values and your personality type than others. As you investigate each job or career, consider whether the responsibilities and requirements are compatible with your own values and personality type.

WORKING CONDITIONS

You will probably spend about forty hours each week (that's two thousand hours each year) on a job, so investigate the working conditions of any job or career you consider. Most office work is done in a pleasant environment, usually indoors and often in air-conditioned, well-lighted offices. Even so, situations can vary considerably. Some offices lack air conditioning and thus are often too hot. Others are noisy or are located in cramped quarters.

The level of stress on a job, whether physical, mental, or emotional, also falls into the category of working conditions. Most office jobs are not physically demanding, but many require more work than you can comfortably complete in eight hours a day—which leads to mental and emotional stress.

Other working conditions worth considering include data-people-things relationships and hours of work.

OPPORTUNITIES AND BENEFITS

When you discover several careers in which the work activities and working conditions appeal to you, research their opportunities and benefits to workers.

Check on the usual salary for beginning workers, and find out how much you can earn after working two, three, five, and ten years. Are the fringe benefits appealing? **Fringe benefits** are the extra payments or services, in addition to salary, that you get from your employer. They usually include medical and dental insurance, paid sick days, and paid vacations. More and more companies are providing child care, too. Some companies provide recreational facilities for employees to use during the lunch hour or other free time.

When you find one or several careers in which you feel you can succeed and that are interesting and rewarding, investigate the expected availability of jobs. You may not want to prepare for work that has limited opportunities or that would require you to move to another city or section of the country.

EMERGING CAREER OPTIONS

Several career options have become more available to office workers in recent years. The most prevalent are temporary work assignments, flextime, and working at home. These primarily affect where and when you work rather than the type of work you do.

Temporary Work Assignments   Several nationwide companies (such as Manpower and Kelly Temporary Services) and many smaller companies have for many years provided temporary office workers for businesses. These companies have also, in turn, provided opportunities for many office workers to experience a variety of working environments.

Office workers have more opportunities than ever to work for temporary agencies, and doing so has some obvious advantages. If you are a beginning worker with good office skills, your limited experience may disqualify you from some desirable jobs. Your good skills will probably qualify you as a temporary worker, however. Many beginning workers are gaining experience and sharpening their skills as temporary workers.

Another reason to consider working for a temporary agency is the opportunity to try a variety of jobs and environments. You can then decide how you want to spend the next forty years.

Large Office/Small Office: What's Your Preference?

CAREERS

You will usually find many more career advancement opportunities in a large office than you will find in a small one. The main reason is that more positions are available in a large office. The more employee positions, the more chances for advancement. In a large office, it is common to find advancement positions such as office assistant I, office assistant II, and office assistant III. These steps up the career ladder often result in higher salaries and more work responsibility. Also, large offices are often part of big companies that have more offices in other locations, which means even more advancement possibilities and more options if you are willing to relocate to a different part of the country.

Career advancement opportunities in small offices are usually limited. This is because fewer positions are available in them. Once an employee reaches a certain level in a small office, he or she finds little chance for career advancement. In many cases, the only possibility for promotion is to accept a position in a new job category. For example, if you are an office support worker in an insurance office, your only advancement option might be to become a claims adjuster.

Are you the kind of person who will want to move up the career ladder, or will you be content with a steady job that you know you can do well? To advance, would you prefer to try new and different kinds of jobs, or would you rather continue using your office skills and training at higher levels?

Most full-time office jobs require working about forty hours per week. Some people—especially mothers with small children—may want to work less than full-time. If you want to work a schedule other than eight to five, most temporary agencies will give you work assignments to match your schedule.

Just-in-Time Hiring   Some companies have begun the practice of **just-in-time hiring,** or not hiring employees until just before they are needed. They may be hired on either a temporary or permanent basis. This is an efficient way of utilizing human resources. It is similar to the way manufacturers use material resources by "just-in-time" delivery of parts. Just-in-time hiring occurs most often when there are high levels of unemployment, and there is a large pool of experienced workers ready to start work on short notice.

Flextime   Some companies allow workers certain latitude in setting their own hours for coming to work. **Flextime** means a system for allowing workers to set their own times for beginning and finishing

Ethics on the Job

You are employed in the office of a small publishing firm that is just getting started. You are very knowledgeable about the computer graphics programs that your company uses, and your boss has come to rely on your expertise. The stress of meeting publication deadlines is always part of your job. Increasingly, your boss has been asking you to take projects home on the weekend to help with the workload. She has purchased all of the necessary software programs and has provided a computer for you to use at home.

You are very happy with your job but you feel dissatisfied with having to spend all of this extra time working on weekends. Your boss trusts you to keep track of the hours you work at home and pays you at your regular rate for them. She then attempts to give you additional time off when the workload is light. You would prefer to be compensated for overtime. Friends suggest that you should simply bill your boss for more hours than you actually work.

1. Does this seem like an ethical solution to you? Explain your answer.
2. What other solutions can you suggest?

work within a range of available hours. The concept of flextime has been around for years, and it's now being accepted by more and more companies.

Job Sharing   Some companies have taken the concept of flextime to a new level by allowing employees to share a job. **Job sharing** is seldom a written policy and always requires the approval of company management. More organizations today are willing to give it a try when two employees like doing the same job but neither wants to work at it full-time. Usually one full-time job is shared by two people who each work half days. Or, one person may work two days a week and another three days a week. Lots of combinations are possible, depending on the job and the willingness of company management to allow such flexibility. Some jobs lend themselves to job sharing more than others. Most companies look more favorably on job sharing that involves relatively routine jobs. Jobs that require greater continuity of information throughout the day and from day to day would be more difficult to perform on a job-sharing basis.

Working at Home   During the 1990s, as prices of more powerful computers dropped, many people purchased sophisticated desktop computers for home use. These newer machines often are just as powerful as those used in most business offices. They make it possible not only to write letters and reports but also to prepare complicated documents, databases, and graphics at home just as easily as in an office.

◆   *Many companies now allow some employees to work at home, often with computers networked with office computers.*

Some workers are more productive at home because they have fewer interruptions than in the workplace.

More than ever before, companies are hiring part-time or temporary office workers and allowing them to complete all or most of their tasks at home using desktop or laptop computers. Sometimes the computers are provided by the company, and may be networked with company computers.

By working at home, you save the time you would spend going to and from an office every day. You also save on gasoline and other car costs, and you eliminate the frustration you would have to endure if you passed through congested traffic. Some companies allow parents of small children to work at home. This allows parents to stay home with their children and also save on child care costs.

Many types of work that do not require the use of a computer are done at home, too. However, the computer has made it feasible for more office workers to stay at home and complete their tasks. An increasing number of people have begun their own office services businesses in their homes, too. You may want to consider this alternative as you think about your career options.

Virtual Organizations, Virtual Workers   A new form of organization is emerging that uses information technology to collapse space and time. These organizations have the ability to change rapidly in structure and function. They are known as **virtual organizations.** They are not defined by buildings but by collaborative networks that link hundreds or thousands of people together. Why keep a hundred offices open all year long to accommodate four or five months of rush business? A virtual business will hire a hundred virtual workers and provide them with laptop computers at a fraction of the cost of maintaining offices for them. And these virtual workers can be scattered across the country or around the world, yet operate as if they were all in the company home office. The driving force behind this trend is global competition. In business today, it's "survival of the fastest." And collaborative networks can deliver better products faster, making greater profits for the company.

In virtual organizations, there may be little need for office managers. Each worker will likely manage information systems as a team member in a horizontal organization.

Sources of Career Information

Numerous sources of career information are available. You can find many of them in your school library, a local public library, or elsewhere within your community.

THE LIBRARY

Begin your career research in your school library or local public library. Most libraries have career books, magazines, pamphlets, films, and videotapes. Your school library may have a special section devoted

◆ *With a laptop computer, cell phone, and briefcase, a worker can set up an "office" almost anywhere and communicate with co-workers.*

to career information. In many schools, this section is called a *career information center.* Many of these centers have computerized career guidance programs that facilitate career research. These programs don't require any previous experience with computers.

Most libraries have copies of the following three books published by the U.S. Department of Labor. They provide a wealth of career information.

◆ *Occupational Outlook Handbook*
◆ *Guide for Occupational Exploration*
◆ *Dictionary of Occupational Titles*

The **Occupational Outlook Handbook (OOH)** includes detailed information on more than 250 occupations (the jobs held by 87 percent of American workers), and it is updated every two years. The *OOH* is easy to use and provides the following types of information:

◆ nature of the work
◆ working conditions
◆ employment
◆ training, other qualifications, and advancement
◆ job outlook
◆ earnings
◆ related occupations
◆ sources of additional information

The **Guide for Occupational Exploration (GOE)** organizes jobs into twelve interest areas. Each interest area is further divided into work groups and subgroups. The *GOE* provides the following types of information:

◆ the kind of work done
◆ skills and abilities needed
◆ interests and aptitudes
◆ how to prepare for this kind of work

The **Dictionary of Occupational Titles (DOT)** includes descriptions of more than twenty thousand jobs. In the main section, "Occupational Group Arrangement," it lists an identification number for and describes in some detail the duties of each job. Copy down the identification number, then turn to the appendix and learn the data-people-things relationships for the job. The *DOT* is somewhat more complicated to use than the *OOH* or *GOE,* so read the instructions in the front before you start using it.

THE COMMUNITY

The business community in your area can also serve as an excellent source of career information. You can benefit from this source in two ways. First, you can gather career information by interviewing several people who earn their living doing the type of work you are considering. Second, you can get some real on-the-job work experience.

Your library research will likely provide an introduction to several careers that interest you and prompt some specific questions. You can probably find answers to these questions by interviewing someone in your local community who has years of experience in the career that interests you. You may know people who work in the careers you are considering. Call them up, explain your interest in their careers, and ask if you may interview them. Most people are flattered by an interest in their work, and they enjoy talking about what they do. If you can, arrange for an interview at the job site so you can see the equipment and materials used. Before your appointment, prepare a list of questions to guide you during your interview.

If you don't know anyone engaged in a career that interests you, ask your teachers, friends, and parents if they can suggest someone. Or simply look in the Yellow Pages of the telephone book. If you are interested in accounting, for example, look under Accountants.

You will learn more about the duties, responsibilities, and data-people-things relationships of any type of work by actual on-the-job work experience than by any other method. Many high schools have school-to-work programs, mentoring, shadowing, and other work experience activities that allow you to work part-time after school. In many schools, a work experience coordinator will help you find the type of job you would like. Most schools grant credit toward graduation for work completed through the work experience program.

If you are doing productive work, you will be paid at least the minimum wage. However, if you are placed on a job mainly to get some experience and observe other workers, you will not be paid. These nonpaid positions usually provide greater opportunity than do paid positions to explore the many facets of a career. So don't overlook nonpaid work experience.

If your school doesn't have a work experience program, apply for a part-time job on your own. If you can't get a paid job in the type of work you would like, consider becoming a volunteer. Volunteers work without pay, usually for nonprofit organizations. Many young people get their first work experience as volunteers in such organizations as the Young Men's Christian Association (YMCA) or Young Women's Christian Association (YWCA), the American Red Cross, or a local hospital. Many opportunities are available through volunteer work, but it is sometimes difficult to get the type of experience you are seeking.

Choosing a Career

The work you do to earn a living will probably become the central activity in your life. It will influence every aspect of your lifestyle. Perhaps no decision in your life will be more important than your choice of career.

Unfortunately, many people never get around to making a conscious career decision. Some spend more time planning a wardrobe or decid-

WHAT'S YOUR ATTITUDE?

Patty has been sure about her future ever since she can remember. "I definitely want to be a model," Patty declares. But Patty's school counselor advises her to look around a little more before making her final decision. "Patty, I'd like you to take some tests—an interest survey, an aptitude test, and a personality test—just to make sure you are not overlooking other promising careers." To her surprise, Patty discovers a number of career opportunities that appeal to her and that she has never been aware of before. "Wow!" she says. "This is exciting. I never knew about these other possibilities! I like having these new options."

Renee is also convinced that she wants to become a model. When the school counselor asks Renee to take the tests, Renee refuses. "I already know what I want to do!" she states.

1. *Describe Patty's and Renee's attitudes toward choosing their careers.*

2. *How might Patty's attitude be helpful on the job?*

3. *Based on their attitudes, which girl is more likely to succeed?*

ing which car to buy than they do planning a career. They don't seem to understand that the work they do will control much of their future lives. Unable to make a conscious choice, these people fall into some type of work through happenstance and simply drift through life. They do make a decision, but it's an unconscious decision to give away control of their lives.

Having explored your personal attributes and careers, it's time to make your career choice. You may feel reluctant to make such an important decision today, this month, or even this year. However, the sooner you choose a career, the sooner you will have a direction for your life. Remember, no career choice is final, so you can always change your mind. Indeed, you *should* change your career choice whenever you determine another one is better for you.

Developing Your Plan of Action

Some people with good intentions get as far as choosing a career but never get around to developing a plan to reach their goals. If you haven't done so already, plan now how you will reach your career and lifestyle goals. Include the following types of information in your plan:

◆ training and education
◆ money for training and education
◆ jobs leading to your career and lifestyle goals
◆ major changes in your personal life

Begin by setting some planning goals. These are the relatively minor but important goals you must reach before you can achieve your bigger goals.

Goals must be specific. Saying you want to be a success or you want a simple lifestyle is much too general. Describe your lifestyle goal in detail.

Goals must be realistic. Setting goals that are impossible to reach is worse than having no goals at all because such goals will constantly frustrate you.

Write your goals clearly and completely, and set a "due date" for each one. Begin with the lifestyle and career goals you want to achieve after five, ten, and twenty years. Then decide what long-range, medium-range, and short-range planning goals will enable you to reach your ultimate goals.

Your ultimate career goal might be to become a certified public accountant (CPA) by the time you are twenty-five years old. You might set a long-range goal to graduate with a bachelor of arts (BA) degree in accounting by the time you are twenty-two. A medium-range goal might be acceptance by a certain college when you graduate from high school. A short-range goal might be to earn an A in this class.

With better planning, most people could have a more satisfying lifestyle than the one they live. You can have a satisfying lifestyle because you know how to take control of your life. You know how to explore your personal attributes, investigate careers, and make important decisions. You also know how to develop a plan of action that will guide you toward your ultimate career and lifestyle goals. Your plan of action can do these four things for you:

◆ Organize your activities.
◆ Keep you on schedule.
◆ Help you set priorities.
◆ Give you a feeling of accomplishment when you reach your goals.

As you achieve your short-range goals, you will become more confident. You will know that you can achieve your longer-range goals, too.

Recall Time

Answer the following questions:

1. Suzy is considering a front-office administrative assistant job for a busy trucking company. What should she find out about her potential working conditions before she makes her final decision?

2. What are some advantages to temporary office work through an agency?

3. Jorge is interested in department store customer service. What sources can he find in the library to research this career?

4. If your long-range career goal is to be a bookkeeper, what might be a short-range goal that you can accomplish during high school?

Summary

Your career choice will be one of the most important decisions of your life. Your work will affect every aspect of your daily life. Such an important decision requires a step-by-step decision-making procedure in which you define your desired future lifestyle; analyze your skills and aptitudes; identify your career alternatives; get information about those alternatives; evaluate the alternatives; make your decision; develop a plan of action to reach your career goal; and continue to evaluate your decision until you are convinced it is the best for you, or decide to change your career goal to one that suits you better.

Exploring your personal attributes can be helpful in selecting a career that makes you happy. In assessing your own personal characteristics, include a description of the lifestyle you hope to lead; your personal and work values; your interests; your preferences for working with data, people, or things; your skills and aptitudes; and your personality type.

Exploring career characteristics is equally as important as assessing yourself. The most vital information about jobs and careers concerns their duties and responsibilities. Try to find a match between your own needs, values, interests, and skills and the requirements of a job. Examine the working conditions of a job or career. Are they compatible with your personal preferences? Are the job opportunities and benefits agreeable to you? Investigate the expected availability of jobs in a certain field. Include temporary work, job sharing, and working at home in your list of options.

Use your school and public libraries as valuable sources of information about careers. Many libraries contain extensive resources for your career research. Three books published by the U.S. Department of Labor provide particularly detailed information about jobs and careers: the *Occupational Outlook Handbook (OOH)*, the *Guide for Occupational Exploration (GOE)*, and the *Dictionary of Occupational Titles (DOT)*.

Contact with your local business community can also provide excellent career information. One approach is to interview people who are working in jobs that interest you. Perhaps the best way to find out about a particular job or career is firsthand experience. Work experience programs or part-time jobs allow you to try out a type of work with on-the-job experience.

Choosing a career goal is truly taking control of your life. It is like sitting in the driver's seat and choosing a destination. To make sure you arrive at the destination, you take along a road map—a plan to reach your journey's end. This plan of action includes setting goals for the training, education, and jobs that will lead to your ultimate career and lifestyle goals.

When preparing for and choosing your office career, you need to:

◆ Think about how you would like to live in the future.
◆ Ask yourself how different types of work would affect your overall lifestyle.
◆ Believe that career choices should sometimes be changed.

Ethics on the Job

You work for a marketing firm as a team member in the animation department. Your supervisor, Luis, is pleased with your work and has offered to spend time teaching you more about the art of animation. You are eager to learn, and accept his offer. The more time you spend with Luis, the more you both come to realize that you have an aptitude for this kind of work.

During a team meeting, Luis announces that he has been asked to prepare a presentation for a prospective client. It is a big account, and securing the business is very important to your firm's management. Luis requests that you serve as his assistant on this project. You are pleased at the invitation, but dismayed by the fact that the prospective client is a tobacco company. You are even more upset when you realize that this company is looking for a way to market its products to young people. Such a project conflicts strongly with your personal values, but you realize that a successful presentation will help both you and Luis to advance within the marketing firm.

1. What must you consider before making a decision?
2. What solution can you offer?

◆ Want to take control of your own life.
◆ Use a decision-making procedure for important decisions.
◆ Record all your career information in a notebook.
◆ Consider what your family and friends think is important, but decide for yourself what is important to you.
◆ Know the types of work that would interest you.

IN CONCLUSION . . .

When you have completed this chapter, answer the following questions:

1. What personal attributes should be considered when choosing a career?

2. What types of career information should be considered when choosing a career?

3. What types of information should be included in a plan of action to reach your lifestyle and career goals?

REVIEW AND APPLICATION

✔ CHECK YOUR KNOWLEDGE

1. How do office careers provide a wide variety of work when the office skills used are so similar?
2. "Your work will be the central activity of your life." Is this statement true or false? Why?
3. Why is it important to daydream about the lifestyle you want to live?
4. List three things you will probably consider when thinking about your hoped-for future life.
5. List three things that have influenced your values.
6. What are some examples of work values?
7. Why would someone take an interest survey?
8. Would a librarian work mostly with data, people, or things?
9. What are some indications of a person's aptitudes?
10. What kinds of work activities would an extrovert enjoy?
11. What is the most important information you will need about jobs and careers?
12. List three examples of working conditions.
13. What is it called when a company provides child care?
14. What are the advantages of working at home?
15. What are the two best sources of career information?
16. What is the *DOT*?
17. List the three career information books published by the U.S. Department of Labor.
18. What are the two ways you can use your business community as a source of career information?
19. When choosing a career, what is the importance of developing a plan of action?
20. What are the ingredients in a career plan of action?
21. Why is it important that goals be realistic?

REVIEW YOUR VOCABULARY

On a separate paper, write the letter of the vocabulary word that is described below.

____ 1. system for allowing workers to set their own work hours
____ 2. outward reflection of your inner self, apparent in how you look, speak, and act
____ 3. person who has an outgoing personality
____ 4. extra payments or services, in addition to salary, that you get from your employer
____ 5. a business organization composed of workers scattered throughout the country or the world, and linked electronically rather than being grouped within one building
____ 6. resource that organizes jobs into twelve interest areas
____ 7. person with a quiet personality
____ 8. way you want to live in the future
____ 9. needs we expect to fulfill through work
____ 10. resource that includes descriptions of more than twenty thousand jobs
____ 11. the practice of hiring employees just before they are needed, on either a temporary or a permanent basis
____ 12. ideas and feelings you believe are desirable and important
____ 13. potential for learning a skill
____ 14. list of statements describing a variety of activities
____ 15. resource that includes detailed information on more than 250 occupations and is updated every two years

a. aptitude
b. *Dictionary of Occupational Titles (DOT)*
c. extrovert
d. flextime
e. fringe benefits
f. *Guide for Occupational Exploration (GOE)*
g. just-in-time hiring
h. interest survey
i. introvert
j. lifestyle goal
k. *Occupational Outlook Handbook (OOH)*
l. personality
m. values
n. work values
o. virtual organization

DISCUSS AND ANALYZE AN OFFICE SITUATION

1. James has accepted an office job with an accounting firm. The job promises to be a perfect match with James's interests and skills. During the first few weeks of work, however, his employer asks James to change his work hours—to come in later and stay later. This conflicts with the schedule James has arranged in order to spend time with his family. James's family is very important to him, but he doesn't want to lose his new job.

    What should James do?

2. Robert enjoys and is skilled at working on cars. He thinks it would be great to someday have his own garage. But when a job at McDonald's came up, Robert took it for the extra money. After two years, Robert is still at McDonald's—and the idea of having his own garage has become just a dream.

    What was missing in Robert's approach to his career? What could he have done differently?

PRACTICE BASIC SKILLS

MATH

1. When considering your lifestyle goals, part of what you must consider is how much money you wish to earn. If you earn $25,000 in one year when the inflation rate is 5 percent, you must earn an extra 5 percent the following year just to stay even.

    Suppose you will earn $25,000 in one year, and the inflation rate remains at 5 percent over the following twenty years. How much will you need to earn in five years to have the same buying power? in ten years? in twenty years? (Note: You will need to calculate each year separately.)

ENGLISH

1. Regardless of what career you choose, you will be required to use standard English on the job. It is a good idea to begin now using standard English so that it becomes a habit for you. On a separate paper, write the words that are not standard English in the following paragraph.

Look, Jack, I'm kinda' lookin' for a gig. Can you turn me on to something? I dig on music, computers, sports, and cars. Maybe I could get a gig doin' somethin' with those kinda' things. Can you lay any ideas on me about what I might do? I'm a pretty hard worker and a strong dude. What do ya think?

PROOFREADING

1. Whatever your new career entails, you will probably be required to write with correct spelling, punctuation, and grammar. On a separate paper, rewrite the passage below, correcting all errors.

Report on the Monday Morning Meeting

The mondya morning meeting was tttenned by jane smith, Mary Ann Worsley, George atwood, and mee. The prolims with the new action plan was discussed in detale with everyon finally agreein that it filled the needs it was deesigned to fill.

Next there was a descussion about the recycling of our newspapers. We worked out a methud of picking up the pappers each tuesday to take to the down town center.

The meetin was over by ten oclock.

APPLY YOUR KNOWLEDGE

1. Write out a description of your desired future lifestyle.
2. What is your long-range career goal? If you haven't made your decision yet, write down one of the career goals in which you are most interested. List some short-range and medium-range goals that will help you achieve your long-range goal.
3. Many schools require students to take a foreign language in order to graduate. Think about your future career and decide which foreign language you think would be most helpful in that field. Write a paragraph explaining your choice. Determine how many years you will need to study this language in order to enhance your career prospects. Write a plan for your course of study.

USING THE REFERENCE MANUAL

Retrieve the file CH18REF on the data disk. Use the proofreaders' marks section of the Reference Manual at the back of the book as well as information learned in this chapter to help you make the corrections. Save and print.

When you prepare for and choose your office career, do you do the following?

1. ~~Consider~~ _Think about_ how you would like to live in the future.

2. Ask yourself how different type**s** of work would ^a effect your overall life-style.

3. Believe that a career choices should sometimes be changed.

4. Want to take con trol of your life.

5. Use a decision making procedure for important decisions.

6. Record all your career information in a notebook.

7. Consider what your family and friends think is important, but decide for yourself what is important to you.

8. Know the types of work ~~areas~~ that would interest you.

CHAPTER 19

Finding and Applying for a Job

OBJECTIVES

After completing this chapter, you will be able to do the following:

1. Name two legal records that you must have before you can begin working.
2. List seven sources of job leads.
3. Organize your job hunt, including the use of job lead cards.
4. Secure job leads from a variety of sources.
5. Fill out an application form correctly.
6. Write a letter of application.
7. Write a résumé and a cover letter.
8. Prepare for and dress appropriately for an interview.
9. Conduct yourself properly and answer questions appropriately in a job interview.
10. Use standard English in a job interview.
11. Follow up a job interview properly.

NEW OFFICE TERMS

cover letter
employment tests
job lead card
letter of application
letter of inquiry
networking

private employment agencies
public employment agencies
résumé
reverse chronological order
standard English

BEFORE YOU BEGIN . . .

Answer the following questions to the best of your ability:

1. How will you go about looking for a job?

2. When you hear about a job that you would like, what action will you take?

3. What will you do to prepare for a job interview?

Y ou may have chosen your ultimate career goal—or you may at least have some ideas about the job you would like for now. If not, first answer this important question: What jobs can you do well and would you enjoy? You will probably think of several related office jobs. It is important to know the type of work you would like and the names of one, two, or several jobs for which you wish to apply *before* you start looking.

You may want an office job to gain experience as a stepping-stone into the career you have chosen. Even if you haven't made your career choice, you still may want a part-time job. You may want to earn some money for recreational activities, new clothes, a car, or college expenses.

Looking for a Job

Whatever your reason for wanting to work, getting the job you want will be a job in itself. You may be well qualified, but so are many others. You will be up against some good competition, and you must convince the employer that *you* are the best candidate. You can do this better than most others if you are motivated, energetic, and prepared.

If you really want to find a job, and you're willing to spend the time required, there are some proven techniques that will make your job hunt more efficient and effective. Begin with the two important hints below that will put you ahead of your competition. Then learn where to look for job leads, how to follow them up with an application, and how to prepare for and conduct yourself in a job interview.

First, most people spend less than five hours a week looking for a job. That's not enough. Plan to invest as much time per week looking for a job as you will spend working on the job after you're hired.

Second, most people aren't well organized for a successful job hunt. In this chapter, you will learn how to spend your job-hunting time efficiently, how to go about organizing your job hunt, how and where to find job leads, how to expand your collection of job leads, and even how to find a job without any job leads.

"Ross! Guess what?" hollers Yolanda. "I found a good job lead this morning! When I was waiting for the bus, I spotted an ad in the newspaper for part-time clerical help at Mesa Realty."

"Really? What are the qualifications?" asks Ross.

"Oh, they're all listed in the ad . . . . You know, 'no experience necessary, bilingual desired' and . . . oh, I've got the ad here in my purse."

Yolanda unsuccessfully digs around in her purse for the little ad. In frustration, she dumps her purse contents onto her desk. "I can't find it!

I'll just have to find another copy of the newspaper."

1. *Will Yolanda conduct a well-organized job search?*

2. *Is it likely that Yolanda will be able to keep paperwork organized as an office clerk?*

3. *Is it likely that the job at Mesa Realty will still be available by the time Yolanda applies for it?*

ORGANIZING YOUR JOB HUNT

Remember, job hunting is quite a job itself, and you must be willing to work hard at finding the right one. You will be using a variety of sources to secure job leads. Write down all your job leads so you will be able to follow up on them.

Before you begin your hunt, set up a base of operations and collect the supplies you will need. Then be sure you have the necessary legal documents.

Base of Operations   A good way to organize your job hunt is to set up a base of operations. This can be a section of your bedroom or another room in your house or apartment. If you have a study desk, designate one drawer for job-hunting materials. You will need a chair and a telephone nearby—preferably at your desk. These are the basics. A section of a filing cabinet will help you organize your job hunt, too. You will need a typewriter or computer with a word processing program when you begin to prepare application documents.

Supplies   You will also need some supplies. The following should be enough to get you started:

◆ *a logbook.* Any loose-leaf notebook will serve this purpose. If you have a computer at home, use the word processing program to keep a log of your progress.

◆ *one hundred index cards for recording job leads.* Use 4-×-6-inch or 5-×-8-inch size.

◆ *an appointment calendar.* Get one that has room for hour-by-hour notations.

◆ *lined notebook paper.* If you don't have a computer readily available, you will need some lined notebook paper for rough drafts of application documents. You probably already have this on hand.

◆ *one hundred sheets of good-quality bond paper.* Use twenty-pound or twenty-four-pound weight and 8½-×-11-inch size. This will be used for résumés and cover letters. White, cream, or light gray are the most preferred colors. About fifty matching envelopes should be enough.

◆ *stamps.* Use these for mailing application documents.

◆ *other helpful office supplies.* These include colored pencils or highlighters, scissors, paper clips, a stapler, transparent tape, and a wastebasket.

Finding the right job is difficult even when you're well organized. Good organization allows you to concentrate your time and effort on getting and following up leads, completing application documents, and going to interviews. If you aren't well organized, you will waste time waiting in line at the post office for stamps or making repeated trips to the stationery store.

Use your computer or logbook to record everything connected with your job hunt. Record the calls you've made, the calls you plan to make, names, numbers, ideas. Do this every day. Then, each evening, go through your logbook and cross out items you have completed and those that are no longer important.

Use your index cards to make job lead cards like the one shown in Figure 19.1. A **job lead card** is an index card on which you record all relevant information about an available job. This is an efficient system because you can easily rearrange your leads however you want, perhaps placing the most promising ones on the top. You may want to keep a separate set of cards in order by time and date of scheduled interviews.

Write the name of the person you should contact and the company name, address, and phone number on the front of the card. Write the source of the lead in the lower left corner. If your source is a newspaper want ad, tape the ad to the card as shown in Figure 19.1. Use the back side of the card to record whatever you do to follow up the lead. Record the date when you call to request an interview, and the time and date of the interview. Also write down the name of the person you are to see, and, if necessary, directions to the company. Later, write down your impression of the interview and whether you are offered the job.

Use a second card to write down whatever information you can learn about the company, such as the product it makes, the service it provides, or other pertinent information. (The "know the company" section later in this chapter explains how to find information about companies.) Then staple this second card, with information about the company, to your job lead card. Just before your interview, review your notes about the company.

If you have a computer that you can use daily in your job search, set up your job lead information using a database program. Record the same information you would if you were using job lead cards. Then print out the information you will need before each application or interview.

FIGURE 19.1 ◆ Sample Job Lead Card

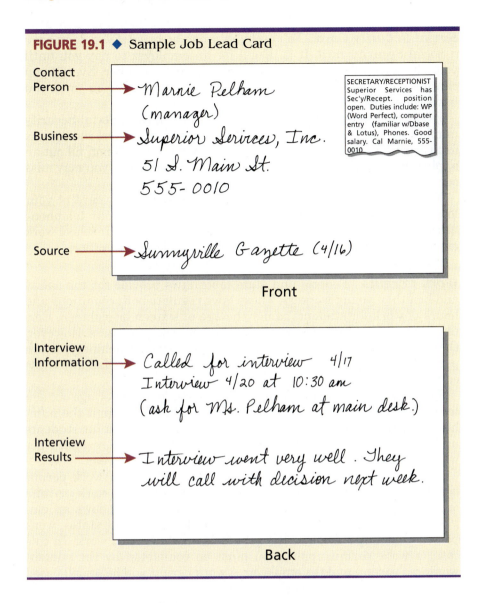

Contact Person

Business

Source

*Marnie Pelham
(manager)
Superior Services, Inc.
51 S. Main St.
555-0010*

Sunnyville Gazette (4/16)

SECRETARY/RECEPTIONIST Superior Services has Sec'y/Recept. position open. Duties include: WP (Word Perfect), computer entry (familiar w/Dbase & Lotus), Phones. Good salary. Cal Marnie, 555-0010

Front

Interview Information

Interview Results

*Called for interview 4/17
Interview 4/20 at 10:30 am
(ask for Ms. Pelham at main desk.)*

Interview went very well. They will call with decision next week.

Back

Use your appointment calendar to keep track of any appointment related to your job hunt. In fact, it's a good idea to put all your appointments in this calendar. Then you won't schedule an interview at the same time you have a dental appointment.

Many calendar programs are available for personal computers. If you are using a computer for other job search functions, you may want to use a calendar program, too.

Your lined notebook paper, bond paper, stamps, and other office supplies will all come in handy when you start writing letters, filling out application forms, and preparing résumés.

Legal Documents   The final part of preparing for your job hunt is to be sure you have all the legal documents you will need for employment. These include a Social Security card and perhaps a work permit.

You work in the personnel office of your local high school district. One of your responsibilities is to mail notices to applicants who are being considered for positions and to arrange interview appointments with them.

Your good friend, Kevin, is being invited to interview for a position in the media services department. When you call to set up his interview appointment, he tells you how eager he is to have this job.

Later that week, you see Kevin socially. He asks you if you can tell him any information that will give him an advantage in his interview. You have access to the questions that will be asked of each candidate, and you know that Kevin would make an excellent employee. You would like to help him.

1. **What would you do?**
2. **What are the ethical implications of your decision?**

Social Security Card   You probably won't be hired if you don't have a Social Security card. It is illegal for an employer to pay you until you have given her or him your Social Security number. Even if you can get someone to hire you, the employer can't pay you until you have your card.

Every person over the age of one year must have a Social Security number in order to be claimed as a dependent on federal income tax form 1040. Therefore, you probably already have one. If not, fill out an application and mail it right away. If you don't have one, you may miss out on a job that you would really like.

You can get an application form for a Social Security card at your local Social Security office. Look up the address in your telephone directory. These applications may also be available in your school work experience or job placement office and at your local post office.

Work Permits   Federal and state labor laws provide for the safety and health of young workers. These laws regulate both conditions and hours of work for students under the age of sixteen or eighteen. Certain jobs are designated as too dangerous for young workers. However, these dangerous jobs usually utilize power-driven machinery or are performed in a hazardous environment. Office jobs don't fall into these categories.

The Fair Labor Standards Act prohibits students under age sixteen from working during school hours. Various state laws limit the number of hours that can be worked in one day or in a week for students under age eighteen. Students are allowed to work more hours per week during summer vacations than during the school year.

If you are under the age of sixteen, you will need a work permit before you can legally begin work. Some states require work permits for all employees under age eighteen. A work permit shows an employer the type and hours of work that are legal. In some states, work permits must specify the exact job duties and hours of work. In this case, a work permit application must be completed by the student worker, a parent, and the employer. A work permit will be issued based on the information in the application.

Ask your counselor if you will need a work permit. They are usually issued by a designated school official. Find out about this now, and you can avoid a delay when you do find a job.

FINDING JOB LEADS

How do you go about finding job leads? The first step is to contact all the sources available that might produce one. Sometimes job lead information is incomplete. For example, you may learn that a local insurance company is looking for an office worker. You don't know the job title or the qualifications for the job. You may not even know who you need to see to apply for it. Follow up even skimpy leads and fill in the missing information yourself. Finding a job you can do well and enjoy requires finding as many job leads as possible and then following up promptly on each one.

Where do you begin looking for sources of job leads? Among the most productive are members of your own family and friends, former employers, in-school sources, newspaper advertisements, and employment agencies.

Family and Friends   Like many young people, you may find your most productive source of job leads right in your own home. Members of your family may hear about job openings where they work. Even if they don't know of any openings, they may have contacts at work and among their adult friends who know that a company is looking for someone with your qualifications.

Job leads often come indirectly through several sources. You probably know one or two people who just recently started new jobs. If you do, they may be able to provide information on jobs from their own job hunts.

Write down the names of family friends and your own personal friends who might help you find job leads. Consider, especially, adult family friends who work for companies where you would like to work. Give them a call. (This is often referred to as **networking.**) But don't ask them if any jobs are available. Instead, ask them either for advice on finding a job or for permission to list them as a reference for a job. Do, though, try to work into the conversation the type of job you are seeking. This approach avoids the usual "Sorry, we don't have anything now, but we'll keep you in mind," answer. This kind of promise

◆ *For young people looking for their first jobs, a family member is sometimes the best source of job leads.*

◆ *Friends can be a good source of job leads, as some of them may have recently searched for and found jobs.*

Large Office/Small Office: What's Your Preference?

FINDING AND APPLYING FOR A JOB

Most people find jobs by looking in the employment section of a newspaper and calling or writing to a company. Large businesses often place detailed ads describing a position and starting salary. Some companies use an employment agency to advertise, interview, and find a suitable employee for them. Many large businesses have a personnel department, sometimes called the *human resource department*. The people who work in this department place newspaper ads for job openings, review applications, and do the initial interviewing and screening. If you pass this screening process, then you interview with the manager or supervisor of the department for which you will be working. You might go through several interviewing steps before you get a job.

Small companies usually don't have a personnel department. The managers or supervisors themselves may place an ad, receive applications, and conduct interviews. This often means that you have fewer interview stages than when applying for jobs in large firms. Another difference is that in small companies, employees are more aware of job openings and have more direct access to the person doing the hiring. As a result, they often suggest friends and relatives for job openings before ads are even placed in a newspaper. This type of "word-of-mouth" communication often plays a much bigger part in finding a job in a small office than it does in a large one.

Would you stand a better chance of getting a job in a large office or a small one? Why?

---

is usually forgotten by day's end. Most people are flattered when asked for advice, and being considered important enough to provide a reference is also complimentary. Using this approach, you aren't asking for something a person probably cannot deliver—an immediate job. However, you are getting your point across that you are available if the right job comes along.

Some young people wonder whether it is appropriate to contact influential family friends when looking for a job. It is, as long as you are qualified to do the work. Many of the best jobs are never advertised at all because they are filled by friends of company employees.

Former Employers Have you previously held a job? Former employers are often good sources of job leads whether you worked in an office or just held a temporary baby-sitting job. Former employers who were satisfied with your work will most likely want to help you find a job.

In-School Sources   Businesses often call school personnel when they need qualified students for temporary or part-time jobs. Many schools today have school-to-work programs, mentoring, shadowing, and various other work experience education activities. Does your school have a cooperative vocational or work experience program or a school placement office—perhaps combined with a career center? If so, employers might call that office when they have job openings, so check there and make your interests known.

Some employers prefer calling school counselors when they need student employees, as a counselor will know which students are best suited for a particular job. So let your school counselor know when you are looking for a job. He or she may be able to give you a job lead for exactly the job you want.

Business and vocational education teachers usually have contacts in the business community, too. Talk with your teacher about the work you want to do and ask if you may list her or his name as a reference. Teachers are usually proud to recommend their students, and you may get another job lead as well.

School personnel do provide a lot of job leads for students, but don't depend totally on your counselor or someone else in your school to take care of finding the right job for you. There are usually more students looking for jobs than there are openings, and several students may be referred for every job. Because of this competition, you might follow up some good leads and still not get a job through in-school sources.

Newspaper Advertisements   Many employers place classified ads in the local newspaper when they need to fill office jobs. Make it a habit to read the help-wanted ads. Some papers separate jobs according to type, such as accounting, clerical, and so on. Newspaper ads are a good source of job leads, and you will also learn a lot about the local

◆ *Help-wanted ads in the local newspaper can tell you enough about a job opening to let you decide whether to apply for it.*

job market. You may discover how much money is offered for each type of work and the qualifications needed for the jobs that interest you.

Follow up promptly every ad that might lead to the job you want. If you wait even a day or two, you may be too late.

Avoid ads that require you to make a deposit of money or enroll in a course and pay a fee. Such ads are not offering jobs at all, but are attempts to sell you something.

Public and Private Employment Agencies Employment agencies match workers with jobs. When employers call an agency about a job opening, agency representatives write out the qualifications, salary offered, and other details on a job order form, review the records of applicants, and refer several applicants for interviews.

Most cities have both public and private employment agencies. **Public employment agencies** provide free job referral service because they are supported by taxes and operated by the federal or state government. Fill out an application form at the public employment agency near you. You will be interviewed to determine your interests and qualifications. Then, when a job is listed that matches them, the agency will call you. You will be told about the company and the job duties, then referred for an interview if you are still interested.

Private employment agencies are not supported by taxes, so they must charge a fee for finding you a job. The fee is either a flat rate or a percentage of the first few months' salary. Employers are often willing to pay the placement fee for higher-level professional jobs; however, if you are a beginning worker, you will probably have to pay the fee yourself. Private employment agencies sometimes have job leads that aren't listed with public agencies. If you aren't getting all the leads you want, you may want to consider applying at a private agency.

The Internet An increasing number of companies are listing job openings on the Internet. You may want to check this out. However, both the presentations and the methods of accessing job listings on the Internet change frequently. Unless you are familiar with current presentations and methods of access, you may need assistance from someone familiar with this process when you are ready to look at job listings.

EXPANDING YOUR COLLECTION OF JOB LEADS

Get all the leads that you can from firsthand sources. Then expand your collection based on the leads you already have. Every time you follow up a lead that does not result in a job, ask for suggestions about whom else you might contact. From each lead that doesn't result in a job, try to get at least one or two new leads.

A lot of other people are looking for work, too. You may not get just exactly the job you want, and you may turn down some jobs offered to you. If you have a lot of leads, you can simply follow up the next one. Having a lot of leads will keep you from getting discouraged when you are turned down or if one particular job isn't what you want.

◆ *Some companies list job openings on the Internet.*

FINDING A JOB WITHOUT LEADS

The ideal is to have a lot of job leads. The more leads you have, the better your chances of getting a job you can do well and will enjoy. However, if you don't have a lot of leads, you may need to do some direct calling. *Direct calling* is contacting employers by telephone or in person when you don't know whether they have any job openings. This is a much less effective way to go out job hunting than knowing where the jobs are at the start.

◆ *Check job vacancies listed on bulletin boards of companies where you would like to work. Schools and colleges frequently have bulletin boards in their career centers.*

If you decide to try direct calling, you may be successful by contacting the personnel offices of companies where you would like to work. Some companies list jobs available on a bulletin board, and you can check regularly for any new openings that have been listed.

For ideas, company names, and addresses of places you might call directly, refer to the Yellow Pages of the telephone directory. You will probably have better luck going in person than inquiring about a job on the telephone. Either way, direct calling takes a lot of time. However, if you contact enough employers, you may find a job this way.

A variation of direct calling is writing a letter of inquiry. A **letter of inquiry** is simply a letter asking whether a specified type of job is available. Suppose you would like to work in an office of a certain company, but you don't know whether the company has a vacancy. Look up the company's number in the telephone directory and call. Ask the person who answers for the name of the person who hires new employees. If you learn that department heads hire new employees, ask for the name of the head of the department in which you would like to work. Confirm the spelling of any names you get, and thank the person who gave them to you. Then write down the address of the company and write a letter of inquiry. Address your letter to the person who does the hiring. An example of a letter of inquiry is shown in Figure 19.2.

Recall Time

Answer the following questions:

1. Fred says he has been looking for a job for three weeks, but he is always downtown relaxing with his friends after school and on weekends. What suggestions can you give him to help make his search more fruitful?

2. What two legal documents should a young person have obtained before beginning to look for work?

3. What are seven common sources of job leads?

4. How would you use index cards to record job leads and your response to them?

Applying for a Job

As you continue to seek new job leads, follow up promptly on the ones you have. You should continue to get more leads because the very next one may be the perfect job. However, you must follow up on each one as soon as you get it. If you don't, someone else may already be working on that job by the time you get around to calling for an interview.

Employers are looking for the person best qualified to fill a job. They will decide whom to hire based generally on their overall impression of each applicant and more specifically on their appraisal of an applicant's ability to do the work.

FIGURE 19.2 ◆ Sample Letter of Inquiry

120 San Marcos Rd.
Orlando, FL 32802
March 1, 1998

Ms. Carole White
Personnel Director
Jensen Computers
710 Chapala Street
Orlando, FL 32802

Dear Ms. White:

My computer science teacher, Mr. Reynolds, recently advised me to write
to learn whether you expect to hire additional word processors for the
summer.

I have completed courses in Word Perfect and Microsoft Word, and I type
75 words per minute on five-minute speed tests.

If you expect to hire additional word processors for the summer, may I
have an application form? If you wish to call me, my home telephone is
832-1246.

Sincerely,

Caitlin Justice

Caitlin Justice

How do employers get the information they need in order to choose
the best applicant for a job? From the applicants themselves. Before
your first interview, prepare a personal data sheet listing all the information about yourself that an employer may need.

Most employers will ask you to fill out an application form. This is
a form used to summarize your job qualifications. Forms are usually
short—from one to four pages—and ask the same or similar questions.
However, most companies design their own application forms, so each
one is a little different from the next.

For many office jobs, employers expect an applicant to present a
résumé (pronounced rez-oo-may). A **résumé** organizes, usually on one
or two pages, all the facts about you related to the job you want. A
résumé should always be accompanied by a cover letter, which is an
abbreviated **letter of application.**

A complete letter of application—a sales letter in which you, as the
applicant, try to convince an employer that you are the best person for
a particular job—includes a description of all your qualifications. How-

Fran finds out through her computer club that a member's company is about to expand its local offices. The member, Nick Petersen, suggests that Fran call Ms. Wiley to find out if Coleman Accounting is hiring yet.

The next morning, Fran calls Ms. Wiley and introduces herself. She tells Ms. Wiley that she had heard Coleman Accounting might need some clerical help and that Nick Petersen suggested she call to find out. Ms. Wiley says the company has already started interviewing for two positions but is still accepting applications.

"Why don't you come to our office today and fill out an application?" she suggests. "I will be here this afternoon and I could meet with you."

"That would be great, Ms. Wiley," says Fran.

"All right then, can you come by around four-thirty with your résumé?" asks Ms. Wiley.

"Yes," says Fran. "I'll see you then. Good-bye."

"I'll have to bring my personal data with me to fill out the application efficiently," thinks Fran.

Kofi also finds a good job lead. He locates an ad on the bulletin board at his school for an assistant to the manager of a local insurance company. The ad reads "Must type 40 WPM. No experience necessary. Will train."

"A management assistant," says Kofi. "Imagine the skills I can sharpen and the new things I can learn in the insurance industry! I need to compose a cover letter and send it with my résumé right away!"

1. *Are Fran and Kofi prepared to put their best efforts into following up job leads?*

2. *What attitudes will guide the way you follow up job leads?*

ever, if you prepare a résumé, your cover letter should not duplicate anything in your résumé. Instead, the cover letter should simply introduce you to the employer and perhaps explain how you learned about the job. The cover letter also provides an opportunity to highlight one particular qualification that makes you appear especially well qualified for the job.

For some jobs, you may be asked to take one or even several **employment tests.** These may include skills and aptitude tests, psychological tests, and general abilities tests. The test most often given to applicants for office jobs is a typing test.

Performing well on employment tests doesn't guarantee you will be hired. Almost all employers will require an interview before deciding to hire you.

If you are not qualified for a job, you probably won't get it. Of course, you don't want a job for which you aren't qualified, anyway. Taking such a position would be setting yourself up for failure. If you are qualified for it, however, the way you present your qualifications may determine whether you are hired.

What influences employers most in forming an overall impression of each applicant? A most important factor is the use of standard English. Make it a habit always to use standard English in a business setting.

STANDARD ENGLISH

Usually, an employer will first learn about your qualifications by reading your application form, résumé, or letter of application. Later, in the interview, you will have a chance to explain why you think you can do the work. Use standard English in everything you write and say to an employer. **Standard English** is the correct style of speaking and writing that you have learned in school. It is the standard way to communicate in business, because its meaning is the same to everyone.

Most people don't use standard English for all their communication. Standard English is not always necessary, or even appropriate. When you write a note to a friend, you probably don't worry much about form. When you're chatting with an acquaintance, you may use slang or other popular words. That is informal communication, and it makes for interesting conversation. However, in business, most communication is formal—and that means using standard English.

Standard English means standard grammar, spelling, and usage (vocabulary). "Arleen wants a job interview" is standard English; "Arleen want a job interview" is not. Some people use standard grammar but nonstandard pronunciation, so they are not speaking standard English.

Employers will have several chances to judge your language use. From the application form, they can see whether you use and spell words correctly. If you submit a résumé or letter of application, they will notice your ability, or inability, to use standard English. If they see poor grammar or misspelled words, your application will probably be filed in the wastebasket. Employers get a lot of applications, and they don't usually waste their time interviewing those who don't use standard English. Finally, during the interview, they will listen as you speak, and note your grammar and pronunciation.

YOUR PERSONAL DATA SHEET

A good way to prepare for the job application process is to complete a *personal data sheet*. This is simply an outline of all the information you may need later when you fill out application forms or prepare résumés.

When you're in an employer's office filling out a form, you may have difficulty remembering the correct spelling of former employers' names, their addresses, and their telephone numbers. Maybe you will forget the exact dates that you attended a former school. You will avoid these problems if you prepare a personal data sheet in advance. An example is shown in Figure 19.3.

APPLICATION FORMS

An application form summarizes information about an applicant's qualifications so an employer can decide which applicants to interview. The application form is an opportunity for you to show that you are qualified to do the job. Follow these suggestions to improve your chances of being chosen for an interview:

◆ Complete the application form as neatly as possible. Many forms ask you to print. Make sure all words are spelled correctly by taking a pocket dictionary with you when you expect to fill out an application form.

Personal Data Sheet

Name _____   Social Security Number _____
Address _____
Date of Birth _____   Place of Birth _____
Telephone _____
Hobbies/Interests _____
Awards/Honors/Offices _____
Activities/Sports _____
Other _____
_____

Educational Background

	Name	Address	Dates Attended From	To
Junior High School	_____	_____	_____	_____
High School	_____	_____	_____	_____
Course of Study	_____ GPA		_____	
Favorite Subject(s)	_____			
	_____			

Employment History (Begin with current or most recent.)

Company _____   Telephone _____
Address _____
Dates of Employment: From _____   To _____
Job Title and Duties _____
_____
Supervisor _____
Last Wage _____   Reason for Leaving _____

Company _____   Telephone _____
Address _____
Dates of Employment: From _____   To _____
Job Title and Duties _____
_____
Supervisor _____
Last Wage _____   Reason for Leaving _____

Company _____   Telephone _____
Address _____
Dates of Employment: From _____   To _____
Job Title and Duties _____
_____
Supervisor _____
Last Wage _____   Reason for Leaving _____

References (Name of persons who can provide information about your personal, school, or work background.)

	Name	Address	Telephone Home	Work	Relationship
1.	_____	_____	_____	_____	_____
2.	_____	_____	_____	_____	_____
3.	_____	_____	_____	_____	_____

◆ If you complete the application form at an employer's office, use a pen. However, you can usually take the application form home and fill it out. If so, use a typewriter—unless the form specifically requests that you print. If you type your form, carefully align the typing on the printed lines. Practice on an extra form so that your application will look professional and neat.

◆ Don't skip over any questions. If a question doesn't apply to you, put "NA," meaning "Not Applicable," or draw a short line in the space.

◆ Use your correct name on the form. Include your first name, middle initial, and last name. State your complete address, including your ZIP code.

◆ Some applications ask for your marital status. Employers cannot legally require you to answer this. If you do, just state whether you are single or married.

◆ Many applications ask for your job preference. List a specific job title. Never use the word *anything*. Employers want a specific answer here.

◆ Most application forms ask for a listing of schools you have attended. Include the name of all the schools you have attended along with the dates of attendance. You may refer to your personal data sheet for this.

◆ The application will ask about your previous work experience. Fill out this section in **reverse chronological order,** beginning with your most recent job. If you haven't had much experience, include even short-term jobs or volunteer work.

◆ Most forms ask for references. These are the names of people who know you well and will recommend you for the job. Plan ahead and ask permission to list people's names as references. Good references include teachers or friends established in business. Don't list classmates.

◆ Most forms request your signature at the end. Write—don't print—your name using your first name, middle initial, and last name.

Review carefully the application form shown in Figure 19.4.

RÉSUMÉS

Employers hiring for office jobs often request applicants to submit a résumé. Your résumé may be typed on a typewriter or word processor, or prepared on a computer using a word processing program. If you use a typewriter, clean the typewriter keys and put in a new ribbon before you start.

Some typewriters, word processors, and computer programs offer different type styles, called fonts. If you have a choice, choose an easy-to-read style such as Times Roman or Helvetica. Avoid italicized and unusual fonts. Word processors and computer programs allow the use of boldface (heavy-faced) type for main headings, which is a nice touch.

Most people use twenty-pound paper for their résumés. But twenty-four-pound paper with some cotton content, though slightly more

FIGURE 19.4 ◆ Sample Application Form

Application For Employment

All qualified applicants will receive consideration for employment and promotion without regard to race, creed, religion, color, age sex, national origin, handicap, marital status or sexual orientation. This application is effective for 90 days. If you wish to be considered for employment therafter, you must complete a new application.

Date _____

Name _____ Telephone (_____) _____
　　　　Last　　　First　　　Middle Initial　　　　　　　　Area Code

Address _____
　　　　　Number & Street　　　　　　　Apt.#　　　City　　　　　　State　　　Zip

Length of time at that address _____ Previous Address _____

Position you are applying for _____ Rate of pay expected $ _____ per month

Were you previously employed by us? _____ If yes, when? _____

Typewriting words per minute _____ Shorthand or speedwriting words per minute _____

Other Business Machines _____

State any other experiences, skills or qualifications which you feel would especially fit you for work with the company

_____

Applying for: Full-time _____ Part-time _____ Days _____ Evenings _____ Midnight _____ Alternating _____ Any _____

Location Preferred:　Downtown St. Paul _____ Eagan _____ Westbury_____ Other _____

Are you at least 18 years of age? _____ Will you take a physical examination? _____

List any friends or relatives working for us _____
　　　　　　　　　　　　　　　　　　　Name　　　　　　　　　　　Relationship

_____
　　　　　　　　　　　　　　　　　　　Name　　　　　　　　　　　Relationship

Referred to our company by _____

School	Name and Location	Course of Major	Graduated
Elementary _____			☐ Yes ☐ No
High School _____			☐ Yes ☐ No
College _____			☐ Yes ☐ No
Business or Trade _____			☐ Yes ☐ No
Other (Specify) _____			☐ Yes ☐ No

Do you plan any additional education? _____ If yes, describe _____

_____

List in order all employers, begin with your most recent employment:

Name and Location of Company	From Mo Yr	To Mo Yr	Salary	Supervisor	Reason for Leaving

1) _____

2) _____

3) _____

Describe the work you did with:

Company #1. _____

Company #2. _____

Company #3. _____

May we contact the employers listed above? _____ If not indicate by number which one(s) you do not wish us to contact _____

CERTIFICATION OF APPLICANT

I hereby certify that the facts set forth in the above employment application are true and complete to the best of my knowledge. I understand that if I am employed, falsified statements on this application shall be considered sufficient cause for dismissal, and that no contractual rights or obligations are created by said employment application.

Signature of Applicant _____

Some intervi
eral hours. How
and found that
first impression
interviewer to fe
don't impress th
very good regard

The interview
seeking process.
cessful interview

1. Prepare for tl
2. Communicate
3. Sense when t
4. Follow up the

PREPARE FC

Preparing has se
ahead of time, y
something about
to phrase your
boost your confi
impression.

Your preparati
ing the clothing
materials you w
things ahead of t
interview. You m
ber or a friend, bi

Know the Com
that you are inte
earn from workin
view is to do som
you know who m
know any of the
ously worked the

Many compani
products or servic
what the company
company well b
releases may prov
information that
and remember to

As you research
may be asked tha
interviewers ask s
company?" or "Wh

As you learn ab
want to ask the i

expensive, is more impressive. White, cream, and light gray are probably the best colors. Avoid pink, green, or any dark colors, as they don't photocopy cleanly. Purchase matching envelopes and extra paper for cover letters when you choose your résumé paper.

If you have completed a personal data sheet, then you already have most of the information you will need to prepare your résumé. Many styles of résumés are used. If you want to see a variety of ways to present this information, you can buy an inexpensive book on résumés at your local bookstore. However, if you are a student or a recent graduate, use a chronological résumé format such as the one shown in Figure 19.5.

As a young job seeker, you can probably provide all pertinent information on a one-page résumé. Employers are busy, and they prefer

---

FIGURE 19.5 ◆ Sample Chronological Résumé

Mizuko Matsuoko
1715 Bliss Street
Winfield, KS 67156
(314) 221-4565

Objective

An entry-level position as a bookkeeper, with opportunities for advancement.

Education

1994-1997 Winfield High School. Graduated in upper 10%, Class of '97. Courses included:

Office Procedures, 2 semesters
Bookkeeping, 4 semesters
Word Processing, 2 semesters
Business Math, 2 semesters

Special Skills

Keyboarding speed test score: 81 WPM

Experience

6/96-9/97   BOOKKEEPER (part-time)
              Merchandise Mart
              Winfield, KS.

              Used DAC Easy computer accounting program to record cash receipts and payments and to maintain accounts receivable and accounts payable ledgers. Assisted in preparing payroll records and printing payroll checks.

6/95-9/96   WORD PROCESSOR
              Stevenson Junior High School
              Winfield, KS.

              Used a computer to write letters and memos. Scanned and updated end-of-school reports.

Personal

Hobbies include solving difficult math problems and conundrums.

References

Available upon request.

ask how the job became available, what your working relationship with other employees will be, and what opportunities exist for advancement within the company.

You will probably be a little nervous at the beginning of every interview. However, if you know what to do and say, you may be more self-confident—and you will likely become less nervous as the interview progresses. Knowing some things about the company helps. The best confidence builder is to prepare for the interview by practicing your interviewing skills. Perhaps your teacher will allow you and others in your class to do some role-playing of interviewing situations.

Dress Appropriately Generally, avoid extremes and dress appropriately for the office where you hope to work. In the business world, this usually means a conservative, dark suit and tie for men. Dresses or skirts and blouses that are modestly tailored are favored for women, and a young woman makes a better impression wearing stockings and dress shoes than wearing casual sports shoes.

To most employers, personal cleanliness and neatness are even more important than the clothes you wear. If you need a haircut, get it before your interview. Bathe or shower, wash your hair, clean and trim your nails, and brush your teeth. Avoid strong-smelling after-shave lotions or heavy perfume. Use makeup sparingly.

Because only about a fourth of all adults smoke, the person who interviews you will probably be a nonsmoker. If you smoke, don't do it on the day of your interview, even if you are offered a cigarette. Many companies now prohibit smoking in the office, and more are adopting nonsmoking policies all the time.

Don't wear a lot of jewelry to a job interview; it may be distracting.

Take the Things You Need Assemble the items that you want to take with you to the interview. Include your job lead card and notes on the company, your personal data sheet, your résumé, and your list of questions to ask. Also, take along a listing of the names and addresses of former employers, schools, and references. If you have completed a personal data sheet like the one shown on page 468, you will have your materials in good order. You will probably take some notes, and you may need to fill out some forms, so take a good pen and a notebook. If you need a work permit form to begin work, take it with you.

Allow Enough Time If it's been a week or more since you made your appointment, call to confirm that the interviewer is still expecting you. Then start getting ready early. After you are dressed, read your résumé through carefully several times. This will help you answer questions about your qualifications. Check your job lead card for the address and leave in time to arrive about ten minutes early. Allow some extra time if you have to travel across town—you might be delayed in traffic. On your way to the interview, mentally review what you've prepared.

Go Alone Never take anyone with you for a job interview. Some young people take along a friend for support, but employers are not favorably impressed by this. When you arrive, introduce yourself to the receptionist and give the name of the person with whom you have the interview appointment.

COMMUNICATE EFFECTIVELY

When you meet the person who will interview you, smile. Smiling will help more than anything to create a favorable first impression.

The second thing you can do to create a good impression is to shake hands properly. Wait for the interviewer to offer his or her hand. When he or she does so, grasp the person's hand firmly. Some employers think a wimpy, "limp fish" handshake reveals a weak personality. But don't squeeze too hard, either. You don't want to begin by hurting the interviewer! Some interviewers don't offer to shake hands. In that case, you won't do it.

Don't sit down until you are invited. If you aren't asked to sit, then remain standing—the interview will be a short one. The interviewer will probably suggest that you sit beside or in front of the desk. If you have a choice of where to sit, take a seat beside the desk. With no barrier between the two of you, you have a psychological advantage. As you sit, lean slightly toward the interviewer. This indicates that you are interested.

You should have a folder containing your résumé and other papers, and you may have a briefcase or purse. Keep your folder in your lap and place your briefcase or purse on the floor by your chair. Even if there is room to do so, never put anything on the interviewer's desk.

Don't let your eyes roam across papers on the desk—what's there is none of your business! Look the interviewer in the eye most of the time, shifting your eyes only occasionally so you don't appear to be staring. Those who fail to maintain good eye contact are often considered insecure or are suspected of trying to conceal something.

The interviewer will determine the tone, pace, and style. Some interviewers will be serious and businesslike, others will be more outgoing and cheerful. Try to respond with the same tone and pace that the interviewer projects. In the usual style of interviewing, you will be asked a series of questions, and eventually you will get a turn to ask your own.

During the interview, speak clearly, listen closely, and show by gestures or facial expressions that you understand and are receptive to the interviewer's thoughts.

Table 19.1 gives a list of questions commonly asked during interviews. When answering questions, pause to give yourself time to compose an answer that is concise but thoughtful. This requires listening very carefully to complete questions before you formulate your answer. It is all right to write down a word or two to help you remember something you want to say in answer to a question, but never interrupt. Good listening skills will help you pick out patterns in the interviewer's questions. You may be able to detect the direction of a line of questioning—organization skills, leadership qualities, or other qualifications. If so, focus your answers on these areas of interest.

◆ *If the interviewer offers to shake hands, clasp his or her hand firmly. But don't squeeze too hard, and don't pump when you shake hands.*

OFFICE TIP

Test your handshake with a friend, and ask if it should be firmer, shorter, or gentler. This is important because people don't usually volunteer to tell you if you have a lousy handshake. Remember, a handshake is often part of your first impression, and it's worth it to perfect a pleasing one.

TABLE 19.1 ◆ Questions Often Asked during an Interview

1. What type of work are you looking for?
2. Have you done this type of work before?
3. Why are you leaving your present job?
4. How often were you absent from your last (or present) job?
5. How did you get along with your boss and co-workers?
6. What are your greatest strengths?
7. What are your greatest weaknesses?
8. What do you hope to be doing in five years?
9. How do you feel about this position?
10. Can we check your references?
11. How does your experience qualify you for this job?
12. How do you take direction?
13. Can you take criticism without feeling hurt or upset?
14. Can you work under pressure?
15. Do you like detail work?
16. Do you prefer working alone or with others?
17. Have you ever been fired or asked to resign?
18. With what type of people do you find it difficult to work?
19. How well do you work with difficult people?
20. What salary do you expect?
21. What did you like most about your last job?
22. What did you dislike about your last job?
23. What do you know about this company?
24. Do you have any questions?

When asked about your skills and experience, elaborate somewhat. Answer questions concisely, but avoid one-word or one-line answers. Refer to your résumé or other notes to help you with answers. If you think that the interviewer hasn't understood your answer or that you haven't expressed yourself clearly, try again. Stay on the topic until you are sure that your message has been received.

When preparing for an interview, many people overlook specific approaches to interview communication. These include how the interviewer may open the interview and certain questions that are either illegal to ask or difficult to answer. Others include nonverbal communication (body language) and being prepared to ask appropriate questions of the interviewer.

Some Problem Areas   Some interviewers begin by asking, "Tell me about yourself" or "What can I do for you?" This type of opening is difficult because the question is so broad. Your task is to narrow the focus and direct your answer to support your candidacy for the job.

By preparing for such questions, you can respond appropriately without rambling. State that you are interested in a particular job and explain why you are qualified to do the work. Don't describe your career goals—the interviewer will be interested mainly in what you can do now.

INDUSTRY FOCUS

Priscilla Azcueta
Director of Professional Services
Manpower, Inc./California Peninsula

Q.   Ms. Azcueta, what do you look for when interviewing applicants for clerical positions?

A.   We look for a concise, articulate, and appropriate reply to questions. For example, an applicant should not give too much information about their personal life or interests. The applicant needs to be aware of the interviewer/interviewee boundaries. The applicant should be able to interact with the interviewer.

   We look to see if the applicant has personality, is outgoing, and will work as a team player. We look to see if the applicant can work independently.

   If the interviewer was off-schedule, we look to see if the applicant is flustered or if the applicant has allowed for the disruption of their interview schedule and time.

Q.   What recommendation do you have for an applicant to prepare for an interview?

A.   Be prepared to talk about your strengths and weaknesses and your ability to handle problem-solving situations which may come up in interview questions.

   Be prepared for the companies that conduct "behavioral interviews." During these interviews, the interviewer will observe the applicant's body language, and look to see if the applicant breaks eye contact to think about their answer before responding to the question. The interviewer will see if the applicant really listens to the question and responds appropriately to the question.

   Wear something that makes you feel good, is comfortable, and appropriate for the position you are applying for. Also, consider your personal hygiene and your overall appearance from top to bottom.

Some personal questions are illegal, but the interviewer may ask them anyway. Questions about marital status, family planning, child care arrangements, and age are illegal—unless they are real job qualifications. But if they are asked, it may be to your advantage to deal with them as honestly and tactfully as possible.

   Other difficult questions that you should prepare for are probing questions, such as "What are your greatest weaknesses?" These questions are variations of "Tell me about yourself." Again, disregard the general question and focus your answer on your strengths—your personal skills and abilities that pertain directly to the job. Try to match the company's needs with your aptitudes. Give examples to support your answers. You can even use a question on your greatest weakness to your advantage. You might mention a weakness that will enhance your qualifications for this particular job. For example, on a job that requires great organization skills, you might say that your greatest weakness is that you simply can't stand disorder and tend to overorganize things. Do not reveal a weakness that will disqualify you for the job.

You may be asked whether you quit or were fired from your last job. Avoid saying anything negative about former employers. Most interviewers will identify with other employers and will interpret your criticism as incompetence or uncooperativeness on your part. Simply explain, briefly and unemotionally, why you left your last job. Don't make any excuses. If you expect to receive a bad recommendation from an employer, suggest other references who will attest to your qualifications.

Nonverbal Communication   Two of the first interactions you will have with the interviewer are shaking hands and making eye contact. These are nonverbal ways of communicating, usually called body language. If this topic interests you, you can find a number of books on body language in your local library.

You will communicate in other nonverbal ways during an interview, and how you do this will significantly affect your chances of being offered the job. In answering questions, the *manner* in which you speak conveys messages to the interviewer. The tone and volume of voice, rising and falling inflections, and facial expressions are all meaningful. They will impart enthusiasm for the job and the company—or lack of it. Be aware of the mood of the conversation and be ready with either a smile or a serious expression, depending on what's appropriate.

Be aware, too, of your interviewer's body language. You will usually notice some nonverbal clues that will help you understand whether you are coming across effectively. If the interviewer appears disinterested or impatient, you might want to move on to another topic that may elicit more interest, and express more enthusiasm yourself to change the mood.

Appropriate Questions to Ask   The interviewer will expect you to ask some questions. If you aren't invited to ask questions and a pause occurs in the conversation after the interview is well under way, inquire if you may ask some questions. Your first questions should show a sincere interest in the company, in the job, and in the employer's needs as related to the job. If the interviewer hasn't discussed salary and fringe benefits, it's all right to ask about them—but ask these questions last.

Make a list of questions you may want to ask before you go for your interview. Then you will be more likely to remember them and to ask them in an appropriate order. The interviewer will probably cover

HUMAN RELATIONS

It was four-thirty on Friday afternoon. Jack Tuttle entered the personnel office of the Harcourt Accounting Corporation five minutes prior to his scheduled interview with the personnel director. When he introduced himself to the receptionist, Ms. Woodruff, she told Jack that she was very sorry, but the director, Ms. Johnson, would be unable to meet with him that day. Ms. Woodruff said that she would be happy to reschedule the interview for the following week.

Jack was visibly disappointed. He had given up a date with his girlfriend to attend an out-of-town school football game for this interview.

"Why can't Ms. Johnson interview me today?" Jack asked.

"Something unexpected came up, I'm sorry," replied Ms. Woodruff. "Can you come in on Monday afternoon?"

"Then why didn't you call me or leave a message at school? I cancelled an important meeting myself to be here." Jack felt angry toward Ms. Woodruff.

"I would have called you, but she just told me twenty minutes ago that she would be unable to interview any more applicants today. Would you like to come in next week?"

"I guess so." Jack was still unhappy, but he was resigned to returning another day. "I'll check my calendar and call you on Monday."

Based on Jack's conversation with Ms. Woodruff, respond to these questions:

1. *What was Ms. Woodruff's first impression of Jack? If the personnel director asks Ms. Woodruff about the applicants she couldn't interview on Friday, how will this affect Jack's chances of getting the job?*

2. *When Jack does get a job, how well will he get along with the other employees?*

3. *What could Jack do to improve his relationships with others on the job?*

some of the topics on your list during the interview, so you won't have to ask all your questions. If you think of others as the interview progresses, make a brief note to remind yourself to ask them later.

Use good judgment about how much time to take up asking questions. If you sense that the interviewer is on a tight schedule, ask only your most important ones.

SENSE WHEN THE INTERVIEW IS OVER

Try to get a feeling for when the interview has run its course. Many interviewers will stand and say something like, "Well, I think I have all the information I need," or "Do you have any other questions?" Unless the interviewer looks rushed, it's all right to ask one or two brief questions at this point—but don't delay your exit more than a minute or two. If the interviewer hasn't mentioned when a decision will be made on the selection of a candidate for the job, ask about that.

In some cases, you may have to take responsibility for closing the interview. If the conversation seems to be drifting, reemphasize your strong points, say that you want the job (if you do), thank the interviewer for her or his time, and leave. On your way out, thank the receptionist or secretary.

FOLLOW UP THE INTERVIEW

You can profit from every interview, no matter what the outcome, if you take time to evaluate the experience. Ask yourself if a little more planning and preparation would have helped. Did you mention everything about your qualifications that would have helped you get the job? Jot down your notes as soon as possible. This will help you to remember the interview discussion for future reference.

In the evening after the interview, write a thank-you note to your interviewer. It should go into the mail the very next morning. While the interview is still fresh in your mind, you can refer to a particular point discussed. Mention some fact that sets you apart from other applicants. The thank-you letter is an opportunity to add any important information in support of your application that you may have neglected to mention or emphasize during the interview. Figure 19.7 shows a sample thank-you letter.

FIGURE 19.7 ◆ Sample Thank-You Letter

1715 Bliss Street
Winfield, KS 67156
April 26, 1998

Ms. Julie Atkins
Kennedy Accounting Services
1700 South Main Street
Arkansas City, KS 67005

Dear Ms. Atkins:

Thank you for the interview yesterday afternoon regarding the position as bookkeeper. I enjoyed talking with you and learning more about your bookkeeping needs.

Having discussed this position in greater detail, I am more interested in the job than ever. I also feel even more certain that I can fulfill your needs.

If I may provide any further information for your consideration, please call me at home any afternoon after three o'clock. My number is 221-4565.

Sincerely,

Mizuko Matsuoko

Mizuko Matsuoko

If you haven't heard from the company within a week to ten days, give the interviewer a call. State your name and that you were interviewed for a particular job. Then ask, "Have you made a decision on who will be hired for this job?" If you are told that a decision hasn't been made, say something like, "I would very much like to work for your company, and I know that I can do a really fine job for you." Showing this extra interest may tip the scales in your favor.

Americans with Disabilities

If you are one of the more than 40 million Americans with a disability, don't be discouraged about finding a job. In fact, the Americans with Disabilities Act of 1990 was passed to encourage those with disabilities to pursue careers.

Title I of the ADA prohibits discrimination against any otherwise qualified applicant in any company with fifteen or more employees. It further requires the employer to make reasonable accommodations for disabled workers. This means that an employer must make reasonable adjustments in a job or work environment that will enable any qualified applicant to perform the essential functions of the job.

For example, employers must make existing facilities more readily accessible, and make changes in work schedules or equipment used on the job. However, employers are not required to lower either the quality or quantity of the work expected of disabled workers.

Recall Time

Answer the following questions:

1. Why is the first minute of an interview important? What do you need to do in the first minute to improve your chance of being chosen for the job?

2. Joe and Laura are both interviewed for the same typing job at Hayward Lumber. Joe answers all the questions Ms. Hayward asks and is very polite and quiet. Laura asks Ms. Hayward several questions about the company and tells her she has heard the company is thinking of opening another branch. Even though her typing skills are not as good as Joe's, Laura gets the job. Why does Ms. Hayward choose Laura?

3. What will you wear to an interview with Ms. Bailey at the National Bank's main office downtown?

4. You are applying for a job as a receptionist in a physician's office. The doctor opens the interview with, "Tell me about yourself." How do you best respond?

5. What items will you bring with you to an interview to be sure you are well prepared?

Summary

Finding openings and applying for jobs is the last step before entering the world of work. How well you perform this step will determine whether you get the job you would most like or have to settle for something much less interesting. Following certain guidelines will help make your search for a good job successful.

First, when beginning your job search, give it plenty of time. You will need to be well organized and have a logical system for keeping track of leads and follow-ups. Before you begin to call prospective employers, be sure that you have a Social Security number and a work permit, if necessary. Also, have a general idea of the jobs for which you qualify.

Make use of as many different sources of job leads as possible, from newspaper ads to employment offices to school and family. Follow up all leads promptly, either calling an employer directly or writing a letter of inquiry if that is required. When you are asked to fill out an application, be prepared. Have all the information you may need with you on a personal data sheet, and type or print the application clearly. Take time to write a concise résumé, and have copies of it available. Brush up on the math or English skills you may be tested on, and be sure to use standard English when speaking or writing to prospective employers.

Before you go to be interviewed for a job, be certain you are well groomed and properly dressed. Make sure you have discovered enough about the company to let the employer see that you are interested in more than just the salary. Take your résumé and notes on any questions you may have about the job and company. Be prepared by anticipating the types of question you are likely to be asked and thinking about how you will answer them. Practice describing your qualifications out loud, perhaps in front of a mirror.

Remember that the first minute of an interview is extremely important. Try to make a good impression through a firm handshake, a smile, and a pleasant, enthusiastic demeanor, and by responding appropriately to the interviewer's tone and body language. Look the interviewer in the eye and try to overcome any nervousness. Ask pertinent questions, but don't be pushy or aggressive. Use common sense and good manners.

Be aware of when the interviewer is trying to conclude the interview. Bring the interview to a close yourself if it begins to move to general conversation and you sense the interviewer has all the information he or she needs. Follow up the interview with a call or a letter, emphasizing your special qualifications and thanking the interviewer for her or his consideration.

When looking for and applying for a job, do the following:

◆ Keep records of all your leads and how you followed up on them.
◆ Use all available sources for job leads.
◆ Follow up leads promptly.
◆ Keep a personal data sheet handy for filling out applications.
◆ Have copies of a résumé ready when needed.

◆ Recognize the need to use standard English in both speaking and writing.
◆ Be clean, neat, and well dressed for interviews.
◆ Find out all you can about the company before an interview.
◆ Be prepared to explain your qualifications and interest in a job.
◆ Appear relaxed and competent in an interview.
◆ Ask questions to show your interest in a company.
◆ Sense when an interview is over, and leave on a high note.
◆ Evaluate your performance at an interview.
◆ Write a follow-up letter.

IN CONCLUSION . . .

When you have completed this chapter, answer the following questions:

1. How will you go about looking for a job?

2. When you hear about a job that you would like, what action will you take?

3. What will you do to prepare for a job interview?

REVIEW AND APPLICATION

✔ CHECK YOUR KNOWLEDGE

1. How much time should you ideally spend each week looking for a job?
2. Who needs a Social Security card? a work permit?
3. List all the information you should collect on a job lead card.
4. What office supplies will you need to conduct your job search efficiently?
5. Where should you keep a record of all the actions you have taken in trying to land a job?
6. What are the seven most common sources of job leads?
7. Define direct calling. When should you use it?
8. What information does a résumé contain? How is it arranged?
9. If you need to fill out an application at a company office, how should you prepare yourself to be sure you have all the needed information?
10. What is standard English? Why is it necessary in business?
11. Should you always apply for a specific job? Would an employer be more likely to hire you if you said you were willing to do anything?
12. Which of your previous jobs do you list first on an application form?
13. What types of people make good references on your application form?
14. What is the purpose of a cover letter?
15. Describe what is meant by the halo effect.
16. What are some steps you can take to prepare yourself for an interview?
17. How can you find information about a company to which you are applying?
18. How can you become more confident about the interview process before actually going to an interview?
19. What things do you need to remember when calling for an interview?
20. What type of clothes are appropriate for an interview at a law office? What type of makeup and jewelry are acceptable?
21. When should you arrive for an interview?
22. What are six things you should take with you to an interview? Which of them should you put on the interviewer's desk?
23. Who should go with you to an interview?
24. What tone should you use in speaking with an interviewer?
25. What should you do if an interviewer's questions are very general, not pertaining to the specific job you've come for?
26. If you had a terrible time with your last employer, and felt he was gravely unfair to you, what should you say about him to an interviewer?
27. When should you ask about possible salary and fringe benefits?
28. How can you tell when an interview is over? What are some signs?
29. After an interview, what can you do to make the interviewer remember you well?

REVIEW YOUR VOCABULARY

On a separate paper, write the letter of the vocabulary word that is described below.

____ 1. form that organizes all the facts about you related to the job you want
____ 2. organizations that charge a fee for finding you a job
____ 3. letter inquiring whether a specific type of job is available
____ 4. letter that always accompanies a résumé
____ 5. method where your most recent job is listed first
____ 6. correct style of speaking and writing
____ 7. item on which you record all relevant information about an available job
____ 8. items that may include skills and aptitude tests, psychological tests, and general abilities tests
____ 9. organizations that provide free job referral service

____ 10. written request for work

a. cover letter
b. employment tests
c. job lead card
d. letter of application
e. letter of inquiry
f. private employment agencies
g. public employment agencies
h. résumé
i. reverse chronological order
j. standard English

DISCUSS AND ANALYZE AN OFFICE SITUATION

1. Bradley hears about a general office work job that has just opened up at a local real estate office. He thinks the job would be perfect for him, especially since he hopes to make his career in real estate. However, he has made a date with his girlfriend for this afternoon, and is reluctant to change the date. He decides to call the real estate office tomorrow instead.

   What might Bradley have done differently, to better his chances of getting the job?

2. Alice is going to an interview with Mr. Beasely of Beasely Electronics. Her friend Judy used to work there. Judy tells Alice that Mr. Beasely is a nice guy, always joking around with the employees and buying them coffee on their breaks. When Judy sees that Alice is dressing quite conservatively for her interview, she tells her it isn't necessary—everyone just wears jeans at work, even Mr. Beasely. She laughs when she sees Alice's résumé, saying her previous experience at a pizza restaurant won't help her get this job—and she should leave the résumé at home. Alice is confused.

   Should Alice take Judy's advice? Why or why not? How can Alice have the best chance of getting the job?

PRACTICE BASIC SKILLS

MATH

1. You think you will like both the jobs you have been offered, but you are trying to decide which will be the best for you financially.

   The job at Jones Lumber pays $4.18 per hour for the first forty hours each week and double time ($8.36 per hour) for any hours after the first forty each week. It pays $50 per month toward health insurance, and allows full-time workers one paid sick day per month.

   The job at Smith's Electrical pays $5.08 per hour, with $1.00 per hour extra on Saturdays. No health insurance is paid for part-time employees.

   You plan to work about twenty hours per week during the school year—eight hours on Saturday and a few afternoons after school. Which job gives you the most income per month, including fringe benefits? Assume a four-week month.

ENGLISH

1. Remember that it is important to use standard English in the business world. On a separate paper, rewrite the following passage, underlining examples of nonstandard English.

   When I start my first job, I'm gonna really do good. I know I will really rip. The boss is a friend of my dad's, and he like me already. If can maintain, I'm sure I will get a raise soon, and I know the guy is gonna be impressed with my performance. I tole him I couldn't wait to get started, cause this job is radical, it's just perfect.

PROOFREADING

1. Retype or rewrite the following paragraphs of a letter of application, correcting all errors.

   Im a student at Roosevelt high school, and will graduate in june this year. I have been in the business education, porgram all three years, and worked as a aide in the office with the principal and his secretery, I also worked for a semester at lawrence radio and TV, where I ansered the phone on Saturday and wrote some checks as well.

I am going to college at state hoping to get a degree in accounting, and I have a good undertanding of math and bookkeeping. I really think this this job would be good for me, and I no I could do it well. May I call for aninterview? My phone number is 9632145.

APPLY YOUR KNOWLEDGE

1. Using an electronic typewriter or PC, write a letter of inquiry to a local business to learn whether any office positions are open.
2. Using a PC and a word processing program, prepare a résumé, including all the parts in the sample résumé shown in Figure 19.5.
3. Assume that you are applying for a job with a company that does business in other countries.

Using a word processing program or a typewriter, write a cover letter highlighting the reasons you would like to work for such a company. Emphasize any special skills that would make you valuable to a company doing business internationally.

USING THE REFERENCE MANUAL

Use the résumé section of the Reference Manual at the back of the book to key your résumé. If you have already prepared a personal data sheet, then you should have most of the information you will need to prepare your résumé.

Save as file CH19REF and print one copy. (If you have access to a laser printer and it is configured correctly to your hardware and software, print a professional copy for your own use when job hunting.)

On the Job:
What to Expect

OBJECTIVES

After completing this chapter, you will be able to do the following:

1. List the purposes for which an employer usually withholds money from earnings.
2. List the topics usually covered by a company's written policies and procedures.
3. List and describe what most employers expect of their employees.
4. List and describe what you may reasonably expect from your employer.
5. Explain how you should behave if you are fired or laid off.

NEW OFFICE TERMS

grievance process
performance evaluation
probation
productivity

severance pay
termination
unemployment compensation
W-4 form

You have spent most of your life in a school setting, experiencing only an occasional transition (change), like going from elementary school to junior high school and from junior high school to high school. During your time as a student, you may have had one or several part-time jobs. Although some people hold formal jobs while also attending school, most of the jobs you have had were probably less structured and less demanding than those you will soon begin to experience.

Soon you will make a major transition, into the world of work. Look on your new life as an adventure—a serious one, but an adventure nonetheless. You will have the opportunity to learn new ways of thinking, new methods of doing things, and special styles of organizing new kinds of tasks. You will meet different people in a new kind of setting. You will have much to learn, much to understand, and many new responsibilities.

Millions of people have successfully made this transition. It may help if you understand what to expect when you are new on the job. You will likely want to know what the first days will be like, what your employer will expect of you, and what you can expect of your employer. You may even want to know what to expect if your employment is terminated.

Your First Days on the Job

Before you do any work, you will be required to fill out certain paper-work. You have probably already filled out an application for employment, which includes your address and telephone number, education, and prior work experience. You will need to fill out the top section of an employment eligibility verification form. (See Figure 20.1 a and b.) Your employer will use this form to review and verify that you are either a U.S. citizen or an alien who is permitted to work in the United States. You will also need to fill out forms for tax withholding and other payroll forms. During your first days on the job, you will likely be introduced to other workers, read certain written policies and procedures, and even learn some unwritten rules.

FIGURE 20.1a ◆ Sample Employment Eligibility Verification Form

U.S. Department of Justice
Immigration and Naturalization Service

OMB No. 1115-0136

Employment Eligibility Verification

Please read instructions carefully before completing this form. The instructions must be available during completion of this form. **ANTI-DISCRIMINATION NOTICE.** It is illegal to discriminate against work eligible individuals. Employers **CANNOT** specify which document(s) they will accept from an employee. The refusal to hire an individual because of a future expiration date may also constitute illegal discrimination.

Section 1. Employee Information and Verification. To be completed and signed by employee at the time employment begins

Print Name: Last	First	Middle Initial	Maiden Name
Address *(Street Name and Number)*		Apt. #	Date of Birth *(month/day/year)*
City	State	Zip Code	Social Security #

I am aware that federal law provides for imprisonment and/or fines for false statements or use of false documents in connection with the completion of this form.	I attest, under penalty of perjury, that I am (check one of the following): ☐ A citizen or national of the United States ☐ A Lawful Permanent Resident (Alien # A _____) ☐ An alien authorized to work until ____/____/_____ (Alien # or Admission # _____)
Employee's Signature	Date *(month/day/year)*

Preparer and/or Translator Certification. *(To be completed and signed if Section 1 is prepared by a person other than the employee.) I attest, under penalty of perjury, that I have assisted in the completion of this form and that to the best of my knowledge the information is true and correct.*

Preparer's/Translator's Signature	Print Name
Address *(Street Name and Number, City, State, Zip Code)*	Date *(month/day/year)*

Section 2. Employer Review and Verification. To be completed and signed by employer. Examine one document from List A OR examine one document from List B **and** one from List C as listed on the reverse of this form and record the title, number and expiration date, if any, of the document(s)

List A	OR	List B	AND	List C
Document title: _____		_____		_____
Issuing authority: _____		_____		_____
Document #: _____		_____		_____
Expiration Date *(if any)*: ___/___/___		___/___/___		___/___/___
Document #: _____				
Expiration Date *(if any)*: ___/___/___				

CERTIFICATION - I attest, under penalty of perjury, that I have examined the document(s) presented by the above-named employee, that the above-listed document(s) appear to be genuine and to relate to the employee named, that the employee began employment on *(month/day/year)* ___/___/___ **and that to the best of my knowledge the employee is eligible to work in the United States. (State employment agencies may omit the date the employee began employment).**

Signature of Employer or Authorized Representative	Print Name	Title PERSONNEL CLERK IV
Business or Organization Name	Address *(Street Name and Number, City, State, Zip Code)*	Date *(month/day/year)*
SANTA BARBARA SCHOOL DISTRICTS, 723 E. COTA ST., SANTA BARBARA, CA 93103		

Section 3. Updating and Reverification. To be completed and signed by employer

A. New Name *(if applicable)*	B. Date of rehire *(month/day/year)* *(if applicable)*

C. If employee's previous grant of work authorization has expired, provide the information below for the document that establishes current employment eligibility.

Document Title: _____ Document #: _____ Expiration Date (if any): ___/___/___

I attest, under penalty of perjury, that to the best of my knowledge, this employee is eligible to work in the United States, and if the employee presented document(s), the document(s) I have examined appear to be genuine and to relate to the individual.

Signature of Employer or Authorized Representative	Date *(month/day/year)*

Form I-9 (Rev. 11-21-91) N

FIGURE 20.1b ◆ Sample Employment Eligibility Verification Form

LISTS OF ACCEPTABLE DOCUMENTS

LIST A	LIST B	LIST C
Documents that Establish Both Identity and Employment Eligibility	**Documents that Establish Identity**	**Documents that Establish Employment Eligibility**

OR ... **AND**

LIST A — Documents that Establish Both Identity and Employment Eligibility

1. U.S. Passport (unexpired or expired)

2. Certificate of U.S. Citizenship (INS Form N-560 or N-561)

3. Certificate of Naturalization (INS Form N-550 or N-570)

4. Unexpired foreign passport, with I-551 stamp or attached INS Form I-94 indicating unexpired employment authorization

5. Alien Registration Receipt Card with photograph (INS Form I-151 or I-551)

6. Unexpired Temporary Resident Card (INS Form I-688)

7. Unexpired Employment Authorization Card (INS Form I-688A)

8. Unexpired Reentry Permit (INS Form I-327)

9. Unexpired Refugee Travel Document (INS Form I-571)

10. Unexpired Employment Authorization Document issued by the INS which contains a photograph (INS Form I-688B)

LIST B — Documents that Establish Identity

1. Driver's license or ID card issued by a state or outlying possession of the United States provided it contains a photograph or information such as name, date of birth, sex, height, eye color, and address

2. ID card issued by federal, state, or local government agencies or entities provided it contains a photograph or information such as name, date of birth, sex, height, eye color, and address

3. School ID card with a photograph

4. Voter's registration card

5. U.S. Military card or draft record

6. Military dependent's ID card

7. U.S. Coast Guard Merchant Mariner Card

8. Native American tribal document

9. Driver's license issued by a Canadian government authority

For persons under age 18 who are unable to present a document listed above:

10. School record or report card

11. Clinic, doctor, or hospital record

12. Day-care or nursery school record

LIST C — Documents that Establish Employment Eligibility

1. U.S. social security card issued by the Social Security Administration (other than a card stating it is not valid for employment)

2. Certification of Birth Abroad issued by the Department of State (Form FS-545 or Form DS-1350)

3. Original or certified copy of a birth certificate issued by a state, county, municipal authority or outlying possession of the United States bearing an official seal

4. Native American tribal document

5. U.S. Citizen ID Card (INS Form I-197)

6. ID Card for use of Resident Citizen in the United States (INS Form I-179)

7. Unexpired employment authorization document issued by the INS (other than those listed under List A)

Illustrations of many of these documents appear in Part 8 of the Handbook for Employers (M-274)

Form I-9 (Rev. 11-21-91) N

TAX FORMS, WITHHOLDING, AND PAYROLL

The state and federal governments require all workers to pay taxes on the money they earn. The money collected in taxes supports the work of these governments and pays the salaries of government employees.

You are required by law to fill out a **W-4 form,** which provides certain information about the amount of taxes you will be paying (see Figure 20.2). The amount you pay depends on how much money you earn (your gross salary), whether you are married, and how many allowances you claim. Each allowance represents one person for whom you provide financial support. An additional allowance is permitted for those who are blind or over age 65. The more allowances you have, the less income tax you will have to pay. A single person usually has one allowance. A family has an allowance for the employee plus as many allowances as there are children claimed by this employee.

The information requested on the W-4 form includes the following:

◆ your name with middle initial and your complete address (number and street name, city, state, and ZIP code)
◆ your Social Security number
◆ your marital status
◆ your total number of allowances
◆ a notation if you wish to have money withheld from your paycheck for other purposes

---

FIGURE 20.2 ◆ A Sample W-4 Form

Form **W-4** Department of the Treasury Internal Revenue Service	**Employee's Withholding Allowance Certificate** ▶ For Privacy Act and Paperwork Reduction Act Notice, see reverse.	OMB No. 1545-0010 **1997**
1 Type or print your first name and middle initial	Last name	**2** Your social security number
Home address (number and street or rural route)	**3** ☐ Single ☐ Married ☐ Married, but withhold at higher Single rate. Note: *If married, but legally separated, or spouse is a nonresident alien, check the Single box.*	
City or town, state, and ZIP code	**4** If your last name differs from that on your social security card, check here and call 1-800-772-1213 for a new card . . . . . ▶ ☐	

5 Total number of allowances you are claiming (from line G above or from the worksheets on page 2 if they apply) . **5**
6 Additional amount, if any, you want withheld from each paycheck . . . . **6** $
7 I claim exemption from withholding for 1997, and I certify that I meet **BOTH** of the following conditions for exemption:
  • Last year I had a right to a refund of **ALL** Federal income tax withheld because I had **NO** tax liability; **AND**
  • This year I expect a refund of **ALL** Federal income tax withheld because I expect to have **NO** tax liability.
  If you meet both conditions, enter "EXEMPT" here . . . . ▶ **7**

Under penalties of perjury, I certify that I am entitled to the number of withholding allowances claimed on this certificate or entitled to claim exempt status.

Employee's signature ▶   **Date** ▶   , 19

8 Employer's name and address (Employer: Complete 8 and 10 only if sending to the IRS)	**9** Office code (optional)	**10** Employer identification number

◆ other information concerning a possible exemption (Information on the W-4 form lists reasons why you may not be required to have money withheld, and are thus exempt from withholding.)
◆ a notation if you are a student
◆ your signature and the date you signed this document

Your employer will keep track of how much money you earn. In addition, on the basis of the information you supplied on your W-4 form, your employer will determine how much money to withhold from each of your paychecks. Charts provide this information and computer programs do all the payroll calculations after the basic information is input.

Besides state and federal taxes, Social Security tax is withheld according to the percentage currently designated by the federal government. Your employer also pays part of your Social Security contribution. Other deductions may be made for disability insurance, health insurance, or a retirement fund. Your employer also pays into one or two other funds for your benefit. It may seem complicated, but you should receive a complete statement of money withheld with every paycheck (see Figure 20.3).

You may be required to keep a time card, or you may be instructed to keep track of the time you spend on the job by some other method. You may be asked to write down the time you arrive in the morning, the time you go out for lunch, the time you return from lunch, and the time you leave in the evening. This record enables your employer to determine how much money you have earned. You should have agreed on your rate of pay when you accepted the job. Figure 20.4 shows a sample time card.

INTRODUCTIONS

After you have finished your paperwork, your supervisor will probably take you around to the other employees for introductions. If you have the opportunity before these introductions are made, ask your employer for a list of employee names with their telephone extensions. If not, then ask for this list following the introductions. It will help you remember your co-workers' names. If no one conducts these introductions, your co-workers should come to you and introduce themselves.

Make it your policy to learn your co-workers' names and titles as quickly as possible. If you have a list of employee names, make notes that will help you remember those to whom you are introduced. For example, you might write titles or the office in which each person works. Go over these names several times so you can commit them to memory. Your new co-workers will be pleased if you are interested enough to call them by name.

It's good manners to determine how people in the office are addressed. Different levels of formality are used in different offices. In some offices, people are addressed by their last names, such as Ms. Adams, Miss Brown, Mrs. Jones, or Mr. Green. In other offices, everyone is called by his or her first name. Make note of who gets called

OFFICE TIP

Your employers and the other people who work in your office are only human, and sometimes they make mistakes. Keep track of the hours you spend on the job, separate from your time card. You can jot your hours on the calendar for that day. Then, when you receive your paycheck and the stub that supplies you with all the withholding information, you are better able to check it for accuracy.

FIGURE 20.3 ◆ A Sample Paycheck

	Current		Year to Date		Taxes Deductions	Year to Date
Restaurants, Inc. Fort Worth, Texas		Morisot, Ramona R. Pay Rate: $7.00/hr				
Description	Hours	Earnings	Hours	Earnings	Federal Tax	$21.17	$508.08
					Social Security	16.06	385.54
					Medicare	3.76	90.24
Regular	37	259 00	888	6,216 00	Dental	3.00	72.00
Overtime	0	0 00			Company Stock	0.00	0.00

	Earnings	Taxes	Deductions	Net Pay	Pay Period
Current	259.00	40.99	3.00	215.01	11-28-97
Year to Date	6,216.00	93.76	72.00	5,160.24	12-12-97

No. 311264

Restaurants, Inc.
Fort Worth, Texas 76179

Date ___ **Dec. 12** 19 **99**

Pay to the Order of ___ **Ramona R. Morisot** ___

Amount **Two hundred fifteen and 01/100** ___ Dollars

Dollars	Cents
215.01	

Texas Federal S&L

Ramona Morisot
2418 Hadley Street
Fort Worth, Texas 76179

Ann Winchell

---

what and how visitors and customers are addressed, then follow these practices. It will help you fit into the work environment more quickly.

WRITTEN POLICIES AND PROCEDURES

Most companies have written policies and procedures. If your new job is with a large company, you may attend a formal orientation meeting for all recently hired employees. At this time, you may be given a policies and procedures manual, sometimes called a policies and rules manual. The policies, procedures, and rules will likely be explained to you in detail at the orientation meeting.

If you do not attend an orientation meeting and no one explains the contents of a policies and rules manual, read through the manual very carefully. This can be important to your future employment with the company, so ask questions about any items you don't understand.

FIGURE 20.4 ◆ A Sample Time Card

Week Ending: September 24, 1999

Employee No.: 541-18-4324

Name: Paul Thornton

DAY	IN	OUT	IN	OUT	TOTAL
Mon	8:02	12:02	1:01	5:03	8
Tue	7:59	11:58	1:01	5:08	8
Wed	8:01	12:02	1:03	5:06	8
Thu	8:01	12:06	1:00	5:08	8¼
Fri	7:59	12:02	1:02	5:01	8
Sat					
Sun					

Total time: 40¼ hours

Rate Per Hour: $10.00

Total Wages: $403.75 (inc. ¼hr. OT)

Policies and rules manuals contain different information in different companies. Some are large documents; others may be just a few pages. In companies that are unionized, you will also receive documents about policies and rules related to the union. The complexities of these documents depend, to some degree, on the complexities of your new company's structure. In some firms, management feels that extensive definition is not necessary, and there are only a few rules and policies. The topics addressed in a policies manual often include hiring procedures; work schedules and records; salaries, wages, and benefits; probation periods; performance evaluations; termination of employment; the grievance process; expenses and reimbursement procedures; and other categories. Every company's manual is unique, created especially for an individual company to meet its own needs.

Hiring Procedures   One section of a policies and rules manual is usually devoted to explaining the procedures the company follows when hiring new employees. Only one interview may be necessary, or a company may use a screening process that requires more than one visit. If a company is hiring a large number of people, it may interview several prospects at one time.

◆ *Find out what level of formality is expected on your new job. Your supervisor might feel uneasy hearing you call her Maria if everyone else addresses her as Mrs. Martinez.*

Many companies have personnel departments that do all the hiring. If this is the case, you might not meet your direct supervisor until your first day of work. Companies hire people in many ways, and the hiring procedures section of the policies manual will describe how your company does it.

Work Schedule and Records One section of the manual usually describes the work schedule, lunch breaks, coffee breaks, overtime, and so on. It also discusses the necessary records to document the work schedule kept by the employee and employer.

Salaries, Wages, and Benefits The salaries, wages, and benefits section of the manual describes how salaries are decided and how and when overtime is paid. Overtime refers to any hours worked over forty hours per week, unless other arrangements have been agreed on. Labor laws govern how many hours each day people may work. This section of the manual also details the availability of special programs that affect the pay schedule, such as medical insurance and retirement plans.

Other Benefits Other benefits include, for example, vacation time, sick leave, outside training opportunities, and bonus days for good performance. This section of the manual indicates how many vacation days you accrue (earn). It is common to earn one week's vacation for every six months worked. It is also common to earn one week's vaca-

OFFICE TIP

Read simple documents once and take action. Highlight the important points as you read. Reading a document and setting it aside for later rereading can waste time you could use for other projects. Of course, complex documents may need to be reread and studied.

tion after the first year, then two weeks' vacation after each subsequent year.

The number of paid sick days that an employee may accrue varies greatly from company to company. Some companies give one day of sick leave each month, to be used only if you are ill. Other companies allow a paid sick day when a member of your family is ill and you need to stay home to care for her or him.

Probation Periods   **Probation** is a period of time usually lasting three to six months after you are hired. During this time, you will accrue no benefits. At the end of the probation period, a formal evaluation should be conducted in a meeting between you and your immediate supervisor. If your job performance is unsatisfactory, you may be terminated. If your job performance is satisfactory, you will become a permanent employee and will be eligible for all available benefits.

Performance Evaluation   A **performance evaluation** is a written statement outlining the strengths and weaknesses of your job performance. You will probably be evaluated at least once each year. Probation may be reinstated with poor job performance, and again termination is a possibility. You should learn to use the evaluation process to your advantage, discovering which things about your work you need to improve and taking steps to improve them. Your performance evaluation may show that you are doing exceptionally good work. In that case, you might be given a merit pay raise.

Termination of Employment   **Termination** means a request for you to leave a job. In other words, you are fired. One reason for termination is a poor review. Other possible reasons are being absent or tardy too often, stealing from the company, coming to work under the influence of alcohol or drugs, and disregarding company rules.

Grievance Process   Your supervisor may do something you think is unfair. For example, he or she may give you a negative evaluation that you don't think is accurate or justified. The **grievance process** refers to the method a company uses to allow you to state your side in disputes with supervisors or other employees.

Expenses and Reimbursement   Companies generally reimburse employees for certain expenses. For example, expenses incurred by an employee on business trips are reimbursable. These expenses will usually be spelled out in a policies manual along with the methods used to document them and methods of reimbursement.

Other Categories   You may find some other categories in your new company's policies document. The ones listed here are only some of the possibilities. It is your responsibility to read your manual completely, making sure that you have a thorough understanding of all topics it covers.

WHAT'S YOUR ATTITUDE?

Dorothy and Hooshang are hired at the same time at a large company that holds an orientation meeting for all new employees. The meeting is conducted on a Saturday morning and takes several hours. The company policies and rules manual is the main topic of discussion.

Dorothy is careful to take notes on the proceedings. She notices what people who work for the company wear. She also notices how they act toward one another, discovering that they are rather formal and businesslike. She is glad to have the opportunity to discover everything about the company so she can quickly fit in and do a good job.

Hooshang sits next to Dorothy. He complains bitterly about having to spend his Saturday morning in a meeting of this sort. He had expected to be working Monday through Friday and resents having to cancel his Saturday plans. He spends time in the meeting grumbling and being a distraction, not bothering to take notes or really pay much attention to the proceedings. Neither does he bother to notice how people who work for the company act. He feels he can read the documents later and find out all he needs to know.

At one point, Dorothy is forced to ask Hooshang to be quiet because he is becoming a real bother. The company representatives also notice Hooshang's behavior. Though they do not speak to him about it at the meeting, they make notes to put in his personnel file about his unpleasant and uncooperative attitude.

1. *How would you describe Dorothy's attitude in the orientation meeting? Do you think she will carry this same attitude over into the office?*

2. *How would you describe Hooshang's attitude in the orientation meeting? Do you think he will carry this same attitude over into the office?*

Unwritten Rules Throughout this book, discussions have focused on what you might expect and what is expected of you in your office job. Many of these rules are not written, but are nonetheless rules of the job. They are part of the way the business office has been run— probably for a long while. You might refer to these as the *culture* of the office—its system of knowledge, beliefs, and behavior. Usually, the tone and style of an office culture is set by the company's owner or chief executive officer (CEO)—in other words, the main boss.

Some offices are very formal and frown on informal behavior. Some offices are so casual that they have no dress code or expectations of any kind except that you get done the tasks that are assigned to you, on time and efficiently.

The unwritten rules in your new office must be learned through observing and asking questions. For example, recall the importance of understanding how people in the office are addressed. What are the special ways of getting work done, of passing information, of maintaining a specific attitude that might be part of the office behavior? Is casual dress the order of the day? Is informal English acceptable? You can acquaint yourself with the unwritten rules of your office by watching how other employees act.

Recall Time

Answer the following questions:

1. Before you do any work for your new company, you will be expected to fill out certain papers. One of these will be a W-4 form from the Internal Revenue Service. What information is requested on this form?

2. What do you understand about a policies and procedures manual? What kinds of information will this provide a new employee?

3. Every office has unwritten rules. How do you discover what these are in your new office?

4. You may have a formal orientation meeting. What sort of information will you expect to receive at such a meeting?

5. Some offices are formal and others are more informal. Who generally sets the style of an office?

Employer Expectations

Expectations that your new employer will have of you include, for example, a good attitude, cooperation, honesty, willingness to learn, dependability, enthusiasm, and initiative (resourcefulness). These are important components of your successful relationship with your employer. On your first day at work, begin to attempt to live up to these expectations.

The expectations listed above relate to your attitude. Expectations related to job performance include producing high-quality work, arriving on time, and not being absent frequently. Other performance-related expectations include skillful decision making and problem solving, caring for office equipment, and safety awareness.

QUALITY OF WORK

Your employer will expect high-quality work from you. The success of your company will depend on the employees' producing good-quality work. Whether your company provides a service or a product, customers will not return for repeat business if the goods or services provided are of low quality.

A poorly typed letter or a mistake in an order is an error in quality of work, and it affects the productivity of your company. Pride in your work helps create a sense of ownership in the tasks that you perform and helps you maintain a high standard. If you do quality work, your employer and your co-workers will notice and praise you for it. Likewise, if you do subquality work, your boss and co-workers will know that, too, and will not be happy about it.

PRODUCTIVITY

Quality of work can affect productivity throughout the company. But what does productivity mean and how is it measured? **Productivity** in the office is the total work accomplished in a given time. If you work next to another office assistant all day long and she or he keyboards thirty pages in a day and you keyboard twenty-five, you know that your neighbor's rate of productivity is higher than yours.

Generally, being productive requires working at a steady pace and staying at the job, except for breaks, for all of the eight hours for which you are being paid. If you spend time on the telephone making personal calls, or spend time visiting with other employees while you're supposed to be working, your productivity level will suffer. Bosses don't like to see people standing around chatting or talking on the telephone when they are supposed to be working. This kind of interference with your productivity can cost you your job.

TARDINESS AND ABSENTEEISM

You should have signed on to your new position fully understanding what your working hours will be. Some jobs are forty hours each week, some are thirty-seven and one-half hours each week. Whatever your schedule, your employer will expect you to arrive on time and leave at the agreed-on hour.

Some people always arrive a few minutes after starting time. Then, after they arrive, they spend several minutes chatting, fixing their clothing, arranging their personal belongings, and getting set for the day. Just because you're already in the building does not mean you have begun to work. Get all your organizing done before starting time.

Plan to arrive a few minutes early so you can say hello to everyone and so you won't feel rushed. Arriving five minutes earlier takes only a little planning, such as setting your alarm to awaken you five minutes earlier.

Getting into the bad habit of arriving late, or even starting work late, can cause resentment on the part of your co-workers. They have to arrive and begin on time; why shouldn't you?

Absenteeism can be a real problem for employers. It signals loss of productivity and a heavier load for the employees who are at work. Occasionally, you will have reasons that you cannot attend work. Generally, the only acceptable reason is illness. If you are ill, call your immediate supervisor as early as possible to tell him or her that you have a problem and will not be able to attend work.

Regular attendance and punctuality (being on time) are attributes of dependability. It is vital to the successful functioning of an office that you be dependable and reliable, that you come to work every day, and that you always arrive on time.

DECISION MAKING AND PROBLEM SOLVING

Learning when to seek advice on the job and when to make a decision yourself can be a tricky aspect of your new position. You can't go to

OFFICE TIP

While applying for a job, Bud was asked how many sick days he might expect to take. His response was, "Maybe just one each month," which he believed made perfect sense. The person who was interviewing Bud was appalled. She felt it was entirely unacceptable for an employee to expect to be taking twelve sick days each year. If you are asked this question, simply say that you are very healthy and don't expect to be sick at all.

Large Office/Small Office: What's Your Preference?

WHAT TO EXPECT ON THE JOB

A large company often has an employee manual with written information regarding the company's policies and expectations. Usually, it will list the company's benefits, such as vacation and sick leave, insurance, pensions plans, and severance pay. Other information, such as rules regarding work behavior, is also included. The manual should detail the specific steps for handling grievances and problems, as well as information regarding performance reviews, pay raises, and promotions. Often, a large company has detailed descriptions and salary ranges for each position, with progressive steps, or levels. For example, it may have three levels of administrative assistant positions, such as administrative assistant I, administrative assistant II, and administrative assistant III. Training is sometimes more formal and extensive in a large company than in a small one. Some companies place a great deal of importance on appearance and dressing well, and sometimes this can even affect job advancement. Often, a hierarchy of reporting and procedures exists. Sometimes, it takes a longer period to get something accomplished because a request has to go through many levels of management before it is approved.

A small company may not have an employee manual. Often, information is given informally, usually verbally, and procedures are less formal. You may not have anyone to train you, and you may have to find out how to do things by asking any number of people. More direct interaction and communication occur, and changes or requests are often acted upon quickly without having to go through many people to get approval. Small companies tend to have a more relaxed attitude about dress codes, and people are generally less formal in their communications.

Which would you prefer—the formal, clearly defined procedures and policies of a large office, or the more loosely structured, informal methods of a small office? Why?

your boss every time a small problem requires a decision. You must devise strategies that will help you make some decisions yourself. If you don't, job advancement will be out of the question for you.

If you are puzzled by a problem, take some time to think it through. Don't be hasty and don't be rash. If the consequences of your decision will not be too dramatic, go ahead and test your decision making. The more initiative you take and the more work you get done on your own without interrupting your supervisor and co-workers with questions, the more successful you will be on the job.

Part of the process of being able to make good judgments is to be able to foresee possible outcomes. If a decision seems to be leading to a very important outcome, perhaps you should get other opinions; but if the outcome will be more or less inconsequential, make the decision yourself.

At the beginning of your new employment, you will need to ask many questions—and you will be *expected* to ask them. However, after you have become more familiar with your job, you will be expected to make more and more job-related decisions yourself.

CARE OF OFFICE EQUIPMENT

A major expense in any office is equipment. Typewriters, computer systems, photocopy machines, and calculators all come with a high price tag. Sometimes we don't realize it, but even the telephone system can be elaborate and expensive. The furnishings—desks, chairs, tables, shelves—are also costly.

You will be expected to take care of the furniture and equipment assigned for your use. Don't eat or drink near your typewriter or computer keyboard. Dropping food into the works can cause damage to these machines. Arrange for regular maintenance and cleaning of your machines if someone else does not have that responsibility.

Treat your machines with respect. Don't drop things onto them or force parts that are supposed to release easily. Learn how to change ribbons and tapes. Treat your machines as though they were your good friends. The better you care for them, the more they will help you accomplish what you need to do.

◆ *Office machines, such as photocopiers, are expensive and require regular servicing to keep them in good working order. Be sure you know how to operate them correctly, as carelessness can cause the need for extra repair and maintenance.*

SAFETY AWARENESS

Concern for the safety of employees is not as big an issue in an office as it is in a machine shop. Still, your company will probably have some safety rules and procedures, and you should be aware of certain steps that can help ensure the safety of others in your environment.

Most large offices have procedures to follow in the event of a major disaster such as fire or earthquake. A diagram of the building's emergency exits should be posted on a wall along with some instructions about what to do in an emergency. Make yourself aware of these directions. Some offices have regular fire drills so that everyone can practice what to do. Your cooperation in these drills may later save you from injury, and may even save your life.

Other little details can help ensure safety in an office. For example, don't string electrical wires across floors where people are walking. Be careful about the placement of items on high shelves so that they do not tumble down on people below. Look around your office to check for safety; you may be able to think of other safety tips.

OFFICE ROMANCES

While you are in school, you see many other people every day. You have opportunities to talk with many young men and women about your own age. You can make friends, date, even meet your life partner at school.

◆ *Be cautious about becoming romantically involved with a co-worker. If the romance ends, continuing to work together could be difficult.*

When you no longer attend classes daily, your circle of potential friends, and dates, may become much smaller. One of the places where many people look for friends and possible romantic interests is on the job. Most people do make friends at work, but it's best to go slow and get to know a co-worker before you decide to spend a lot of time with him or her. Sometimes it's difficult to break off a friendship that you let grow too fast.

Those who look for romantic interests on the job need to use at least as much caution as they would in making friends. Go slow. A person who catches your eye may seem like someone with whom you would like to pursue a romantic relationship. But if you move too quickly, you may find it very difficult to break off. Carmen, a young woman in Chicago, got involved too quickly with a young man to whom she was very much attracted. Soon she was thinking, "If only I'd waited a couple of weeks, it would have been obvious that I didn't want to get involved with this man." He became quite upset when Carmen broke off the relationship.

Broken relationships in the office are often a problem. It can be difficult to work with someone with whom you've had a close relationship that went sour. And poor working relationships are a major reason employees are fired. So be cautious. Romance in the office can be risky!

Employee Expectations

Your new employer will expect many things of you. It is reasonable for you to expect certain things from your employer, too. These include a tour of the office and introductions, training, timely paychecks, communication to keep you informed, evaluation of your work, safe working conditions, and honesty.

TOUR OF THE OFFICE AND INTRODUCTIONS

You can expect that someone in the company will provide you with a tour of the office. This person will show you where materials and supplies are kept, will probably tell you who occupies which offices, and will show you the rest room and lunchroom.

At the same time that this tour is being conducted, you will probably be introduced to your co-workers. You can expect that people will be open, friendly, and helpful in welcoming you to your new office.

TRAINING

It is in the company's best interest to train you carefully and thoroughly. This training will probably include information about company policy and rules, and you should receive a clear statement of what is expected of you. You will likely learn who your immediate supervisor is—this is the person to whom you will be accountable.

Although you may have learned in school many of the basic skills you need to perform your new job, you will still require some training. For example, you will need to know the details about the job, what pre-

◆   *Your new job could require some extensive training to get you familiar with specific duties for your position and details about the company.*

cisely your duties will be, and how you should accomplish them. Take advantage of this training, and learn as much as you can now, because in a short while, you will be on your own.

In many companies, there is increased emphasis on cross training; that is, training employees to perform the tasks usually done by other workers. This helps employers because when someone is ill or on vacation, another worker can step in and do the work.

If you have an opportunity to learn how to do the work usually done by other workers, take advantage of it. *You* will become more valuable to the company.

TIMELY PAYCHECKS

If you come to work each day on time and work all the hours you are assigned, you can expect to get paid for your work. The policies and procedures manual will tell you when paydays are. For some companies, this will be every Friday; for others, it will be the first and the fifteenth days of the month. Government offices often pay only once a month, usually on the tenth of the month following the month when the money was earned. Every company has established paydays, and you can expect to be paid on those days so you can plan accordingly.

Along with your paycheck, you can expect an accounting of the money earned and the money withheld for taxes and other items.

COMMUNICATION TO KEEP YOU INFORMED

Your employer should keep you informed about changes in company policy, potential changes in your workload or responsibilities, and other changes in the company that might affect you. A good company has a system of communication that allows employees to feel involved and a part of the ongoing business of the company. This communication often takes place in staff meetings, but it can also be accomplished by memos, bulletins, and newsletters. You will receive a lot of information verbally, from either your supervisor or your co-workers. Pay attention. Some of the things you hear may directly affect your work with the company.

EVALUATION OF YOUR WORK

You can expect periodic evaluations that should help you be a better employee. Having careful, thoughtful feedback from your supervisor about the quality and productivity of your work, your attitude, and how you fit into the office environment is a reasonable expectation. The evaluation is also part of the company's communication system.

Part of your evaluation may be criticism of how you work. Don't be defensive. Listen carefully to any criticism. Think about it later, and use this information to become a better worker.

Your employer should also tell you what you are doing exceptionally well. Use both criticism and praise to improve your work skills.

SAFE WORKING CONDITIONS

On-the-job safety is your new employer's responsibility. It should be constantly monitoring the safety of the environment in which you are expected to work.

Although this is a larger concern in certain kinds of machine shops and factories than in an office, your employer should be vigilant in seeing to it that safety precautions are taken. Your employer should also have a plan of action for an emergency.

HONESTY

After you work for a few years, you may discover that honesty is probably the most important expectation you will have of your employers. Smart companies invariably have a policy of straight shooting with their employees. *Straight shooting* means direct communication about what you can expect of your employers along the lines of advancement, salary, salary raises, benefits, and so on.

If you think your employer has been unfair, you may want to discuss the problem with her or him. Don't begin the discussion with accusations. Simply say that you are confused about what has gone on, and you need to clarify the issues so that you can understand them. Yes, this can be risky, but you don't want to be in a situation where you are being used or manipulated. In such a case, you would be happier leaving this job to seek other employment.

Companies that make promises and don't deliver have serious personnel problems and don't last long in the business world.

Be sure you know exactly the sort of business your new company is in before you agree to take the job. Some people have become involved in shady businesses through naiveté (trustfulness) and innocence. If you have any doubts about the nature of the business your company is involved in, find out.

Most companies deal honestly with their employees. You need to be able to trust your employers, as they expect to be able to trust you.

MANAGING STRESS

Stress is anything that triggers your fight-or-flight response. Our distant ancestors found stress very helpful. It motivated them to battle or to run like crazy when confronted by an enemy or a wild and hungry predator. Today, stress can be either positive or negative. An example of positive stress is the excitement a musician feels just before a production. In this case, the fight-or-flight response helps to improve the performance. The excitement a basketball player feels just before a big game can lift the level of play.

Negative stress can be short term (such as the pressure to make a quick decision when a car swerves into your path). Or it can be long term (such as the stress you might feel in a high-pressure job). Too much stress, especially over a long period of time, can cause a loss of energy and leave you vulnerable to illness and even premature aging. Photos of presidents taken before and after four years in one of the most stressful jobs in the world provide a vivid example.

There are two major types of stress, *physical stress* and *psychological stress.* Physical stress is caused by physical demands on the body (such as illness, accidents, or even prolonged psychological stress). Psychological stress can be simply the result of physical stress. But psychological stress is usually caused by emotional demands in your personal life (family, friends) or from your work. Psychological, or emotional stress is often the most damaging type in today's society. And, fortunately, we have ways to ease this stress.

There are four basic types of psychological, or emotional stress. The first is *pressure,* which is an internal or external demand to complete a task in a limited time or in a certain way. The second is *frustration,* which is the blocking of your needs or wants. The third is *conflict,* which is the need to make a choice between two or more options. The fourth is *anxiety or fear,* which is one of two basic emotional responses to a perceived threat (the other is anger).

When stress triggers your fight-or-flight response, your body provides you with physical energy not needed to cope with a modern-day situation. This generates anxiety. Your body responds to any thought as if it concerns the present, even when you think about the past or the future. A vivid thought (with a strong emotional component) about a past bad experience or a possible future problem can bring on the fight-or-flight response. People who experience prolonged stress usually have attitudes, beliefs, and thinking patterns that perpetuate it.

You can't eliminate stress from your life. That's unrealistic in today's world. Reducing stress through good stress management should be your goal.

The first step in stress management is to treat your body like a machine that needs regular rest, maintenance, and care to work properly. You begin each day with a limited amount of energy. Your energy

◆ *Learning good stress management techniques can help you avoid burnout and health problems related to prolonged stress.*

HUMAN RELATIONS

Angela, a word processor, was the newest employee in the office. Her keyboarding skills, however, were better than anyone in the department. When her supervisor, Mr. Bracken, brought work into the department, he would usually give new work to those who were nearly finished with their prior assignments.

Because Angela was the most productive, she was often given big projects near the end of the day and would have to work late to complete them. Angela felt that Mr. Bracken was taking unfair advantage of her because she was a productive worker. She objected to this, but she didn't know what to do about it.

Then Angela came up with an idea. She would simply try to avoid Mr. Bracken. Her desk was situated so that she could easily see anyone approaching the department down a long hall.

So the next time she saw Mr. Bracken approaching, she quickly left her station and went to the ladies' room. By doing this several times a week, she avoided several big projects that might have caused her to work late. Instead, Bob and Judy began getting these projects.

Based on what you know about Angela's approach to solving her problem, answer these questions:

1. *How do you think Angela's behavior will affect her chances for promotion?*

2. *How do you think her practice of avoiding Mr. Bracken will affect Angela's relationships with her co-workers?*

3. *What would have been a better way for Angela to solve her problem?*

level varies from day to day, and it's different from that of other people. When you use up your energy supply, you can replace it only by resting and getting proper nourishment. If you don't, your body will begin to break down.

Learn to recognize the signs of stress. They include physical, mental, emotional, and relational symptoms, such as the ones listed below.

Physical Symptoms

Frequent colds or flu	Fatigue
Frequent sighing	Headaches
Increased accidents	Insomnia
Hyperventilation	Pounding heart
Restlessness	Weight change

Mental Symptoms

Boredom	Confusion
Forgetfulness	Negative attitude
Reduced ability to concentrate	"Weird" thoughts

Emotional Symptoms

Anxiety	Bad dreams
Crying spells	Depression
Frustration	Increased use of profanity
Sarcasm	Irritability
Mood swings	Short temper

Relational Symptoms

Avoidance of people	Blaming others for problems
Distrusting others	Fewer contacts with friends

Increased arguing   Intolerance
Lack of intimacy   Resentment

You probably noticed that some of these symptoms apply to you. Everyone has some of these symptoms. However, if many apply to you, it is likely that you are not managing the stress in your life as well as you should for good health.

Some people have highly reactive bodies. They often experience many anxiety-related problems while those around them remain calm. Scientists feel that being highly reactive is often an inherited trait. If you fall into this category, it doesn't mean that you are doomed to severe anxiety for life, but that you must understand the symptoms and take care of your needs. These needs may be physical, mental, emotional, or relational.

The following are ways others have learned to manage stress in their lives. You may find some of them helpful in your own stress management plan.

◆ **Set Priorities and Reduce Overall Activity.** At certain times in your life, you will face periods of high stress. Everyone does. When this happens, reduce your activities. This is not a time to set new performance records! Set priorities. Do what's most important, and cut back on what's not quite as crucial for now. Sometimes stress can lead you to give small details an exaggerated importance. Try to keep a proper perspective of what's vital and what can wait until later. Set some short-term goals. Give your body a rest and you will recover your energy level.

◆ *Regular exercise, as well as relaxation, is important to your overall well-being and good job performance.*

◆ **Exercise.** Physical exercise can help you work off emotional stress. You probably know that aerobic exercise is vigorous exercise that makes your heart beat faster and requires you to use a lot of oxygen. This changes your body chemistry. Many people use running, bicycling, aerobic dancing, tennis, or other vigorous physical exercise to lower their stress levels. Exercise can even give you an emotional, natural "high" feeling because it causes increased levels of endorphins to be produced in the brain. (*Endorphins* are hormones that have a tranquilizing or pain-killing effect on the body.)

◆ **Take Time to Relax.** You know that regular rest is necessary to regain energy. One way to assure time for rest and relaxation is to schedule it. Scheduling regular relaxation is as important for your mind and body as scheduling regular maintenance on your car— only a lot more is at stake!

Some proven forms of relaxation include the following. Find a couple you haven't used and give them a try.

Passive Forms of Relaxation	**Active Forms of Relaxation**
Biofeedback	Hobbies and crafts
Diaphragmatic breathing	Dancing
Massage	Tennis, golf
Meditation	Jogging, swimming
Reading	Team sports
Television	Gardening
Yoga	Walking

◆ **Talk Out Your Problems.** Talk with someone you trust and respect, perhaps a friend, family member, minister, or counselor. When you hold a problem in, you tend to obsess on it (think about it constantly). Most problems aren't as big as we think they are when we hold them in. When you talk about a difficulty, you can usually see that it is solvable, let go of it, and move on with your life. When you talk about a problem, a compromise usually seems more acceptable, too.

◆ **Accept What You Can't Change.** Most people want as much control over their lives as possible, but in the real world, there are a lot of things we simply can't change. It is self-defeating to worry about things that aren't changeable. When you learn to accept what you can't change, life gets a lot easier—and the stress level goes down.

◆ **Keep a Balanced Lifestyle.** In today's world, both marriage partners often must bring home a paycheck to cover the high cost of living. Many people are even working at two jobs. Caring for young children, arranging for baby-sitters, and driving children to and from school or activities add more responsibilities—and more stress—to the mix. One way to relieve the stress level is to schedule time for regular recreation, to do something that gets your mind off both work and family responsibilities. Sometimes this isn't easy. You can't add any more hours to the day. But spending some time in a leisure activity or enjoying a favorite hobby almost guarantees you will be more relaxed. It may well be worth quitting a second job or reducing your responsibilities elsewhere. A balanced lifestyle really works!

◆ **Eat and Sleep Well.** Of course you would never fall for junk food advertising (at least not on a regular basis). But it may be hard to obtain nutritionally balanced meals every day. Try to make good eating habits a priority in your life. If you don't, your health will likely be compromised. Many nutritionists recommend vitamin and mineral supplements, too.

Sleep needs vary; some people need more than others. But many people don't get enough sleep and find themselves drowsy in class or on the job. This is most common in the early afternoon, following lunch. If you feel tired or drowsy during the day, you probably need more sleep.

An improper diet and insufficient sleep can increase your level of stress from any source. So eat well and get enough sleep!

Stress in your personal life can affect your performance on the job. Personal stress is distracting, causing a lack of concentration on the task at hand, and it may cause you to be less cooperative with your co-workers.

On the job, tasks that you dislike or cannot do well can cause stress. Your employer or certain co-workers may pressure you to perform in a way that makes you uncomfortable. Working on a stressful job for a long period of time can cause burnout. A person with burnout has reached a point where he or she can no longer perform job tasks effectively; he or she should take a rest, perhaps a long vacation, or should move on to other work. Companies lose an estimated $68 billion each year from stress-related disability claims.

Just as personal stress can affect work performance, job stress can carry over into your personal life as well. Both on and off the job, much stress is caused by personal relationships. You don't usually get to choose your co-workers. And even if you are exceptionally cooperative, you will run into people who will cause you stress. Most of us have stressful conflicts with members of our own families, or even friends whom we have chosen.

Some say that stress is a bigger problem today than ever before. Some say stress is a twentieth-century phenomenon. It is true that stress has been recognized as a debilitating problem only in the last few years, but it has been around for a long time. (Would you trade your stress for that of the prehistoric man or woman? Every night was an adventure in trying to evade a pack of hungry wolves, a saber-toothed tiger, or some other predator!)

Freedom from Sexual Harassment

Sexual harassment in the workplace is not a new problem; it's taken place probably since women began working outside the home. Stories of workplace harassment were reported in writings of a hundred

Although the research shows that fashions and acceptable dress vary from city to city throughout the United States, some basic rules apply anywhere.

A skirted suit in a dark blue, beige, or gray, with a contrasting blouse, is the most appropriate office attire for a woman. If you choose to wear a dress, it should not be a floral print, nor should it indicate "fun." Rather, it should also be a dark color, indicating that you are in the office to do business. Knit polyester pantsuits are not acceptable anymore.

Wear plain-colored midheeled or low-heeled pumps with neutral-colored stockings. Avoid flashy jewelry. Wear simple, small earrings, a simple watch, and only one or two rings that are not large.

Never wear a whole row of earrings in a group of holes. Nose, lip, and eyebrow rings are also frowned on by established, successful employees, as well as by most bosses.

MEN'S WARDROBES AND WORK SUCCESS

John T. Molloy's New Dress for Success (Warner Books) tells men all about how to dress in various settings. Extensive research was conducted to arrive at the opinions expressed in this book. The clear message is "Use clothing as a tool."

When you begin your employment in a new industry, one of the first things you might do is research how people dress in that field. Do this systematically by observing several male executives, and keeping notes on what they wear. The most important observations will come from your own office. After reviewing your notes, eliminate the most

◆ *The way you choose to express your individuality might not be viewed favorably by potential employers, especially for an office position in which you would have a lot of contact with customers.*

conservative as well as the most innovative dress, and you will come up with an appropriate range of clothing for yourself.

Shades of blue, beige, and gray in different weaves are the colors of choice for men's suits, slacks, and sports coats. These can be combined with contrasting dress shirts in white, blue, yellow, and occasionally other solid colors, the paler the better.

Ties are the most important status symbol of your attire. Whether or not you wear a tie directly affects how you are perceived in terms of social status. In one experiment, men who wore ties to dinner houses were allowed to pay by check when they explained to the management that they had left their cash and credit cards at home. Men not wearing ties were refused the same courtesy.

In another experiment conducted in several New York restaurants, men who were not wearing ties were assigned the worst house seating. Men with ties were given the more desirable tables.

In yet another experiment, men who did not wear ties to job interviews were much less likely to get the job.

The point is, employers and customers alike will take you more seriously if you wear a tie. A tie is a symbol of respectability. Wearing a tie cannot make you a success in business, but it can help.

Other clothing accessories are important, too. You should wear only dark shoes and socks. Most leather belts are all right, but be careful that the buckle is small; it shouldn't be a large metal decoration. Wear a thin, simple watch—no deep-sea–diving sports watches—and no other jewelry with the exception of a plain wedding band. Many, perhaps most, established office workers do not approve of young men who wear earrings. Why begin with one strike against you? If you want the best shot at a good job, pay raises, and promotions, try for a conservative look. Do not wear tiepins, tie clips, or tie bars—and wear

◆ *Your grooming and dress reflect the way you see yourself. If you want to become a success, you must dress like those who have already attained it.*

FIGURE 21.2 ◆ Sample Performance Evaluation Form

PERFORMANCE EVALUATION FOR EMPLOYEES

Evaluation Report:

Employed _____

Evaluation Status:

_____ 1st Probationary
_____ Final Probationary
_____ Annual
_____ Special Request

Date Issued _____

Date Due _____

_____ Intital Probationary
_____ Permanent

_____ Permanent in prob. assign.
_____ Temporary

Report for _____ to _____

FULL NAME (LAST NAME FIRST)   SOCIAL SECURITY NO.

POSITION TITLE   DEPARTMENT

Exceeds Work Performance Standards —
Meets Work Performance Standards —
Below Work Performance Standards —

If "Below Work Performance Standards" is checked, please give your reasons for this rating and indicate suggestions made to employee on how to improve.

SUGGESTIONS OR COMMENTS MADE BY IMMEDIATE SUPERVISOR

1. **QUALITY OF WORK**   1. ☐ ☐ ☐
   a. Job knowledge   a. ☐ ☐ ☐
   b. Accuracy   b. ☐ ☐ ☐
   c. Neatness   c. ☐ ☐ ☐
   d. Thoroughness   d. ☐ ☐ ☐

2. **QUANTITY OF WORK**   2. ☐ ☐ ☐
   a. Volume of output   a. ☐ ☐ ☐
   b. Meeting schedules   b. ☐ ☐ ☐

3. **WORK HABITS AND ATTITUDES**   3. ☐ ☐ ☐
   a. Dependability   a. ☐ ☐ ☐
   b. Punctuality   b. ☐ ☐ ☐
   c. Orderliness   c. ☐ ☐ ☐
   d. Compliance with instructions, rules and regulations   d. ☐ ☐ ☐
   e. Ability to work without immediate supervision   e. ☐ ☐ ☐
   f. Safety practices   f. ☐ ☐ ☐

4. **PERSONAL QUALITIES**   4. ☐ ☐ ☐
   a. Judgment   a. ☐ ☐ ☐
   b. Initiative   b. ☐ ☐ ☐
   c. Adaptability to emergencies and new situations   c. ☐ ☐ ☐

5. **INTERPERSONAL RELATIONS**   5. ☐ ☐ ☐
   a. Employee contracts   a. ☐ ☐ ☐
   b. Public contracts   b. ☐ ☐ ☐

6. **SUPERVISORY ABILITY (if applicable)**   6. ☐ ☐ ☐
   a. Leadership   a. ☐ ☐ ☐
   b. Fairness & impartiality   b. ☐ ☐ ☐
   c. Decision making   c. ☐ ☐ ☐
   d. Training & instructing   d. ☐ ☐ ☐
   e. Planning & assigning   e. ☐ ☐ ☐
   f. Supervisory control   f. ☐ ☐ ☐
   g. Evaluating performance   g. ☐ ☐ ☐
   h. Productivity   h. ☐ ☐ ☐

7. **OVERALL WORK PERFORMANCE**   7. ☐ ☐ ☐

Recommendation by Supervisor:

☐ Recommend continued employment
☐ Retain in position subject to further evaluation
☐ Recommend termination
☐ Recommend disciplinary action

_____
Signature of Immediate Supervisor

_____
Title   Date

My signature below is an acknowledgment that I have seen and discussed this evaluation, but does not necessarily imply agreement with the conclusions of the supervisor.

_____
Signature of Department head to whom immediate supervisor is responsible

_____
Signature of Employee   Date

_____
Title   Date

Every company designs its own form for evaluation according to its own needs. Generally, a list of categories is on the left side of the page and ratings are on the right side. It is not uncommon to have number ratings, with higher numbers indicating excellent performance and lower numbers indicating poor performance. The rating scale might be from 5 to 1 or from 10 to 1. From these numbers, an overall job performance rating can be calculated.

Some categories found on these forms are attitude toward job, attitude toward co-workers, attendance, tardiness, ability to follow directions, willingness to take initiative, ability to make good judgments, productivity, quality of work, dependability, personal grooming, ability to get along well with others, and willingness to improve through education and information about the job. Many possible categories exist, and they can be broken down in smaller subcategories if management needs that kind of information about individual employees.

During your evaluation meeting, your supervisor will explain the form to you and carefully discuss your ratings. Generally, you will be asked to sign the evaluation form. This does not indicate that you agree with the evaluation, only that you received it. Your evaluation will go into your permanent records with your company, and you will be given a copy for your own records.

THE PURPOSE

The main purpose of the evaluation is to inform both the employer and the employee about the employee's job performance. The information gathered by the job performance evaluation may be utilized in a number of different ways.

◆ *When you are evaluated on your work performance, the form will be explained and your rating will be discussed with you.*

HUMAN RELATIONS

Davis came to work in the office of a new company just after high school. He is younger than most of the other employees and he is a little shy. He does his work meticulously. His attitude is excellent because he continually seeks information about how to do his job more effectively. He is anxious to advance and to take on more responsibility.

His supervisor, Ms. Jordan, knows Davis is a good worker, but she mistakes his shyness for snobbery and unfriendliness. She is not pleased by what she views as an attitude problem.

It is time for Davis's end-of-probation interview, so Ms. Jordan calls him into her office for an evaluation. She has filled out an evaluation form and explains it carefully to Davis. Davis's ratings are very high on all categories except getting along with co-workers.

Davis is puzzled by this and asks Ms. Jordan what it means. As they spend time together chatting, Davis explains to Ms. Jordan that he has a problem with being shy, and it becomes clear to her that what she has perceived as standoffishness is indeed shyness.

Ms. Jordan is sympathetic to Davis's problem and gives him several ideas to overcome the difficulty. She assures him that with time—and as he feels more secure with his work—his shyness will diminish.

1. *What did Ms. Jordan learn about Davis during his end-of-probation interview?*

2. *Will Davis's evaluation and end-of-probation interview prove helpful to him?*

You will probably begin your new job on probation, a period during which you can be fired without cause. At the end of three to six months, you will be given an evaluation to ascertain how you are doing and to upgrade your position to that of a full-time, regular employee. Therefore, one use of the evaluation is for advancement.

Another use is to determine if a pay raise is in order and if so, how much. Most employers understand that good performance should be rewarded. It helps the morale of workers to gain recognition when they are doing a good job.

The evaluation may also be used when new positions open up, to discern who among the employees may be best suited to fill them. Especially in the case of advancement, the evaluation plays a big role in the selection process. The evaluation may make it clear that an employee would be better suited to work in another department at another type of job. In this case, a transfer may be ordered.

The most important benefit the evaluation offers the employee is the opportunity to discover how well he or she is doing and what can be done to improve performance. This is part of ongoing education along your path toward your career goal. Sometimes evaluations can be hurtful, but mostly they will be given in the spirit of **constructive criticism**—suggestions that will help you do your job better—and you should receive them as such.

During the evaluation meeting, you will have the opportunity to ask questions or to air any concerns you may be having. Don't bring up petty difficulties with co-workers. Your supervisor will not be impressed if she or he is forced to spend time in that sort of discussion. Rather, bring up issues about work that have been confusing to you.

For example, you might want to know how to determine which tasks should take priority, or how to improve some skill with which you are having difficulty. Taking this time to solve troubling, important problems can help raise your level of competence.

Taking the information you learn from your evaluation and immediately putting it to work is in your best interests. If you do that, you will learn to view the evaluation process as a benefit that is important to your development.

Salary Increases and Promotions

When you began your job with your new company, you agreed on a rate of pay. That is the best time to inquire about procedures for salary increases so that you will know when to expect them. If you are serious about your ultimate career goal, you should also inquire about the possibilities for advancement and promotion. Do you have a future with this company?

No matter how satisfying your job, you will want to know that your employers appreciate you. The most concrete way employers can express appreciation is through a raise in pay.

Remuneration (compensation, or pay) comes in many other forms. These include the benefits that accrue for you during the length of your employment. For example, you could go from earning one weeks' paid vacation to earning two weeks' paid vacation—a nice benefit, indeed.

As you look to the future, you will set goals that will lead to satisfying your eventual employment needs. These goals will probably include earning increases in pay and may include earning promotions, too. A promotion is another way your employer indicates satisfaction with your work.

You can increase your opportunities for raises and promotions in several ways. Appearance and dress are only part of what you can do to further your career.

TYPES OF COMPENSATION

Several forms of compensation are available, depending on the job you have. You may work in the office of a restaurant, in a real estate office, or in some other type of business. Different types of businesses compensate their employees in different ways, including wages, salaries, pay for work accomplished, bonuses, and benefits. Most companies distribute paychecks once a week, every other week, or once a month.

Wages   People who work in offices often receive a set hourly wage. The amount you will be paid is determined by multiplying the number of hours worked by the agreed-on hourly wage. Generally, your workweek will consist of forty hours. If you work more than forty hours, you are working overtime, and you will be paid one and a half times your hourly wage for each hour of overtime you work.

Salaries   Many office workers—usually those with supervisory responsibilities—receive a set salary instead of an hourly wage. Thus, no matter how many hours they work, they receive the same salary.

Pay for Work Accomplished   Some people are paid for each piece of work they do. For example, a word processor may get paid by the completed page. No consideration is made for how long it took to do the work, only that the work has been completed. When the work is turned in, the worker is paid. Generally, no benefits of any kind are associated with this pay arrangement.

Bonuses   A bonus is extra money rewarded or gifted to employees. It might be a special holiday gift or it might be given because a job was well done. Sometimes, if a company has an especially good season or year, the employer decides to share some of the profits with the employees. Bonuses are an excellent way to boost employee morale.

Benefits   Recall that benefits are the extra expenses your employer is responsible for, such as various kinds of insurance, Social Security taxes, pension plans, and so on. Benefits also include vacations and sick leave. Any or all of these benefits can be expanded, which increases your total compensation from a company.

EVALUATION OF YOUR EMPLOYMENT NEEDS: GOAL SETTING

You will move ahead toward your ultimate career goal faster by setting some career path goals. These might include frequency of raises, guidelines for what you want to achieve regarding advancement and promotion, and what you want to accomplish concerning productivity or training on the job.

Have an idea where you want to be in one year and in five years. Often, potential employers will ask, "What do you expect to be doing in five years?" Knowing this not only helps you answer an employer's question, but also helps guide you toward your ultimate career and lifestyle goals.

Even if your salary range is adequate for a beginning worker, you may have changing obligations that require you to make more money. For example, you may get married, you may decide you want to save money to further your education, or you may leave the family home, so that your expenses increase. All these changing life situations will require that you upgrade your salary and, perhaps your responsibility on the job as well.

From time to time, take a look at your life circumstances. If you are still relatively free of obligations, perhaps you will not need a raise in pay or a promotion for a while. But things change. Be aware of your own situation so that you can bring about adjustments on the job to meet your changing financial needs.

INCREASES IN COMPENSATION

In some companies, automatic pay raises are given at certain intervals, such as every six months or one year. Often these raises are attached to a good performance evaluation. Salary increases are also related to the kind of job performed. For example, the engineers in a company may get more frequent and higher raises than the office workers. Generally, an industry standard of pay exists for different types of jobs.

Not all companies have a standard procedure for awarding pay increases. In companies that do not, it is up to the employer to decide when a pay raise should be granted, and in some cases the employer waits for a request for a raise from the employee. If you must request a raise, you will feel more comfortable doing so if you follow the suggestions given below.

Is It Time to Request a Pay Raise?   If you think it's time to ask for a raise, ask yourself these questions:

1. Have I been on the job a sufficient length of time to warrant asking for a raise?
2. Have I learned my job well and become very efficient, and is my productivity adequate?
3. Do I have good relationships with the other employees?
4. Have I been able to make some crucial decisions and judgments that positively affected my work? In other words, have I acted independently when it was appropriate to do so?
5. Have I had good evaluations and other feedback about my work from my supervisor and co-workers?
6. Does the company seem to be in good condition financially? Can the company afford to pay more now, or would it be better to wait a few weeks until things improve?

With the exception of question 6, asking yourself these questions can help you prepare for requesting a raise. If the answer to any of your questions is no, take some time to improve that area before you go to your boss seeking a raise.

How Do I Ask for a Raise?   If you have decided that the timing is right and that you have, in fact, earned a raise, request an appointment with your supervisor to ask for one. This may be scary, but you will be able to do it. In some companies, if you don't ask, you will stay at the same level of pay for longer than necessary.

First, ask your supervisor what workers must do to get a raise. Your supervisor may then list the requirements for a higher rate of pay. If you have accomplished all of them, say so—and say that you hope to receive your raise soon.

If, on the other hand, your supervisor tells you the company has no set standard to follow, that it has no rules for granting raises, then you must simply state your case. List your good points, and talk with confidence about why you deserve a raise. Be respectful—as you always

should be—to your boss. Show that you believe you have earned a raise, and you want his or her thoughts in the matter.

If you are denied, accept the decision—and ask what your supervisor wants you to improve in order to earn a raise. Take this direction seriously, and begin at once to work on the areas that need improvement so that your raise will be forthcoming at your next request.

PROMOTIONS

By now, you probably know what attributes make a good employee. You have read about a pleasant attitude, the ability to get along with co-workers, good work habits, enthusiasm and desire to learn, and the willingness to take responsibility for your job and decisions related to it. In this chapter you have read about appropriate attire and grooming. If you put into practice all the ideas discussed in this book, you will be a perfect employee. Your bosses will love you and eagerly and regularly promote you along your career path.

Sounds easy, doesn't it? However, you will probably need to consider one more element. You learned about setting goals to guide you toward your ultimate career and lifestyle. The only missing element is your determination.

As you move along your career path, you will need to demonstrate that you are eager and willing to take on new responsibilities and learn new things. Sometimes, you will need to exercise a degree of assertiveness. Often, you will need to demonstrate initiative, taking on a little more than you are asked to do. It's like wearing a sign that says, "I want to get ahead, I want to succeed, I want to do well." Don't be obnoxious and overdo it, but make it clear that you are serious about your job and your career.

Your bosses will be looking for this attitude. They want to advance people who not only have received excellent job performance evaluations, but are also eager to move up. Be aware of when promotions become available and how to apply for them.

When Do Promotions Become Available?   Opportunities for promotions become available for two reasons. The first is when an employee who has greater responsibility than you vacates her or his position. The second is when the company creates a new position with greater responsibility than your present one.

In growing companies, new positions are created fairly often. If, in your initial interview, you asked whether promotions would be possible, your boss already knows you are interested. Your good evaluations and your attitude can help your employer make a promotion decision in your favor.

How Do I Apply for a Promotion?   Your company may make decisions about promotions without input from eligible employees. Some companies, however, advertise that a position is available and that they are seeking someone from within the company to fill it.

INDUSTRY FOCUS

Irene Kinoshita
CEO
Ascolta Training Company

Q. Ms. Kinoshita, what advice would you like to pass on to a group of business students?

A. They should understand that downsizing is the result of asking the workforce to redefine itself. Things are changing fast, so those entering the workforce should always be in the learning mode. Your skills are quickly outdated, and you shouldn't expect that the job you are doing now will be the same that you will be doing next week.

   The other thing that is really important is not to limit yourself. Instead of saying, for instance, I have a wonderful background in finance and that's all I'm going to know, you need to be a whole company person and understand all aspects of a business.

Q. What do you look for when you hire people?

A. Especially in a small company, we need people who are flexible, people who will say, "That wasn't in my job description but it needed to be done."

   I look for communication skills—how well they present themselves, and I expect their writing and speaking skills to be good. I also look for creativity. Are they going to plug along and just do everything I tell them to, or are they going to come up with some good ideas, too?

   If you are seriously interested in promotion, stay alert to changes in the office. Know when someone is vacating a position that might interest you.

   Before you actively seek promotion, ask yourself the questions that were outlined earlier about asking for a raise. Make certain you are ready before you ask to be included in the selection process. Then, let your supervisor know that you are interested and that you eagerly seek more responsibility and opportunity.

   If a formal selection process is used, prepare your application as carefully as you would when applying for a new job.

Further Education and Training

You can further enhance the skills that will take you toward your ultimate career and lifestyle goals through formal education and training.

◆   *There are many opportunities for further education and training. Some companies will even reimburse employees for taking classes to improve their performance on the job.*

When you initially investigated careers, you determined the types of education and training you would need for an entry-level position and for advancement within each career. After you begin work in the career of your choice, you will probably learn of some additional education and training alternatives that will help you advance in your career. An occasional workshop or **seminar** (meeting in which information is presented and discussed) satisfies the education and training requirements to advance in some careers and in some industries. Other careers and industries require years of formal education for advancement.

In some instances, your company will train you for most of the positions it has available. You will receive the training as you receive the advancements—or when you take a new position in a different department. Willingly participate in all the training that your company offers—training will be your ticket to the future.

As you may have already discovered, after you leave high school you can choose from a variety of ways to receive the education and training needed to advance along your career path. These alternatives include on-the-job training programs, vocational schools, community colleges, and colleges and universities.

ON-THE-JOB TRAINING PROGRAMS

On-the-job training is learning by doing. This training is usually provided for jobs that do not require formal education.

VOCATIONAL SCHOOLS

The kinds of skills needed to work in an office are often taught as part of the vocational curriculum offered by most high schools.

If you want more intensive training in office skills, a vocational school in your area can probably provide it. The cost of attending a vocational school varies but may be more than the cost of attending your local community college, where you can usually receive similar training.

COMMUNITY COLLEGES

You can earn up to two years of college-level credit in a community college, and it is relatively inexpensive to attend. Most community colleges offer two types of programs. One program prepares students in general education so that they can transfer to a four-year college or university. The other program provides instruction in vocational skills, such as office skills or computer science, that requires two years to complete.

Community colleges often have close ties to the local business establishment and tailor their programs to meet the needs of local businesses.

COLLEGES AND UNIVERSITIES

Some four-year institutions are less concerned with training students for specific occupations than with providing a general, liberal arts education. However, many four-year colleges and universities offer vocational specialties, such as accounting and computer science.

Although many colleges and universities are supported by the state, a college education can still be very expensive. Give as much thought as possible to what you want to do. If your chosen profession does not require the expense and rigors of a four-year college program, it may be advantageous to participate in another type of educational setting.

Whatever your decision about further education and training, you know what is expected of you, and you know what you can expect of the people for whom you work. You are well on your way to succeeding in your new office career. You can look on your new life as an adventure, with limitless possibilities. You can be and do whatever you choose. With the right information and effort, you will be successful in your new career.

Recall Time

Answer the following questions:

1. What are the main purposes for conducting a job performance evaluation? List the categories that might be rated on an evaluation form.

2. What does your employer pay for you that are considered benefits?

3. What are several questions you might want to ask yourself if you were going to ask your boss for a raise or for a promotion?

4. Several different types of training and educational programs are available to you. What are some of them? Describe why you would choose one or another.

Summary

After you have become successful on your first real job, what's next?

One way you tell your employer that you are ready to do more is by your appearance, which signals many things about you. It is important to look like the person you want to become.

Attending to your health is a major step toward looking well. Exercise, proper eating habits, sufficient sleep, and a reasonable social life are the keys to that healthy, attractive glow.

You also want to be clean, neat, and businesslike. Though trendy clothes are fun for leisure time, if worn to work they imply that you do not take your job seriously.

Much research has been conducted that demonstrates which clothing helps one to achieve a successful career. For women, this includes skirted suits of blue, gray, or beige, with a contrasting blouse, neutral-colored stockings, and plain-colored pumps.

Men should wear suits or slacks and sports coats of blue, gray, or beige with shirts in solid, pale, contrasting colors. Research shows that when you wear a necktie, others perceive you as respectable and responsible.

When planning your wardrobe, select clothing that isn't too expensive and that will hold up well. Taking care of your clothes helps them last, so that over time you can increase the variety of things you have to wear, and you will always look good.

As you seek advancement, you will find that your regular job performance evaluations provide valuable information. These evaluations are conducted by your supervisor, and generally he or she will use a standardized form and procedures so that every employee is treated the same.

At the time of your employment, you may have discussed salary increases. After you have been on the job for a while and you have been doing a good job, you may want to ask for a raise. In some companies, raises are connected with the performance evaluation and are given on a regular basis without a request from the employee. In other companies, you may have to ask your supervisor for a raise.

Setting employment goals will help you determine when you need a pay raise, how rapidly you wish to advance, and what additional training you will need.

When positions become available in your company, check your career goals to see if the new positions advance you in the direction you want to take. You may have to apply formally for a new job, or your bosses may select someone on the basis of her or his job performance evaluations.

When you determine what direction you want to take, you may need to investigate the educational and training requirements for that job.

When you begin to think about your career path and how best to achieve your goals, you will want to consider the following:

◆ Do everything you know to do to be successful in the position you now hold.

◆ Meet the expectations of your employers regarding attitude, productivity, and good work habits.

◆ Be careful about your grooming. Keep yourself clean and neat, with your hair properly combed. If you are a woman, make sure your makeup is right.

◆ Choose your wardrobe carefully to reflect how you feel about advancement and taking on more responsibility. Avoid trendy clothes.

◆ If you are a man, always wear a necktie to important meetings and every day to work if it is appropriate.

◆ Understand the purpose of your job evaluations and use them effectively.

◆ Know how and when to ask for a raise.

◆ Know how to ask for a promotion.

◆ Research what your chosen position will require in terms of education and training. Know the types of training that are available.

IN CONCLUSION . . .

When you have completed this chapter, answer the following questions:

1. What are the names of two guides on how to dress for success?

2. What is the most important status symbol of men's attire?

3. What is the main purpose of an evaluation?

4. What are six questions you should ask yourself before you ask for a raise?

REVIEW AND APPLICATION

 CHECK YOUR KNOWLEDGE

1. How can you assess how well you are progressing on your job?
2. You should keep in mind several things about grooming. Name them.
3. Good health plays an important role in how you look. Discuss several ways you can help take good care of your health.
4. Much research has been done regarding dressing for success. What does this research tell us about what women should wear to work?
5. What does the way we dress say about us?
6. What does the research tell us about men wearing neckties?
7. What are the best colors for men's clothing?
8. Describe the purposes of a job performance evaluation.
9. How can a job performance evaluation be helpful to you?
10. What should you consider when thinking about asking for an increase in salary?
11. What should you consider when thinking about asking for a promotion?
12. How do positions in a company become available?
13. Name three types of training and education.
14. Discuss the advantages of a community college.
15. What is on-the-job training? What kinds of jobs require this type of training?
16. How are vocational schools different from training programs in other kinds of educational settings?

 REVIEW YOUR VOCABULARY

On a separate paper, write the letter of the vocabulary word that is described below.

_____ 1. meeting in which information is presented and discussed
_____ 2. suggestions that will help you do your job better

_____ 3. compensation, or pay

a. constructive criticism
b. remuneration
c. seminar

 DISCUSS AND ANALYZE AN OFFICE SITUATION

1. Garth has done a fine job in his new position. He is respected as a man who has a good attitude, is always willing to take on more responsibility, is reliable, and is capable. A new position has opened up in his department that requires more responsibility and offers a better salary. Garth's supervisor has offered him the position. Garth doesn't know whether to accept the offer because he has not really thought through what he wants to accomplish in the long run.

   Garth has not taken a fundamental planning step. What is it? What would you do if you were Garth?

2. Rosemary has been on the job for several months and she has never had an evaluation. She approaches her supervisor and asks if it isn't time to have the evaluation and, hopefully, a salary increase. At the evaluation meeting, Rosemary's supervisor gives her an evaluation that is not too favorable and denies her request for a pay raise. Rosemary is surprised and hurt by her supervisor's evaluation. She thought she was doing whatever was requested of her.

   How can Rosemary use this evaluation to her advantage?

PRACTICE BASIC SKILLS

MATH

1. A person can be remunerated in several ways for the work she or he does. When agreeing to a certain type of pay, you should be aware of what

you might be making if you were employed under another type of pay structure. For example, compare the following:

◆ *Job 1*. You work forty hours per week at $6 per hour and you expect to work five overtime hours each week at $9 per hour.
◆ *Job 2*. You work the same number of regular and overtime hours as in job 1, but you are offered a flat salary of $300 per week.

Assuming the two jobs are exactly alike except for the method of payment, which job should you take?

ENGLISH

1. When your supervisor evaluates your work, he or she will notice whether you use formal or informal language. In business settings, informal language is not appropriate. Read the paragraph below, then rewrite it in standard, formal English.

I don't really know what I wanna do with myself. I like this job well enough, I mean, it's pretty groovy and it gives me some dough to buy tapes and stuff. Maybe what I need is to go to college for a while. That might be radical. Lots of cool people to meet and swinging parties to go to. This work stuff is for the birds, anyway.

PROOFREADING

1. In your office job, you may have occasion to proofread a letter or report that a supervisor hands you to keyboard. See if you can find the mistakes in the paragraph below, and rewrite it correctly on a separate paper.

We are hapy to anounse that our knew line of clothing is out. We hope you wil join us at our fall sho where our new lien will be shown. The springe fashions wil be off particular interst to you becaus the stiles are fresh, cool, and exciting.
     The shwo will be heald on Mondy, Juli 23rd at 3:00 P.M. at the Coral Room of the Blue Lagoon Hotel. Please let us know if you entend to atend. make your resergvations by callin 714-259-3109.

APPLY YOUR KNOWLEDGE

1. Think about what you want to accomplish in the next five years. Write a comprehensive goal

statement that includes specific steps in a specific time frame.
2. Take a trip to a clothing store. Keep in mind the kinds of statements you want to make with what you wear. Take a notebook and make notes about things you see that you would like to buy. If you bought all the garments that you feel would make up an appropriate wardrobe, what would the clothing items be? How much would the items cost?

USING THE REFERENCE MANUAL

Retrieve the file CH21REF on the data disk. Use the interoffice memorandums section of the Reference Manual at the back of the book to help you follow an acceptable style using the current date. Assume you are the writer and that you are sending this memo to the office staff. Save and print.

Since your appearance on the job affects your progress in our company, I feel it might be well to cover some "unwritten" norms about dressing for success.

1. Dressing for success begins with cleanliness and being neat and attractive in your appearance. People who exercise regularly, get sufficient sleep, eat properly, and do not have excessive social lives tend also to look better.
2. The key to an appropriate office hairstyle is that it be neatly trimmed, brushed and never too faddish. Women might want to seek a consultant to help them decide what colors and amount of makeup to wear. Men who choose not to be clean shaven must be sure to trim a mustache or beard regularly.
3. An overall guideline to follow in dress is to dress like the people who hold the positions to which you aspire. Basically, for women, a skirted suit in a dark blue, beige, or gray—with a contrasting blouse—is the most appropriate office attire. For men, blues, browns, and grays in different weaves are the colors of choice for men's suits, slacks, and sports coats. These can be combined with contrasting dress shirts in white, blue, yellow, and occasionally other colors.

If you have any questions about the above items, please feel free to address them at our next staff meeting on Monday morning.

CAREER PORTFOLIO

PART FIVE: EMPLOYMENT SKILLS

Specific Activities to Complete

Select at least two of the following items for inclusion in your Career Portfolio, using the information from Chapters 18 through 21.

1. *Keyboard the procedure you will follow to locate possible office jobs in the community. Save and print this list. (Be sure you proof according to the instructions given previously on page 92.) Insert this list as the first item in your Career Portfolio binder behind the fifth tab, entitled "Employment Skills."*
2. *Keyboard a sample letter of application. Save, print, and insert this letter behind the fifth tab also.*
3. *Keyboard a current résumé. Show a draft of the résumé to a fellow student and incorporate any suggestions that may improve its appearance. Save, print, and insert your résumé behind the fifth tab.*
4. *Keyboard a listing of where in your town you can go to receive additional training after this course. Consider programs in which people prepare to be office workers by taking courses in business schools, by working on office and computer application certificates in a community college, and by enrolling in business administration courses at a local university. Save, print, and insert the list behind the fifth tab.*

Reference Manual

Letter Styles

This section will expose you to different letter styles. All the rules given here are up-to-date with current business standards. However, when beginning a new office job, always check first with your boss to see if the company has its own rules and preferences.

MAJOR PARTS OF A LETTER

Date—The date is typed 2 to 3 lines below the bottom of the letter-head. If you are not using letterhead paper, begin 12 to 14 lines from the top of the paper.

Inside Address—The inside address is typed 4 to 8 lines below the date. This placement is determined by the size of the letter. Long letters require fewer blank lines. Short letters require a greater number of blank lines between the date and inside address.

Greeting—The greeting is typed a double-space after the inside address.

Body—The body of the letter begins a double-space after the greeting.

Closing—The closing is typed a double-space after the ending of the body of the letter.

Signee's Name—The name of the person who signs the letter is typed 4 lines below the closing.

Typist's Initials—Your initials as typist are typed in small letters a double-space after the signee's name.

Enclosure Notation—The enclosure notation is typed a double-space after the typist's initials.

Copies Notation—The copies notation is typed a double-space after the typist's initials.

FORM

Letter styles will vary from company to company; however, the following are the three most common styles used by business today.

Block Style—The entire letter is typed even with the left margin (see Figure A.1).

Modified Block, or Semiblock, Style—The date and closing begin at the center (see Figure A.2).

FIGURE A.1 ◆ Block-Style Letter

February 2, 19—
(4–8 line returns)

Mr. Jessie Johnson
44 Warren Avenue
San Antonio, TX 76435

Dear Mr. Johnson:

The next meeting of the Southwestern Association of CPAs will be held at the Newport Hyatt in San Antonio on April 8 at 7 p.m. This meeting will be a joint venture of the SACPA and the Future Accountants Association. The topic of the meeting will be, "Automating the Accounting Office."

The main speaker of the evening will be Katherine Cornell, president of the National Association of CPAs. Cornell has just completed designing and installing fully automated facilities for her firm's new location in Atlanta. The office of the future has arrived for this company.

I know you will not want to miss the meeting. Enclosed is your registration form, which must be returned to me by March 1.

Sincerely,

Harriet Yatamoto
Meeting Coordinator

ak

enclosure

AMS (NOMA) Simplified Style—The simplified style of letter is recommended by the Administrative Management Society. The letter has no greeting or closing, has a subject line, uses the block arrangement (see Figure A.3).

PUNCTUATION

Two different rules dominate letter punctuation for the greeting and closing. These rules are as follows:

Mixed Punctuation—For the mixed punctuation rule, a colon goes after the greeting and a comma goes after the closing (see Figure A.1).

Open Punctuation—For the open punctuation rule, no punctuation is used after the greeting and no punctuation after the closing.

FIGURE A.2 ◆ Modified-Block-Style Letter

January 4, 19—

(4–8 line returns)

Robert Alvarez
46 Market Avenue
Plymouth, MA 02360

Dear Mr. Alvarez:
Because styles and popular tastes do change, we make it a point to see that our magazine stays ahead of the times. Apparently we have succeeded. The American Society of Styles recently presented our magazine with a national award.

Because the readers of such a magazine are also ahead of the times, we invite you to extend your subscription now before it expires. We have made it easy for you to do so with the postpaid reply envelope enclosed.

Thank you for your continued support. I look forward to your imminent reply.

Sincerely,

Diane Eastbrook

mk

enclosure

FIGURE A.3 ◆ AMS Simplified Letter

December 12, 19—

(4–8 line returns)

Mrs. Julia Chung
CRANCO
P.O. Box 139
Lowell, MA 02660

(3 line returns)

AMS SIMPLIFIED LETTER STYLE

(3 line returns)

This letter is written in the time-saving simplified style recommended by the Administrative Management Society (formerly called NOMA). To type this style, follow these steps:

1. Use the extreme block format with blocked paragraphs.

2. Type the address three or more blank line spaces below the date.

3. Always omit the formal salutation and complimentary close.

4. Use a subject heading and type it in all-capital letters a triple-space below the address: triple-space from the subject line to the first line of the letter body.

5. Type enumerated items flush at the left margin; indent unnumbered listed items five spaces.

6. Type the writer's name and title in all-capital letters at least three blank line spaces below the letter body.

7. Type reference initials, which consist of the typist's initials only, a double-space below the writer's name.

Correspondents in your company will like the AMS simplified letter style not only for the distinctive "eye appeal" it gives letters but also because it reduces letter-writing costs.

F. JAMES LUCEY—PRESIDENT

kc

c: Sue Rodeo

LETTER PLACEMENT

Before beginning to type a letter, decide where to set your margins. For some typists, this depends on the size of the letter. If you are not sure where to set your margins, use this as a guide:

Size of Letter (Estimated)	**Margin Setting**
Short (fewer than 100 words in body)	50 space line
Average (101–200 words in body)	60 space line
Long (more than 200 words in body)	70 space line

Many progressive typists, especially those with word processing equipment, are leaving their margins at one setting for all work.

Envelope Addressing

Many people blame the post office for lost or delayed mail. However, many times mail is lost or delayed because of errors in the address. This section will discuss good business practice for typing addresses on envelopes.

RETURN ADDRESS

Most companies have their own envelopes with a printed return address. However, if these are not available, begin to type the return address 2 lines down and 3 spaces in.

MAIN ADDRESS

An experienced typist puts the envelope in the machine and turns the roller to the correct place without counting. If you have not typed envelopes before, this can be a problem. Therefore, a good rule to remember is 15/55—go down 15 lines and in 55 spaces—for 12 pitch (15/50 for 10 pitch).

THINGS TO REMEMBER

(1) Always single-space; (2) type all states with two capital letters and no periods; (3) current post office regulations state that the bottom of the envelope (about 6 lines up) must be free of all notations so that the envelope can go through the electronic scanning machines.

NOTATIONS

1. Attention—in the address itself
2. Personal or Confidential—below the return address, about 3 lines

Listed below are some address samples. Table A.1 shows the post office abbreviations for the United States and Canada.

The Noodle Corporation
Attention: Mrs. Shirley Gonzales
2399 Palm Avenue
Burlingame, CA 94010

Ms. Julia Singleton
Buy-Rite Company
9 Almond Way
Boston, MA 02368

Mr. Paul Wong
131 Battery Street
Portland, OR 93616

Miss Rose Marie Frazier
Personnel Department
Save Now Bank
34 Montgomery Street
San Francisco, CA 94115

Please note: The post office prefers all capital letters and no punctuation. This makes it easier for the scanning machines. Therefore, the preferred way to write the above addresses is as follows:

THE NOODLE CORPORATION
ATTENTION MRS SHIRLEY GONZALES
2399 PALM AVENUE
BURLINGAME CA 94010

MS JULIA SINGLETON
BUY RITE COMPANY
9 ALMOND WAY
BOSTON MA 02368

MR PAUL WONG
131 BATTERY STREET
PORTLAND OR 93616

MISS ROSE MARIE FRAZIER
PERSONNEL DEPARTMENT
SAVE NOW BANK
34 MONTGOMERY STREET
SAN FRANCISCO CA 94115

Interoffice Memorandums

Correspondence that stays within a company is typed using interoffice memorandum style. This style is set up in various ways, but always contains the headings: To, From, Date, and Subject. When typing memorandums, keep the following points in mind:

◆ Memorandums are informal and should never contain titles. This also holds true for the terms Mr., Mrs., Miss., Ms. Use no salutation or complimentary close.
◆ Use block style.
◆ Triple-space from the subject to the body of the memo.
◆ Type typist's initials, enclosure notation, and copies notation in the usual spots.

The following are samples of the styles you will find for memorandums:

1. TO:
   FROM:
   DATE:
   SUBJECT:

2.   TO:
      FROM:
      DATE:
      SUBJECT:

TABLE A.1 ◆ Post Office Abbreviations

These two-letter abbreviations have been authorized with the zip code system.

US STATE, DISTRICT POSSESSION, OR TERRITORY	TWO-LETTER ABBREVIATION	US STATE, DISTRICT POSSESSION, OR TERRITORY	TWO-LETTER ABBREVIATION
Alabama	AL	North Carolina	NC
Alaska	AK	North Dakota	ND
Arizona	AZ	Ohio	OH
Arkansas	AR	Oklahoma	OK
California	CA	Oregon	OR
Canal Zone	CZ	Pennsylvania	PA
Colorado	CO	Puerto Rico	PR
Connecticut	CT	Rhode Island	RI
Delaware	DE	South Carolina	SC
District of Columbia	DC	South Dakota	SD
Florida	FL	Tennessee	TN
Georgia	GA	Texas	TX
Guam	GU	Utah	UT
Hawaii	HI	Vermont	VT
Idaho	ID	Virgin Islands	VI
Illinois	IL	Virginia	VA
Indiana	IN	Washington	WA
Iowa	IA	West Virginia	WV
Kansas	KS	Wisconsin	WI
Kentucky	KY	Wyoming	WY
Louisiana	LA		
Maine	ME		
Maryland	MD	**CANADIAN PROVINCE, POSSESSION, OR TERRITORY**	**TWO-LETTER ABBREVIATION**
Massachusetts	MA		
Michigan	MI		
Minnesota	MN	Alberta	AB
Mississippi	MS	British Columbia	BC
Missouri	MO	Labrador	LB
Montana	MT	Manitoba	MB
Nebraska	NE	New Brunswick	NB
Nevada	NV	Newfoundland	NF
New Hampshire	NH	Northwest Territories	NT
New Jersey	NJ	Nova Scotia	NS
New Mexico	NM	Ontario	ON
New York	NY	Prince Edward Island	PE
		Quebec	PQ
		Saskatchewan	SK
		Yukon Territory	YT

3. TO: DATE:
   FROM: SUBJECT:

Punctuation

Punctuation is a means of making written communication easier to read and comprehend. The following rules will provide you with an easy guide to the most common punctuation questions, but it should not be considered a final authority.

COMMA

An often-used form of punctuation, the comma, is also the source of much confusion and many errors. It should be used as follows:

Rule: Before conjunctions that join independent clauses.

Examples: The meeting is at three o'clock, and we will be on time.
             The typist finished the project, but he did not get it mailed before the deadline.

Rule: To set off a subordinate clause preceding a main clause.

Example: If you finish your exam on time, you will be given an extra reward.

Rule: To separate words and phrases in series.

Examples: The company sold tires, batteries, plugs, and mirrors.
             The secretaries in the office, the clerks in the plant, and the managers in the factory are all willing to change to flexible schedules.

Rule: To separate dependent clauses.

Examples: With your help, we will get the task completed by Wednesday.
             As soon as the machines are repaired, we will return to work.

Rule: To set off nonrestrictive clauses.

Examples: Juanita, who is in the other room, unlocked the office this morning.
             The Fifth Avenue bus, which is usually late, is the one for Clover City.

Rule: To set off introductory words or phrases.

Examples: Incidentally, I left the lights on.
             By the way, I saw George yesterday.

Rule:	To separate two or more adjectives when each modifies the same noun. Do not use a comma between the two adjectives if one modifies a combination of the noun and the other adjective.
Examples:	The blue-eyed, blond young woman walked down the street. Mr. Jones was an important American diplomat.
Rule:	Before *Inc.* in a company name.*
Example:	Lewis & Wong, Inc. would like an answer to its letter.
Rule:	Before *Jr.* and *Sr.* in a person's name.*
Example:	Samuel Adams, Jr. was elected to the board of directors.
Rule:	To set off words in direct address.
Examples:	Thank you for the offer, Mr. Pate. Your services were most appreciated, Madam President.
Rule:	To separate the day of the month from the year, and the year when used with the month.
Example:	On July 20, 1991, Susan graduated from college.
Rule:	To set off unrelated numbers.
Example:	In the World Series of 1990, 45 runs were scored.

*Trend is to leave out comma.

SEMICOLON

Use the semicolon as follows:

Rule:	To separate two independent clauses that are not joined by a conjunction.
Examples:	The plane flew low; it began to spray the plants. The new machine arrived; it was broken.
Rule:	To avoid confusion when two independent clauses contain other commas.
Example:	The word processing machine, which was broken, was purchased at Ames & Harris, Inc.; and they will replace it today.
Rule:	To avoid confusion when a sentence contains words in series.

Example:	We have offices in San Francisco, California; Portland, Oregon; Seattle, Washington; Reno, Nevada; and Ogden, Utah.
Rule:	To introduce an illustration composed of an independent clause.
Examples:	Be sure to ask good questions; for example, what is my future with the company. Manuel is the coordinator; that is, he schedules all the classes.

COLON

Use the colon as follows:

Rule:	To introduce a list or a quotation that follows.
Examples:	You may now purchase the following items: shoes, dresses, shirts, and ties. Patrick Henry said: "Give me liberty or give me death."
Rule:	To separate hours and minutes.
Example:	It is now 10:15 p.m. in New York City.
Rule:	After the salutation in a formal business letter.
Example:	Dear Mr. Jones: I am writing in response . . .

HYPHEN

Use the hyphen as follows:

Rule:	To join compound numbers when they are spelled out.
Examples:	We have twenty-nine calculators in the office. We began the employment office with forty-three job orders.
Rule:	To write fractions when they are used as words.
Examples:	Only one-half of the workers attended the party. Exactly three-fourths of the work was done on time.
Rule:	To join compound adjectives modifying the same word.
Examples:	We decided to send the package by third-class mail. She was the most hard-to-reach executive in the whole building.

He received an award for the best-kept plants within the complex.

Rule: Sometimes to join *self, vice,* and *ex* to another word.

Examples: He was known as a self-made man.
She was the first woman to become vice-president of a marketing firm.
His ex-boss was in the audience.

Rule: To be certain your meaning is clear.

Examples: The workers began to re-cover the office sofa.
He was quite mad because he was told to re-lay the carpet.

APOSTROPHE

Use the apostrophe as follows:

Rule: To indicate the plural form of uncapitalized letters, symbols, and words.

Examples: Your typing exercise had three *b*'s typed as *v*'s.
For line 3, use #'s and not #s.
Six misspelled *and*'s appear in the sentence.

Rule: To indicate the omission of numbers and to indicate the omission of letters in contractions.

Examples: She is from the class of '73.
I'll be at the office by 3 p.m.

APOSTROPHE IN POSSESSIVE

Rule: For the possessive form of a noun that does not end in *s,* add " 's."

Examples: cat's paw, clerk's pay, men's hats, children's milk

Rule: For the possessive form of a noun that ends in *s,* if the word is singular, add "'s" unless the word is awkward to pronounce; if the word is plural, add the apostrophe only.

Examples: singular—class's pet, press's ink, distress' signs, plaster of Paris' reputation;
plural—clerks' union, streets' lights, trucks' tires, houses' numbers

Rule: For the possessive form of proper names; if the name is singular and has one syllable, add " 's"; if the name is singular and has more than one syllable, add the apostrophe only; if the name is plural and ends in *s,* add the apostrophe only.

Examples: Ross's, Glenis', Hings', Charles's, Ulysis', Andersons'

Rule: For the possessive form of compound nouns, add the apostrophe to the last word. (If the compound is plural, it may be best to reword the sentence and not use the possessive form.)

Examples: mother-in-law's house
passer-by's reaction
(Instead of saying my sister-in-law's children, it would be wise to say the children of my sisters-in law.)

QUOTATION MARKS

Use quotation marks as follows:

Rule: To enclose direct quotations.

Example: Mary asked, "Will you please repeat the assignment?"

Rule: To set off titles of book chapters, short stories, articles, speeches, songs, poems, and movies.

Example: The story was called, "The Boy and His Dog."

Rule: To set off slang words, definitions, and words intended to show irony.

Examples: The girl wore a "rad" outfit.
Recessions cannot be gauged solely by the "gross national product."
It's such a "beautiful" day here in the rain.

QUOTATION MARKS WITH OTHER FORMS OF PUNCTUATION

Rule: Periods and commas are always placed inside the closing quotation marks.

Examples: Julia said, "I would like to go home now."
"I would like to go home now," said Julia.

Rule: Exclamation points and question marks go inside or outside a quotation mark depending on if they are part of the whole sentence or part of the quoted material.

Examples: Mary asked, "Did I miss my dinner?"
Did Mary say, "I must have missed my dinner"?

PARENTHESES

Use parentheses as follows:

Rule: To set off clauses, phrases, or words that clarify or explain part of a sentence but are not essential to the meaning of the sentence.

Examples: The nicest car (the Lexus) was not chosen.
The larger (20 × 20) rooms were much nicer.
The merchandise was damaged (as were all the parcels in the lot) and we returned it unopened.

Rule: To clarify dollar amounts.

Example: The cost to you will be thirty dollars ($30).

Grammar

ABBREVIATIONS

Rule: Spell out titles of persons when they precede last names. Exceptions to this would be Mr., Mrs., Ms., Messrs.

Examples: Captain Poldark
Doctor Singh
Professor Rosario

Rule: Abbreviate Jr., Sr., Esq. when they follow a name.

Examples: Victor Worg, Jr.
Francis Borghi, Esq.

Rule: Abbreviate academic titles when they follow a name.

Example: Patricia Frazier, Ph.D.

Rule: It is good business practice not to abbreviate days, months, addresses.

Examples: The interview will be Thursday, June 11.
The company is located at 246 Corbett Avenue in San Ramon.

SPACING IN THE TYPING OF ABBREVIATIONS

Rule: Abbreviations that consist of all-capital letters usually do not have periods or spaces between the letters.

| *Examples:* | YMCA |
| | FBI |

Rule: The trend is for no periods and no spaces for academic degrees and geographic names.

| *Examples:* | BS degree | USA |
| | MD | CPA |

Rule: For time, use periods but no spaces.

| *Examples:* | a.m. |
| | p.m. |

PLURALS

Rule: The basic rule is to add *s* to form the plural of most words.

Example: pencil, pencils

Rule: If a noun ends in *y* and is preceded by a vowel, add *s* to form the plural.

Example: key, keys

Rule: If a noun ends in *y* and is preceded by a consonant, form the plural by changing the *y* to *i* and adding *es*.

Example: deputy, deputies

Rule: If a noun ends in *o* and is preceded by a vowel, add *s* to form the plural.

Example: trio, trios

Rule: If a noun ends in *o* and is preceded by a consonant, add *es* to form the plural.

Example: cargo, cargoes

Rule: Some nouns form their plurals in irregular ways.

Examples: child, children; mouse, mice; woman, women; ox, oxen

Rule: If a compound noun is a solid word, form the plural by treating the last part of the word as if it were alone.

Examples: doghouse, doghouses; guidebook, guidebooks

Rule:	If compound words are spaced or hyphenated, form the plural to the chief part of the word.
Example:	mother-in-law, mothers-in-law

Please note: The English language has so many exceptions, it is best to consult a dictionary when in doubt.

NUMBERS

Rule:	Spell out numbers one through ten. Use figures for numbers above ten.
Example:	There will be five positions eliminated due to the contract loss.
Rule:	Spell out indefinite numbers.
Example:	There were thousands of people at the concert.
Rule:	Use both words and figures for large numbers.
Examples:	23 billion, 9 million
Rule:	Spell out fractions.
Example:	Nearly one-half of the workers were absent.
Rule:	Spell out numbers that begin a sentence.
Example:	Eleven new restaurants opened in the area.
Rule:	Use both words and figures when two numbers come together.
Example:	Please order twelve 3-inch tapes.
Rule:	For measurements, use figures.
Example:	She gained 12 pounds last month.
Rule:	Use figures for clock time.
Example:	We begin work at 8:30 a.m.
Rule:	Use words for periods of time.
Example:	The project took thirty hours to complete.

Rule:	For numbers of street addresses, use the basic rule of spelling out numbers ten and under.
Examples:	We moved to Seventh Avenue. The meeting will be held at 340 East 27th Street.

CAPITALIZATION

Capitalize words as follows:

Rule:	To begin a sentence.
Example:	The secretarial position is advertised as that of an administrative assistant.
Rule:	When they are proper names of persons, places, and things.
Examples:	My uncle is Walter Gonzales. We will be visiting Plymouth, Massachusetts. They had a picnic on Angel Island in San Francisco.
Rule:	When the title of a person precedes his or her name.
Example:	Tell Uncle Harry to call Senator Wong.
Rule:	For names of organizations and companies.
Examples:	Girl Scouts, Chamber of Commerce, Elks, General Motors
Rule:	For periods of time—months, days, holidays.
Examples:	We will visit on the fourth Tuesday of July. The parade will be on Memorial Day.
Rule:	When an adjective is derived from a proper name.
Examples:	Japanese art, Mexican food, Oriental rugs
Rule:	For titles of books, magazines, newspapers.
Examples:	A popular book in 1990 was *All I Really Need to Know I Learned in Kindergarten.* Many people read the *New York Times.* We have a subscription to *Sunset* magazine.
Rule:	For directions when they refer to specific sections of the country.
Examples:	The office will move to the South for cheaper labor. The job is offered on the East Side of town.

Rule:	For personal titles when they refer to definite persons.
Example:	The President of General Motors will be at the meeting.
Rule:	For the first word of the salutation of a letter and the first word of the closing.
Examples:	Dear Ms. Jones Yours truly
Rule:	For the first word of a direct quotation.
Example:	Mary Jane said, "Please wait for me."
Rule:	In hyphenated words, for the words you would ordinarily capitalize.
Example:	We plan to leave in mid-April.

Word Division

The right-side margin is very important for the overall appearance of your typing work. Many times, you are at the right margin and must decide whether to divide a word—and if so, how to divide it. In current practice, typists are trying to avoid dividing words at the end of lines. However, if it is necessary to divide words, certain rules are to be used. You must remember that words can only be divided between syllables. Following are the preferred rules:

1. Never divide words of one syllable:
   curl, halves, raze
2. Divide compound words where the two words come together:
   hair/line, house/coat, land/lady, over/power
3. Divide hyphenated words at the point of hyphenation:
   self-esteem, one-half
4. Do not divide names, dates, addresses:
   Senator Alvin Wong, January 23, 1992, 239 Lincoln Avenue
5. Do not divide abbreviations or contractions:
   PT&T, PG&E, can't, didn't, wouldn't
6. Divide after a prefix and before a suffix:
   intra/state, post/script, regi/ment, wordi/ness
7. When a single-letter syllable comes within a word, divide between the letters:
   chari/oteer, concili/ation, evalu/ation, extenu/ation

Good business practice also states the following:

- When dividing a word, you must have more than 3 letters to bring to the second line.
- Never leave fewer than 3 letters in the first line.
- Never have more than one hyphenated line together. Appearance-wise, only one hyphen to a paragraph is a good rule to follow.
- Never divide the last word of a paragraph or of a page.

Remember, you, the typist, may be concerned about keeping the right margin even. However, it is much more difficult on the reader to encounter divided words. Think of your clients!

Résumés

Many times, the first step in landing a job is submitting a resume. An ad in the newspaper, a telephone call, or an inquiry may be the impetus to put yourself on paper. It is very important that your resume be neatly typed and provide the right information.

The information in the resume must fit the job for which you are applying; however, some basic rules are to be followed. All resumes should contain at least the following:

- identification
- education
- experience

Many resumes also contain these:

- personal data
- references

Resumes will vary according to the person and according to the position that is open. However, some good advice is this:

- Be brief in the description of the job duties. Explain in detail, but use brief phrases. Do not be repetitive.
- Use action words when describing past duties. Examples are *managed, produced, sold, trained, handled.*
- Include any special skills or knowledge you have, such as a foreign language.
- Be neat. Be sure the copy is free of errors. Place the information evenly on the paper.
- Try to keep the resume to one page and definitely no more than two.
- If you photocopy your resume, be sure the copy is top grade.

Figures A.4 and A.5 show samples of resumes.

Manuscripts and Reports

Many times, on your job, you will be asked to type a business report. Sometimes, you may have a manuscript to prepare for a publisher or

FIGURE A.4 ◆ Sample Resume 1

Elvira Lopez
115 Eastmont Drive
Eastmont, MA 02365
(213) 861-4352

EDUCATION

1990	Eastmont Business College Eastmont, MA 02364	AA in Secretarial Science
1984	Eastmont High School Eastmont, MA 02363	Graduated with a major in business

EXPERIENCE

1986 to present	Boston Insurance 236 Coly Street Boston, MA 02385	Word Processor Typed correspondence from transcription machines
1984 to 1986	Action Realty One Plaza Brookline, MA 02397	General Office Clerk Answered telephones, Typed letters, typed forms, sorted mail, made bank deposits

REFERENCES

Joyce Wong 963 Eighth Avenue Eastmont, MA 02365	Walter Alverez 67 Warren Avenue Eastmont, MA 02365	Dr. Sheila Wakem 26 Second Avenue Eastmont, MA 02365

a college class. Following are instructions for preparing these reports and manuscripts.

SPACING AND MARGINS

Manuscripts may be single-space, double-space, or space-and-a-half. Double-spacing is the easiest to read; however, many businesses presently tend to use the space-and-a-half.

Setting margins will depend on whether your report will be bound or unbound. For reports to be bound at the top, use the following guidelines:

◆ First page has 2½-inch top margin.
◆ All other pages have 1½-inch top margin.
◆ All pages have 1-inch bottom margin.
◆ Side margins are 1 inch.

Floater An employee who works in different departments of a company for various periods of time.

Fraction equivalents Fractions that are equal to given percentages.

Fringe benefits The extra payments or services, in addition to a salary or wage, that people get from their employer.

Full-time work schedule A plan under which employees work a standard forty-hour week.

G

Geographic filing system The method of arranging, or grouping, files according to geographic location.

Gigabyte A measure of computer storage capacity equal to approximately 1 billion bytes.

Grapevine The transmission of information by word of mouth without regard for organizational levels.

Graphic User Interface (GUI) A operating system that instructs the computer through visual methods rather than text-based commands. The operator uses icons to represent programs, files, and menus in a windows environment.

Graphics software Computer programs that present numerical data clearly and quickly in visual form.

Greeting In a business letter, the part that follows the inside address and usually consists of the word *dear* followed by the name of the person receiving the letter.

Grievance process The method a company uses to allow employees to state their side in disputes with supervisors or other employees.

Groupthink The tendency of members of highly cohesive groups to lose their critical individual evaluative abilities, and out of a desire for unanimity, to overlook realistic, meaningful alternatives as attitudes are formed and decisions are made.

Groupware A combination of electronic technology and group processes that allows individual computer users to be part of a team and share information.

Guide for Occupational Exploration (GOE) A U.S. Department of Labor publication that organizes jobs into twelve interest areas and further divides those areas into work groups and subgroups.

H

Hard copy From a computer, output that is created at a printer and gives a permanent printed copy of processed information.

Hard disk Thin, rigid metallic platters that record data in magnetic form, providing non-volatile, or permanent storage usually within the system unit.

Hidden agenda A personal goal based on attitudes and feelings that an individual brings to the group.

Horizontal organization A company that has a skeleton group of senior executives at the top in traditional support functions such as finance and human resources, with everyone else working together in cross-functional teams that perform the core processes such as production and sales.

Human relations How people get along with one another. Also called interpersonal relations.

I

Income statement A summary of all income and expenses for a certain time period, such as a month or a year.

Indexing The process of typing the name of a person or company in its proper order on a file folder or card.

Inside address In a business letter, the part that follows the date and includes the name, title, company, and address of the person receiving the letter.

Integrated software The combination of several independent software packages, such as word processing, spreadsheet, graphics, and database, for coordinated use in one package.

Interest survey An instrument that lists statements describing a variety of activities. Sometimes called an interest inventory or interest test.

Internet An international "network of networks" made up of government, academic, and business-related networks that allows people around the world to communicate through electronic mail and have access to millions of computer files through a collection of huge supercomputers, telephone cables, and satellite transmission systems around the world.

Interpersonal relations Same as **Human relations.**

Introvert A person with a quiet personality.

Itinerary An outline of travel plans that includes flight numbers, departure and arrival times and places, hotel accommodation information, and car rental information.

J

Job lead card An index card on which a job seeker records all relevant information about an available job.

Job sharing An arrangement in which two people divide responsibility for a single job.

Just-in-time hiring The practice of employing temporary workers to complete only a specific project, on short notice, and without a training period.

K

Keyboard The input device usually used in an office to enter data and instructions into a computer. Most *keyboards* consist of the typewriter keypad, the cursor movement–numeric keypad, and the function keypad. Also called a terminal when connected with a monitor.

L

Lateral communication Horizontal communication that occurs between departments or functional units, usually as a coordinating or problem-solving effort.

Lateral files Collections of records in which file folders are arranged vertically, from side to side, inside drawers that rest sideways in metal cabinets.

Leaders Periods used across the space between a topic name and its page number in a table of contents.

Letter of application A sales letter in which an applicant describes all of his or her qualifications and tries to convince an employer that he or she is the best person for a particular job.

Letter of inquiry A letter asking whether a specified type of job is available.

Liabilities A business's financial obligations or debts.

Lifestyle goal The way a person wants to live in the future.

Local area network (LAN) A computer and communications network covering a limited geographical area. Does not require a central node or processor.

Lose-lose negotiating style A bargaining method used by one party who attempts to win at the expense of the other but ultimately creates problems for both parties.

M

Mainframe A powerful, large computer that can handle many users at the same time, process large volumes of data at incredibly high speeds, and in many cases store millions of characters in primary memory.

Management information system (MIS) An integrated system, usually computer based, which provides information critical for decision making.

Memorandum A written document that is less formal than a letter; stays within a company; and contains the headings To, From, Date, and Subject. Also called a memo.

Microcomputer A computer system unit containing memory, a keyboard for entering data, a monitor for displaying what is entered through the keyboard, one or two disk drives for storing files on disks, and a printer for producing final copy. Also called a personal computer (PC).

Photo Credits

Page 2 © Index Stock Photography; **4** © Bruce Ayres, Tony Stone Images; **6** © John Feingersh, Uniphoto; **10** © Sheryl Pomerenk for West; **11** © Billy Hustace, Tony Stone Images; **14** © Robert Brenner, PhotoEdit; **22** © Kim Karpeles, New England Stock; **27** © Sheryl Pomerenk for West; **29** © Peter M. Fisher, The Stock Market; **30** © Llewellyn; **32** © Giancarlo de Bellis, Omni-Photo Communications; **34** © Index Stock Photography; **35** © Jeff Kaufman, FPG; **42** © José L. Pelaez, The Stock Market; **46** © Tony Freeman, PhotoEdit; **47** © Elena Rooraid, PhotoEdit; **49** © Esbin-Anderson, Photo Network; **51** © Sheryl Pomerenk for West; **52** © José L. Pelaez, The Stock Market; **53** © Bruce Ayres, Tony Stone Images; **64** © Bachmann, Photo Network; **67** © Rob Lewine, The Stock Market; **70** © Walter Hodges, Tony Stone Images; **76** © Ariel Skelley, The Stock Market; **81** © José L. Pelaez, The Stock Market; **94** © Index Stock Photography; **98** Photo courtesy of Hewlett-Packard Company; **99** Top left, Courtesy of Apple Computer, Inc.; **99** Top right, © Gateway 2000, Inc.; **99** Bottom, photo courtesy of Hewlett-Packard Company; **100** Top, © George Haling, Tony Stone Images; **100** Bottom, © Uniphoto; **101** © Roger Ball, The Stock Market; **103** Top left, courtesy of International Business Machines Corporation. Unauthorized use not permitted; **103** Middle left, courtesy of International Business Machines Corporation. Unauthorized use not permitted; **103** Top right, courtesy of Apple Computer, Inc.; **103** Bottom, photo courtesy of Hewlett-Packard Company; **104** Courtesy of Intel Corporation; **106** Left, courtesy of Apple Computer, Inc.; **106** Middle, photo used with permission from Microsoft Corporation; **106** Right, courtesy of Logitech, Inc.; **107** Courtesy of US Robotics; **108** Photo courtesy of Hewlett-Packard Company; **120** © Comstock; **124** © Index Stock Photography; **131** © Jon Feingersh, The Stock Market; **132** © Sheryl Pomerenk for West; **134** © Don Smetzer, Tony Stone Images; **142** © Mugshots/Gabe Palmer, The Stock Market; **147** © Zigy Kaluzny, Tony Stone Images; **150** © John Turner, Tony Stone Images; **151** © Robert E. Daemmrich, Tony Stone Images; **153** Top © David Young-Wolff, PhotoEdit; **153** Bottom, photo courtesy of Hewlett-Packard Company; **160** © Michael Goldman, FPG; **163** © Don Smetzer, Tony Stone Images; **165** © José L. Pelaez, The Stock Market; **166** © Frank Siteman, New England Stock; **168** © Tom Wilson, FPG; **175** © Sheryl Pomerenk for West; **182** © Robert E. Daemmrich, Tony Stone Images; **184** © Index Stock Photography; **193** Top © Tony Freeman, PhotoEdit; **193** Bottom © Michael Newman, PhotoEdit; **199** © Daemmrich, Uniphoto; **200** Courtesy of Imation; **201** Top, courtesy of Verbatim Corporation; **201** Bottom, courtesy of Iomega Corporation; **210** © Frank Herholdt, Tony Stone Images; **212** © Dick Luria, FPG; **219** © Michael Newman, PhotoEdit; **225** © Sheryl Pomerenk for West; **227** © Tom & Dee Ann McCarthy, The Stock Market; **238** © Don Smetzer, Tony Stone Images; **240** © Jean Miele, The Stock Market; **241** Courtesy of Peachtree Software; **242** Courtesy of International Business Machines Corporation. Unauthorized use not permitted; **253** © Gerold Lim, Unicorn Stock Photos; **266** © Billy Hustace, Tony Stone Images; **269** © Mark Sherman, Photo Network; **280** Top © David Hanover, West; **280** Middle © Jeff Zaruba, The Stock Market; **280** Bottom © Alan Schein, The Stock Market; **281** © Cathy Melloan, Tony Stone Images; **292** © Index Stock Photography; **296** © Frank Siteman, Tony Stone Images; **301** © Peter Fownes, Photo Network; **306** © Devaney Stock Photos; **310** © Steven Peters, Tony Stone Images; **317** © Sheryl Pomerenk for West; **326** © Chuck Keeler, Tony Stone Images; **329** © José L. Pelaez, The Stock Market; **331** © Jon Feingersh, The Stock Market; **332** © José L. Pelaez, The Stock Market; **334**